The Brave New World of eHRM 2.0

A Volume in:
Research in Human Resource Management

Series Editors

Dianna L. Stone
James H. Dulebohn

D1404218

Research in Human Resource Management

Series Editors

Dianna L. Stone
University at Albany, University of New Mexico, and Virginia Tech

James H. Dulebohn
Michigan State University

The Brave New World of eHRM 2.0

Edited by

James H. Dulebohn
Dianna L. Stone

INFORMATION AGE PUBLISHING, INC.
Charlotte, NC • www.infoagepub.com

Library of Congress Cataloging-in-Publication Data

The CIP data for this book can be found on the Library of Congress website (loc.gov).

Paperback: 9781641131551
Hardcover: 9781641131568
eBook: 9781641131575

Printed in the United States of America

CONTENTS

CHAPTER 1

THE TRANSFORMATION OF HUMAN RESOURCES MANAGEMENT THROUGH TECHNOLOGY AND E-HRM

James H. Dulebohn and Dianna L. Stone

ABSTRACT

This article considers the evolution of the field of electronic human resource management (eHRM), and its impact on human resource management (HR). It also reviews the transformation of HR since the 1980s and the influence of computer technology and e-HRM in enabling HR to function as a core business function and play a strategic role in organizations. We define e-HRM as web-based interactive human resource management systems (HRMS) that provide real time information and enable organizations and employee end-users to access HR functions and enter and retrieve HR related data from anywhere through a web browser (Stone & Dulebohn, 2013). This will set the stage for discussing more recent trends in e-HRM and briefly describing papers included in this issue of *Research in Human Resource Management*.

The Brave New World of eHRM 2.0, pages 1–9.

Human resource management (HR) is the organization science and management function that deals with the entire employment relationship and all the policies and activities for managing the relationship. HR has evolved since its beginnings as an administrative function in the second decade of the twentieth century. More recently beginning in the 1980s, HR has experience a dramatic transformation. This transformation has involved HR moving from being an administrative and maintenance oriented function to operating in many organizations as a core business function and as a strategic business partner. The application and implementation of computer technology to HR functional activities also began in the 1980s, and this occurrence has represented one of the primary drivers and facilitators of the transformation of HR.

The following will provide a brief discussion of the evolution of HR, the transformation of HR since the 1980s and the influence of computer technology and e-HRM in enabling HR to function as a core business function and play a strategic role in organizations. We define e-HRM as web-based interactive human resource management systems (HRMS) that provide real time information and enable organizations and employee end-users to access HR functions and enter and retrieve HR related data from anywhere through a web browser. This will set the stage for discussing more recent trends in e-HRM and briefly describing papers included in this issue of *Research in Human Resource Management*.

The late 19th century and early twentieth century witnessed the emergence of the modern corporation along with increasingly complex and large organizations. HR emerged in response to these changes and organizational challenges such as high turnover and low productivity (Dulebohn, Ferris, & Stodd, 1995). The overall objective of *personnel management* (the initial label given to HR) was to rationalize and bureaucratize the employment relationship and adopt standardized employment practices to effectively manage labor and employment in organizations (Baron, Jennings, & Dobbin, 1988; Bloomfield, 1923). Standardized personnel management practices prior to 1940's, represent many that continue today, included centralized employment, manpower (i.e., human resource) planning, job analysis, job descriptions, selection testing, performance appraisal, job evaluation and wage surveys, promotion systems, record keeping, and codified employment policies and procedures, etc. (Baron, Jennings, & Dobbin, 1988). Once organizations implemented standardized employment practices, the role of personnel management up to the late 1970s was primarily administrative oriented. Organizations generally viewed personnel management as a non-core and non-value adding business function and personnel management activities as perfunctory and as not essential to contributing to organizational success.

Following the passage of the National Labor Relations Act in 1935, providing workers the right to unionize and engage in collective bargaining, HR was distinguished by two disparate roles up through the 1970s. These were personnel management and labor relations. During this period the US economy was manufacturing-oriented, management's priority for managing the employment relationship was to deal with unions and collective bargaining. Consequently, the labor relations side of HR rose in prominence. In contrast, organizations continued to view the personnel management side as a necessary but a lower level function responsible for administrating and enforcing standardized employment practices.

TRANSFORMATIONAL EFFECT OF INFORMATION TECHNOLOGY ON HR

Larger organizations began adopting computer technology in the 1960s. Programming languages such as Fortran and Cobol had been developed in the 1950s. During the 1960s, third generation computers based on integrated circuits such as the IBM System/360 mainframe resulted in the proliferation of commercial computer hardware and integrated operating systems and programming language software. Organizations began designing, developing (primarily in-house), and implementing centralized computing systems for applications such as inventory control. Some major vendors such as SAP came on the scene in the 1970s and began producing and selling mainframe programs, such as for payroll and accounting, based on a centralized database architecture.

The adoption of computer technology and the development of computer application programs in organizations up through the 1970s primarily focused on core business functions related to organization profitability, such as accounting, payroll, operations, and financials. Organizational application of computer technology to personnel management functions (other than payroll) was given low priority by organizations during the 1960s and 1970s because of the continued view of personnel management as administrative, non-core, and maintenance-oriented. Among those organizations that had the resources to acquire mainframe computer resources, relatively few shifted employee record keeping and payroll processing to mainframe computers. This state of affairs was highlighted by research conducted by Tomeski and Lazarus (1973) in a survey of 87 large US organizations. They concluded, "human resource systems have failed to keep pace with the general advance of computer technology and its other applications, such as the financial ones" (p. 61).

The advent of the microcomputer resulted in a proliferation of computer technology to organizations along with the development of pre-packaged software for business functions, including those related to personnel management functions, as well as client-server systems. The widespread application of computer technology to HR functional activities that began in the 1980s was one of the primary catalysts and enablers of the transformation of HR in its emergence from being primarily transaction oriented to representing a core business function and operating as a strategic business partner. Therefore, concurrent with the introduction and widespread adoption of micro-computers (i.e., following IBM's release of the PC in 1984) was the beginning of the transformation of the view, role, and importance of personnel management from being ancillary to core business functions to becoming a core business function that could impact organizational success. The transformation of HR included the adoption of the label *human resources* in place of the administrative *personnel management*.

A number of external and internal organizational factors converged to contribute to this transformation. Some external factors included the shift from a manufacturing to a service and knowledge-based economy (that heightened the importance of human capital), a decrease in unionization, an increase in government regulation of the employment environment that began with Equal Pay Act of 1963 and Title 7 of the Civil Rights Act of 1964, an increase in domestic and international competition, and structural changes in the employment relationship. Internal factors included a widespread change in the view of labor (i.e., an organization's employees), from primarily representing a cost to be minimized to representing a critical resource to be cultivated and a potential competitive advantage. Specifically, organizations began to realize that the collective skills, abilities, and expertise, resulting from investments in human resources, contributed to organizational success and advantages such as the ability to respond to customers, to innovate, and to rapidly develop and introduce new products to the market (Ulrich & Dulebohn, 2015).

The introduction of the PC in the early 1980s was followed by networking technology, client server architecture, and a proliferation of packaged software to automate separate HR functions. Functions included applicant tracking, performance management, compensation and benefits, training and development, and regulatory compliance. In the late 1980s software vendors began releasing integrated HR software suites that included the ability to automate and manage different HR functions. Later in the 1980s vendors began providing integrated software solutions to manage and coordinate the major transactional HR functions to work together and collect, store and share information in a single database. For example, PeopleSoft version 1 was released in 1989 as the first client-server human resource management system (HRMS). During the 1990s enterprise resource planning systems (ERPs) became more complex to include modules that enabled the management and sharing of data among the major business functions including operations, accounting, finance, HR, supply chain, and customer relations. In 2000, PeopleSoft released PeopleSoft 8, based on the software company's complete rewrite of the prior client-server version code to be fully web-enabled and thus this version allowed end users to access all the ERP modules, including HRMS, through a web-browser. This occurrence represented the first fully functional e-HR human resource management system.

The application of computer technology transformed HR in several ways. First, it automated many of the transactional processes that characterize much of the administrative activity of HR and personnel management. In addition, computer technology enabled HR administration functions to be decentralized and outsourced to external vendors, organizational service centers, and employees through self-service, using e-HR technology. The automation of HR transactional functions has enhanced HR administrative efficiency, automated workflow, and enabled the decentralization of administrative HR to line management and employees. Consequently, it has freed HR professionals to engage in managerial and strategic activities, as business partners, and be involved in strategic planning and execution through the alignment of HR activities with the strategic plan. Critical current HR roles include planning, change management, organizational development, human capital acquisition and development, and assessment of human capital capabilities. In addition, computer technology has enabled HR to focus on and measure its bottom line impact, monitor the environment and incorporate labor market data in HR decision-making, integrate the varied HR functions with each other, and align HR functions with business strategy in strategic implementation.

e-HRM has further transformed HR in a number of ways such as by connecting the organization with the external environment, and thereby extending organizational reach in acquiring its human resources and serving employees and customers. For example, the effectiveness of HR is often measured in part by the degree the organization has the human capital it needs in meeting human resource planning gaps. Recruitment and selection prior to the mid–1990s was paper based, typically face-to-face and was conducted in a similar manner as personnel managers had done it for the prior half century, e.g., hire at the entry level, promote from within, structuring advancement through seniority systems, etc. The changing employment relationship since the 1980s, the departure from a focus on recruitment at the entry level and life-long employment, and the emergence of protean careers and talent wars have contributed to the need for organizations to hire at all organizational levels. Although it is often taken for granted today, e-HRM has enabled organizations to recruit talent from distinct and varied geographical labor markets, post jobs globally, automatically scan resumes, administer selection tests, conduct interviews online, and has enabled job seekers to apply on-line through web portals. Other examples of e-HRM enabling organizations include functionality such as global compensation features that incorporate different legal and tax parameters in countries, in which an organization operates, and the existence of shared services centers to provide HR services to organizational units. Further, e-HRM provides both HR professionals and line managers with features such time and labor and performance management capabilities (line managers can access to enter employee data and performance appraisal information that is stored and accessible through central databases) and analytic capabilities to inform planning and decision-making. On the employee side, e-HRM provides self-service capabilities that provide employees with anywhere access to enroll in benefits and query their employment data and information relevant to their jobs

Similar to a computer operating system, running behind the scene, that controls and manages the hardware and software programs of a computer, e-HRM has become a critical part of organizational infrastructure and HR's capabilities and effectiveness. A defining characteristic of e-HRM is that it provides web access to an organization's HRMS and an interactive environment between end-users and HRMS (Stone & Dulebohn, 2013). Because of its continued development and the ever increasing functionality provided by e-HRM systems and HRMS, research and theory on these systems, and their components and capabilities is warranted.

In 2005, one of the first academically oriented books on eHRM was published (Gueutal & Stone, 2005), and this prompted an interest in theory and research on eHRM. Since that time, research has examined the acceptance and effectiveness of these new systems including e-recruitment (Chapman & Gollodei, 2017), e-learning (Johnson & Brown, 2017), e-selection (Stone, Lukaszewski, Stone-Romero & Johnson, 2013; Tippins, 2015), e-performance management (Payne, Horner, Boswell, Schroeder, & Stine-Cheyne, 2009), and the impact of eHRM on HR effectiveness, HR metrics, and strategic planning (Dulebohn & Johnson, 2013; Marler & Fisher, 2013; Ruel & Bondarouk, 2007; Strohmeier, 2007). However, eHRM continues to evolve with changes in technology, and therefore additional research is needed to examine its effectiveness.

ARTICLES INCLUDED IN THE ISSUE

Toward this end, in the current volume we have included a very interesting set of nine chapters on an array of eHRM issues. The first six chapters address critical HR activities enabled by e-HRM. These include e-recruitment, e-selection, use of gamification in assessment, e-socialization of new employees, e-performance management, and e-learning. The next three chapters address emerging issues in e-HR including cyberdeviance, using technology to manage the new task-oriented employment relationship, and examining the assumptions underlying the use of technology in eHRM. A brief description of each chapter is as follows. It merits noting that all of the articles described below offer directions for future research.

First, an article by Sara Murphy, Peter Fisher, Lisa Keeping, and Douglas Brown provides a review of the literature on the website characteristics that influence the effectiveness of e-recruitment. They base their review on a model of e-recruitment developed by Cober, Brown, Keeping, and Levy (2004), and find that a number of website characteristics influence applicant attraction including aesthetic features, website façade elements, website attitudes, navigability, and content features. Second, a chapter by David Dickter and Victor Jockin offers a very interesting review of the history and future of technology in employee selection. They provide a review of the existing empirical research, and consider the advances and concerns of using technology in selection for practitioners. For example, they suggest that HR researchers and practitioners must be conversant in both technology and selection to keep up with the science of selection. They also indicate that societal issues will magnify the importance of e-selection over time because of the increased use of technology at home and work, and the fact that nature of work is changing (e.g., use of artificial intelligence, robotics). The third article by Sarena Bhatia and Ann Marie Ryan explores the use of new game-based assessment in selection, assessment that incorporates game elements to evoke and measure relevant constructs in the hiring process. They consider such topics as the development of game-based assessment, psychometric properties, applicant reactions, scoring, and cross-cultural ramifications of using these new assessment methods.

Fourth, an article by Jamie Gruman and Alan Saks introduces the new issue of e-socialization, the process of facilitating newcomer adjustment, through the use of information and communication technology. They specify the main challenges and opportunities presented by e-socialization, and discuss such issues as e-orientation, e-training, e-socialization agents, e-socialization tactics, and proactive behaviors. The fifth article by Richard Johnson and Jason Randall considers design issues in e-learning. They suggest that there is considerable research on e-learning in fields such as education, human resource management, information systems, and industrial and organizational psychology. However, they note that the literature has not been integrated. Thus, they revisit and expand on the design issues considered by Salas, DeRouin, and Littrell (2005) including learner control, organizational support, trainee interaction, and interface design. The authors also review research that indicates how technological design can enhance the psychological learning process and trainee engagement. The sixth article is by Stephanie Payne, Anjelica Mendoza and Margaret Horner who focus on electronic performance management (e-PM). They note that e-PM is widely used in organizations, but has not received much attention in the HR research literature. Their review describes how e-PM can address ongoing concerns about the effectiveness of performance management in organizations, and suggests that it can automate, document, integrate, structure, and make the process more accessible.

The seventh article is by Elizabeth Cassady, Sandra Fisher, and Shaunee Olsen, and addresses a very new and innovative application of technology in HR. The authors argue that technology can be used to manage new task workers, a new type of contingent worker that utilizes online platforms to complete short-term tasks for clients. They suggest that relational eHRM systems can be used to create more productive work relationships, facilitate communication, offer training and development, and analyze how their performance can be enhanced. The eighth article by Markus Ellmer and Astried Riechel examines the assumptions and conceptions of technology used in eHRM. They suggest that technology is viewed from a very general and generic level, and these authors call for more complex considerations of technology in the field. The final article by Amber Schroeder and Julia Whitaker examines a very new and intriguing issue in eHRM, cyberdeviance. They examine different forms of cyberdeviance based on the Robinson and Bennett (1995) typology, and consider issues associated with cyberbullying, online incivility, cyberloafing, and cybercrime. The authors also consider the antecedents and consequences associated with each of these forms of cyberdeviance.

CONCLUSION

This introductory article has briefly reviewed the significant impact of technology and eHRM on the evolution and transformation of the field of HR. We argued that computer technology and eHRM has enabled HR to function as an important core business function, and play a strategic role in organizations. However, we believe that additional theory and research is needed on these new systems in order to examine their effectiveness. Thus, the primary goal of this issue of *Research in Human Resource Management* is to provide reviews of the existing literature on a number of key topics (e.g., e-recruitment, e-selection, e-performance management, e-learning, new employment relationships), and offer directions for future research and practice. We hope that the reviews will contribute to increased understanding of aspects and capabilities of eHRM as well as foster additional research on eHRM that will add to further understanding as well as enable HR to continue its trajectory in adding value to organizations.

REFERENCES

Baron, J. N., Jennings, P. D., & Dobbin, F. R. (1988). Mission control? The development of personnel systems in US industry. *American Sociological Review*, 497–514.

Bloomfield, D. (Ed.). (1923). *Problems in personnel management*. HW Wilson Company.

Chapman, D., & Godollei, A. (2017). E-Recruiting: Using technology to attract job applicants. In G. Hertel, D. L. Stone, R. D. Johnson, & J. Passmore (Eds.). *The Handbook of the Psychology of the Internet at Work*. London: Wiley/Blackwell.

Cober, R. T., Brown, D. J., Keeping, L. M., & Levy, P. E. (2004). Recruitment on the net: How do organizational web site characteristics influence applicant attraction? *Journal of Management, 30*, 623–624.

Dulebohn, J. H., & Johnson, R. D. (2013). Human resource metrics and decision support: A classification framework. *Human Resource Management Review, 23*(1), 71–83.

Gueutal, H. G., & Stone, D. L. (2006). *The brave new world of e HR: Human resource management in the digital age*. San Francisco: Jossey Bass.

Johnson, R. D., & Brown, K. G. (2017). Toward an integrative model of e-Learning: A literature review. In G. Hertel, D. L. Stone, R. D. Johnson, & J. Passmore (Eds.). *The Handbook of the Psychology of the Internet at Work*. London: Wiley/Blackwell.

Marler, J. H., & Fisher, S. L. (2013). An evidence-based review of e-HRM and strategic human resource management. *Human Resource Management Review, 23*(1), 18–36.

Payne, S. C., Horner, M. T., Boswell, W. R., Schroeder, A. N., & Stine-Cheyne, K. J. (2009). Comparison of online and traditional performance appraisal systems. *Journal of Managerial Psychology, 24*(6), 526–544.

Robinson, S. L., & Bennett, R. L. (1995). A typology of deviant workplace behavior: A multidimensional scaling study. *Academy of Management Journal, 38*, 555–572.

Rüel, H. J., Bondarouk, T. V., & Van der Velde, M. (2007). The contribution of e-HRM to HRM effectiveness: Results from a quantitative study in a Dutch Ministry. *Employee relations, 29*(3), 280–291.

Salas, E., DeRouin, R., & Littrell, L. (2005). Research-based guidelines for designing distance learning. In H. Gueutal & D. L. Stone (Eds), *The brave new world of e HR:*

Human resource management in the digital age (pp. 104–137): San Francisco, CA: Jossey-Bass.

Stone, D. L., & Dulebohn, J. H. (2013). Emerging issues in theory and research on electronic human resource management (eHRM). *Human Resource Management Review, 23*(1), 1–5.

Stone, D. L., Lukaszewski, K. M., Stone-Romero, E. F., & Johnson, T. L. (2013). Factors affecting the effectiveness and acceptance of electronic selection systems. *Human Resource Management Review, 23*(1), 50–70.

Strohmeier, S. (2007). Research in e-HRM: Review and implications. *Human resource management review, 17*(1), 19–37.

Tippins, N.T. (2015). Technology and assessment in selection. *Annual Review of Organizational Behavior, 2,* 551–582.

Tomeski, E. A., & Lazarus, H. (1973). The computer and the personnel department: Keys to modernizing human resource systems. *Business Horizons, 16*(3), 61–66.

Ulrich, D., & Dulebohn, J. H. (2015). Are we there yet? What's next for HR? *Human Resource Management Review, 25*(2), 188–204.

CHAPTER 2

"POUNDING THE PAVEMENT" IN THE 21ST CENTURY

A Review of the Literature Regarding Organizational Recruitment Websites

Sara A. Murphy, Peter A. Fisher,
Lisa M. Keeping, and Douglas J. Brown

ABSTRACT

Organizations often use their own websites for recruitment purposes (Maurer & Cook, 2011). For over a decade, the use of these organizational recruitment websites (ORWs) has proliferated, as has the research investigating the role these websites play in organizational recruitment. This research has examined a wide array of constructs relating to ORWs and how they predict recruitment outcomes (Gregory, Meade, &Thompson, 2013; Kraichy & Chapman, 2014; Maurer & Cook 2011). We conducted a comprehensive narrative review of the empirical literature in this area utilizing the model developed by Cober, Brown, Keeping, and Levy (2004) as an organizing framework. Cober et al's model delineates the process by which website characteristics impact e-recruitment outcomes. Thirty-three articles were identified as capturing constructs within the model. Our review discusses these articles by

The Brave New World of eHRM 2.0, pages 11–46.

highlighting aspects of the model that have been supported and unsupported, discussing new relationships that have been uncovered, and identifying gaps for future research to explore.

Keywords: e-recruitment, organizational recruitment websites, applicant attraction

As recent as a decade ago, job seekers submitted applications and resumés in person when applying for jobs. Job hunts were conducted using newspaper advertisements, and recruiters reached out to potential applicants at events and job fairs. Although these traditional methods are still used today, the recruitment literature has seen a pronounced shift as organizations have come to rely on online tools for recruitment (Maurer & Cook, 2011; Mulvey, 2013; Ployhart, 2006). These include, but are not limited to, job advertisements on online job boards (e.g., Monster.com) as well as career-related sections of organizations' websites where job openings and job-relevant information can be posted. In fact, up to 96% of organizations report relying on these online methods for recruitment (Maurer & Cook, 2011), highlighting the significance of this trend and supporting Stone, Lukaszewski, and Isenhour's (2005) prediction that over 95% of organizations would come to use these electronic recruitment methods.

The use of online recruitment methods is an attractive option for organizations; they make applicant pool generation more efficient (Chapman & Webster, 2003) and reduce the costs associated with recruitment by up to 87% per employee hired (Maurer & Liu, 2007). Other attractive qualities of e- recruitment include the ability to streamline the administrative burden of early stage recruitment (Stone et al., 2005) and the ability to customize recruitment messages to individual job seekers (Chapman & Godollei, 2017). For example, Holm (2012) found that the shift to an e-recruitment approach enabled organizations to attract and communicate with job seekers simultaneously, and fully automated the processing of applications. In addition, Dineen and Noe (2009) found that customizing the way that information was presented to viewers impacted the effectiveness of recruitment websites. It is no surprise that many organizations have come to rely on e-recruitment, fueling ample research in this domain.

Among the new e-recruitments tools, the use of organizations' own websites for recruitment purposes has become increasingly prominent (Breaugh, 2013). Within the literature these websites have been referred to with a variety of labels such as *recruitment websites* (Williamson, King, Lepak, & Sarma, 2010), *organizational webpages* (Thompson, Braddy, & Wuensch, 2008), and *corporate websites* (Pfieffelmann, Wagner, & Libkuman, 2010; van Birgelen, Wetzels, & van Dolen, 2008) to name a few. Throughout this paper, we use the term *organizational recruitment website* (ORW) as it specifically conveys the recruitment context and the use of the word "organizational" is inclusive of both for- and not-for-profit organizations.

As the variety of features present in ORWs has grown, so too has the variety of constructs examined by researchers. Over the past two decades, research has examined a wide array of characteristics associated with these websites and how they influence recruitment outcomes (Sylva & Mol, 2009). Results emerging from these studies have expanded our understanding of ORWs. However, there has yet to be a comprehensive review of the state of the ORW literature. To this end, the focus of this paper is to review the relevant empirical literature on ORWs to support the continuation of the already considerable research conducted in this field. We contribute to a better understanding of what has been examined, what we have learned, and what we still need to understand. We use the model introduced by Cober, Brown, Keeping, & Levy (2004) as an organizing framework to structure this review. Although developed over a decade ago, this model remains the primary theoretical framework outlining the constructs presumed to be relevant to how job seekers perceive and use ORWs as well as how these websites affect recruitment outcomes.

This review answers calls in the literature for a more developed understanding of how characteristics of ORWs affect early stage recruitment outcomes (Breaugh, 2013; Ployhart, 2006). To orient the reader, we first provide a brief overview of Cober, Brown, Keeping, and Levy's (2004) model and its constructs. Next, we summarize and discuss the empirical findings that have emerged in relation to each construct within the model. Finally, we reflect on the state of the literature today and discuss possible extensions of the model that future research should consider, and practical implications based on the findings we summarize.

OVERVIEW OF MODEL

In the early days of e-recruitment, Cober, Brown, Keeping, and Levy (2004) proposed a conceptual model of applicant attraction via ORWs. The original model expanded on extant theory and conceptualizations of the recruitment process, describing the process by which ORWs generate applicant attraction. Specifically, the model proposed a series of interrelated constructs specific to website design, and relationships between these constructs, ultimately leading to applicant attraction. Figure 2.1 presents Cober et al.'s conceptual model, and Table 2.1 defines the constructs proposed in the original paper.

NARRATIVE REVIEW OF THE ORW LITERATURE

Inclusion Criteria and Review Structure

Our review focuses on studies that empirically tested relationships involving one or more of the constructs identified by Cober, Brown, Keeping, and Levy;s (2004) model. To identify articles to include in this review, we first examined the conceptual definitions of variables of interest. Articles that included constructs reflecting the definitions outlined by Cober, Brown, Keeping, and Levy (2004) were included. Since no study has tested the model in its entirety and conflicting

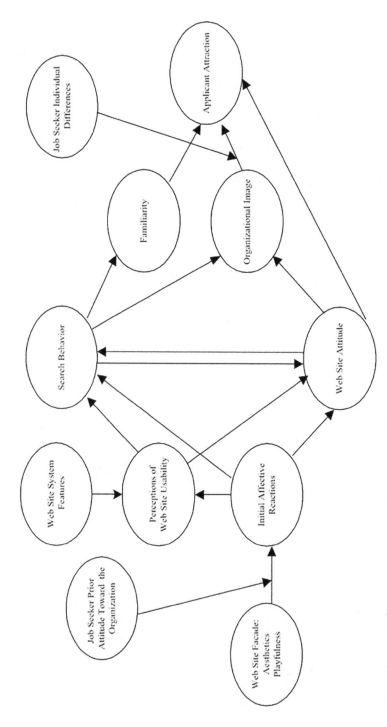

FIGURE 2.1. Cober, Brown, Keeping, and Levy's model (2004).

TABLE 2.1. Definitions of Constructs included in Cober, Brown, Keeping, and Levy (2004).

Construct	Original Definition
Website Façade: Aesthetics and Playfulness	The appearance and presence of a website. Aesthetics include features such as color, fonts, pictures and the use of whitespace, as well as adherence to Gestalt principles, such as repetition, alignment and proximity. Playfulness refers to the degree to which design elements of the website provide users with a vivid experience, including images, sound, video and animations.
Job Seekers' Initial Affective Reactions	The immediate, spontaneous emotion evoked by a website, with a particular focus on positive affective reactions, which serve as "the backdrop upon which organization messages are conveyed to prospective employees." (p. 629)
Job Seekers' Prior Attitude Toward the Organization	The strength and direction of a job seekers pre-conceived attitudes towards an organization. For example, an employee with strong attitudes towards a company may be less strongly affected by the website's facade in their initial affective reactions.
Perceptions of Website Usability	The degree to which the recruitment message is both coherent and understandable to job seekers, and the extent to which the website's design positively affects user access to valued information.
Website System Features	• Navigation: the logic behind the system of organization that allows users to acquire information and navigate within the website. • Responsiveness: the degree to which the website provides feedback and response to the user's actions and input. • Metaphor: the use of familiar models and ideas in the graphical user interface, and the degree to which they make sense to the user. • Content: the availability of goal-congruent information available on a website, and the variety of information available. • Transition speed: the timeliness of transitions such as initial access to the website and navigation within the website.
Search Behavior	The degree to which users obtain information about the organization from the website. This includes the depth of the user's search (amount of time spent reviewing each piece of information they access), the breadth of the user's search (the number of options the job seekers choose), and effort expended by job seekers (the total amount of time spent searching the website for information).
Familiarity	The extent to which a job seeker is familiar with the organization, which should be expected to increase proportionally to the amount of time they spend searching the organization's website.
Website Attitude	Both affective (feelings) and cognitive (thoughts) considerations regarding a website that are held by job seekers. This may include (to a degree) the initial affective reactions a job seeker experiences when accessing a website, but also more nuanced emotions and evaluations of the website which take place over time.
Organizational Image	Job seekers' more general perceptions of the organization itself after being exposed to the organization's website.

(continues)

TABLE 2.1. Continued

Construct	Original Definition
Job Seeker Individual Differences	The degree to which a job seeker's own interests and values align with those projected by an organization's website. For example, an extroverted job seeker may be more favorably affected by an organization that projects a team-oriented image.
Applicant Attraction	The conversion from a job seeker to an applicant.

results have emerged for some of the proposed relationships, we opted to speak to the parts of the model that were tested in relation to each construct. We first examined those articles that cite Cober, Brown, Keeping, and Levy (2004) and then expanded our search to include other articles in the e-recruitment literature that capture constructs within the model. A total of 33 articles met our criteria.

Cober, Brown, Keeping, and Levy's model (2004) explicates how job seekers are drawn to organizations through the exploration of ORWs. As such, our discussion begins with a description of the empirical work focused on the construct that appears first to job seekers upon entering an ORW: the website façade. Each subsequent construct will be discussed in the order that it appears in the model, allowing a picture of the model, as it stands today, to emerge. We structure our review around each of the model's constructs. Within our discussion of each construct, we first introduce the construct and describe its role in the original model. We then summarize the existing literature relevant to each construct in three different sections:

1. Research that supports the model's propositions,
2. Research that conflicts with the original model, and
3. Research that is relevant to the construct, but that considers other factors that were not originally proposed as influential in attracting job seekers.

CONSTRUCTS

Website Façade

A website's façade encompasses those features related to the aesthetics and playfulness of the website. The aesthetic and interactive features of an ORW's façade are of particular importance to recruitment because they elicit reactions from users, which influence attitudes toward the organization as well as behaviors (Cober, Brown, Keeping, & Levy, 2004). Analyses of various ORWs supports that the features included on recruitment websites *do* differ appreciably from one organization to another (Cober, Brown, & Levy, 2004), and that features such as fonts, colors, and interactive components typically aim to draw applicants to the organization and these features are related to e-recruiting outcomes (Dineen, Ling, Ash, & DelVecchio, 2007).

Although each feature has individual effects on attitudes and behaviors, we can also learn about the e-recruitment process by studying the ways in which these components work together to affect outcomes. Cober, Brown, Keeping, and Levy (2004) originally proposed that the higher the degree of unity (i.e., degree that visual components are meaningfully linked), contrast (i.e., purposeful differences between elements that should be distinct), and playfulness (i.e., elements that provide an interactive entertainment experience) on an ORW, the more favorable job seekers' initial affective reactions would be. Given the interplay of these characteristics to capture and maintain job seekers' attention, trigger information processing, impact decision making, and impact attitudes and behaviors (Dineen et al., 2007), changing the aesthetic and playful features of the website can influence how recruiting outcomes emerge. Thus, the way that individual façade elements work together as a whole to create unity, contrast, and playfulness is proposed to be of particular importance in predicting applicant attraction by way of other mediating mechanisms.

Façade: Consistent with model. Although few studies specifically investigate the effects of unity and contrast on the emergence of attraction, research has established that the aesthetic components of the website façade *do* predict organizational attraction (Braddy, Meade, & Kroustalis, 2008; Chen, Lin, & Chen, 2012; Walker, Feild, Giles, & Bernerth, 2008) and intentions to pursue employment (Allen, Biggane, Pitts, Otondo, & Van Scotter, 2013; Thompson et al., 2008; Walker et al., 2008). More specifically, the attractiveness of individuals pictured on ORWs (Walker et al., 2008), the attractiveness of the web page formatting (Braddy et al., 2008; Thompson et al., 2008), perceptions about website design and communication features (Allen et al., 2013; Chen et al., 2012; Lyons & Marler, 2011), and the degree of playfulness and technological advancement present on an ORW (Howardson & Behrend, 2014; Parzinger, Ward, Langford, & Greehey, 2013; Walker, Feild, Giles, Armenakis, & Bernerth, 2009) all influence e-recruiting outcomes. As ORWs continue to become more technologically advanced and interactive (Howardson & Behrend, 2014), deeper investigation into how façade elements work together to create a more interactive experience for job seekers, and how these more interactive experiences affect recruitment, continue to be interesting research topics.

Wills (2007) tested the relationship of façade unity and contrast to initial affective reactions, supporting the proposition that higher levels of unity and contrast would elicit more positive affective reactions than websites with less unity and contrast (Cober, Brown, Keeping, & Levy, 2004). Several studies have further expanded on the relationship between façade elements and e-recruitment outcomes, suggesting that it may be driven by other constructs, such as initial affective reactions (Parzinger et al., 2013), usability perceptions (Howardson & Behrend, 2014), and organizational image (Lyons & Marler, 2011). In addition, Stone,

Baker-Eveleth, and Eveleth (2015) found that more pleasing aesthetics were positively and directly related to website usefulness perceptions, and other research linked pleasing aesthetics to the attitudes that applicants form about the ORW after exposure (Gregory et al., 2013; Kroustalis, 2009) as well as their evaluation of the website (Allen et al., 2013). Thus, it seems that empirical support is leaning in the predicted direction, as façade elements (e.g., vividness, presentation style) are related to the attitudes and perceptions that applicants form about ORWs. Further, the relationship between aesthetics and attraction to organizations after exposure to an ORW seems to be driven by a number of mediating perceptual mechanisms.

Façade: Conflicting with model. Although much of the research reports a positive relationship between website presentation components and organizational attraction, one study presents conflicting findings. That is, no direct relationship between the vividness of a company's recruitment website and applicant attraction to the organization was found (Williamson et al., 2010). As will be discussed later, moderating elements (i.e., the amount of information presented on the ORW and firm reputation) explain the lack of a direct relationship between vividness and attraction. Future research is required to investigate whether additional moderating variables exist for this relationship.

Façade: Additional relevant research. Other relationships have emerged in relation to the façade construct that were not proposed in the model, but that are relevant to our review of recruitment using ORWs. A surprising, but important, finding was that job seekers remembered more information when it was presented in the form of an ORW than when it was presented in the form of a richer format, such as a virtual world (Badger, Kaminsky, & Behrend, 2014). In addition, presenting information in a video format, as opposed to a picture format, predicts more favorable attractiveness ratings (Walker et al., 2009). These findings are consistent with Allen et al.'s (2013) research, finding that people paid more attention to information provided using text and web page content that contained hyperlinks than they did to information presented in graphic image form. Such findings not only support the move from more traditional forms of recruitment to the use of ORWs, but also indicate that increasing media richness might not always lead to better recruitment outcomes. Rather, these findings are exemplary of the curvilinear effect of website complexity on user attitudes and behavior that has emerged in the marketing literature (Deng & Poole, 2010; Mai, Hoffmann, Schwarz, Niemand, & Seidel, 2013). More specifically, research in this domain has found that using rich façade characteristics, such as avatars that present website information, affects user perceptions of website informativeness and entertainment, as well as customer satisfaction, attitudes about products, and behavioral intentions (Holzwarth, Janiszewski, & Neumann, 2006). Thus, for website design features to be effective at persuading job seekers, they need to work in tandem with the information type and quantity available on the website.

It is possible that there are other moderating variables that affect whether the façade characteristics of a website are going to impact outcome variables. For example, the inclusion of more customized information on e-recruitment websites impacts how long job seekers look at the content of a job posting and, subsequently, their recall of the website information, but this effect was stronger when aesthetics were favorable, as opposed to when they were poor (Dineen et al., 2007). Further, research in marketing and HCI (human-computer interaction) contexts tells us that animation features differentially affect users' attention to different types of website characteristics (Kuisma, Simola, Uusitalo, & Öörni, 2010), and the level of customer involvement in online purchases can affect the degree to which different types of avatars effectively persuade users (Holzwarth et al., 2006). Cober, Brown, Keeping, and Levy's model (2004) proposes that prior attitudes about the organization moderate the relationship between façade characteristics and affective reactions, however the HCI and marketing literatures suggest that additional moderators of this relationship might exist. For example, ORW façade characteristics might have different effects for different types of job seekers, in accordance with how invested they are in working for a specific type of company.

Job Seekers' Prior Attitudes

The ways in which people process information, react and behave towards organizations can be largely influenced by the preconceived notions they have about those organizations (Hinojosa, Walker, & Payne, 2015; Kanar, Collins, & Bell, 2010). Since applicants may have been exposed in the past to organizations to which they are applying, it is possible that they have formed attitudes about those organizations; this might impact how they process characteristics of the ORW. Although Cober, Brown, Keeping, and Levy (2004) proposed that the effects of façade characteristics on initial affective reactions would be weaker for individuals with more strongly rooted prior attitudes about the organization, Stone and colleagues (2005) proposed the opposite, suggesting that e-recruitment, as a method, would be more effective for those organizations that are well-known to job seekers. These predictions conflict, but they speak to the instrumental role that familiarity with the organization prior to ORW exposure has on recruitment outcomes, such as attraction to the organization and intentions to pursue employment.

Prior attitudes: Consistent with model. Recent research supports the idea that the prior images job seekers have of organizations influence the images that they form after looking at ORWs (Allen, Mahto, & Otondo, 2007; Gregory et al., 2013). Walker, Feild, Giles, Bernerth, & Short (2011) found further support for the notion that the effects of website façade elements on organizational image perceptions are less strong when job seekers have previously formed attitudes about the organization than when the organization is unfamiliar to them (Cober, Brown, Keeping, & Levy, 2004). Williamson and colleagues (2010) went one step further, revealing that website vividness does, in fact, impact applicant attraction, however the effect only emerged when the organization had a favorable reputation and the website lacked important information. Together, this research agrees with Cober, Brown, Keeping, and Levy's rationale (2004) about the role of prior attitudes towards the website. It also suggests that having prior attitudes about the organization does not eliminate any effect of website façade features on attraction. Instead, Williamson et al.'s (2010) study suggests that although façade elements do not impact attraction when organizations have a poor reputation, they *can* impact attraction when job seekers consider the organization to have a favorable reputation prior to seeing the website and when the website lacks information.

Other work finds that intentions about applying for open positions within an organization before having looked at the ORW impact the amount of time job seekers spend viewing the website and website information processing (Hinojosa et al., 2015). For example, pre-recruitment job pursuit intentions are more positively related to job pursuit intentions after exposure to the ORW and website information recall when perceived fit with the organization is low (Hinojosa et al., 2015). This supports the notion that prior attitudes about an organization as a potential place of employment influences job seeker decision making (Hinojosa et al., 2015).

Prior attitudes: Conflicting with model. Some interesting findings have emerged that conflict with Cober, Brown, Keeping, and Levy's model (2004) . For example, Braddy and colleagues (2008) found that exposure to an ORW impacts organizational favorability, overall image as an employer, and organizational attractiveness, but that prior familiarity levels with the organization did not affect the nature of these relationships. Wills (2007) found that prior attitudes toward the organization did not change the nature of the relationship between aesthetic website characteristics and initial affective reactions. Moreover, Williamson and colleagues (2010) failed to find a moderating effect of a firm's prior reputation on the effect of website vividness on applicant attraction when the amount of information provided on the website was not considered.

Based on the research conducted to date on the moderating role of prior attitudes towards the organization, it seems that more research is required to fully understand the effect of prior attitudes on applicant attraction. Although many findings generally support Cober, Brown, Keeping, and Levy's model (2004), only one study looked at the specific relationship that was predicted to be affected by prior attitudes towards the organization, and no support was found for the proposition. Although research conducted to date generally supports the idea that prior attitudes about an organization influence applicant attraction, more research testing the proposed moderating role of this construct is required before we can draw any firm conclusions.

Prior attitudes: Additional relevant research. Attitudes formed prior to exposure to organizational information have been shown to impact attitudinal and behavioral outcomes across a variety of literatures. For example, a person's perception of an organization's reputation has been shown to impact consumer loyalty (Casaló, Flavián, & Guinalíu, 2008), emotions, and purchase behavior (Kim & Lennon, 2013). Online peer reviews have also been shown to shape consumers' attitudes and considerations (Moore, 2015; Lee, Park, & Han, 2008; Purnawirawan, De Pelsmacker, & Dens, 2012). Thus, in a recruitment context, it is possible that reviews of the organization on other websites could affect job seekers' attitudes about that organization prior to viewing the ORW, though more research is required to say so definitively.

Initial Affective Reactions

Affective responses are often evoked due to objects and situations, and often influence attitudes, decision-making, and subsequent behaviors (Elfenbein, 2007; Forgas & George, 2001). ORWs provide job seekers with cues about the organization, and affective reactions to recruitment materials on ORWs typically influence job seekers' subsequent evaluations (Reeve, Highhouse, & Brooks, 2006). As such, affective responses that accompany exposure to ORWs will likely have important implications for attracting talent.

Initial affective reactions: Consistent with model. Research testing this piece of the model remains scarce, however a few studies have looked at the role of affective reactions in eliciting organizational attraction. Consistent with Cober, Brown, Keeping, and Levy's propositions (2004) , higher positive affect is associated with more favorable attitudes towards the website (Wills, 2007) and initial affective reactions influence usability perceptions (Cho, Lee, & Liu, 2011; Wills, 2007). Positive affect also mediates the relationship between ORW façade (i.e., aesthetics and playfulness) and the viewer's interest in employment with the organization (Parzinger et al., 2013), partially supporting affective reactions as a mediator in driving recruitment outcomes.

Initial affective reactions: Additional relevant research. Other interesting results speak to how initial affective reactions influence organizational image perceptions and attraction to the organization. Specifically, average levels of positive and negative affective reactions to ORWs predict the website's attractiveness levels as well as job seekers' organizational image perceptions (Cho et al., 2011; Reeve et al., 2006). Reeve and colleagues (2006) took this line of research one step further, suggesting that the *intensity* of the positive and negative reactions to various pieces of recruitment information are particularly important. More specifically, they found that one intense negative reaction to a piece of recruitment information can effectively diminish any positive effects of exposure to other pieces of recruitment information (Reeve et al., 2006). Such an effect is consistent with previous work finding that the presence of negative information about organizations has a larger impact on job seekers' attraction to the organization than positive information (Kanar et al., 2010). A similar finding has also emerged in the HCI literature, where perceived irritation due to visual website design features, such as colors, images, and layout, have been shown to negatively impact consumer behavior (Hasan, 2016). Moreover, the stronger impact of negative information and negative affective reactions is consistent with the substantial body of literature supporting the "bad is stronger than good" principle, which states that negative events, such as experiencing negative affect, have a stronger impact on outcomes than positive events (e.g., Baumeister, Bratslavsky, Finkenauer, & Vohs, 2001). The influence of affective reactions on recruitment outcomes could, then, be impacted by not only the type of affective reaction a job seeker has (i.e., positive or negative), but also the intensity of a job seeker's affective reaction.

Another interesting avenue that has not yet been fully explored is how individual differences impact initial affective reactions. Reeve and colleagues (2006) found that higher levels of extraversion and state positive affect prior to website exposure were associated with more positive reactions to negative information, whereas higher levels of neuroticism and higher general mental ability were associated with more intense negative reactions to negative information. Although Reeve and colleagues (2006) did not find the same effects in response to positive information, it is possible that state levels of affectivity and individual differences play a role in dictating the intensity of affective reactions to recruitment websites. Although Cober, Brown, Keeping, and Levy's model (2004) did not propose that individual differences would play a role in determining affective reactions, their impact on affective reactions suggests that attitudes and perceptions towards ORWs and the organization itself could also be affected by these individual differences.

Finally, job seekers' affective reactions have been shown to directly influence perceptions of how easy the website is to use (Cho et al., 2011). These findings suggest that job seekers' initial affective reactions to ORW façade elements influence their perceptions of website system features. More research is required, however, to establish whether reactions to aesthetic and interactive aspects of the website play a critical role in explaining job seeker responses to technical aspects of the website, and how this influences organizational attraction.

Website System Features

Cober, Brown, Keeping, and Levy (2004) define website system features as antecedent features that affect user perceptions of website usability. Although several specific features were described in the model (i.e., navigability, responsiveness, metaphor, content, and transition speed), much of the recent research in this domain focuses on two specific system features: content and navigability. As such, our discussion of the recent research will be structured to first outline the supporting and conflicting findings that emerged for content and navigability features of ORWs. This will be followed by a discussion of additional research relevant to the topic of website system features in an e-recruitment context.

Content. Conceptually, this element is described as the amount and variety of information that aligns with job seekers' goals, and it was originally expected to influence the usability perceptions that job seekers form (Cober, Brown, Keeping, & Levy, 2004).

Content: Consistent with model. Not only do employers manipulate the content features of their websites to project different images of their organizations

(Cober, Brown, & Levy, 2004), but job seekers also tend to give more attention to these content features than to other types of features, such as design and communication components. Consistent with the original model, content features are related to usability perceptions (Gregory et al., 2013; Kroustalis, 2009; Thoms, Chinn, Goodrich, & Howard, 2004), website evaluations (Allen et al., 2007; Allen et al., 2013; Gregory et al., 2013; Kroustalis, 2009; van Birgelen et al., 2008), and intentions to pursue employment (Allen et al., 2013). The amount and variety of information provided on an ORW is also related to the image that job seekers form about the organization (Allen et al., 2013) and organizational attraction (Baum & Kabst, 2014; Lyons & Marler, 2011; Williamson et al., 2010).

Several mediating mechanisms related to website content have also been tested. Specifically, the relationship between the amount of job and organization information presented on ORWs and employment intentions is mediated by the attitudes job seekers form towards the website (Allen et al., 2007) and towards the organization (Allen et al., 2007; Behrend, Baker, & Thompson, 2009; Kroustalis, 2009). Although there is still much research that needs to be conducted to test other mediating mechanisms involved in the emergence of applicant attraction, these results provide a promising foundation for future research investigating content features of recruitment websites.

Content: Conflicting with model. Interestingly, a few results have emerged which conflict with the model as it relates to ORW content. Thoms and colleagues (2004) manipulated whether or not recruitment websites listed job tasks to investigate whether the presence of this information would be related to ratings of usability (i.e., informativeness), but found that no relationship emerged. On the other hand, since Thoms and colleagues (2004) found that the inclusion of pictures of current employees affected usability perceptions, it is possible that job seekers merely value individual content elements differently when exploring ORWs. Further, one study found no relationship between the employment information content provided on an ORW and the organizational image formed after exposure to the ORW (Lyons & Marler, 2011). In a similar vein, another study found a negative relationship between the quality of content displayed on a website and the amount of applications received per job opening (Selden & Orenstein, 2011). Although these findings are counter-intuitive, one possible explanation is that high-quality information allows job seekers to make better person-organization (P-O) fit judgments, leading those who feel they would fit poorly with the organization to self-select out of the application process (Selden & Orenstein, 2011). The presence of such conflicting results with respect to content suggests that additional moderating and mediating variables may exist that have not yet been identified, and that perhaps job seekers value certain types of job and organization information more highly than others.

Navigability. Navigability is defined as whether the website is organized to allow for information acquisition through logical exploration of the website (Cober, Brown, Keeping, & Levy, 2004; Palmer, 2002). Navigability features of ORWs were originally proposed to directly predict usability perceptions, which would subsequently impact other attitudes and behaviors driving attraction (Cober, Brown, Keeping, & Levy, 2004).

Navigability: Consistent with model. Research conducted since 2004 supports the proposed model, finding that navigability positively influences usability perceptions (Cho et al., 2011; Stone et al., 2015). Navigability has also been directly linked to attitudes towards the website (Cho et al., 2011; Kashi & Zheng, 2013; van Birgelen et al., 2008), but the role of usability as a driving force behind the relationship between the navigability features and attitudes towards the website has, unfortunately, not yet been formally tested. Perceived usefulness, defined as the viewer's perception of the website's instrumental value for attaining goals, was identified as a driver of the relationship between navigability and attraction (Stone et al., 2015), providing partial support for Cober, Brown, Keeping, and Levy's proposition (2004).

Navigability: Conflicting with model. Kashi and Zheng (2013) were the only ones to find no relationship between the website ease of use and usability perceptions. Thus, a closer inspection of the relationship between the navigability elements of a website and the perceived usefulness of the website for gathering goal-related information is needed.

Website features: Additional relevant research. Other website features in the model consist of website responsiveness, metaphor, and transition speed (Cober, Brown, Keeping, & Levy, 2004). These refer to whether the website provides feedback to users, whether the navigation elements make sense to users, and the timeliness of any web page changes, respectively. Unfortunately, we could not find research that explicitly investigated these elements within an e-recruitment context, though other types of website features have been studied. For example, one study found that providing customized fit feedback affected attraction to the organization (Dineen et al., 2007) and another found that the inclusion of features that allow job seekers to contact current employees actually *diminished* attraction (Johnson, 2013), however, there remains a dearth of research regarding the effects of including these system features on recruitment outcomes.

Although research in e-recruitment has not focused on all of the website features outlined in Cober, Brown, Keeping, & Levy's model (2004), research in the HCI literature has explored several of the effects that some of these system features may have on perceptions of usability. Studies have found that metaphor (Antle, Corness, & Droumeva, 2009), responsiveness (Lee & Kozar, 2012) and download speed (Tarafdar & Zhang, 2005) are related to usability perceptions. In addition, other features of the online environment, such as security and information clarity, can influence consumer decision-making and behavior (Darley, Blankson, & Luethge, 2010), and overall website quality impacts perceptions of website usefulness and playfulness (Ahn, Ryu, & Han, 2007). Thus, the consumer behavior and HCI literatures present us with other possible factors that could impact e-recruitment outcomes and provide researchers with some direction for investigating the role that these system features play in predicting e-recruiting outcomes.

Finally, a few studies have investigated how other variables that were not included in the model might influence the effect of system features on recruitment outcomes. For example, general attitudes toward technology are related to perceptions of website ease of use (Stone et al., 2015), and P-O fit mediates of the relationship between navigability and attraction (Chen et al., 2012). Such findings are consistent with the notion that older job seekers, who often have less experience and more negative attitudes towards technology, are less comfortable with ORWs than younger job seekers (Bartram, 2000), and may therefore possess less favorable P-O fit perceptions and lower organizational attraction. As older workers stay in the workforce longer, it is important to consider their attitudes towards technology and their ability to use the Internet to find employment as factors that might impact the effectiveness of e-recruitment methods.

Perceptions of Usability

User interface design has come a long way since the first computers were developed for cracking military communications in World War II (IBM, 2003). From punch cards to Siri™ voice commands, computers are becoming ever more intuitively usable in response to consumer preferences (Doug Engelbart Institute, 2017; Porat & Tractinsky, 2012). Although the advent of the Internet and websites was more recent than computers, website designers have been forced to keep up with users' demands for usable interfaces. Website users need to be able to easily access the information they are seeking, and the information needs to be presented in a coherent manner to hold users' attention (Lee & Benbasat, 2003).

In the case of job seekers, who are actively seeking out employment information, recruitment websites need to be coherent and understandable (Cober, Brown, Keeping, & Levy, 2004). This is particularly important because navigating *away* from a website is *always* very easy, and there is very little sunk cost involved in navigating away from a recruitment website if it is too difficult to access, goal-related information. Since Cober, Brown, Keeping, and Levy's original model (2004) on e-recruitment was published, website design standards and best practices, as well as consumer preferences, have changed at an almost unbelievable rate (Huang & Benyoucef, 2013). However, despite these changes, it remains universal that highly usable websites elicit positive attitudes about the website and the organization as an employer.

Usability: Consistent with model. Much like many of the other constructs involved in the original model, a notable amount of support has been found for the direct relationship between perceptions of website usability and e-recruiting outcomes such as organizational attractiveness and behavioral intentions to apply (Braddy et al., 2008; Ehrhart, Mayer, & Ziegert, 2012; Kashi & Zheng, 2013; Pfieffelmann et al., 2010; Selden & Orenstein, 2011; Stone, Baker-Eveleth, & Eveleth, 2015; Thompson et al., 2008; Thoms et al., 2004). Interestingly, Pfieffelmann and colleagues (2010) found a moderating effect of gender on the relationship between perceptions of website usability and applicant attraction, such that the relationship was positive for women, but was unsubstantial for men. The authors argue that women tend to perceive Internet searches as more effortful than men, thus indicating a stronger relationship between ease-of-use and applicant attraction. This is particularly important for organizations in industries suffering from low participation by women, such as Science, Technology, Engineering and Math (STEM), which can't afford to deter female applicants (Beede et al., 2011).

Consistent with Cober, Brown, Keeping, and Levy's model (2004), empirical research has supported the link between perceptions of website usability and attitudes towards ORWs (Cho et al., 2011; Gregory et al., 2013; Kashi & Zheng, 2013; Kroustalis, 2009; Wills, 2007). Furthermore, support was found for the relationship between usability perceptions and organizational image (Braddy et al., 2008), as well as the mediating role of organizational image between perceptions of usability and organizational attractiveness (i.e., applicant attraction; Kroustalis, 2009). Only a single test of the mediating role of website attitudes in the relationship between perceptions of usability and organizational image has been undertaken. Although it supports Cober, Brown, Keeping, and Levy's (2004) original proposition (Wills, 2007), it has not been replicated, and thus remains a relatively open and theoretically interesting question.

Usability: Additional relevant research. Although the original model only proposed a single antecedent of perceived website usability (i.e., website system features), empirical support has been found for several other predictors of usability, including enjoyment derived from the website (Cho et al., 2011) and expectations that the website will be usable (perceptions of usability mediated the relationship between expectations and applicant attraction; Howardson & Behrend, 2014). These findings match research in related literatures, which has found that confirmation or disconfirmation of expectations can affect outcomes such as e-loyalty (Song et al., 2016) and that levels of user engagement with a website can impact advertising effectiveness (Calder, Malthouse, & Schaedel, 2009).

Website Attitudes and Organizational Image

Engendering positive attitudes towards a website is the underlying reason for employing many of the aesthetic and website features previously discussed. Whether an organization uses its website as a virtual storefront (e.g., Amazon.com), to provide a service (e.g., YouTube.com), or to disseminate information and recruit job applicants, it is important for websites to not only provoke positive affect in the short term, but also to create lasting, positive impressions. In the age of social media, where Internet sensations can be easily shared between users and "go viral" overnight, it is crucial that recruitment websites engender lasting, positive attitudes. Furthermore, with many organizations using their websites as an extension of their brand, signaling theory (Spence, 1973) suggests that potential applicants will build their impressions of organizations as employers based on the information and reactions they draw from the organization's website. This would suggest that organizational image could be very strongly influenced by website attitudes and that the two are very closely tied. Although image has long been established to be tightly tied to applicant attraction (Gatewood, Gowan, & Lautenschlager, 1993), research on the impact of ORWs on organizational image has only recently been undertaken.

Attitudes and image: Consistent with model. Considerable empirical support has been found for the positive relationship proposed (Cober, Brown, Keeping, & Levy, 2004) between attitudes towards an organization's website, and the image job seekers hold about the organization (Allen, Mahto, & Otondo, 2007; Gregory et al., 2013; Kashi & Zheng, 2013; Kroustalis, 2009). Similarly, and consistent with the original model, empirical support has been found for the direct relationship between website attitudes and applicant attraction (Cho et al., 2011; van Birgelen et al., 2008; Wills, 2007). These findings underscore the importance of carefully constructing recruitment websites. Research by Allen et al. (2007) as well as Cho et al. (2011) took the relationship one step further and found support for the proposed mediating role of organizational image in the relationship between website attitudes and applicant attraction.

Attitudes and image: Conflicting with model. In contrast to the proposed model and findings presented by Allen et al. (2007), Gregory et al. (2013) did not find support for the mediating role of organizational image on the relationship between website attitudes and applicant attraction, suggesting that there may be moderating variables affecting the relationship.

Attitudes and image: Additional relevant research. Independent of website attitudes, organizational image was also found to be affected by the quality of the job ad (Gregory et al., 2013), and overall website attractiveness (Braddy et al., 2008). Interestingly, organizational image was also found to be negatively related to general mental ability (GMA), as a result of negative information having a stronger impact on job seekers with higher GMA (Reeve, Highhouse, & Brooks, 2006). Other antecedents of the attitudes formed towards websites have also emerged in the marketing and HCI literatures. For example, experiencing more website interactivity and flow throughout the use of a website affects cognitive, affective, and behavioral outcomes (van Noort, Voorveld, & van Reijmersdal, 2012), and displaying websites with the optimal levels of complexity increases attitudes towards the website (Mai et al., 2013). The branding literature also finds that a user's subjective cognitive and affective response to contact with a brand influences behavioral intentions (Morgan-Thomas & Veloutsou, 2013). Considering the overlap between this construct and organizational image perceptions, it may be fruitful to consider research from the branding literature to better understand how exposure to ORWs influences image perceptions and behavioral intentions.

Finally, we were unable to find any research examining the proposed relationship between website attitudes and search behavior. As we will later discuss, however, little research has been conducted regarding website search behaviors in an e-recruitment context in general.

Individual Differences

Cober, Brown, Keeping, and Levy (2004) proposed that individual differences would impact the relationship between image perceptions and attraction to the organization. The underlying rationale for this proposition is that the effect of image perceptions on attraction will depend on the personal preferences and characteristics that job seekers bring to the experience of exploring ORWs. This logic has received some support in other literatures, where researchers find that user values influence user preferences and intentions towards an Internet retailer (Overby & Lee, 2006). Although the specific proposition outlined in the model has yet to be empirically tested, the construct of fit, which embodies individual differences to some degree, has been tested for its impact on organizational attraction. We will therefore discuss the research investigating the role of job seekers' fit perceptions on e-recruitment outcomes.

Individual differences: Additional relevant research. Fit perceptions are based on how well the organization's core values appear to match job seekers' own values and preferences (Chapman, Uggerslev, Carrol, Piasentin, & Jones, 2005). Research to date links P-O fit perceptions to organizational attraction (Chapman et al., 2005; Chen et al., 2012; Hu, Su, & Chen, 2006; Johnson, 2013) and job application intentions (Johnson, 2013), and some research also links person-job (P-J) fit perceptions and organizational attraction (Lyons & Marler, 2011). In addition, job seekers' work-life balance and usability perceptions each predict organizational attraction, and P-O fit perceptions drive both of these relationships (Ehrhart et al., 2012).

Research has also begun to unearth how individual differences can predict fit, supporting research in the consumer behavior literature finding that individual differences not only influence perceptions of an organization (Bart, Shankar, Sultan, & Urban, 2005), but that they also influence consumer behavior (Zhu & Zhang, 2010). For example, Kraichy and Chapman (2014) found that more positive fit perceptions emerged in response to affective recruitment messages (i.e., cheerful, as opposed to formal), that those with a high need for cognition tended to perceive better fit with cognition-oriented ORWs, and that those with a lower need for cognition perceived better fit with affect-oriented ORWs. Further, Johnson (2013) found that individuals with less collectivism displayed better fit with organizations promoting individual achievement values whereas applicants displaying higher levels of collectivism are a better fit for organizations that promote relationship orientation. Given that individual differences also seem to predict fit perceptions it is likely that both individual difference variables and fit perceptions are instrumental in e-recruitment.

Other research has begun to explore how receiving personalized feedback from the website influences fit. Application rates and reports of organizational attraction are found to be higher when websites offer more feedback about whether the job seeker would be a good fit for the organization (Dineen & Noe, 2009; Hu et al., 2006). A configure customization (i.e., depicting fit information in accordance with the job seekers' preferred order; Dineen & Noe, 2009) can also impact job seekers' information processing, fit perceptions, and ultimately their behavior. It therefore appears that not only do job seekers' perceptions of fit influence their attraction, but the way that this information is presented to them can influence e-recruitment outcomes as well.

Job seekers who display more favorable fit perceptions after being exposed to culture-related website content tend to be more attracted to the organization (Braddy, Meade, Michael, & Fleenor, 2009). Other work looking at how the presence of certain information (i.e., diversity cues) elicits different website search behavior for Black and White job seekers finds that the presence of cues that are of interest to job seekers elicits more information processing, which influences their attraction and their ORW search behavior. The preferences, values, and personality traits that an individual possesses can then impact job seekers' emergent perceptions of fit, but it appears that they can also impact how the job seeker experiences the ORW and processes recruitment information.

Search Behavior

Search behavior is described as the amount of time spent viewing ORWs, the breadth of the search, and the effort put in by the job seeker (Cober, Brown, Keeping, & Levy, 2004). The model originally proposed that search behavior would influence job seekers' attitudes towards the ORW as well as the image they form about the organization. Further, it was proposed that it would impact applicant attraction by increasing job seekers' sense of familiarity with the organization after having explored the ORW. Although these three elements are included in the conceptual definition, to our knowledge research has only begun to investigate the effects of viewing time on e-recruitment outcomes. Thus, the typical operationalization of search behavior in the e-recruitment literature is the amount of time spent viewing recruitment features of an ORW.

Search behavior: Consistent with model. Although job seekers do tend to spend more time attending to recruitment content features (e.g., text, hyperlinks) than website graphics, design features related to presentation elements of the website do catch the viewer's attention as well (Allen et al., 2013). For example, one study found that the presence of diversity cues on a fabricated ORW (i.e., signals that the organization values diversity; Walker, Feild, Bernerth, & Becton, 2012) influenced the search behavior of Black and White job seekers differently. More specifically, Black job seekers spent more time viewing the website than White job seekers. Whether the company displays support for a diverse workforce is therefore considered important to minority job seekers as these cues influence not only search behavior but also job seekers' affective reactions and organizational attraction (Walker et al., 2012).

Search behavior: Additional relevant research. Although the Walker et al. (2012) study was fairly specific in terms of the type of website features studied, it also found that presenting diversity cues on recruitment websites impacts search behavior by eliciting positive organizational attractiveness perceptions. Thus, it might be possible that organizational attractiveness perceptions are not only an "ultimate dependent variable" as originally proposed by Cober, Brown, Keeping, and Levy (2004). Rather, attractiveness perceptions might also drive the search behaviors exhibited by job seekers as well.

Another line of research that has emerged in relation to search behavior focuses on the effect of customized information on the amount of time job seekers spend viewing recruitment-related content. Customized information is defined as "information tailored to individual job seekers in response to information those job seekers initially provide about themselves" (Dineen et al., 2007, p. 357). Applicants spend more time viewing recruitment-related content when the website provides customized information, but this is only true when the aesthetic properties of the website are also favorable (Dineen et al., 2007). The researchers reasoned that when aesthetic properties are poor, applicants may direct more attention and viewing time to website content than to the façade elements of the website (Dineen et al., 2007). Although the effects of website customization have garnered little research in an e-recruitment context, the HCI and marketing literatures have responded to calls for more research on customization (Zeithaml, Parasuraman, & Malhotra, 2002). For example, customization has been shown to influence user browsing behaviors (Danaher, Mullarkey, & Essegaier, 2006; Kalyanaraman & Sundar, 2006), supporting the idea that website customization is an important topic to consider for e-recruitment research.

Other research finds that job seekers spend more time viewing recruitment websites when they have prerecruitment perceptions about the organization as a potential employer but also report lower levels of subjective fit with the organization (Hinojosa et al., 2015). Based on this research it seems that ORW design features and job seeker prerecruitment perceptions influence the degree to which job seekers attend to and evaluate ORW content. By using system features that customize information for job seekers, organizations are combining elements of website content and aesthetic presentation. This introduces an interesting element to consider, as applying these types of website features could backfire if the aesthetic elements are not appealing to job seekers. Related research in the HCI literature speaks to other factors that could be of interest to researchers studying search behaviors in an e-recruitment context. For example, individual differences affect how long a person visits a website (Danaher et al., 2006), website viewing time influences user enjoyment and trust (Cyr & Head, 2013), website quality drives the effect of attitudes towards the Internet on Internet search behavior (Ho, Kuo, & Lin, 2012), and user motivation impacts website search behavior (Huang, Lurie, & Mitra, 2009).

Familiarity

In the original model, the familiarity construct is described as the increased level of familiarity job seekers exhibit as a result of having spent time exploring the ORW, and is proposed to be the key mechanisms in explaining the relationship between search behavior and applicant attraction to the organization (Cober, Brown, Keeping, & Levy, 2004). The notion that attitudes and behavior are affected by the experience job seekers have navigating the ORW continues to be supported in the HCI and marketing literatures (Galletta, Henry, McCoy, & Polak, 2006; van Noort, Voorveld, & van Reijmersdal, 2012). However, very little research has studied acquired familiarity with the organization as a result of website exploration in an e-recruitment context.

Familiarity: Additional relevant research. The only study that looked at familiarity after exposure to an ORW focused on the role that familiarity plays in explaining the relationship between the richness of the recruitment medium (i.e., print or website) and attraction to the employer. Results indicated that applicants become more attracted to organizations when the richer recruitment medium is used (i.e., website) as a result of being exposed to more information that is considered to be credible, accurate, and reflective of the organization (Baum & Kabst, 2014). This exposure tended to increase familiarity and decrease uncertainty, which contributed to applicants' attraction to the organization as an employer (Baum & Kabst, 2014). These findings also coincide with previous research in the marketing literature, finding that user familiarity influences the effect of usability perceptions on the formation of customer loyalty (Casaló et al., 2008)

Although Baum and Kabst (2014) provide support for the inclusion of familiarity in Cober, Brown, Keeping, and Levy's model (2004), the specific proposition outlining the role that familiarity plays in driving organizational attraction has not yet been tested empirically. Additional research is required before any conclusions can be drawn about the role that familiarity plays in early stages of recruitment in an online environment.

DISCUSSION

Research investigating the mechanisms involved in the emergence of e-recruitment outcomes remains limited (Chapman & Godollei, 2017). However, it appears that many of the constructs proposed to impact applicant attraction from exploring ORWs are, in fact, instrumental. Figure 2.2 visually summarizes the state of the literature today based on the empirical work conducted since 2004. We only depicted those relationships that either supported one of Cober, Brown, Keeping, and Levy's propositions (2004) (bolded arrows), were found between two constructs in the model that had not been originally proposed (dashed arrows), or were not supported (hollow arrow). Table 2.2 summarizes the main points that emerged for each construct.

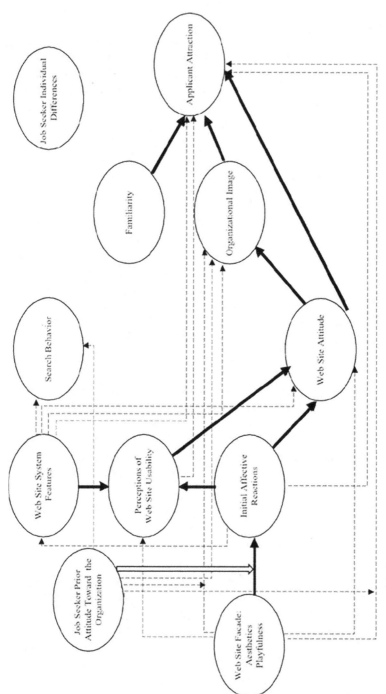

FIGURE 2.2. State of the literature based on empirical work conducted since 2004. Bolded arrows represent relationships that supported original propositions. Dashed arrows represent relationships between two constructs in the model that had not been originally proposed. Hollow arrows represent relationships that were originally proposed but did not emerge in the literature.

TABLE 2.2. Summary of Key Research Takeaways since Cober, Brown, Keeping, and Levy (2004).

Model Construct	Key Outcomes
Website Façade Elements	Linked to more positive affective reactions (Parzinger, et al., 2013; Wills, 2007)
	Linked to usefulness perceptions and attitudes towards ORWs (Stone, et al., 2015; Gregory, et al., 2013)
	Hyperlinks, ORWs, and videos result in better information recall than images or virtual worlds (Allen, et al., 2013)
Job Seekers' Prior Attitudes	Affect search behavior, information recall, and post-exposure intentions (Hinojosa, et al., 2015)
	Moderates the effect of ORW on organization image (Allen, et al., 2007; Braddy, et al., 2008)*
	Moderates the effect of vividness on attraction when ORW lacks information (Williamson, et al., 2010)*
Initial Affective Reactions	Linked to usability perceptions and attitudes towards ORWs (Cho, et al., 2011; Wills, 2007)
	Intense negative affective response can lower organization evaluations (Reeve, et al., 2006)
	Individual differences can affect the intensity of affective responses (Reeve, et al., 2006)
Website System Features	Content features impact usability and overall ORW evaluations (Allen, et al., 2013)
	General attitudes towards technology can influence perceptions of ORW ease of use (Howardson & Behrend, 2014; Stone, et al., 2015; Gregory, et al., 2013)
	Presenting a list of job tasks does not affect usability, but including employee pictures does (Thoms et al, 2004)
Perceptions of Usability	Linked to attraction, attitudes towards ORWs, and organization image (Braddy, et al., 2008; Erhart, et al., 2012)
	The relationship between usability and attraction is positive for women but unsubstantial for men (Pfieffelmann, et al., 2010)
	Mediates the relationship between website façade and applicant attraction (Pfieffelmann, et al., 2010; Selden & Orenstein, 2011; Wills, 2007) *
Attitudes Towards the Website	Linked to applicant attraction (Cho, et al., 2011; Wills, 2007)
	Linked to image perceptions (Braddy, et al., 2008)
	Mediates the relationship between ORW usability and organization image (Wills, 2007)
Organizational Image	Mediates the relationship between website façade and applicant attraction (Lyons & Marler, 2011)
	Mediates the relationship between ORW usability and applicant attraction (Kroustalis, 2009)
	Quality of job advertisement and overall ORW attractiveness influence organization image (Walker, et al., 2008)
Individual Differences	Cheerful recruitment messages elicit more positive fit perceptions, moderated by need for cognition (Kraichy & Chapman, 2014)
	General mental ability and extraversion impact the intensity of affective reactions (Reeve, et al., 2006)
	Personalized feedback about fit predicts applicant attraction and application rates (Dineen & Noe, 2009; Hu, et al., 2006)

(continues)

TABLE 2.2. Continued

Model Construct	Key Outcomes
Website Search Behavior	Increased content is positively linked to search behaviour (Allen, et al., 2013)
	Providing customized information is linked to increased search behavior (Dineen & Noe, 2009)
	Prior attitudes about the organization are linked to search behavior (Hinojosa, et al., 2015)
Familiarity	The richness of the recruitment medium is linked to applicant attraction by increasing familiarity (Baum & Kabst, 2014)

Notes. * = conflicting findings in the literature

Summary of Findings

Support for proposed relationships. Research conducted to date tells us how ORW exploration can foster applicant attraction. We now know that a number of aesthetic features predict applicant attraction and intentions to pursue employment, and that this relationship is driven by mediators such as affective reactions, usability perceptions, and organizational image. Specifically, website façade elements impact affective perceptions, which impact the attitudes that job seekers form towards the website. Website attitudes then influence organizational image perceptions and, subsequently, applicant attraction. Navigability and content features of the website are also predictive of usability perceptions, which are then tied to the attitudes that job seekers form towards the ORW, as well as organizational image perceptions and applicant attraction. The role of job seekers' prior attitudes towards the organization as a moderator of the relationship between façade elements and affective reactions to ORWs has only been tested once, but this relationship did not emerge. Research then supports much of Cober, Brown, Keeping, and Levy's model (2004), providing us with some insight into how applicant attraction to organizations emerges as well as a way forward for future research on e-recruitment.

Conflict with proposed relationships. Although a portion of the model has been supported, a few conflicting findings emerged that should be acknowledged. First, the vividness component of aesthetics only impacts applicant attraction when the organization has a favorable reputation but lacks information (Williamson et al., 2010). The quality of the recruitment website is also negatively related to the amount of applications organizations receive (Selden & Orenstein, 2011), and no notable relationship has emerged between recruitment content and organizational image perceptions (Lyons & Marler, 2011). Other studies indicate that navigability is not related to usability perceptions (Kashi & Zheng, 2013) and that organizational image does not mediate the relationship between website attitudes and applicant attraction (Gregory et al., 2013). Given that the e-recruitment literature is still in its infancy (Chapman & Godollei, 2017), we expect that many of these discrepancies will be resolved as the literature matures. These inconsistencies in the literature, however, highlight opportunities for future research to explore.

Underexplored proposed relationships. Some pieces of Cober, Brown, Keeping, and Levy's model (2004) have not yet been explored in much depth. Specifically, the role that a number of website system features, website search behavior, post-ORW exposure familiarity, and individual difference variables play in predicting applicant attraction requires more attention. Although research investigating the effects of applicant fit perceptions on attraction provides some support for Cober, Brown, Keeping, and Levy's theory (2004) that the values an applicant brings to the e-recruitment experience affect outcomes, any other effects that these values can have on recruitment outcomes have not yet been studied. The effects of website system features, search behavior, and familiarity on decision making and loyalty have been more deeply investigated in the HCI and consumer behavior literatures than in an e-recruitment context.

Model Extensions

Fit. Although the model presented by Cober, Brown, Keeping, and Levy (2004) is quite comprehensive, recent findings also present opportunities for extending the model. One area that seems to have taken off in the literature, but was not explicitly included in the model, is the role of fit on recruitment outcomes within an ORW context (e.g., Gregory et al., 2013; Hu et al., 2006; Pfieffelmann et al., 2010). The literature typically refers to P-O or P-J fit as impactful on applicant attraction, however another interesting variant of fit has recently been brought to light. Person-industry fit, described as how well job seekers' values match the cultural stereotypes associated with the industry in which they work, is related to P-O fit (De Goede, Van Vianen, & Klehe, 2011). Effective website design, however, can actually suppress the effects that industry stereotypes have on job seekers' decisions to apply to the organization, which is consistent with research finding that factors beyond the organization's control, such as word-of-mouth (Van Hoye & Lievens, 2007), can affect the recruitment process and applicant attraction.

Word-of-mouth. Research investigating the effects of word-of-mouth has begun to emerge in the marketing and HCI literatures, especially in relation to online reviews. Online reviews have been shown to influence outcomes such as purchasing decisions (Chen & Xie, 2008) and sales (Zhu & Zhang, 2010). The e-recruitment literature has touched on the effects of displaying employee testimonials on ORWs and how this differs from having received the same information from someone on a company-independent website (Van Hoye & Lievens, 2007), however it has not yet investigated the impact of online employee reviews from a multitude of sources. For example, Glassdoor.com provides reviews from current and former employees about the organization that is posting each job. For organizations with which job seekers are familiar, online reviews might not be effective at influencing attitudes and behaviors. However, for job seekers who are unfamiliar with the organization, external online reviews could be instrumental in their experience of an ORW, and could subsequently impact attraction to the organization. Additional research should therefore consider exploring this topic further.

ORW formats. There are multiple mediums by which job seekers can be exposed to ORWs (Perakakis, Ghinea, & Thanou, 2015). For example, job seekers may not apply to an organization using a mobile device, but they may look at the ORW using a mobile device, highlighting the importance of considering other formats of ORWs. The HCI literature has already begun to explore the effects of mobile website formats, finding that tasks take longer to complete and that users can be less effective at completing tasks when using mobile devices (Arthur, Doverspike, Muñoz, Taylor, & Carr, 2014). Further, some organizations choose to host recruiting information on social media pages rather than setting up their own external ORW. To our knowledge, no recruitment research has investigated the implications associated with hosting recruitment information on social media websites. However, the marketing literature discusses several opportunities and pitfalls for managing customer relationships online, such as issues related to controlling message diffusion, privacy, and data security (Malthouse, Haenlein, Skiera, Wege, & Zhang, 2013). Since ORWs can be presented in different, or multiple, ways, it is likely that the features of these mediums will differ, and that job seekers' attitudes and behaviors will reflect these differences to some degree.

Customization. The effect of customization elements on websites is another potential extension of the model. Organizations began using customized information to inform job seekers whether they would likely be a good fit for the organization in an attempt to reduce the number of applications received from poor-fitting individuals (Dineen et al., 2007). Although we know why organizations have begun including these elements, and we know that they do impact fit and attraction (Dineen et al., 2007; Dineen & Noe, 2009), their impact on other elements involved in the emergence of applicant attraction is not yet fully understood.

Trust and security. As more organizations attempt to customize their ORW content, provide feedback based on information submitted (Dineen et al., 2007), and use social media as well as mobile formats of websites, the need to foster trust among job seekers will become more important. Research in the consumer behavior literature states that trust is increasingly important because it affects buying behavior, and that lower level of trusts can spark apprehensiveness (Darley et al., 2010). Being able to trust not only the security of ORWs, but also the information and the graphical characteristics that are displayed is important to curbing any reluctance from users (Beldad, de Jong, & Steehouder, 2010), and could impact e-recruitment outcomes such as attraction to an organization as well as intentions to apply. There are numerous features on both computer-compatible websites and mobile-compatible websites that could track and record user information. Therefore, job seekers could be apprehensive about visiting certain websites or entering information such as preferences and values on websites.

FUTURE DIRECTIONS AND RESEARCH AGENDA

Considering the nascent state of the e-recruitment literature, there are ample avenues for future research on applicant attraction within the context of ORWs. The advancements in web design over the past decade have been extensive, and given the expectation that organizations will be able to keep up with the technology, some of the earlier research on ORWs may no longer apply. It is therefore crucial for future research to consider branching out into other literatures that study some of these constructs, such as the e-commerce, marketing, and HCI literatures. Although some of the relationships found in these other literatures may emerge differently in an e-recruitment context, the results of studies in these other literatures could give researchers in e-recruitment some guidance going forward.

First, research in e-recruitment should consider using approaches that capture user behavior while they navigate a website. With the exception of Reeve et al.'s (2006) study on the effect of affective intensity on e-recruitment outcomes, much of the research to date asks participants to respond to questionnaires prior to and/or after being exposed to a website stimulus. As a result, researchers are often unable to capture the *process* by which individuals come to form attraction perceptions towards the organization from experiencing ORWs. Some research has taken a step in the right direction by looking at the flow of a website user's experience as influential on consumer behavior and return intentions (e.g., Hausman & Siekpe, 2009), and more research in the HCI literature uses methods such as eye-tracking to capture a user's experience (e.g., Cyr, Head, & Larios, 2010; Zhou & Lu, 2011). The e-recruitment literature may therefore benefit from using these methods.

Second, contextual differences should be considered. As recruitment and selection become more global, it is increasingly important to consider the cultural differences that may exist. Individuals from other cultures may not be as familiar with searching ORWs for recruitment information, and further, the process of developing applicant attraction to the organization may differ as a result. Some research has begun to explore the nature of contextual effects on website usage, finding that cultural differences affect user responses to website color schemes (Cyr et al., 2010), web site evaluation, and usability (Li, Sun, & Zhang, 2007). Research in e-recruitment should consider the possibility that individuals with different cultural backgrounds may have different values and different perceptions of what constitutes an aesthetically pleasing website, as these differences could influence the emergence of recruitment outcomes.

Finally, future research should consider looking into the motivations that job seekers have for seeking out and exploring ORWs. Some research in the e-commerce area has begun to investigate the motivational underpinnings for search behaviors on websites, finding that they affect the amount of time spent searching online for product/service information as well as online shopping behaviors (Joines, Scherer, & Scheufele, 2003). Further, other research has linked motivation to the effects of electronic word-of-mouth (i.e., online reviews) and to the amount of time spent making a product choice and the quality of the product choice (Gupta & Harris, 2010). In an e-recruitment context, it is therefore possible that a person's motivation for being on an ORW will greatly impact not only how they experience it, but also how they perceive the website and how their attitudes towards the website and the organization are formed.

Practical Implications

The practice of e-recruitment has come a long way since the initial publication of Cober, Brown, Keeping, and Levy's model (2004) predicting recruitment outcomes from ORWs. Although research (as in most areas of management research) lags behind organizational practice, the construction and implementation of ORWs is somewhat unique in that organizations' websites are intentionally easy for a wide audience (including other organizations) to access, and much of the computer code behind them is available to anyone who wishes to view it. Thus, design features can proliferate with incredible ease, and the design decisions of successful organizations can be easily copied and iterated on by other organizations. Furthermore, marketing and recruitment research for organizations has existed for substantially longer than the use of ORWs for recruitment itself, so best practices from these research areas have been applied to the design and implementation of ORWs from the very beginning. As a result, many of the findings we have summarized in this review are representative of best practices that recruiters should adhere to for the best e-recruitment outcomes.

First, attractive aesthetic features in an ORW are critical to the ultimate successful implementation of an e-recruitment strategy. Careful design and development of an ORW to ensure that it engenders positive affective reactions, perceptions of usability (that is, it is easy to navigate and find the content of interest), and to ensure that it aligns with a positive organizational image are necessary for positive e-recruitment outcomes. Furthermore, while it was found that prior negative attitudes towards an organization cannot necessarily be rectified with an ORW itself, positive attitudes can be improved, suggesting that even organizations with a positive public image can benefit from care and attention to the ORW development process (Reeve et al., 2006).

Other, more specific findings that are of practical use to managers and HR practitioners include the use of hyperlinks and videos on ORWs to improve information recall (Allen et al., 2013), cheerful recruitment messaging to elicit more positive fit perceptions (Kraichy & Chapman, 2014), and personalizing feedback to increase applicant attraction (Dineen & Noe, 2009; Hu et al., 2006).

It is also important to note that while several researchers have found that ORW aesthetics and quality may *negatively* impact recruitment outcomes, it is entirely possible that these effects are driven by applicant fit and job seekers self-selecting out, thus potentially reducing the costs associated with selecting out ill-fitting candidates for organizations. Although this idea requires additional research, the existing literature points heavily towards a comprehensive, well thought out ORW design process.

CONCLUSION

Given the continued popularity of e-recruitment methods, determining the best ways to implement these tools to attract the right applicants is increasingly important. Utilizing the Cober, Brown, Keeping, and Levy (2004) framework as an organizing framework, we paint a clearer picture of the e-recruitment literature as it relates to ORWs. Research conducted since Cober, Brown, Keeping, and Levy (2004) proposed their model demonstrates that substantial progress has been made in determining how ORWs influence applicant attraction. Further, many of the constructs originally proposed as instrumental in predicting applicant attraction do, in fact, influence e-recruitment outcomes. This knowledge helps us understand the emergence of applicant attraction within a digital context. However, the research reviewed also highlights the complexity associated with attracting applicants using ORWs. Our review provides a summary of the literature as it exists today and highlights that this literature is still rife with questions that require additional research attention.

REFERENCES[1]

Ahn, T., Ryu, S., & Han, I. (2007). The impact of web quality and playfulness on user acceptance of online retailing. *Information & Management, 44,* 263–275.

*Allen, D. G., Biggane, J. E., Pitts, M., Otondo, R., & Van Scotter, J. V. (2013). Reactions to recruitment websites: Visual and verbal attention, attraction, and intentions to pursue employment. *Journal of Business and Psychology, 28,* 263–285.

*Allen, D. G., Mahto, R. V., & Otondo, R. F. (2007). Web-based recruitment: Effects of information, organizational brand, and attitudes toward a web site on applicant attraction. *Journal of Applied Psychology, 92,* 1696–1708.

Antle, A. N., Corness, G., & Doumeva, M. (2009). What the body knows: Exploring the benefits of embodied metaphors in hybrid physical digital environments. *Interacting with Computers, 21,* 66–75.

Arthur, W. Jr., Doverspike, D., Muñoz, G. J., Taylor, J. E., & Carr, A. E. (2014). The use of mobile devices in high-stakes remotely delivered assessments and testing. *International Journal of Selection and Assessment, 22,* 113–123.

*Badger, J. M., Kaminsky, S. E., & Behrend, T. S. (2014). Media richness and information acquisition in internet recruitment. *Journal of Managerial Psychology, 29,* 866–883.

Bart, Y., Shankar, V., Sultan, F., & Urban, G. L. (2005). Are the drivers and role of online trust the same for all web sites and consumers? A large-scale exploratory empirical study. *Journal of Marketing, 69,* 113–152.

Bartram, D. (2000). Internet recruitment and selection: Kissing frogs to find princes. *International Journal of Selection and Assessment, 8,* 261–274.

---

[1] * indicates articles that specifically tested part of Cober, Brown, Keeping, and Levy's model (2004), forming the foundation for Figure 2.2

*Baum, M., & Kabst, R. (2014). The effectiveness of recruitment advertisements and recruitment websites: indirect and interactive effects on applicant attraction. *Human Resource Management, 53,* 353–378.

Baumeister, R. F., Bratslavsky, E., Finkenauer, C., & Vohs, K. D. (2001). Bad is stronger than good. *Review of General Psychology, 5,* 323–370.

Beede, D. N., Julian, T. A., Langdon, D., McKittrick, G., Khan, B., & Doms, M. E. (2011). Women in STEM: A gender gap to innovation. *Economics and Statistics Administration Issue Brief,* (04–11). Retrieved from http://papers.ssrn.com/sol3/papers.cfm?abstract_id=1964782.

*Behrend, T. S., Baker, B. A., & Thompson, L. F. (2009). Effects of pro-environmental recruiting messages: The role of organizational reputation. *Journal of Business and Psychology, 24,* 341–350.

Beldad, A., de Jong, M., & Steehouder, M. (2010). How shall I trust the faceless and intangible? A literature review on the antecedents of online trust. *Computers in Human Behavior, 26,* 857–869.

*Braddy, P. W., Meade, A. W, & Kroustalis, C. M. (2008). Online recruiting: The effects of organizational familiarity, website usability, and website attractiveness on viewers' impressions of organizations. *Computers in Human Behavior, 24,* 2992–3001.

Braddy, P. W., Meade, A. W., Michael, J. J., & Fleenor, J. W. (2009). Internet recruiting: Effects of website content features on viewers' perceptions of organizational culture. *International Journal of Selection and Assessment, 17,* 19–34.

Breaugh, J. A. (2013). Employee recruitment. *Annual Review of Psychology, 34,* 389–416.

Calder, B. J., Malthouse, E. C., & Schaedel, U. (2009). Experimental study of the relationship between online engagement and advertising effectiveness. *Journal of Interactive Marketing, 23,* 321–331.

Casaló, C., Flavián, C., & Guinalíu, M. (2008). The role of perceived usability, reputation, satisfaction and consumer familiarity on the website loyalty formation process. *Computers in Human Behavior, 24,* 325–345.

Chapman, D. S., Godollei, A. (2017). E-recruiting: Using technology to attract job applicants. In G. Hertel, D. L. Stone, R. Johnson, & J. Passmore (Eds.), *The handbook of the psychology of the internet at work.* London: Wiley, Blackwell.

Chapman, D. S., Uggerslev, K. L., Carroll, S. A., Piasentin, K. A., & Jones, D. A. (2005). Applicant attraction to organizations and job choice: A meta-analytic review of the correlates of recruiting outcomes. *Journal of Applied Psychology, 90,* 928–944.

Chapman, D. S., & Webster, J. (2003). The use of technologies in the recruiting, screening, and selection processes for job candidates. *The International Journal of Selection and Assessment, 11,* 113–120.

*Chen, C-C., Lin, M-M., & Chen, C-M. (2012). Exploring the mechanisms of the relationship between website characteristics and organizational attraction. *The International Journal of Human Resource Management, 23,* 867–885.

Chen, Y., & Xie, J. (2008). Online consumer review: Word-of-mouth as a new element of marketing communication mix. *Management Science, 54,* 477–491.

*Cho, S., Lee, W., & Liu, J. (July, 2011). E-recruitment: Effects of enjoyment and attitudes toward websites on corporate image and intention to apply. *International Council on Hotel and Restaurant and Institutional Education Conference,* University of Massachusetts – Amherst, 1–16.

Cober, R. R., Brown, D. J., Keeping, L. M., & Levy, P. E. (2004). Recruitment on the net: How do organizational website characteristics influence applicant attraction? *Journal of Management, 30,* 623–646.

*Cober, R. T, Brown, D. J., & Levy, P. E. (2004). Form, content, and function: An evaluative methodology for corporate employment websites. *Human Resource Management, 43,* 201–218.

Cyr, D., & Head, M. (2013). The impact of task framing and viewing time on user website perceptions and viewing behavior. *International Journal of Human-Computer Studies, 71,* 1089–1102.

Cyr, D., Head, M., & Larios, H. (2010). Colour appeal in website design within and across cultures: A multi-method evaluation. *International Journal of Human-Computer Studies, 68,* 1–21.

Danaher, P. J., Mullarkey, G. W., & Essegaier, S. (2006). Factors affecting web site visit duration: A cross-domain analysis. *Journal of Marketing Research, 43,* 182–194.

Darley, W. K., Blankson, C., & Luethge, D. J. (2010). Toward an integrated framework for online consumer behavior and decision making process: A review. *Psychology & Marketing, 27,* 94–116.

De Goede, M. E. E., Van Vianen, A. E. M., & Klehe, U-C. (2011). Attracting applicants on the web: PO fit, industry culture stereotypes, and website design. *International Journal of Selection and Assessment, 19,* 51–61.

Deng, L., & Poole, M. S. (2010). Affect in web interfaces: A study of the impacts of web page visual complexity and order. *MIS Quarterly, 34,* 711–730

*Dineen, B. R., Ling, J., Ash, S. R., & DelVecchio, D. (2007). Aesthetic properties and message customization: Navigating the dark side of web recruitment. *Journal of Applied Psychology, 92,* 356–372.

Dineen, B. R., & Noe, R. A. (2009). Effects of customization on application decisions and applicant pool characteristics in a web-based recruitment context. *Journal of Applied Psychology, 94,* 224–234.

Doug Engelbart Institute. (2017). Doug's 1968 Demo - Doug Engelbart Institute. Retrieved March 23, 2017, from http://www.dougengelbart.org/firsts/dougs–1968-demo.html

*Ehrhart, K. H., Mayer, D. M., & Ziegert, J. C. (2012). Web-based recruitment in the millennial generation: Work-life balance, website usability, and organizational attraction. *European Journal of Work and Organizational Psychology, 21,* 850–874.

Elfenbein, H. A. (2007). Emotions in organizations. *The Academy of Management Annals, 1,* 315–386.

Forgas, J. P., & George, J. M. (2001). Affective influences on judgments and behavior in organizations: An information processing perspective. *Organizational Behavior and Human Decision Processes, 86,* 3–34.

Galletta, D. F., Henry, R. M., McCoy, S., & Polak, P. (2006). When the wait isn't so bad: The interacting effects of website delay, familiarity, and breadth. *Information Systems Research, 17,* 20–37.

Gatewood, R. D., Gowan, & M. A., Lautenschlager, G. J. (1993). Corporate image, recruitment image, and initial job choice decisions. *The Academy of Management Journal, 36,* 414- 427.

*Gregory, C. K., Meade, A. W., & Thompson, L. F. (2013). Understanding internet recruitment via signaling theory and the elaboration likelihood model. *Computers in Human Behavior, 29,* 1949–1959.

Gupta, P., & Harris, J. (2010). How e-WOM recommendations influence product consideration and quality of choice: A motivation to process information perspective. *Journal of Business Research, 63*, 1041–1049.

Hasan, B. (2016). Perceived irritation in online shopping: The impact of website design characteristics. *Computers in Human Behavior, 54*, 224–230.

Hausman, A. V., & Siekpe, J. S. (2009). The effect of web interface features on consumer online purchase intentions. *Journal of Business Research, 62*, 5–13.

*Hinojosa, A. S., Walker, H. J., & Payne, G. T. (2015). Prerecruitment organizational perceptions and recruitment website information processing. *The International Journal of Human Resource Management, 26*, 2617–2631.

Ho, L-A., Kuo, T-H, & Lin, B. (2012). The mediating effect of website quality on internet searching behavior. *Computers in Human Behavior, 28*, 840–848.

Holm, A. B. (2012). E-recruitment: Towards a ubiquitous recruitment process and candidate relationship management. *Zeitschrift für Personalforschung—German Journal of Human Resource Management, 26*, 241–259.

Holzwarth, M., Janiszewski, C., & Neumann, M. M. (2006). The influence of avatars on online consumer shopping behavior. *Journal of Marketing, 70*, 19–36.

*Howardson, G. N., & Behrend, T. S. (2014). Using the internet to recruit employees: Comparing the effects of usability expectations and objective technological characteristics on internet recruitment outcomes. *Computers in Human Behavior, 21*, 334–342.

Hu, C., Su, H-C, & Chen, C-I, B. (2006). The effect of person-organization fit feedback via recruitment websites on applicant attraction. *Computers in Human Behavior, 23*, 2509–2523.

Huang, Z., & Benyoucef, M. (2013). From e-commerce to social commerce: A closer look at design features. *Electronic commerce research and applications, 12*, 246–259.

Huang, P., Lurie, N. H., & Mitra, S. (2009). Searching for experience on the web: An empirical examination of consumer behavior for search and experience goods. *Journal of Marketing, 73*, 55–69.

IBM. (2003, January 23). IBM - Archives - History of IBM - 1940 - United States [TS200]. Retrieved March 23, 2017 from www-03.ibm.com/ibm/history/history/decade_1940.html

*Johnson, T. L. (2013). *The effects of organizational, website, and applicant characteristics on perceptions of person-organization fit, organizational attraction, and job application intentions* Available from ProQuest Dissertation and Theses (UMI No: 3594572)

Joines, J. L., Sherer, C. W., & Scheufele, D. A. (2003). Exploring motivations for consumer web use and their implications for e-commerce. *Journal of Consumer Marketing, 20*, 90–108.

Jones, D. A., Willness, C. R., & Madey, S. (2014). Why are job seekers attracted by corporate social performance? Experimental and field tests of three signal-based mechanisms. *Academy of Management Journal, 57*, 383–404.

Kalyanaraman, S., & Sundar, S. S. (2006). The psychological appeal of personalized content in web portals: Does customization affect attitudes and behavior? *Journal of Communication, 56*, 110–132.

Kanar, A. M., Collins, C. J., & Bell, B. S. (2010). A comparison of the effects of positive and negative information on job seekers' organizational attraction and attribute recall. *Human Performance, 23,* 193–212.

*Kashi, K., & Zheng, C. (2013). Extending technology acceptance model to the e-recruitment context in Iran. *International Journal of Selection and Assessment, 21,* 121–129.

Kim, J., & Lennon, S. J. (2013). Effects of reputation and website quality on online consumer's emotion, perceived risk and purchase intention. *Journal of Research in Interactive Marketing, 7,* 36–56.

*Kraichy, D., & Chapman, D. S. (2014). Tailoring web-based recruiting messages: Individual differences in the persuasiveness of affective and cognitive messages. *Journal of Business and Psychology, 29,* 253–268.

*Kroustalis, C. M. (2009). *Internet recruitment: Examining the roles of information, attitudes, and perceived fit on applicant attraction.* Available from ProQuest Dissertations and Theses database, (UMI No. 3398516).

Kuisma, J., Simola, J., Uusitalo, L., & Öörni, A. (2010). The effects of animation and format on the perception and memory of online advertising. *Journal of Interactive Marketing, 24,* 269–282.

Lee, Y., & Kozar, K. A. (2012). Understanding of website usability: Specifying and measuring constructs and their relationships. *Decision Support Systems, 52,* 450–463.

Lee, Y. E., & Benbasat, I. (2003). Interface design for mobile commerce. *Communications of the ACM, 46,* 49–52.

Lee, J., Park, D-H., & Han, I. (2008). The effect of negative online consumer reviews on product attitude: An information processing view. *Electronic Commerce, Research and Applications, 7,* 341–352.

Li, H., Sun, X., & Zhang, K. (2007). *Culture-centered design: Cultural factors in interface usability and usability tests.* Proceedings of IEEE Society's ACIS International Conference on Software Engineering, Artificial Intelligence, Networking, and Parallel/Distribute Computing (pp.1084–1088). Washington, DC: IEEE Computer Society.

*Lyons, B. D., & Marler, J. H. (2011). Got image? Examining organizational image in web recruitment. *Journal of Managerial Psychology, 26,* 58–76.

Mai, R., Hoffmann, S., Schwarz, U., Niemand, T., & Seidel, J. (2013). The shifting range of optimal web site complexity. *Journal of Interactive Marketing, 28,* 101–116.

Malthouse, E. C., Haenlein, M., Skiera, B., Wege, E., Zhang, M. (2013). Managing customer relationships in the social media era: Introducing the social CRM house. *Journal of Interactive Marketing, 27,* 270–280.

Malthouse, E. C., & Schaedel, U. (2009). An experimental study of the relationship between online management and advertising effectiveness. *Journal of Interactive Marketing, 23,* 321–331.

Maurer, S. D., & Cook, D. P. (2011). Using company websites to e-recruit qualified applicants: A job marketing based review of theory-based research. *Computers in Human Behavior, 27,* 106–117.

Maurer, S. D., & Liu, Y. (2007). Developing effective e-recruiting websites: Insights for managers from marketers. *Business Horizons, 50,* 305–314.

Moore, S. G. (2015). Attitude predictability and helpfulness in online reviews: The role of explained actions and reactions. *Journal of Consumer Research, 42,* 30–44.

Morgan-Thomas, A., & Veloutsou, C. (2013). Beyond technology acceptance: Brand relationships and online brand experience. *Journal of Business Research, 66,* 21–27.

Mulvey, T. (2013). *SHRM survey findings: Social networking websites and recruiting/selection.* Retrieved from: https://shrm.org/hr-today/trends-and-forecasting/research-and-surveys/Pages/shrm-social-networking-websites-recruiting-job-candidates.aspx

Overby, J. W., & Lee, E-J. (2006). The effects of utilitarian and hedonic online shopping value on consumer preference and intentions. *Journal of Business Research, 59,* 1160–1166.

Palmer, J. W. (2002). Web site usability, design, and performance metrics. *Information Systems Research, 13,* 151–167.

*Parzinger, M. J., Ward, S. G., Langford, M., & Greehey, B. (2013). Web recruitment: Impact of aesthetics and playfulness on user's initial affective reactions as it relates to applicant attraction. *International Journal of the Academic Business World, 8,* 57–66.

Perkakis, E., Ghinea, G., & Thanou, E. (2015). Are websites optimized for mobile devices and smart TVs? *Proceedings from the 8ᵗʰ International Conference on Human System Interaction* (pp. 47–53), Warsaw, Poland, (25–27 June 2015).

*Pfieffelmann, B., Wagner, S. H., & Libkuman, T. (2010). Recruiting on corporate web sites: Perceptions of fit and attraction. *International Journal of Selection and Assessment, 18,* 40–47.

Ployhart, R. E. (2006). Staffing in the 21st century: New challenges and strategic opportunities. *Journal of Management, 32,* 868–897.

Porat, T., & Tractinsky, N. (2012). It's a pleasure buying here: The effects of web-store design on consumers' emotions and attitudes. *Human-Computer Interaction, 27,* 235–276.

Purnawirawan, N., De Pelsmacker, P., & Dens, N. (2012). Balance and sequence in online reviews: How perceived usefulness affects attitudes and intentions. *Journal of Interactive Marketing, 26,* 244–255.

*Reeve, C. L., Highhouse, S., & Brooks, M. E. (2006). A closer look at reactions to realistic recruitment messages. *International Journal of Selection and Assessment, 14,* 1–15.

*Selden, S., & Orenstein, J. (2011). Government e-recruiting websites: The influence of e- recruitment content and usability on recruiting and hiring outcomes in US state governments. *International Journal of Selection and Assessment, 19,* 31–40.

Song, L., Weisstein, F. L., Anderson, R. E., Swaminathan, S., Wu, G. J., Feng, S., & Tan, K. (2016). The effects of expectation disconfirmations of customer outcomes in e-markets: Impact of national culture. *Journal of Marketing Channels, 23,* 217–229.

Spence, M. (1973). Job market signaling. *The Quarterly Journal of Economics, 87,* 355–374

Stone, D. L., Lukaszewski, K. M., & Isenhour, L. C. (2005). E-recruiting: Online strategies for attracting talent. In H. Gueutal & D. L. Stone (Eds.), *The brave new world of EHR: Human resources in the digital age* (pp. 22–53). New York: John Wiley & Sons.

*Stone, R. W., Baker-Eveleth, L., & Eveleth, D. (2015). The influence of the firm's career- website on job seekers' intentions to the firm. *International Journal of Human Resource Studies, 5,* 111–130.

Sylva, J., & Mol, S. T. (2009). E-recruitment: A study into applicant perceptions of an online application system. *International Journal of Selection and Assessment, 17,* 311–323.

Tarafdar, M., & Zhang, J. (2005). Analyzing the influence of website design parameters on website usability. *Information Resources Management Journal, 18,* 62–80.

*Thompson, L. F., Braddy, P. W., Wuensch, K. L. (2008). E-recruitment and the benefits of organizational web appeal. *Computers in Human Behavior, 24,* 2384–2398.

*Thoms, P., Chinn, S. J., Goodrich, J., & Howard, G. (2004). Designing personable and informative job recruiting web sites: Testing the effect of the design on attractiveness and intent to apply. *Psychological Reports,* 1031–1042.

*van Birgelen, M. J. H., Wetzels, M. G. M., & van Dolen, W. M. (2008). Effectiveness of corporate employment websites: How content and form influence intentions to apply. *International Journal of Manpower, 29,* 731–751.

Van Hoye, G., & Lievens, F. (2007). Investigating web-based recruitment sources: Employee testimonials vs. word-of-mouse. *International Journal of Selection and Assessment, 15,* 372–382.

van Noort, G., Voorveld, H. A. M., & van Reijmersdal, E. A. (2012). Interactivity in brand websites: Cognitive, affective, and behavioral responses explained by consumers' online flow experience. *Journal of Interactive Marketing, 26,* 223–234.

*Walker, H. J., Feild, H., Bernerth, J. B., & Becton, J. B. (2012). Diversity cues on recruitment websites: Investigating the effects on job seekers' information processing. *Journal of Applied Psychology, 97,* 214–224.

*Walker, H. J., Feild, H. S., Giles, W. F., Armenakis, A. A., & Bernerth, J. B. (2009). Displaying employee testimonials on recruitment web sites: Effects of communication media, employee race, job seeker race on organizational attraction and information credibility. *Journal of Applied Psychology, 94,* 1354–1364.

*Walker, H. J., Feild, H. S., Giles, W. F., & Bernerth, J. B. (2008). The interactive effects of job advertisement characteristics and applicant experiences on reactions to recruitment messages. *Journal of Occupational and Organizational Psychology, 81,* 619–638.

*Walker, H. J., Feild, H. S., Giles, W. F., Bernerth, J. B., & Short, J. C. (2011). So what do you think of the organization? A contextual priming explanation for recruitment website characteristics as antecedents of job seekers' organizational image perceptions. *Organizational Behavior and Human Decision Processes, 114,* 165.

*Williamson, I. O., King, J. E. Jr, Lepak, D., & Sarma, A. (2010). Firm reputation, recruitment web sites, and attracting applicants. *Human Resource Management, 49,* 669–687.

*Wills, R. (2007). *Organizational recruitment web sites: The influence of web site aesthetics on initial affective reactions to the site and subsequent attraction to the organization.* Retrieved from http://tigerprints.clemson.edu/all_theses/252/

Zeithaml, V. A., Parasuraman, A., & Malhotra, A. (2002). Service quality delivery through web sites: A critical review of extant knowledge. *Journal of the Academy of Marketing Science, 30,* 362–375.

Zhou, T., & Lu, Y. (2011). Examining mobile instant messaging user loyalty from the perspectives of network externalities and flow experience. *Computers in Human Behavior, 27,* 883–889.

Zhu, F., & Zhang, X. (2010). Impact of online consumer reviews on sales: The moderating role of product and consumer characteristics. *Journal of Marketing, 74,* 133–148.

CHAPTER 3

E-SELECTION

The History and Future of Technology in Employment Selection

David N. Dickter and Victor Jockin

ABSTRACT

In this article we offer an update for students, researchers and practitioners about applications and advancements in technology- and internet-enabled assessment (e-selection) tools. We divide the paper into three sections that in general represent the Past, Present, and Future of e-selection. In each, we explore the state of the field, and highlight both relevant research and gaps in the literature. First, we look back at the recent history of e-selection and technological innovations. Next, we highlight various tools and some of the advantages and challenges currently associated with them. We discuss current approaches to supporting the tools' installation, validation, and ongoing use in organizations. Finally, we address the future of e-selection. We believe that changes in work itself will have important consequences regarding how and for whom selection is applied. We address the broader societal, economic and technological trends and implications for the future, including advances in automation and their influences on work and HRM.

The Brave New World of eHRM 2.0, pages 47–79.

OVERVIEW

The use of technology in employment selection has had a profound effect on human resource management (e.g., Stone, Deadrick, Lukaszewski, & Johnson, 2015; Tippins, 2015). In this article we offer an update for students, researchers and practitioners about applications and advancements in technology- and internet-enabled assessment (e-selection) tools. We discuss advances in e-selection and concerns for practice, conclusions from the literature, and societal/economic trends in the workplace that we believe are having or will have an impact on e-selection. We note here that progress to date has been largely practice-based, with much more need for theory development (Stone & Dulebohn, 2013). Our intent is to focus on these practical issues, while also summarizing the available research literature. We divide the paper into three sections that in general represent the Past, Present, and Future of e-selection. In each, we explore the state of the field, and highlight both relevant research and gaps in the literature.

I.   First, we look back at the recent history of e-selection and technological innovations. Each innovation has brought with it some important challenges and concerns that have influenced succeeding waves of innovations.

II. Next, we highlight various tools, and some of the advantages and challenges currently associated with them. We draw also on our experience with e-selection in industry, and with human resource management (HRM) systems. We discuss current approaches to supporting the tools' installation, validation, and ongoing use in organizations. We also touch on the directions the research literature has taken with regard to these tools.

III. Finally, we address the future of e-selection. We believe that changes in work itself will have important consequences regarding how and for whom selection is applied. We address the broader societal, economic and technological trends and implications for the future, including advances in automation and artificial intelligence and their influences on work itself and HRM in particular. We recommend areas for future research given these trends.

As mentioned above, in each section of this paper we provide an overview of the applicable published research literature. We wish to note here that this is a challenge. Studies of both the innovations and concerns lag the application of e-selection in organizations. Most of the literature is practitioner-oriented; Ryan and Derous (2016) describe this as a "tension" between selection research and practice due to the practical desire for innovation and efficiency pushing ahead of academic research agendas. Further, practitioners may not share their work in published form because the academic motivation to publish is lacking, and/or due to concerns about revealing trade secrets.

I. THE HISTORY OF TECHNOLOGY IN SELECTION

Historically, the advantages of e-selection have included process improvements (i.e., efficiency, data-sharing) and changes to the candidate experience (e.g., job previews, simulations, and games as assessments). Here we discuss these historical developments and some corresponding challenges and concerns for HRM.

We must concede that reading an article on HRM and technology is perhaps analogous to ordering the latest computer, only to receive a product that is obsolete when the box is opened. It is therefore helpful to consider what has been accomplished thus far and where e-selection may be heading next. Figure 3.1 displays four types of innovations that have changed or are changing the way e-selection operates, as well as a fifth that we foresee with the rise of artificial agents (i.e., programs, bots, etc.) that currently operate at the computing forefront. To better illustrate them we describe them as different phases in the development of e-selection. Though many of the challenges listed are revisited with subsequent innovations, it is clear that e-selection has been marching forward, from an optional or adjunct role to a necessary and central one. In this section on e-selection's history, we address the first two phases, Digitization and Linkage.

Digitization

We entitle the first innovation as "digitization" to refer to the development of e-selection in the form of analog-to-digital translation of assessments, such as making a computerized multiple-choice ability test with the same items as the paper test. Although HRM achieved efficiencies with digitization, organizations were initially challenged by limited computing resources (see Figure 3.1). Tests were delivered as standalone instruments or combined into a test battery. The original focus was on measurement equivalence (Mead & Drasgow, 1993). This involved demonstrating that the computerized test form measured essentially the same qualities as the original paper form, and had a similar score distribution. For example, if within-person correlations between two administrations of a test are about the same whether study participants complete two paper forms, two computer forms, or one paper and one computer form, then the computer and paper forms appear to be measuring essentially the same qualities. Combined with similar score distributions (means, standard deviations, shape) across those two modes of administration, the computer and paper forms can be described as equivalent, meaning they can be used interchangeably.

At first, the computerized versions of tests were intended to improve efficiency by automating delivery and scoring for test administrators. Testing was administered by organizations using their own computers. Resources were limited and were often insufficient for large-scale delivery with simultaneous tests. There were few established test vendors relative to the current market, and therefore much of the software and processes were homegrown. As organizations and researchers gained more computing abilities, however, technological improvements

Past → Future	1. Digitization	2. Linkage	3. Originality	4. Virtualization	5. Artificial
Sample Achievements	• Analog-to-digital translation of assessments • Efficiency • Improved measurement	• HRM systems connecting assessments to other HR databases • Software-as-a-service • Digital applicant tracking • Self-service for candidates, including unproctored internet assessment (UIT) • Self-service for HR • International, global assessment	• New, digital-only assessments created, no longer only mimicking paper content • UIT becomes standard • Simulated work experiences, fidelity, and job previews • Gaming • Devices multiply: pads, phablets, watches	• Candidate information now available online through social networking and other public sources • New approaches to validating assessments, such as MTurk • Big data	• Natural Language Processing of candidate information • Machine learning and AI programs for validation analyses • Multi-source data gathering from the Internet of Things • Robots/Bots working with/replacing functions of people in workplaces
Challenges or Concerns	• Hardware/software limitations • Resources for developing/operating homegrown systems • Measurement equivalence • Candidate acceptance • The "digital divide" in computing usage	• Standardized protocols for exchanging data between systems • Online test security, candidate identity, cheating • Differing national standards for data privacy, protection	• Lack of models, research to understand reasons for candidate performance differences on different devices • UIT issues (security, identity, cheating) remain	• Data scientists without HRM/assessment background move into e-selection space • Ethics, legality in unintended or unauthorized information used for selection • Security against hacking	• HRM's increasing need for computing, programming skills • Candidate acceptance of new data collection sources • Candidate/employee adjustment to ubiquity of computing, "cyber"-sourcing of co-workers and work functions

FIGURE 3.1. Past, Present and Future of E-selection: Five Innovations in HRM and Computing

such as computerized adaptive testing (CAT; e.g., McCloy & Gibby, 2011) were developed to make the tests themselves more efficient. This method presented different items to candidates based on their performance on previous items and therefore was more tailored than a traditional fixed-form examination (e.g., Embretson, 2000; see also the section below on cognitive ability tests). Using the CAT approach, it became possible for candidates to receive items whose difficulties were known from prior research. Their correct/incorrect responses were used to determine which items will be presented subsequently, and an item response function was computed to estimate the candidate's true score (Embretson, 2000).

State of the Research Literature Associated with Digitization

In a review of selection over the prior century, Ryan and Ployhart (2014) noted that technology has become an essential part of the field, yet the e-selection research literature suffers from a dearth of empirical publications. Much of the e-selection literature has been built on publications that preceded this technology. In some ways this is justifiable, as the central issues have not changed, and the research categories Ryan and Tippins described still apply. These include design (e.g., outcomes, and constructs measured), implementation (e.g., globalization, retesting practices), and evaluation (e.g., validation, fairness, stakeholder perceptions; Ryan & Tippins, 2014).

Design

Computerized testing has required candidates to adjust to some new conditions and perhaps adjust their test-taking strategies (for example, they could no longer cross off incorrect answers on the test form) as well as some trust in the system (e.g., the security of their answers to personality and interest questions). The research literature supports the equivalence of computerized and conventional (i.e., paper) assessments of "non-cognitive" tests such as personality and interest assessments, as well cognitive ability tests such as verbal and mathematical ability as long as they are not speeded (i.e., there is ample time for most examinees to finish without the pressure of time; Mead & Drasgow, 1993; Reynolds & Dickter, 2017). Results of speeded cognitive ability tests, on the other hand, will vary by mode of administration (Mead & Drasgow, 1993).

Other studies have concluded that the constructs measured are the same, for example, when a test of five personality factors is measured via paper-pencil or a computer (Arthur, Doverspike, Muñoz, Taylor, & Carr, 2014; Morelli, Mahan, & Illingworth, 2014). Perhaps one of the biggest research opportunities, however, lies in investigating the potential of e-selection for measuring new job-relevant constructs (characteristics) of candidates, such as abilities or skills. Despite the many types of e-selection assessments available (see Section II for a survey of several types) and the advantages of each (e.g., the promise of novelty and candidate engagement in the experience, simulated job tasks, improved score estimation through computing, etc.), it is unclear from the empirical literature that e-selection research is actually uncovering and measuring new constructs, rather than merely translating traditional constructs into a more realistic presentation.

Implementation

Implementation includes a variety of dimensions, yet has received insufficient empirical research and theory development. Many authors have considered the mechanics of implementation and ongoing use of e-selection, and considerations for access to tests, security, training or maintenance (e.g., Dickter, Jockin, & Delany, 2017; Kehoe, Dickter, Russell, & Sacco, 2005; Reynolds & Rupp, 2010). Some research has explored the method of deployment by varying types of technology (e.g., computers, phones, tablets) and types of access (internet, WIFI, etc.; e.g., Brown & Grossenbacher, 2017). However, there are very few models that would explain how and why test results might vary (for one example, see Potosky, 2008). Morelli, Potosky, Arthur, and Tippins (2017) issued a call for conceptual models to explain how score differences occur between different modes or testing (e.g., paper vs. computer) and different types of technology. Without such models it is difficult to tell whether observed differences are due to how the candidate interacts the technology, how the test content itself might be affected by the technology, how the environment affects the technology, or some combination (Morelli et al., 2017).

As noted above, there are far more handbooks and practical guides than there are published empirical studies about the effects of new technologies on test scores and validity. A sample of the edited handbooks for practitioners across the years includes Hertel, Stone, Johnson, & Passmore (2017); Kavanagh, Thite, and Johnson (2015); Tippins and Adler (2011); and Gueutal and Stone (2005). Thus there is ample opportunity for the HRM researcher to contribute to the field.

Evaluation

E-selection is widely regarded by practitioners to be appropriate and practical based on equivalence research as mentioned above. However, applicants must be considered stakeholders along with practitioners such as HRM staff and administrators (e.g., Kehoe, et al., 2005). Both perceived and actual fairness to these stakeholders have been subjects of research. For example, there have been concerns about adverse impact against examinees who might not be computer savvy (i.e., that there is a "digital divide" of the haves and have-nots in computer access and/or proficiency that could affect pass rates, and further, that legally protected groups might be disadvantaged by it; Tippins, 2015). Under the Civil Rights Act of 1991, adverse impact is defined as a hire rate for a group of interest (for example, Hispanic or female candidates) that is less than 80% of the hire rate for a reference group (usually Caucasians or men). Below this threshold, employers may be legally required to prove that this adverse impact results from selection based on legitimate job requirements, and not to unrelated factors. Although the digital divide is surely shrinking with the uptake of new computing devices, and equivalence studies support computerization for non-cognitive tests as described above, there are few large-scale studies of passing rates for actual applicant pools (i.e., not student samples). This represents yet another gap in the literature, where expedience and convenience have led practitioners to forge ahead despite limited empirical research.

Linkage

A second innovation we will call "linkage" (see Figure 3.1) has connected assessments not only to each other but also to other portions of the human resources information system (HRIS; Lukaszewski, Dickter, Lyons, & Kehoe, 2015). For example, commercial applicant tracking systems were developed and standardized information-exchange protocols were established to allow assessment systems to export data to them. Exchanges also were possible between different assessment vendors. (This challenge was met successfully, as vendors recognized the need for compatibility across software platforms because many clients were using multiple testing and HRIS vendors.) Data exchanges from systems containing assessments and performance information allowed for validation studies to be performed, i.e., by connecting test data with performance evaluations for new hires, in order to determine whether test scores correlated significantly with performance on the job. As more commercial, off-the-shelf tests were developed, a self-service model became possible: applicants, who were more and more likely to own their own computer, could take tests at home at their convenience and unsupervised, and human resources departments could extract, interpret and apply the results. (See also Marler & Dulebohn's 2005 model of self-service acceptance from the employee's perspective. This model can be applied to HR staff, hiring managers and other employees of an organization who use e-selection systems.) Many researchers and practitioners wrote about the perils of keeping test materials secure, and working to prevent cheating on this "unproctored" internet testing (UIT; e.g., Ryan & Ployhart, 2014; Tippins et al., 2006). Nevertheless, a thriving industry of software-as-a-service developed (internet-based systems with little or no customer maintenance of assessment programs required) and customers began to make use of UIT, sometimes with subsequent verification (repetition of testing under proctored conditions) as the International Test Commission has recommended (2006) and sometimes without. (Note that statistics on the number of organizations currently using each approach are needed.)

Concerns about maintaining test security and applicant privacy are inherent in e-selection (Bauer et al., 2006; Zafar & Stone, 2015). Hacking of organizational data, including HRIS records, has gained prominence and can be seen worldwide (e.g., Passeri, 2014), giving candidates yet another concern about what might happen to information they release about themselves in order to gain employment (Dorsey, Martin, Howard, & Coovert, 2017). These concerns also have been complicated at multinational organizations due to regulated differences in data protection and privacy in different countries (Dickter et al., 2017). For example, the EU (European Union)-U.S. Privacy Shield was developed to protect the privacy of European Union citizens. The privacy shield allows for companies to certify that they are protecting and securing personal data that is transferred from the EU and Switzerland to the United States. However, the requirements are dynamic and obligate HRM professionals to stay current on developments (for example, at privacyshield.gov/NewsEvents). As of this writing U.S. privacy protections are not extended to non-U.S. citizens and the Privacy Shield is contested. Another consideration is the protection of individuals against information that may be publicly available but if used in a hiring decision could wrongly harm the individual's prospects for employment. Certainly this includes information related to protected groups (e.g., race, ethnicity, sex, disability), but also could include a variety of other information, whether historical facts (e.g., prior debt), or personal information or digital media posted by the individual or by another person. With more and more information about individuals becoming tracked and brokered on the internet, this issue will become increasingly salient in employment decisions and in everyday life.

State of the Research Literature Associated with Linkage

Little published research is available about the effects of linking e-selection tools and HRM systems together. However, the development of internet-based testing has resulted in a variety of published empirical investigations on unproctored internet testing (UIT). With UIT now a common mode of testing, and the ability of various computing devices to connect to the internet, there is a need for research on the effects of testing using different types of devices under different conditions (Arthur et al., 2017). It remains unclear what the effects of taking an assessment, particularly a cognitive ability test, on various types of computing devices might be under various conditions, and whether scores should somehow be adjusted based on the device. Researchers need to develop models to understand how and why different devices and testing conditions might affect test scores, and whether they disadvantage some groups of test-takers who might be more likely to use one type of device or condition over another (Potosky, 2008; Reynolds & Dickter, 2017; Stone, Lukaszewski, Stone-Romero, & Johnson, 2013). For example, to what extent might taking a cognitive ability test on a small-screen smartphone matter under different conditions (e.g., proctored, unproctored, various levels of distractions, timed or untimed)? Also, would certain demographic groups be more likely to do so because they would be less likely to have access to a computer to take the test?

Beaty et al. (2011) conducted a meta-analysis of validation studies with non-cognitive tests (e.g., personality) in UIT and proctored conditions and found consistent validity across conditions. These findings are consistent with conclusions by practitioners, as well as more recent studies in academic settings. King, Ryan,

Kantrowitz, Grelle, and Dainis (2015) found that test scores for customer service attitude and judgment in managerial situations were equivalent whether they were delivered via personal computer or mobile internet device. This was not the case for cognitive ability tests (King et al., 2015). Subjects in the study also rated all tests easier to take on a PC than on a mobile device. Other researchers have pointed out the need to consider type of device and not only whether the test is UIT. Brown and Grossenbacher (2017) found that scores on a cognitive ability test were slightly higher when taken on devices with larger screen sizes. Arthur et al. (2014) conducted a large study (nearly 3 million candidates) and found similar scores and measurement properties for personality tests taken in person or remote on mobile devices, but lower scores for cognitive ability tests taken on mobile devices. Illingworth, Morelli, Scott, and Boyd (2015) found no practical score differences between UIT tests taken on desktop computers or mobile devices.

II. THE PRESENT STATE OF E-SELECTION

Technology has facilitated selection across a broad range of products and processes, including resume processing, application blanks, interviews, tests of cognitive ability and personality, and simulations. As summarizing the array of e-selection tools has been done effectively elsewhere (e.g., see Stone et al., 2013 for a summary of research issue by type of e-selection tool), this section surveys and discusses a few of the tools that are currently common or growing in use, including: resumes and interviews; cognitive ability tests; personality testing and situational judgment tests; simulations and assessment games. First, we discuss two e-selection innovations currently taking place, which we refer to as Originality and Virtualization.

Originality

Referring back to Figure 3.1, the third innovation we call "originality" continues the development of new assessments, often without paper analogues, in order to measure new capabilities of people or improve presentation and realism using digital representation. For example, computer screens and menus used by customer service representatives can be recreated faithfully, and programs can simulate other work experiences such as managerial in-baskets (Fetzer & Tuzinski, 2013). This innovation also allows candidates to preview the job. Also, some test developers have created game-like assessments that blur the line between testing and leisure activity and increase user engagement (e.g., see Arthur, Doverspike, Kinney, & O'Connell, 2017). Another avenue for new assessments is the availability of new computing devices such as iPads and tablets of various sizes.

State of the Research Literature Associated with Originality

Research topics associated with new assessments (resumes, interviews, cognitive ability tests, personality tests, situational judgment tests, simulations and game-like assessments) will be discussed below (see "Overview of E-Selection Tools). Tippins (2015) provided a range of research questions on e-selection yet to be explored. Categories of research topics included costs and benefits, effects on reliability and validity, effects on adverse impact, applicant reactions, impact on the applicant pool, and legal concerns (Tippins, 2015).

Virtualization

The fourth innovation from Figure 3.1, "virtualization" has been the use of the e-selection information itself. The internet has matured to a point that many candidates have a virtual footprint on the internet that can be mined for the purpose of selection. Data scientists at organizations such as Google have been conducting their own proprietary analyses with these data for years, but in general this is a frontier research area for HRM. Organizations can assemble large datasets to research numerous correlations between job success and data available both within and outside the company. The term "big data" has been coined to loosely encompass this kind of information. Specifically, big data is characterized by three general attributes: its enormous quantity (volume), its dynamic and frequently changing nature (velocity), and its highly inconsistent and unstructured format (variety, Landers, Fink, & Collmus, 2017)). All of these factors present substantial challenges in summarizing and analyzing this information, challenges that greatly exceed those faced when evaluating traditional datasets. Big data might include information stored by an employer, or other types of information such as those on social media. For example, on social networking sites such as LinkedIn, passive job candidates volunteer information about their work history and self-assessments of job-related competencies. In other cases, it has become possible to mine the internet for candidate data. Researchers have reported being able to assemble profiles of personality characteristics from posts on social media such as LinkedIn, Twitter, Instagram, or Facebook (Park et al., 2015; see "Digital Applications, Resumes and Profiles" below).

Naturally this new avenue of research opens up new concerns: it blurs the line between information that is volunteered freely by the job candidate versus harvested without the candidate's knowledge or consent (Black, Stone, & Johnson, 2015). Prior concerns about data privacy and hacking remain, and now there are concerns about the conclusions that are drawn from these various data sources, how that information will be used and where it will be kept. Another concern for HRM and industrial/organizational psychology is keeping selection and assessment work within the purview of these fields. Data scientists are mining and utilizing this information without awareness of legal requirements protecting applicants from misuse of the data. A number of organizations—several Silicon Valley startups, as well as others established players in the HR and IT space—are attempting to provide tools to evaluate and leverage this kind of information for purposes of recruitment and selection. These systems may also attempt to locate and categorize negative or disqualifying behavior, such as inappropriate social media or discussion group posts from a job candidate.

The new data points and screening tools described above present challenges for the validation of personnel selection systems. The extent to which social media profiles predict job performance, for example, remains largely untested. Further, by the nature of this kind of information, it is not standardized across candidates, which raises a host of potential issues for organizations wishing to formally incorporate such information into hiring systems. Social media participation, or internet access, for instance, can vary substantially between individuals for reasons unrelated to potential job performance. Further, the relationship between ethnic or class differences and social media participation, or sophistication in understanding privacy settings, or perhaps even cultural conventions of social exchange, all might introduce bias into a selection system that incorporates such results. In the event a selection system shows adverse impact against certain subgroups and is subsequently challenged, it is currently unclear whether research exists that would adequately address any of these potential concerns.

For these reasons, data from these new methods can perhaps augment traditional recruitment tools, and may provide additional information about prospective job applications in some contexts. However, they cannot currently replace traditional hiring methods, and are unlikely to do so. Interviews and other standardized forms of employee screening and evaluation remain the most defensible and understood methods of selecting employees (Schmidt & Hunter, 1998).

State of the Research Literature Associated with Virtualization

Research on the use of internet information for selection is a new frontier with a limited literature and many opportunities for interesting work. For example, Kluemper, Rosen, and Mossholder (2012) arranged for raters to review student social networking profiles in order to estimate their personality characteristics in five areas: openness to experience, conscientiousness, extraversion, agreeableness and neuroticism. The rated students completed a self-assessment in these same areas. Ratings based on the internet profiles were not only correlated in all five areas, but also added value (variance) in predicting grade point average over and above the information from self-ratings.

Other researchers have appropriately investigated perceived fairness. Stoughton, Thompson, and Meade (2015) investigated reactions among students to screening using social networking data, finding overall adverse reactions to the selection process and perceptions of fairness. Black, Stone, and Johnson (2015) updated a model of privacy by Stone and Stone (1990) to explain when the use of social networking data might be perceived as a violation of privacy. A key aspect of the model is the extent to which the candidate perceives having control over the information and the impressions that are produced by it (Black et al., 2015; Stone & Stone, 1990). Roulin and Bangerter (2013) describe ways in which individuals can signal their potential fit to recruiters through the use of publicly-accessible social networking profiles.

Virtualization has also offered a new avenue for research in the form of voluntary subjects for assessment research, such as Amazon MTurk subjects who participate in assessments for a small amount of compensation (e.g., see Woo, Keith, & Thornton, 2015, as well as discussion of MTurk below). Initial testing of new assessments (pilot testing) or studies examining the relationship between test scores and important outcome variables (criterion validation) could proceed more rapidly with this approach, though it may be appropriate to argue that such applicants might be different from "real" candidates.

An Overview of E-Selection Tools

Digital Applications, Resumes, and Profiles

This traditional step of completing an application or sending a resume has been re-defined into an assembly of selection-related profile information. Technology has transformed the candidate screening process by unclogging the bottleneck of a mountain of resumes, cover letters and applications, with the machinery of keyword-based data mining. Applicant tracking systems and other programs can search for and parse necessary and desired terms among submitted materials, and prioritize candidates. Other systems may also attempt to bypass this need to parse resume data by forcing the re-entry of data into a structured format. In addition, some workforce analytics or applicant tracking systems can aggregate and analyze resume data and attempt to identify candidates suitable for particular openings. For example, they might attempt to flag candidates meeting certain criteria, such as specific types of experience or specific academic credentials. As mentioned above, passive candidates can be searched on social media accounts such as LinkedIn in a similar fashion (as resume keywords) and as self-assessed or peer-endorsed lists of competencies. The internet has transformed not only how candidates are found and evaluated, but also how individuals develop their skills and qualifications. For example, online profiles may include records of completion of educational experiences such as Massively Open Online Courses (MOOCs) that are offered free at some universities, and industry-developed online course results (e.g., online courses on a range of topics on LinkedIn from Lynda.com, including many that are not software-related, such as photography). Individuals voluntarily assemble their own profiles on career-related social networking sites such as LinkedIn, However, the internet also contains a large amount of publically available information about many job candidates, beyond what they may list on their resumes and what might be discovered by examining a candidate's work history or following up with references. It may be fair to say that almost anything a person places online might be considered relevant data in a "job profile" by a recruiter (whether the person intends this or not, and whether using this data for selection would be legally defensible if identified and challenged), and further, that that profile could be subject to analysis as mentioned earlier based on social media activity, such as posts and mentions on social media. As a proof-of-concept, consider the work of Park et al. (2015) using Facebook data. These researchers conducted a statistical and semantic analysis of the language (e.g., words, symbols, phrases; a "language-based assessment") associated with five personality characteristics using internet data from Facebook and assessments that volunteers had completed, as well as assessments completed by people who knew the volunteers ("informants"). The researchers built a model for each personality characteristic and applied the models to data from a separate sample of 5,000 volunteers. They obtained intriguing results, including significant correlations between the Facebook language-based assessment scores and ratings by informants. The results were consistent after a six-month re-test interval. The study is noteworthy for the results, but perhaps equally so for its demonstration that an automated "judge" can be programmed to make these assessments.

Interviews

Long the staple of employment selection, interviews have also been technology-enabled, including the preparation of the interview (e.g., automated questions generated based on the candidates' answers to application questions or personality assessments) and its delivery (technology-mediated interviews such as videoconferencing). Although the convenience and cost savings of technology-mediated interviews are clear, it is also reasonable to ask whether they affect applicant reactions or performance relative to face-to-face interviews. For example, Bauer, Truxillo, Paronto, Weekley, and Campion (2004) found that applicants viewed a variety of interview methods as procedurally fair (face-to-face, live telephone and interactive voice-response). However, Chapman and Rowe (2002) found that the extent to which candidates were attracted to (and presumably likely to join) an organization after an in-person or teleconference interview varied by the degree of structure in the interview. Teleconference interviewees tended to prefer more structure (i.e., standardized and scripted questions) than face-to-face interviewees, who preferred unscripted, conversational interviews. (Note that the research literature supports structured over unstructured interviews, however; e.g., Schmidt & Hunter, 1998). Blacksmith, Willford, & Behrend (2016) conducted a meta-analysis to test their hypotheses that technology-mediated interviews— including telephone, videoconferencing or computer-mediated, and interactive voice response interviews—were less-favorably viewed by applicants and also resulted in lower ratings than face-to-face interviews. The authors reasoned that technology-mediated interviews might reduce or frustrate the opportunity for interpersonal connections (e.g., eye contact and other demonstration of social skills, and impression management techniques) relative to face-to-face interviews. Results supported the hypothesis that applicants favored face-to-face interviews and also provided some support for the hypothesis of higher ratings from face-to-face interviewers. However, moderators were found, such as recency of study and whether the research was a field or lab study, that limited the interpretation of the latter result. Blacksmith et al.'s. (2016) study was also based on a modest sample (11 studies of interviewer ratings and 5 of applicant reactions) and may not reflect the latest technological capabilities for interviewing (e.g., videoconferencing software) that should be the subject of future studies.

Similarly, there is a need to better understand the scoring implications of a related technology, video-recorded interviews. In this type of interview, candidates can respond to written or video-delivered interview questions in a video-recorded session at a time and place of their choosing (or in a testing center if they do not have access to a web camera), for later scoring by a third party (i.e., programmed interviews; Milne-Tyte, 2011). In some professions such as computer science this may be less likely to be perceived as impersonal, though one can imagine the downside for the same reasons that Blacksmith et al. (2016) discussed, as well as the elimination of the possibility of real-time feedback. It remains to be seen whether such interviews are equally valid, more so (for example, by focusing on the candidate's knowledge and experience) or less so (for example, by removing the opportunity for real-time demonstration of job-relevant interpersonal skills). In the future, it may also be commonplace to use natural language programs to score their answers. With interactive, language-based devices and programs (e.g., Amazon's Alexa, Google Home) becoming more conversational and natural language processing and machine learning coming to HR (IBM's Watson; Dickter et al., 2017), artificial agents that "conduct" interviews themselves appear to be on the horizon (see additional discussion in Section III).

Personality and Attitude Assessment

Personality and attitude measures have become a common form for workplace assessment, and as with cognitive ability tests these instruments are now typically delivered online. Personality assessments are generally administered in the form of surveys. For instance, job candidates might be asked to indicate whether they agree or disagree with various statements about themselves, or about work behavior in general. Responses are generally recorded using a multiple-point rating scale (e.g., five points ranging from Strongly Agree to Strongly Disagree) or simply by indicating true or false.

Because this format so closely models responding in a paper format, and because such assessments are typically not speeded, researchers have concluded that personality and attitude surveys measure the same attributes in a computer-based vs. paper setting and results collected in either context can be used interchangeably (e.g., Bartram & Brown, 2004; Chuah, Drasgow, & Roberts, 2006; Salgado & Moscoso, 2003).

In addition, the advent of computer-based personality and attitude assessment has brought several advantages. Among these are the ability to enforce a complete set of responses. When responses are left blank on a knowledge test or cognitive ability test it is reasonable and standard practice to assign zero points for that item. When responses are left blank on a paper-based personality survey, on the other hand, we learn nothing about the attributes the survey is intended to measure. For this reason, personality surveys typically require that some minimum percentage of items with a scale score are answered, and then responses are averaged (and then possibly rescaled) effectively ignoring the skipped content. With computer-based personality assessment, complete responding can be enforced. This creates a more reliable and consistent assessment across individuals. Another advantage of computerization for personality assessments is the ability to provide the computerized adaptive tests (CAT) mentioned above, allowing for the presentation of items that are best tailored to individual applicants by automatically choosing items from a pool whose measurement on the desired characteristic are known (Stark, Chernyshenko, Drasgow, & Williams, 2006).

Traditional Cognitive Ability Tests

Cognitive ability tests measure mental capabilities involved in thinking, such as reasoning, mathematical ability and verbal ability. Traditional cognitive assessments started as paper-based instruments, many using a multiple-choice format, though most of these tests have now been adapted for online delivery. General cognitive ability has long been recognized as among the most effective predictors of job performance (Schmidt & Hunter, 1998). Among these reasons is that it is required to learn and apply job knowledge (Schmidt & Hunter, 2004). E-selection has changed cognitive tests in some ways, and in others has left them the same. As described above, early electronic versions of cognitive tests used in employment were generally the same multiple-choice items, now presented on a computer screen. Test scores were found to be equivalent when tests were delivered untimed, but could be different when the test was timed (Mead & Drasgow, 1993), due, for example, to the mechanics of paging through items online vs. on paper, pressing a key versus using a pencil, etc. Computerized tests have allowed for different response formats (e.g., matching or re-ordering items) that would be more cumbersome with a paper-pencil format. Computerized adaptive testing (CAT) and Item Response Theory (IRT) have had bigger effects on testing by allowing candidates to receive shorter versions of tests tailored to their responses and abilities, and improved estimation of scores over classical test theory. One of many advantages of IRT is the ability to present fewer items to the candidate, and just the ones needed to compute a score, rather than a larger set of items on a fixed form (Embretson, 2000; Stark, Chernyshenko, & Drasgow, 2017).

E-selection with cognitive testing has other potential advantages. For example, cognitive items can be imbedded into scenarios or simulations to improve the realism and therefore the applicant's perception of the item as job-related, and to seem less like a test (see also the gamification section below). Some studies have provided evidence that e-selection might broaden the domain of cognitive abilities that could be tested (e.g., spatial movement; for example, Ventura, Shute, Wright, & Zhao, 2013). However, research on general mental ability and employment testing has not indicated that adding such specific abilities (for example, comparing information, solving word problems, etc.) to a test of general mental ability will increase validity in most instances (Ones, Dilchert, Viswesvaran, & Salgado, 2010).

Situational Judgment Tests

Situational Judgment Tests (SJTs) present candidates with a series of situations, and then ask them to evaluate a set of possible responses to those situations (Weekley & Ployhart, 2006). When used as pre-employment assessments, these scenarios generally model workplace situations (e.g., sales scenarios, or customer service scenarios, etc.). SJT assessments have been shown to predict job performance across a range of jobs, while also showing smaller ethnic group differences, and thus lower adverse impact in selection settings, than typical cognitive ability measures (McDaniel & Nguyen, 2001; McDaniel et al., 2011; Motowidlo, Dunnette, & Carter, 1990).

The concept of evaluating responses to situations is clearly a very broad domain that can, depending on the content of the scenarios and the response alternatives presented, call upon an array of different knowledge areas and psychological traits. As such, unlike targeted personality or cognitive ability measures, SJTs are properly viewed as a type of measurement method (like surveys, for instance) rather than as specific trait measures (Schmitt & Chan, 2006). The psychological traits assessed can vary depending on SJT content, but they are likely to relate at least in part to important traits such as general cognitive ability, conscientiousness, and job knowledge (Clevenger et al., 2001; McDaniel & Nguyen, 2001; Weekly & Jones, 1999).

SJTs also can vary by response format and scoring methodology. For instance, candidates might be asked to identify the best response, or to identify the best and worst response, or to provide effectiveness ratings for each response. To derive scores, these responses are then compared in some fashion to similar ratings provided by experts (Motowidlo, Dunnette, & Carter, 1990). The greater the resemblance between candidate responses and expert responses, the higher the candidate's score. This similarity can be measured in a number of ways: for example, as the mean expert effectiveness rating of the response identified as best by the candidate; or the difference between the expert mean effectiveness values of the best and worst response identified by the candidate; or as the Euclidian distance between candidate and expert rating profiles (smaller distance corresponds to a higher score); or a correlation between the candidate's response profile and the expert profile (Legree et al., 2010).

SJTs are among the employment assessments that have most benefited and advanced as a result of computerization. For instance, the scenarios can now practically be presented as videos rather than narrative passages. This allows for greater realism, and also allows facial expression and other social cues to come across in scenarios, as well as impacting candidates' perceptions of the company and of the assessment's job relatedness. This could be relevant, for example, in customer service scenarios or other interpersonal settings. In addition, some studies have also found that the use of audio or video presentation of SJT scenarios results in reduced ethnic group score differences without reducing SJT validity (Chan & Schmitt, 2002; Konradt, Hertel, & Joder, 2003; O'Connell et al., 2007).

Computerization has also facilitated the use of some of the more advanced scoring methods mentioned earlier. Distance and correlational scoring, for instance, are so computationally intensive that they became practical and widespread only after the advent of computerization. Thus technology has advanced both presentation and scoring of SJTs.

Simulations and Work Samples

Work simulations used in selection will generally take components of jobs and model them in a way that attempts to capture the same skills required to perform those job tasks. Simulations and work samples used for employee selection predate the computerization of assessment and may take many forms. For manufacturing positions, simple tests of manual dexterity—for instance, moving pegs to set locations on a board—have been used for decades (Salvendy, 1975). For white collar professions, assessment centers, which also pre-date computerization, present job candidates with a series of assessments, many of which are job task simulations (Lievens & Thornton, 2005; Thornton & Rupp, 2006). Examples of assessment center evaluation elements include in-box exercises, which require that job candidates to respond to various simulated business correspondence, and presentation exercises, which require that candidates prepare for and deliver presentations.

Like SJTs, there is some evidence that simulations produce smaller ethnic group score differences than traditional cognitive ability tests, and that they are also perceived more favorably by job applicants (Lievens & De Soete, 2012). There is also some evidence that well-designed simulations can be incrementally valid beyond SJTs, which can be viewed as lower-fidelity simulations (Lievens & Patterson, 2011). Also similar to SJTs, computerization has led to large advances in range and capabilities of simulation-based assessments, as well as their scoring. This trend towards computer-based job simulations has been facilitated by the computerization of many job functions. A simple example is a keyboarding test, a computer-based test in which a job applicant is presented with a section of text that he or she must then transcribe (Yamaguchi, Crump, & Logan, 2013). Scores are based on some combination of speed and accuracy. Simulations for more complex and multifaceted aspects of jobs include computerized in-box exercises, machine operation simulations, or call center simulations. In call center simulations, for example, the candidate is presented with a computer interface similar to those call center agents must use (Holland & Lambert, 2013). Using this interface, candidates must respond to recorded simulated customer calls (or increasingly, instant messaging or email) of the type a company's customer service department typically receives. Candidates must, for instance, locate the customer's account and information within it, or research questions regarding company policy, or record data or notes about the call for reference by future agents, etc. These computerized tasks are highly amenable to computer-based simulation and online delivery.

With respect to scoring, computerization has allowed for the capture of many relatively subtle aspects of the candidate's behavior, which can now contribute to score profiles (Sydell et al., 2013). Response time is a good example. During a call center simulation, a computerized assessment can easily capture not only whether the candidate has provided a correct response, but how long it took him or her to provide that response. If the candidate has to locate some information within the interface, the number of steps taken to reach that information, and any missteps to the wrong location, can also be recorded.

Combining all of the data points that emerge from something like a call center into a score or set of scores thus becomes a highly complex problem, one that as with traditional personnel assessment must be guided by considerations of reliability, validity, and fairness. The complexity and scope of the data collected during such simulations has led to a diversity of scoring approaches, and to continued advances in the technology of combining such data into useful predictions of employee performance (Lobene, 2017).

Game-Like Assessments

Game-like or gamified simulations have recently become a topic of discussion and research (Aldrich, 2009). Though there are a range of features and elements that have fallen under the label of gamification, some common examples include aspects of competition (e.g., leaderboards), earning rewards (e.g., badges, etc.) or advancing levels. The principle behind these enhancements is generally to engage and motivate participants. Gamification has made notable inroads recently into areas such as training, sale management, recruitment, and employee engagement (Dale, 2014) or as a hybrid recruitment and selection step occurring early in the selection process (Derous & De Fruyt, 2016). Several IT-focused companies have sprung up in recent years with a focus on gamifying aspects of HR software systems for organizations to help motivate employees or track performance.

However, the extent to which gamification will enhance or improve personnel selection remains unclear. To date, despite the notable inroads of gamification within other areas of HR, there has been little to no research evaluating gamified assessments for use in personnel selection (Arthur et al., 2017). Further, there is some reason to suspect that the impact of gamification within the selection space will remain minimal. Computer-based simulations are perhaps the class of assessments most amenable to the introduction of game-like features, such as goals, feedback, and or progress indicators. But recall that simulations derive their value from modeling job tasks, and that superfluous motivators, guides, or information provided during the assessment might actually diminish their resemblance to actual job tasks. Simulations are often justified to organizations for specific selection settings, at least initially, on the basis of content validity (that is, on the basis of the resemblance between the tasks performed on the assessment and those performed on the job). To the extent that gamification reduces this resemblance, the case for content validity is reduced. Additional potential concerns are that age or class differences in the exposure to gaming could in principle introduce additional job-irrelevant sources of score variance.

We do not mean to dismiss the notion that gamification may at some point augment the array of instruments available for personnel selection. Though game-like elements can be designed that bear little resemblance to job tasks, traditional cognitive ability assessments tend to be highly predictive of job performance even when they bear little or no resemblance to the job (Schmidt & Hunter, 1998). Today, however, it remains to be seen whether such instruments will materially advance the science of personnel selection.

III. THE FUTURE OF E-SELECTION: TECHNOLOGY AND THE CHANGING NATURE OF SELECTION, VALIDATION AND WORK ITSELF

Advances in automation and information technologies continue to reshape jobs, the workplace, and the challenges faced by HR professionals. These global technological trends have implications for the skills needed to succeed in today's jobs, but also offer new tools to select employees and to develop and validate pre-employment assessments. In this section, we take a broad view of those technological trends, and discuss some of their more salient implications for the HR professional.

New Tools for Assessment Development and Validation

The increasing computerization and accessibility of candidate, applicant, and employee data has opened up new avenues for the development and validation of employment tests. For instance, the consolidation of vendors providing assessment and performance information has brought increased access and order to employee and applicant information, making it possible to collect the test records and performance data from subsequent hires in one place. In addition, information related to jobs and job requirements, which is important for both the selection of employment assessments and for their validation, has become more readily accessible online. Further, the growing scale and penetration of the internet has created avenues for discovering new sources of job applicant information potentially relevant for recruitment and selection.

Online Job Analysis Data

Job analysis data, or descriptive information about job tasks and requirements, can be important for numerous HR functions. This is in part because skill dimensions required for a particular job can in part inform the selection of appropriate pre-employment assessments. If reasoning and problem solving are important job skills, for instance, a cognitive ability assessment would become more important. Job analysis skill dimensions might further guide the design of performance evaluation instruments. Such instruments could call for ratings or evaluations on the range of skills determined to be related to success in that job.

With the advent of the internet, this kind of descriptive information is now more readily available. Most notably, the U.S. Department of Labor maintains an online database of job information called the Occupational Information Network (O*NET; see Rivkin, Gregory, Norton, Craven, & Lewis, 2017). For nearly all major jobs within the US economy, O*NET catalogs important personal requirements (knowledge or skills), personal characteristics (abilities, interests, or values), and experience requirements necessary to succeed in each job. Task and activities performed in these jobs are also described.

For those wishing to analyze jobs within their organization, finding a similar job title in O*NET and taking that job analysis data at face value is likely of some preliminary usefulness, but is not in itself entirely sufficient (Gatewood, Feild, & Barrick, 2010). Because job requirements may vary across organizations, some level of direct confirmation is recommended. Further, from a legal standpoint, direct local confirmation of some form (for instance, surveys of job incumbents about the tasks they perform) would be required to meet the job analysis standards outlined in the EEOC's Uniform Guidelines of Employee Selection (EEOC, 1978; Stone et al., 2013). A promising option for the collection of such local job analysis information was described by Reiter-Palmon et al. (2006). Their web-based job analysis method, which elicited more timely and detailed job descriptions than traditional job analysis methods, was based in part on the Generalized Work Activities dimensions that are part of the O*NET job description framework.

Crowdsourced Assessment Development

Another advance in data collection is Amazon's Mechanical Turk (or MTurk), a crowdsourcing platform that allows researchers to access the services of human subjects and assistants with unprecedented efficiency. This platform provides access to a global network of small contractors (workers) who can be employed for the completion of small tasks. MTurk now routinely enables researchers to collect samples of several hundred respondents within a matter of hours and at minimal cost. Similar studies would have been vastly more time-consuming and often appreciably more expensive using traditional in-person research samples. Sheehan and Pittman (2016), in their summary of MTurk as a research tool, estimated that by 2015, nearly 15,000 published scholarly papers had employed MTurk samples for all or part of their research, a six-fold increase over the preceding ten years.

The MTurk platform offers significant efficiencies for HR professionals seeking to develop and validate employment assessments. As part of assessment development, MTurk workers could be asked to, for example, complete a set of cognitive ability items, or a set of personality or attitude survey items. They might also be asked to complete related assessments, like marker tests to distinguish ways in which tests are similar or different. The resulting item data would be useful in assessing basic statistics such as difficulty and response variance, or in the case of marker assessments, construct validity. Rapid iterations of modified assessment content informed by these results become practical and economical for the first time during the assessment development process, because of the efficiency and low cost of collecting such data.

Limited criterion-related validation studies (demonstrating that a test predicts an outcome such as job performance or learning during training) are also possible using MTurk, notably if the performance criterion is a relatively modest training success measure. MTurk workers could, for example, complete a series of pre-employment assessment tools, and then be asked to complete an online training course relevant to the job in question, followed by a knowledge test assessing what they had learned. Correlations between assessment content and the training success measure could form the basis of an economical, though relatively limited, criterion-related validity study.

Representativeness of samples, as well as levels of attention and motivation, are important factors in any research study. Survey content requesting demographic variables from MTurk workers can be included, and MTurk groups are generally diverse, enabling adequate representation among various ethnic groups. It is further possible to place prior conditions upon participation, such as English proficiency or geographical location, to further refine the makeup of the research sample in a way that approximates applicant samples. Regarding participant motivation and involvement, Sheehan and Pittman (2016) cite several studies suggesting that MTurk workers are actually more likely to take tasks seriously and provide useable data than are many other samples of convenience, such as student or volunteer samples. By and large, results from MTurk samples appear to be comparable to those obtained from in-person samples (Casler, Bickel, & Hackett, 2013).

Results of MTurk validation studies, by virtue of not involving actual applicants, incumbents, or trainees, would likely be most useful as initial estimates of training success validity. But the ease and minimal cost of such a study would often justify such research as a first step in a subsequent broader validation effort.

Artificial Agency

The fifth innovation in Figure 3.1, "artificial agency," is new as of this writing but is likely to develop quickly: the use of cognitive computing or machine learning to collect, score and analyze candidate information. These developments can be seen as a continuation of a broader trend towards mechanization and automation that began with the industrial revolution, and which just now, with advances in information technology, are beginning to expand beyond manufacturing and into the realm of knowledge work. These recent advances include data, as described in the prior innovations, as well as new information such as natural language processing of human speech (Landers, 2017). Artificial intelligence (AI) programs such as IBM's Watson are already being put to use for HRM. In addition, a multitude of possible new data sources such as internet-enabled devices (the Internet of Things; Gartner, 2017) could permit a variety of new information sensors. These sensors could collect more of current data types (e.g., devices with cameras) as well as newer data types (e.g., heart rate collected from a wearable device). Combining machine learning and ubiquitous, internet-enabled devices could result in a surge of new data and analysis.

The prospect of using these data to make selection decisions is both fascinating and worrisome, and points to the need to review and update the standards and guidelines for the ethical use of testing (e.g., American Educational Research Association, American Psychological Association, National Council on Measurement in Education, Joint Committee on Standards for Educational, & Psychological Testing, 2014). In addition to data collection, delivery of assessments with devices such as conversational chat bots for interviewing are now possible and could become mainstream. Importantly, these technological advancements are likely to transform the work itself, such that the ability to work productively with an AI on the job might need to be assessed as a condition of employment just as use of word processing software is required today.

Technology and the Changing Nature of Work

From the dawn of the industrial revolution, advances in technology have been reshaping the nature of work. With the advent of computers and the information revolution in the second half of the 20th century, these trends have only accelerated and broadened in scope, creating a series of evolving challenges for HR professionals related to hiring, training, and managing workers. Because our topic is personnel selection, we will focus on how these recent global technological trends have affected the cognitive and non-cognitive skills required to perform successfully in today's jobs, which in turn has implications for the relative predictive value of different personnel selection instruments.

To begin, we consider the impact of technology on job complexity, or the degree to which jobs require substantial learning and reasoning. Not surprisingly, the extent to which cognitive ability assessments predict job performance increases as jobs become more complex (Schmidt & Hunter, 2004). As job complexity increases, therefore, both the traditional and the simulation-based cognitive ability assessments, discussed previously in this chapter, become more important for selection into such jobs. We consider how technological advances have affected the ratio of more complex to less complex jobs within the economy as a whole, but also how the complexity of specific jobs has changed with the introduction of technology.

Workplace Technology and Complexity across Jobs

When the balance of job types across the economy is examined, it is clear that for more than a century the average job within the US economy has become increasingly complex. Using US Census data, Wyatt and Hecker (2006) divided all jobs in the US economy into one of seven major job families, and then reported the percent of all jobs that each job family represented in 1910, and again in 2000. From the information in this paper, it is clear that job complexity has increased in the U.S. economy as a whole over that 90 year period. Lower complexity jobs such as farm work have substantially decreased as a percentage of the economy and higher complexity jobs such as technical and computing jobs have increased dramatically (almost five-fold; Wyatt & Hecker, 2006). All indications are that these trends have not only continued through today, but are accelerating (Brynjolfsson & McAfee, 2014). In light of Schmidt and Hunter's (2004) observation that cognitive ability testing becomes more predictive of job performance as job complexity increases, this argues for the increasing importance of such assessments.

Workplace Technology and Complexity within Jobs

In addition to a general increase in the number of complex jobs, such as professional and technical positions, relative to less complex jobs, like farm laborers, there is also evidence that the introduction of technology can often increase the complexity within specific jobs. The trend here is somewhat less clear, however, because technology and automation can both replace and add required job skills (Lewis, 1996). On balance, however, there is evidence that technology has maintained or increased complexity for many existing job categories.

Manufacturing: No sector of the economy has been more profoundly transformed by technology than manufacturing. Though early literature on manufacturing automation argued that this trend would "deskill" some lower-level jobs (Braverman, 1974), thus possibly reducing their complexity and hence the importance pre-employment cognitive ability testing, several more recent analyses indicate that remaining manufacturing jobs are actually often now higher-skilled (Acemoglu & Autor, 2011). This is because the operation of computerized machines, and with it aspects of programming, are often important components of many manufacturing jobs that had previously employed a greater number of workers utilizing only more basic mechanical skills (Bravo Orellana, 2015). This advancing complexity of manufacturing work is mirrored in part by an increased utilization of college-educated workers within mining and manufacturing industries today (Autor, Levy, & Murnane, 2003).

As with changes in average job complexity in the US economy as a whole, these changes within jobs also have implications for employment testing and personnel selection, as cognitive skills required to learn these more advanced tasks become of increased importance, and skills that might previously have been central, such as manual dexterity, diminish in importance.

Knowledge Workers: Technology and automation are now transforming a growing list of roles in the broader economy. This trend has emerged not so much due to advances in robotics, which replicate highly structured mechanical tasks, but to advances in software, which are beginning to enable the replication of an increasing range of cognitive, information processing, and learning tasks (Brynjolfsson & McAfee, 2014). A range of technology companies are working on these kinds of products, including Google, IBM, and Microsoft. IBM's Watson is a leading example. As the result of these technologies, a number of complicated cognitive tasks that involve complex perception, information processing, and judgment are now on the cusp of being at least partially automated. Examples include medicine, where medical diagnosis software such as IBM's Watson Healthcare is under development (Lorenzetti, 2016).

The impact of technology, automation, and the emergence of AI on the overall job complexity of white-collar professions and other knowledge workers remains less certain, and therefore the HR implications for personnel selection are at this point also less clear. This is in part because in the case of manufacturing, computerization and automation displaced some physical or mechanical skills but often added the need for certain computer and information processing skills, maintaining or increasing job complexity. In the case of the introduction of AI into the domain of knowledge workers, however, it is cognitive tasks and skills such as business forecasting, actuarial work, or medical diagnoses that are being at least in part displaced.

That said, we are in the early phases of the AI trend, and current levels of automation are not eliminating the need for substantial human knowledge and judgement in how to use and interpret the results of AI software. Accordingly, much of what has been written on this topic to date is speculation regarding where this trend might lead (Ford, 2015). As of today, the level of cognitive demand within white collar positions that are being partially automated remains relatively high. For these reasons, the importance of cognitive ability when selecting into these jobs, as well as the earnings premium associated with higher education, are not under immediate threat and are more likely than not to continue into the immediate future for white collar professions (e.g., Lohr, 2017). Cognitive ability assessments such as those reviewed in this chapter will remain an important component of personnel selection in such professions, even as some level of outright technological displacement will begin to occur within these areas of the economy within the coming decades.

Workplace Technology and Personality

The Challenges of Virtual Teams: The advent of the internet and mobile communication technology have also led to a substantial increase in telecommuting and virtual work teams, or even virtual organizations, consisting of workers tied together principally through electronic means (Bureau of Labor Statistics, 2016). These advances in communications technology have also accelerated globalization and corporate outsourcing, changing not only the manner in which team members communicate, but often also the team's national and cultural diversity. As with the technological advances in computerization and automation, these trends have the potential to alter the relative importance of various personal attributes linked to successful job performance, and thus impact HR management and personnel selection decisions.

Kraut et al. (1999) outlined four attributes of virtual organizations, and we adapt their criteria slightly here to encompass virtual teams within organizations as well. First, because of increased globalization and outsourcing, teams are more likely to represent multiple organizations and/or include members from various countries and nationalities. Second, team members are often not in the same time zone, reducing overlap in working hours and potentially complicating or changing the nature of collaboration and team decision making. Third, the group is geographically dispersed, and therefore, fourth and finally, must communicate primarily, if not exclusively, via electronic rather than face-to-face means. The extent to which particular teams and organizations face each of these four conditions may, of course, vary.

As physical proximity and direct interpersonal contact diminishes, virtual teams can become less cohesive than traditional face-to-face teams (Hertel, Geister, & Konradt, 2005). However, there is also evidence that this effect may be reduced or eliminated if workers are higher in openness to experience. Openness to experience is one of the five major dimensions of personality, and it encompasses attributes such as intellectual curiosity, flexibility, and creativity (Costa & McCrae, 1988). Jacques et al. (2009), for instance, have found that openness to experience is associated with managers' increased perceived usefulness and intentions to adopt virtual teams. Similarly, MacDonnell et al. (2009) found that in comparison to traditional face-to-face teams, openness to experience among team members was more strongly related to team cohesion than it was for face-to-face teams.

With respect to personnel selection, therefore, there is at least some initial evidence that openness to experience could be considered as a component of the profile used to evaluate candidates for positions in virtual teams or organizations. However, research on this topic is thus far limited and results are not entirely consistent (Krumm et al., 2016). What is clear, however, is that technological advances in the workplace can change the balance of personal attributes that contribute to successful job performance, and that simply relying on prior summaries may not be adequate. Research into the role of technology in changing the psychological requirements of work must therefore be ongoing.

CONCLUSIONS

Opportunities for Future Research

As described throughout the paper there is ample opportunity for new research on e-selection. In addition to the review by Tippins (2015), the chapter on e-selection by Reynolds and Dickter (2017) offers a range of topics for which there are gaps in the literature. These include: 1) examining test differences or equivalence on multiple types of devices; 2) developing empirical and theory-based "taxonomies" of effects of administering assessments in UIT conditions and with mobile devices; 3) studying the added value of virtual-reality simulations over other types of assessments, and whether measuring biometric data or other non-traditional test performance improves validity over other types of tests; and 4) considering the value and ethical implications of using big data. Aside from the practical matters and frameworks, it is also important to consider what opportunities there may be for the further development of psychological models and theories related to e-selection and HRM. Examples mentioned in this paper included a model of acceptance of self-service, a model of perceived fairness of the selection process, and a model of privacy. All of these seem appropriate given that the nature of e-selection requires acceptance; that is, willingness to share personal information, to expend effort to provide it to an HRIS, and to trust that the information will be used appropriately and kept safe.

E-Selection and Society

Advances in e-selection may be viewed within the context of societal trends in the use of technology at work and in everyday life. Given the pace of change in HRM, a number of priorities are clear. First, it is important for HR researchers and practitioners to be conversant in both technology and selection in order to keep up with the science of selection. Data scientists have moved into selection work (Ones, Kaiser, Chamorro-Premuzic, & Svensson, 2017) and there is a concern that they will be conducting their own form of "dustbowl empiricism" without an awareness of the need for more underlying theory, appropriate methodology, and consideration of legal and ethical concerns as discussed in this paper. Second, societal trends will only magnify the importance of e-selection over time with the increased use of technology in work, at home, and the continued automation of jobs. In HRM and e-selection, it will be important to be aware of the changing nature of work itself. This includes artificial intelligence moving into service sectors and formerly human-only analytical roles, and the emergence of AI in everyday applications (e.g., electronic concierges), human-robotic (or AI) teams, and other labor force movements between people-oriented and AI/bot-centered work. Although professional jobs requiring an advanced education are not yet replaceable, it is noteworthy to us that in a recent issue of The Industrial Psychologist, the editor wonders if robot/AI programs might replace many of the functions of industrial/organizational psychologists (Behrend, 2017).

REFERENCES

Acemoglu, D., & Autor, D. H. (2011). Skills, tasks and technologies: Implications for employment and earnings. *Handbook of Labor Economics, 4,* 1043–1171.

Aldrich, C. (2009). *The complete guide to simulations and serious games.* San Francisco: Pfeiffer.

American Educational Research Association, American Psychological Association, National Council on Measurement in Education, Joint Committee on Standards for Educational, & Psychological Testing. (2014). *Standards for educational and psychological testing.* Washington, DC: American Educational Research Association.

Arthur, W., Doverspike, D. Kinney, T.B., & O'Connell, M. (2017). The impact of emerging technologies on selection models and research: Mobile devices and gamification as exemplars. In J. L. Farr & N.T. Tippins (Eds). *Handbook of employee selection* (2nd ed., pp. 967–986). New York, NY: Routledge.

Arthur, W., Doverspike, D., Muñoz, G. J., Taylor, J. E., & Carr, A. E. (2014). The use of mobile devices in high-stakes remotely delivered assessments and testing. *International Journal of Selection and Assessment, 22,* 113–123.

Autor, D. H., Levy, F., & Murnane, R. J. (2003). The skill content of recent technological change: An empirical exploration. *Quarterly Journal of Economics, 118*(4), 1279–1333.

Bartram, D., & Brown, A. (2004). Online testing: Mode of administration and the stability of OPQ 32i scores. *International Journal of Selection and Assessment, 12,* 278–284.

Bauer, T. N., Truxillo, D. M., Paronto, M. E., Weekley, J. A., & Campion, M. A. (2004). Applicant reactions to different selection technology: Face-to-face, interactive voice response, and computer-assisted telephone screening interviews. *International Journal of Selection and Assessment, 12,* 135–148.

Bauer, T. N., Truxillo, D. M., Tucker, J. S., Weathers, V., Bertolino, M., Erdogan, B., & Campion, M. A. (2006). Selection in the Information Age: The impact of privacy concerns and computer experience on applicant reactions. *Journal of Management, 32,* 601–621.

Beaty J. C., Nye, C. D., Borneman M. J., Kantrowitz, T. M., Drasgow, F., & Grauer, E.(2011). Proctored versus unproctored Internet tests: Are unproctored noncognitive tests as predictive of job performance? *International Journal of Selection and Assessment, 19,* 1–10.

Behrend, T. (2017). From the editor: Player piano. *The Industrial Psychologist, 54 (4),* 1–2.

Black, S., Stone, D. L., & Johnson, A. (2015). Use of social media and applicants' privacy. *Employee Responsibilities and Rights Journal, 27*(2), 115–159.

Blacksmith, N., Willford, J. C., & Behrend, T. S. (2016). Technology in the employment interview: A meta-analysis and future research agenda. *Personnel Assessment and Predictions, 2*(1), 12–20.

Braverman, H. (1974). *Labor and monopoly capital: The degradation of work in the twentieth century.* New York: Monthly Press Review.

Bravo Orellana, E. R. (2015). *Deskilling, up-skilling or reskilling? Effects of automation in information systems context.* Paper presented at the 21st Americas Conference on Information Systems, Puerto Rico.

Brown, M. I., & Grossenbacher, M. A. (2017). Can you test me now? Equivalence of GMA tests on mobile and non-mobile devices. *International Journal of Selection and Assessment, 25,* 61–71.

Brynjolfsson, E., & McAfee, A. (2014). *The second machine age: Work, progress, and prosperity in a time of brilliant technologies.* New York: W.W. Norton & Co.

Bureau of Labor Statistics (2016). Percent of employed people did some or all of their work at home in 2015. *The Economics Daily,* 24.

Casler, K. L. Bickel, L., & Hackett, E. (2013). Separate but equal? A comparison of participants and data gathered via Amazon's MTurk, social media, and face-to-face behavioral testing. *Computers in Human Behavior, 29*(6), 2156–2160.

Chan, D., & Schmitt, N. (2002). Situational judgment and job performance, *Human Performance, 15,* 233–254.

Chapman, D. S., & Rowe, P. M. (2002). The influence of videoconference technology and interview structure on the recruiting function of the employment interview: A field experiment. *International Journal of Selection and Assessment, 10,* 185–197.

Chuah, S. C., Drasgow, F., & Roberts, B. W. (2006). Personality assessment: Does the medium matter? No. *Journal of Research in Personality, 40*(4), 359–376.

Clevenger, J., Pereira, G. M., Wiechmann, D., Schmitt, N., & Harvey, V. S. (2001). Incremental validity of situational judgment tests. *Journal of Applied Psychology, 86,* 410–417.

Costa, P. T., & McCrae, R. R. (1988). Personality in adulthood: A six-year longitudinal study of self-reports and spouse ratings on the NEO Personality Inventory. *Journal of Personality and Social Psychology, 54,* 853–863.

Dale, S. (2014). Gamification: Making work fun, or making fun of work? *Business Information Review, 31*(2), 82–90.

Derous, E., & De Fryt, F. (2016). Developments in recruitment and selection research. International *Journal of Selection and Assessment, 24*(1), 1–3.

Dickter, D. N., Jockin, V., & Delany, T. (2017, in press). The evolution of e-selection. In G. Hertel, D. L. Stone, R. D. Johnson, & J. Passmore (Eds.), *The handbook of psychology of the internet at work.* Chichester, United Kingdom: Wiley-Blackwell.

Dorsey, D. W., Martin, J., Howard, D. J., & Coovert, M. D. (2017). Cybersecurity issues in selection. In L. L. Farr & N. T. Tippins (Eds.), *Handbook of employee selection* (pp. 913–930). New York, NY: Routledge.

Equal Employment Opportunity Commission (EEOC) (1978). Guidelines on employee selection procedures. *Federal Register, 35,* 12333–12336.

Embretson, S. E. (2000). *Item response theory for psychologists.* Mahwah, NJ: Lawrence Erlbaum.

Fetzer, M., & Tuzinski, K. (Eds). (2013). *Simulations for personnel selection.* New York, NY: Springer.

Ford, M. (2015). *The rise of the robots: Technology and the threat of a jobless future.* New York, NY: Basic Books.

Gartner. (2017). *Gartner says 8.4 billion connected "things" will be in use in 2017, up 31 percent from 2016.* Retrieved from http://www.gartner.com/newsroom/id/3598917

Gatewood, R. D., Feild, H. S., & Barrick, M. (2010). *Human resource selection* (7th ed.). Mason, OH: South-Western.

Gueutal, H. G., & Stone, D. L. (Eds.) (2005). *The brave new world of eHR: Human resources in the digital age.* San Francisco, CA: Jossey-Bass.

Hertel, G., Geister, S., & Konradt, U. (2005). Managing virtual teams: A review of current empirical research. *Human Resources Management Review, 15,* 69–95.

Hertel, G., Stone, D. L., Johnson, R. D., & Passmore, J. (Eds.). (2017-in press). *The handbook of the psychology of the internet at work.* Chichester, United Kingdom: Wiley-Blackwell.

Holland, B., & Lambert, D. (2013). How to measure contact center skills using multimedia simulations. In M. Fetzer & K. Tuzinski (Eds.), *Simulations for personnel selection* (pp. 129–156). New York: Springer.

Illingworth, A. J., Morelli, N. A., Scott, J .C., & Boyd, S. L. (2015). Internet-based, unproctored assessments on mobile and non-mobile devices: Usage, measurement equivalence, and outcomes. *Journal of Business Psychology, 30*, 325–343.

International Test Commission (2006). Guidelines for computer-based and Internet-delivered testing. *International Journal of Testing, 6*, 143–172.

Jacques, P. H, Garger, J., Brown, C .A., & Deale, C. S. (2009). Team candidates: The roles of personality traits, technology anxiety and trust as predictors of perceptions of virtual reality teams. *Journal of Business and Management, 15*(2), 143–157.

Kavanagh, M. J., Thite, M., & Johnson, R. D. (Eds). (2015). *Human resource information systems: Basics, applications, and future directions* (3rd ed.). Thousand Oaks, CA: Sage.

Kehoe, J. F., Dickter, D. N., Russell, D. P., & Sacco, J. M. (2005). e-Selection. In H. Gueutal & D. L. Stone (Eds.), *The brave new world of eHR: Human resources in the digital age* (pp.54–103). New York, NY: Wiley & Sons.

King, D. D., Ryan, A. M., Kantrowitz, T., Grelle, D., & Dainis, A. (2015). Mobile internet testing: An analysis of equivalence, individual differences, and reactions. *International Journal of Selection and Assessment, 23*(4), 382–394.

Kluemper, D. H., Rosen, P. A., & Mossholder, K. W. (2012). Social networking websites, personality ratings, and the organizational context: More than meets the eye? *Journal of Applied Social Psychology, 42*(5), 1143–1172.

Konradt, U., Hertel, G., & Joder, K. (2003). Web-based assessment of call center agents: Development and validation of a computerized instrument. *International Journal of Selection and Assessment, 11*, 184–193.

Kraut, R., Steinfield, C., Chan, A. P., Butler, B., & Hoag, A. (1999). Coordination and virtualization: The role of electronic networks and personal relationships. *Organization Science, 10*(6), 722–740.

Krumm, S., Kanthak, J., Hartmann, K., & Hertel, G. (2016). What does it take to be a virtual team player? What does it take to be a virtual team player? The knowledge, skills, abilities, and other characteristics required in virtual teams. *Human Performance, 29*, 123–142.

Landers, R. N. (2017). A crash course in natural language processing. *The Industrial Psychologist, 54*(4), 5–16.

Landers, R. N., Fink, A. A., & Collmus, A. B. (2017). Using big data to enhance staffing: Vast untapped resources or tempting honeypot? In L. L. Farr & N. T. Tippins (Eds.), *Handbook of employee selection* (pp. 949–966). New York, NY: Routledge.

Legree, P. J., Kilcullen, R., Psotka, J., Putka, D., & Ginter, R. N. (2010). *Scoring situational judgment tests using profile similarity metrics (Technical Report 1272).* Arlington, VA: US Army Research Institute for the Behavioral and Social Sciences.

Lievens, F., & De Soete, B. (2012). Simulations. In N. Schmitt (Ed.), *The Oxford handbook of personnel assessment and selection* (pp. 383–410). Oxford, UK: Oxford University Press.

Lievens, F., & Patterson, F. (2011). The validity and incremental validity of knowledge tests, low-fidelity simulations, and high-fidelity simulations for predicting job performance in advanced-level high-stakes selection. *Journal of Applied Psychology, 96*(5), 927–940.

Lievens, F., & Thornton, G. C. III (2005). Assessment centers: recent developments in practice and research. In A. Evers, O. Smit-Voskuijl, & N. Anderson (Eds.) *Handbook of selection* (pp. 243–264). Malden, MA: Blackwell Publishing.

Lobene, E. V. (2017, April). *High-fidelity simulation scoring practices: Tricks of the trade revealed!* Symposium conducted at the meeting of the Society for Industrial and Organizational Psychology, Orlando, FL.

Lohr, S. (2017, March 19). A.I. is doing legal work. But it won't replace lawyers, yet. *The New York Times*. Retrieved from https://www.nytimes.com/2017/03/19/technology/lawyers-artificial-intelligence.html

Lorenzetti, L. (2016, April 5). Here's how IBM Watson Health is transforming the healthcare industry. *Fortune*. Retrieved from http://fortune.com/ibm-watson-health-business-strategy/

Lukaszewski, K. M., Dickter, D. N., Lyons, B. D., & Kehoe, J. (2015). Recruitment and selection in an internet context. In M.J. Kavanagh, M. Thite, & R. D. Johnson (Eds.). *Human resource information systems: Basics, applications, and future directions* (3rd ed., pp. 368–387). Thousand Oaks, CA: Sage.

Marler, J. H., & Dulebohn, J. H. (2005). A model of employee self-service technology acceptance. In J. J. Martocchio (Ed.), *Research in personnel and human resources management, Volume 24* (pp. 137–180). Boston: Elsevier.

MacDonnell, R., O'Neill, T., Kline, T., & Hambley, L. (2009). Bringing group-level personality to the electronic realm: A comparison of face-to-face and virtual contexts. *The Psychologist-Manager Journal, 12*(1), 1.

McCloy, R. A., & Gibby, R. E. (2011). Computerized adaptive Testing. In N.T. Tippins & S. Adler (Eds.) *Technology-enhanced assessment of talent* (pp. 153–189). San Francisco, CA: Jossey-Bass.

McDaniel, M. A., & Nguyen, N. T. (2001). Situational judgment tests: A review of practice and constructs assessed. *International Journal of Selection and Assessment, 9*, 103–113.

McDaniel, M. A., Psotka, J. , Legree, P. J., Yost, A. P., & Weekley, J. A. (2011). Toward and understanding of situational judgment item validity and group differences. *Journal of Applied Psychology, 96*, 327–336.

Mead, A. D., & Drasgow, F. (1993). Equivalence of computerized and paper-and-pencil cognitive ability tests: A meta-analysis. *Psychological Bulletin, 114*, 449–458.

Milne-Tyte, A. (2011, September 26). Seeking work? Ready your webcam. *The Wall Street Journal*. Retrieved from https://www.wsj.com/articles/SB10001424053111904537404576554943587087926

Morelli, N. A., Mahan, R. P., & Illingworth, A. J. (2014). Establishing the measurement equivalence of online selection assessments delivered on mobile versus nonmobile devices. *International Journal of Selection and Assessment, 22*, 124–138.

Morelli, N., Potosky, D., Arthur, W., & Tippins, N. (2017). A call for conceptual models of technology in I-O Psychology: An example from technology-based talent assessment. *Industrial and Organizational Psychology: Perspectives on Science and Practice. 10*(4), 1–36.

Motowidlo, S. J., Dunnette, M. D., & Carter, G. W. (1990). An alternative selection procedure: The low fidelity simulation. *Journal of Applied Psychology, 75*, 640–647.

O'Connell, M. S., Hartman, N. S., McDaniel, M. A., Grubb, W. E. III, & Lawrence, A. (2007). Incremental validity of situational judgment tests for task and contextual job performance. *International Journal of Selection and Assessment, 15*(1), 19–29.

Ones, D. S., Dilchert, S., Viswesvaran, C., & Salgado, J.W. (2010). Cognitive abilities. In J. L. Farr & N. T. Tippins (Eds.), *Handbook of employee selection* (pp. 255–275). New York, NY: Routledge.

Ones, D. S., Kaiser, R. B., Chamorro-Premuzic, T., & Svensson, C. (2017). Has industrial-organizational psychology lost its way? *The Industrial Psychologist, 54*(4), 67–74.

Park, G., Schwartz, H. A., Eichstaedt, J. C., Kern, M. L., Kosinski, M., Stillwell, D. J., Ungar, L. H., & Seligman, M. E. P. (2015). Automatic personality assessment through social media language. *Journal of Personality and Social Psychology, 108*, 934–952.

Passeri, P. (2014). *Fortune 500 cyber attacks timeline*. Retrieved from http://www.hackmageddon.com/2014/11/25/fortune–500-cyber-attacks-timeline/

Potosky, D. (2008). A conceptual framework for the role of administration medium in the personnel assessment process. *Academy of Management Review, 33*(3), 629–648.

Reiter-Palmon, R., Brown, M., Sandall, D. L., Buboltz, C., & Nimps, T. (2006). Development of an O*NET web-based job analysis and its implementation in the U.S. Navy: Lessons learned. *Human Resource Management Review, 16,* 294–309.

Reynolds, D. H., & Dickter, D. N. (2017). Technology and employee selection: An overview. In J. L. Farr & N. T. Tippins (Eds.), *Handbook of employee selection* (2nd ed., pp. 855–873). New York, NY: Routledge.

Reynolds, D. H., & Rupp D. E., (2010). Advances in technology-facilitated assessment. In J. Scott & D. Reynolds (Eds.), *Handbook of workplace assessment* (pp. 609–641). San Francisco, CA: Jossey-Bass.

Rivkin, D., Gregory, C. M., Norton, J. J., Craven, D. E., & Lewis, P. M. (2017). Advancing O*NET data, application and uses. In J. L. Farr & N. T. Tippins (Eds). *Handbook of employee selection* (pp. 874–912). New York, NY: Routledge.

Roulin, N., & Bangerter, A. (2013). Social networking sites in personnel selection: A signaling perspective on recruiters' and applicants' perceptions. *Journal of Personnel Psychology, 12*(3), 143–151.

Ryan, A. M., & Derous, E. (2016). Highlighting tensions in recruitment and selection practice and research. *International Journal of Selection and Assessment, 24*(1), 54–62.

Ryan A. M., & Ployhart, R. E. (2014). A century of selection. *Annual Review of Psychology, 65*, 693–717.

Salvendy, G. (1975). Selection of industrial operators: The one-hole test. *International Journal of Production Research, 13*(3), 303–321.

Salgado, J. F., & Moscoso, S. (2003). Internet-based personality testing: Equivalence of measures and assessees' perceptions and reactions. *International Journal of Assessment and Selection, 11*, 194–203.

Schmidt, F. L., & Hunter, J. E. (1998). The validity and utility of selection methods in personnel psychology: Practical and theoretical implications of 85 years of research findings. *Psychological Bulletin, 124*(2), 262–274.

Schmidt, F. L., & Hunter, J. E. (2004). General mental ability in the world of work: Occupational attainment and job performance. *Journal of Personality and Social Psychology, 86*(1), 162–173.

Schmitt, N., & Chan, D. (2006). Situational judgment tests: Method or construct? In Weekley, J. A., & Ployhart, R. E. (Eds), *Situational judgment tests: Theory, measurement, and application* (pp. 135–155). Mahwah, NJ, US: Lawrence Erlbaum Associates.

Sheehan, K. B., & Pittman, M. (2016). *Amazon's Mechanical Turk for academics: The HIT handbook for social science research.* Irvine, CA: Melvin & Leigh.

Stark, S. Chernyshenko, O.S., & Drasgow, F. (2017). Modern psychometric theory to support personnel assessment and selection. In J. L. Farr & N. T. Tippins (Eds.), *Handbook of employee selection* (2nd ed., (pp. 931–948). New York, NY: Routledge.

Stark, S., Chernyshenko, O. S., Drasgow, F., & Williams, B.A. (2006). Item responding in personality assessment: Should ideal point methods be considered for scale development and scoring? *Journal of Applied Psychology, 91*, 25–39.

Stone, D. L., Deadrick, D. L., Lukaszewski, K. M., & Johnson, R. (2015). The influence of technology on the future of human resource management. *Human Resource Management Review, 25*(2), 216–231.

Stone, D. L., & Dulebohn, J. H. (2013). Emerging issues in theory and research on electronic human resource management (eHRM). *Human Resource Management Review, 23*(1), 1–5.

Stone, D. L., Lukaszewski, K.M., Stone-Romero, E .F., & Johnson, T. L. (2013). Factors affecting the effectiveness and acceptance of electronic selection systems. *Human Resource Management Review, 23*, 50–70.

Stone, E. F., & Stone, D. L. (1990). Privacy in organizations: theoretical issues, research findings, and protection strategies. In G. Ferris & K. Rowland (Eds.), *Research in personnel and human resources management, 8* (pp. 549–411). Greenwich: JAI Press.

Stoughton, J. W., Thompson, L. F., & Meade, A. W. (2015). Examining applicant reactions to the use of social networking websites in pre-employment screening. *Journal of Business and Psychology, 30*(1), 73–88.

Sydell, E., Ferrell, J., Carpenter, J., Frost, C., & Brodbeck, C. C. (2013). Simulation scoring. In M. Fetzer & K. Tuzinski (Eds.), *Simulations for personnel selection* (pp. 83–107). New York, NY: Springer.

Thornton, G. C., III, & Rupp, D. R. (2006). *Assessment centers in human resource management: Strategies for prediction, diagnosis, and development.* Mahwah, NJ: Lawrence Erlbaum.

Tippins, N.T. (2015). Technology and assessment in selection. *Annual Review of Organizational Behavior, 2*, 551–582.

Tippins, N. T., & Adler, S. (Eds.) (2011). *Technology-enhanced assessment of talent.* San Francisco, CA: Wiley.

Tippins, N. T., Beaty, J., Drasgow, F., Gibson, W. M., Pearlman, K., Segall, D. O., & Shepherd, W. (2006). Unproctored Internet testing in employment settings. *Personnel Psychology, 59*, 189–225.

Ventura, M., Shute, V., Wright, T., & Zhao, W. (2013). An investigation of the validity of the virtual spatial navigation assessment. *Frontiers in Psychology, 4*, 1–7.

Weekley, J. A., & Jones, C. (1999). Further studies of situational tests. *Personnel Psychology, 52*, 679–700.

Weekley, J. A., & Ployhart, R. E. (Eds.). (2006). *Situational judgment tests: Theory, measurement, and application.* Mahwah, NJ: Lawrence Erlbaum Associates.

Woo, S. E., Keith, M., & Thornton, M. A. (2015). Amazon Mechanical Turk for industrial and organizational psychology: Advantages, challenges, and practical recommendations. *Industrial and Organizational Psychology, 8*(2), 171–179.

Wyatt, I. D., & Hecker, D. E. (2006, March). Occupational changes during the 20th century. *Monthly Labor Review*, 35–57.

Yamaguchi, M., Crump, M. J. C., & Logan, G. D. (2013). Speed-accuracy trade-off in skilled typewriting: Decomposing the contributions of hierarchical control loops. *Journal of Experimental Psychology. Human Perception & Performance, 39*(3), 678–699.

Zafar, H., & Stone, D. L. (2015). HRIS security and privacy. In M. Kavanagh, M. Thite, & R. Johnson (Eds.), *Human Resource Information Systems: Basics, applications, and future directions* (3rd ed.). Thousand Oaks, CA: Sage.

CHAPTER 4

HIRING FOR THE WIN

Game-Based Assessment in Employee Selection

Sarena Bhatia and Ann Marie Ryan

ABSTRACT

Game-thinking, or the use of game elements and principles in non-game settings, is becoming more prevalent in human resource management systems. This chapter explores the burgeoning trend as it relates to game-based assessments (GBAs), or assessments that incorporate game elements to evoke and measure relevant constructs in employee selection. The authors provide a background for how game-thinking is being applied in organizations, including a discussion of game elements and the differences between gamification and game-based processes. They then conduct a thorough review of the advantages and disadvantages of GBAs in hiring contexts, covering topics such as assessment development, psychometric considerations, applicant reactions, scoring, and cross-cultural ramifications. The chapter concludes with areas for future research, which are ample considering how nascent GBAs are.

The Brave New World of eHRM 2.0, pages 81–110.

INTRODUCTION

The world has been swept by the pace of technological change. Many of these effects can be seen in the human resource management (HRM) processes in organizations. Assessments are offered on mobile devices, due to the increasing interest from applicants to engage with these tools outside of a traditional computerized setting (Kantrowitz, 2014). Interviews are being conducted virtually (Bolch, 2007), and companies are offering virtual job previews and tryouts in which applicants interact with an online environment that parallels their potential work environment (Winkler, 2006). Smartphone apps and health tracking devices are being used to incentivize and reward participation in employee wellness programs (Goth, 2017), and organizational learning programs are taking place in online environments where employees can interact (Lahey, 2014).

Many of the technological changes in HRM are easier to implement and less costly for the organization over the long-term relative to using less advanced methods, but they are also tailored to give the applicant or employee a more attractive, immersive experience. In keeping with this focus on engagement, game-thinking and gamification are experiencing a burgeoning use in assessment contexts (Chou, 2015), due in part to how much more accessible gamified systems are with advances in technology. Game-thinking refers to process of using game principles and game elements in nongame situations (Collmus, Armstrong, & Landers, 2016). Games have a long history prior to their widespread use in organizational settings; they have been used in training and educational fields for decades (Chin, Dukes, & Gamson, 2009). Their more recent introduction to HRM applications has manifested in several ways.

First, in the recruitment space gamified tools are used to give prospective candidates insight into the job, or help funnel them to the jobs for which they are best-suited. L'Oreal, for example, offers an online game in which students virtually engage with real-life scenarios, ask questions, and experience different sectors of the organization (Tims, 2010). Marriott and PriceWaterhouseCoopers are using gamified recruitment in similar ways, with the goal of providing a realistic job preview and showing the young workforce that these companies are attractive places to work (Zielinski, 2015). Gamified systems are also being applied to learning- Deloitte is an example of this, having incorporated several game elements into its online learning system, such as awarding badges for completing learning modules and providing leaderboards that allow employees to see their rankings relative to their peers. The company has enjoyed increased participation in its training programs, to the tune of a 37% increase of users on the site each week (Meister, 2013). Game-based thinking has also been incorporated into the fabric of work, with some companies using it to make mundane tasks more interesting. Qualcomm incorporated a points system to their online boards to encourage knowledge sharing within the organization (Meister, 2015).

While there is much to explore when it comes to game-thinking in HRM, in this chapter we focus on the use of game-thinking in assessments for employee selection. We believe this area deserves special focus, both because of its burgeoning use (evidenced by the increasing number of test publishers offering gamified tools for hiring) and the special considerations that surround selection tools. There are few areas within HRM that are as high-stakes and as potentially litigious as selection, and we strive to provide a thorough review of the existing evidence as well as a critical lens of how much there is still to do when it comes to games and selection. We first begin with a deeper dive into game-thinking and game elements to help the reader understand the context for this chapter.

DEFINING GAME-BASED ASSESSMENTS

Despite this widespread use of game-thinking, there is a level of nuance that is often overlooked when organizations adopt gamification and game-based systems, and that nuance is the *extent* to which games are truly integrated into these tools. At the heart of this distinction are game elements, defined as a set of building blocks or features shared by games (rather than a necessary set of conditions for a game) said to be "characteristic to games... readily associated with games, and found to play a significant role in gameplay" (Deterding, Dixon, Khaled, & Nacke, 2011, p. 4). Game elements vary widely in scope, ranging from the abstract such as *fantasy,* or the portrayal of an imaginary world (Garris, Ahlers, & Driskell, 2002) to a more concrete *avatar,* or a digital self-representation (Reeves & Read, 2009). Some game element taxonomies are more theoretical, and illustrate the way the game is conceptualized, designed, and structured. These kinds of taxonomies group many game elements into superordinate categories. (i.e., Deterding et al., 2011; King, Delfabbro, & Griffiths, 2010). Others are much more concrete (i.e., Garris, Ahlers, & Driskell, 2002). Taxonomies of game elements vary widely in the discipline from which they stem and in what they include, though most of them contain some form of focused goals/rules, feedback, challenge, interaction, and sensory stimuli (Dickey, 2005; Gee, 2009; Prensky, 2001; Shute & Ke, 2012; Wilson et al., 2009). These elements are common to many games, and the inherent motivating quality of these elements helps explain why games are able to captivate and intrigue such a large audience (Locke & Latham, 2002; Ryan, Rigby, & Przybylski, 2006). A selection of game element taxonomies can be seen in Table 4.1.

The various game elements mentioned in Table 4.1 can be incorporated into selection assessment tools in two primary ways: they can be layered on top of existing tools in a process called *gamification* (Deterding et al., 2011) or they can be built into the structure of the process in a way that we and other researchers refer to as *game-based* (Landers, 2015; Mislevy et al., 2014).

An example is helpful to illustrate the difference: imagine there is an assessment tool that has innovation, interpersonal skill, and cognitive reasoning portions. A gamified assessment may introduce an avatar at the beginning to guide the user through the multiple parts of the assessment, and give instructions for each section. This assessment could also use a points system to alert the user

TABLE 4.1. Game Element Taxonomies.

Author and Year	Discipline	Elements
Deterding et al. (2011)	Media research	Game interface design patterns, Game design patterns and mechanics, Game design principles and heuristics, Game models, Game design methods
Dickey (2005)	Educational technology research and development	Focused goals, Challenging tasks, Clear and compelling standards, Protection from adverse consequences for initial failures, Affirmation of performance, Affiliation with others, Novelty and variety, Choice
Floryan (2009)	Computer science	Goals, Content and user tasks, Simulation fidelity, User freedom
Garris, Ahlers, & Driskell (2002)	Gaming	Fantasy, Rules/goals, Sensory stimuli, Challenge, Mystery, Control
Gee (2009)	Game-based learning	Underlying rule system and game goal to which player is attached, Micro-control that creates sense of intimacy and power, Experiences that offer good learning opportunities, Match between affordance and effectivity, Modeling to make learning more general and abstract, Encouragement to players to enact their own unique trajectory in game
King, Delfabbro, & Griffiths (2010)	Clinical psychology	Social features, Manipulation and control features, Narrative and identity features, Reward and punishment features, Presentation features
Prensky (2001)	Game-based learning	Rules, Goals and objectives, Outcomes, Feedback, Conflict (competition, challenge, opposition), Interaction, Representation (story)
Reeves & Read (2009)	Business technology	Self-representation with avatars, 3D environments, Narrative context, Feedback, Reputation, ranks, and levels, Marketplaces and economies, Competition under rules that are explicit and enforced, Parallel communication systems that can be easily configured, Time pressure
Shute & Ke (2012)	Game-based learning	Interactive problem solving, Specific goals/rules, Adaptive challenge, Control, Ongoing feedback, Uncertainty, Sensory stimuli
Sweetser & Wyeth (2005)	Computer science	Concentration, Challenge, Player skills, Control, Clear goals, Feedback, Immersion, Social interaction
Wilson et al. (2009)	Gaming	Adaptation, Assessment, Challenge, Conflict, Control, Fantasy, Interaction (equipment), Interaction (interpersonal), Interaction (social), Language/communication, Location, Mystery, Pieces or players, Progress and surprise, Representation, Rules/goals, Safety, Sensory stimuli
Wood, Griffiths, Chappell, & Davies (2004)	Cyber psychology	Sound, Graphics, Background and setting, Duration of game, Rate of play, Advancement rate, Use of humor, Control options, Game dynamics, Winning and losing features, Character development, Brand assurance, Multiplayer features

that he or she is progressing through the assessment, and incorporate sound to add sensory stimulation. However, the actual content of the assessment is not changed; the elements are simply layered onto the tool so we would describe it as gamified. In contrast, in a game-based assessment, the game elements would aid in the evoking and measuring of the relevant constructs. An assessment of innovation may parallel real life by presenting a challenging task, multiple pathways to success, high levels of control, and competition while measuring an applicant's ability to create and execute innovation solutions. A cognitive reasoning module could use time restraints, feedback, and clear goals to produce a stimulating situation that assesses processing capacity. In these cases the use of game elements is fundamentally changing how behaviors are elicited from a job candidate, and are built into the fabric of the assessment.

These game-based assessments (GBAs) are more difficult to develop and score because they require evidence of psychometric support with the added difficulty of dependencies across points in the game, multiple skills and abilities being assessed in different ways, and the need to derive meaningful measurement from thousands of data points. However, introducing game elements without considering implications for psychometric properties can introduce construct-irrelevant variance, lack of consistency, or test bias to name a few potential issues. For this reason, we focus on GBAs rather than gamified assessments, as the elements are not simply used to motivate or entertain but are truly integral to the measurement of the relevant constructs. This is not to say that gamified assessments are not useful; they may offer many of the same benefits of GBAs in terms of engagement and motivation (Armstrong, Ferrell, Collmus, & Landers, 2016). In fact, assessment methods such as situational judgment tests or assessment centers can be gamified. However, GBAs are a new and unique kind of assessment method and go beyond simply adding of a few game elements to an SJT, in-basket exercise, or similar established selection method.

In the following sections, we explore the current body of knowledge on GBAs in order to shed light on one of the newest, most complex, and least understood selection methods. Current research that applies to GBAs lives in several different disciplines, so we draw on educational psychology and organizational training research in addition to the literature on personnel selection to articulate the current state of these tools. We use the frame of advantages and disadvantages for the ease of organizing the review; however, because so little work on GBAs exists it is impossible to definitively claim anything as an established advantage or disadvantage. We will conclude the chapter with the primary directions for future research.

ADVANTAGES

Some of the suggested advantages for using GBAs in employee selection relative to other methods are more positive candidate perceptions of the hiring process, more positive organizational image, and greater fidelity of the assessment to the work context.

Perceptions of the Selection Process

There is an extensive body of research that links applicants' reactions to the process by which they apply for jobs to meaningful outcomes (Ryan & Ployhart, 2000). These reactions can have an impact on organizations, including whether applicants will accept offers, what applicants will share with their networks about their experiences, and whether applicants will continue to engage with the company (Hausknecht, Day, & Thomas, 2004). For these reasons, organizations care about how applicants feel during the hiring process, and what kinds of attributions they make about the organization. In the following section, we focus on the role GBAs can play in shaping perceptions about the hiring process. Organizations want to mitigate negative or stressful experiences during this evaluation, and want to keep talented applicants involved. One of the primary reasons for incorporating games into assessment processes, therefore, is increased engagement and fun in order to produce positive reactions (Anderson & Rainie, 2012).

While applicant reactions to GBAs have rarely been explicitly tested, related research can help us anticipate how applicants may feel. Much of the work in the gaming literature, serious and otherwise, indicates that participants enjoy interacting with game-based tools. For example, a recent meta-analysis indicated that perceived ease of use of games related to perceived usefulness and enjoyment (Hamari & Keronen, 2017). Perceived usefulness in turn related to attitude, which then positively related to playing intentions.

Why might these tools elicit greater enjoyment? Some researchers have used the lens of self-determination theory, a motivation theory concerned with people's inherent growth and needs, to explain how game elements relate to autonomy, competence, and relatedness (Ryan et al., 2006). The researchers draw parallels between the game element of control and the need for autonomy, as well as between the feeling of presence and the need for competence. Relatedness can be addressed through the social mechanisms of games like chat functions or group play. As may be expected, in a series of studies testing these relationships, the fulfillment of basic needs (i.e., autonomy, competence and relatedness) during gameplay was positively related to enjoyment and desire to play in the future.

Other studies have framed these positive feelings in the lens of flow, an absorptive state coined by Mihaly Csikszentmihalyi (1990). Flow is a state of complete concentration on the task at hand, during which a person loses sense of time and any separation from the task. A number of studies shown that games induce a state of flow, whether they be video games played for personal leisure or serious games (Bowman, 1982; Chiang, Lin, Cheng, & Liu, 2011; Chou & Ting, 2003; Hamari et al., 2016; Hsu & Lu, 2004; Weibel, Wissmath, Habegger, Steiner, & Groner, 2008). Again, the presence of game elements is responsible for inducing flow. Avatars and narratives can immerse players, unexpected challenges can keep them stimulated, and feedback can incentivize them to continue working towards the game's goals (to name a few).

The takeaway from this body of work is that the incorporation of game elements into assessments makes them more motivating and interesting. While games are fun and enjoyable, they can also serve an important purpose in a selection context: to reduce negative perceptions about tests. One area where GBAs can help is test-taking anxiety. This form of anxiety around tests plagues both those in the educational and organizational world because it introduces error to test validity estimates, can create unfavorable attitudes toward the test and testing organization, and can produce undesirable physical symptoms (Arvey, Strickland, Drauden, & Martin, 1990; McDonald, 2001). Some work has shown initial promise that GBAs can reduce this test-taking anxiety by appearing less intimidating and more user-centered (Collmus et al., 2016; Smits & Charlier, 2011). Additionally, some researchers posit that game-thinking can reduce perceived test length and test fatigue; while this has not been widely tested, a few studies support this postulation (Collmus, 2016; Landers, 2015). The rationale for this is that GBAs are more engaging, and therefore that time spent on them does not feel as tedious. The suggestion that GBAs can reduce perceived test time complements best practices of assessment utility. Longer assessments allow for more reliable measures, and greater validity (Cortina, 1993; Messick, 1995). The dilemma with using longer assessments is that they can relate to attrition, but recent work has found that attrition often happens very early in the selection process and that assessment length is not significantly related to attrition rates (Hardy, Gibson, Sloan, & Carr, 2017). This evidence in conjunction with the use of GBAs may further allay organizational fears that candidates will react negatively to longer tests, thus persuading them to use assessments with greater utility.

Future work may look at whether GBAs can alleviate other negative reactions such as perceived difficulty, lack of concentration, and even stereotype threat (Arvey et al., 1990; Steele & Aronson, 1995). Reducing these negative reactions should be more easily accomplished with GBAs, which often operate as a form of stealth assessments in that the candidate might not attend as heavily to the fact that he or she is being assessed (Shute, 2011). While true stealth assessment is impossible in a selection context because applicants know they are being evaluated, GBAs may offer benefits that mitigate traditional issues with personnel testing. Many of the detrimental cognitive or affective outcomes in traditional test settings occur because the evaluative aspect of testing is very salient. If assessments could more closely mirror play, it is possible these issues could be reduced or eliminated.

Organizational Image

In addition to managing perceptions of the selection process, organizations are also concerned with their image or brand during recruitment and selection. When organizations appear attractive to candidates, applicants are more likely to accept, reapply, and recommend jobs at the company, and are less likely to take litigious action in the case where they feel they have been wronged (Bauer et al., 2001;

Ployhart & Ryan, 1998; Truxillo, Bauer, Campion, & Paronto, 2002). Some work suggests that when sophisticated technology is used, as it often is with GBAs, impressions of the organization are boosted. One recent study found that overall organizational impressions were highest when video-based situational judgment tests (SJTs) were used, following by 3D and lastly, 2D SJTs (Bruk-Lee et al., 2016). Another study found that high technology interactivity, or the extent to which technology uses graphical interface features, was related to organizational attractiveness perceptions (Howardson & Behrend, 2014). While these findings are not unique to GBAs, GBAs are highly technological and are only moving further into this space as virtual and augmented reality become more accessible (Manly, 2015). Therefore organizations may be seen as more attractive when they incorporate GBAs into their selection battery.

It may be that the technology itself is boosting impressions, but more than likely there is an underlying mechanism to these findings. One idea is that using technology and gaming communicates information about what the organization offers and values (Collmus, Armstrong, & Landers, 2016). GBAs may serve as a signal that the organization places emphasis on technology, innovation, and even fun. While much of an organization's image or brand may be solidified for an applicant before he or she reaches the assessment phase because of media, advertising, or the recruitment process (Collins & Stevens, 2002; Walker, Feild, Giles, Bernerth & Short, 2011), the assessment space offers another touchpoint during which the applicant is evaluating fit with the hirer.

Quite a bit of work supports the idea that game-based tools will enhance an organization's image, but some studies run counter to this. The theories of cognitive load suggest that when there is more complexity, applicants are able to process less information. One study found that when an interactive, virtual world was used to share information about a hiring company, applicants acquired less job-related information than those who saw a traditional website (Badger, Kaminsky, & Behrend, 2014). In the case of a GBA that is more technology-heavy and requires high attentional focus, applicants may have less time to process messages about the company while they are completing the assessment.

Fidelity

Fidelity in testing has multiple components; the first is physical fidelity, which relates to the extent to which the test physically reproduces the performance environment of the job (Kozlowski & DeShon, 2004). These situations would attempt to use the equipment needed on the job, mirror the job environment, and have the candidate perform behaviors that are as similar to those performed on the job as possible. The second is psychological fidelity, which has to do with how knowledge, skills, and abilities (KSAs) needed for the job are integrated into the assessment (Truxillo, Donahue, & Kuang, 2004). In this case the underlying psychological processes that are important to performance would be elicited. Physical fidelity is said to be less important than psychological fidelity, particularly in roles where physically-based tasks are not required (Goldstein, Zedeck, & Schnedier, 1993). Fidelity lies along a continuum and to make matters more complex, the stimulus and the response of an assessment may have differing levels of fidelity (for example, a video-based situational judgment test would present its stimulus content via video, which would be considered higher fidelity, but may require applicants to respond in a paper-and-pencil form, which is lower fidelity). Fidelity increases the point-to-point correspondence between the assessment and work, oftentimes also increasing face validity and content validity (Tuzinski, 2013).

GBAs may fall anywhere from the moderate to high end of the fidelity continuum. Tuzinski places serious games in the moderate fidelity range, which is appropriate given the currently developed offerings (2013). Rigorously-developed GBAs are almost always high in psychological fidelity in that they assess KSAs that are needed for the job; they may assess cognitive ability or personality, or they may parallel the work environment more authentically and request that the candidate complete tasks that he or she would likely encounter on the job. For example, a GBA may place the applicant in the role of a manager and ask him or her to create a new business plan or resolve a machinery issue at a plant. In these latter cases, GBAs would be higher on the physical fidelity continuum, and more similar to a tool like a virtual assessment center (though not so high as a work sample in which applicants complete the work almost exactly as it would be done on the job).

GBAs also often include rich media such as high-quality graphics and sensory stimulations (Tippins, 2015). They can include branching as well, in which the applicant's response dictates the next scenario or problem set that he or she sees. Branching is frequently incorporated into games to produce the game elements of control and adaptive challenge. In a selection setting, branching is useful because it more accurately mirrors the choices an individual has on a job, and is seen as more interactive (Kanning, Grewe, Hollenberg, & Hadouch, 2006). However, it requires careful orchestration from a development and scoring perspective. The rich media and branching that is available in GBAs, in combination with moderate levels of fidelity, can elicit more positive reactions than what is accessible with traditional assessments. Related research supports this. For example, one study found that a multimedia assessment that made use of video was perceived as more valid, more job-related, more enjoyable, and shorter than a computerized or paper-and-pencil version of the same assessment (Richman-Hirsch, Olson-Buchanan, & Drasgow, 2000). The study mentioned earlier, in which the video-based SJT was preferred and rated as more realistic than corresponding 3D and 2D measures, complements the idea that rich media fares well with applicants. An earlier study found assessments that included video portions were seen as more face valid than paper-and-pencil tests (Chan & Schmitt, 1997). In a similar vein, Kanning and colleagues found that interactive items were viewed as more positive and useful (2006). The immersion, control, and storytelling of GBAs offers a much different experience than other measures, and applicants may respond well to this experience.

However, there is some work showing that high fidelity and/or richer media assessments are not viewed any more favorably than traditional assessments (Lievens & Sackett, 2006; Potosky & Bobko, 2004; Truxillo & Hunthausen, 1999; Wiechmann & Ryan, 2003). Additionally, GBAs are less likely to have as high physical fidelity as an assessment center or a work sample because they are often administered through a computer or a mobile device (leaving less room for face-to-face interaction that can have high fidelity such as a conflict resolution scenario or a leaderless group discussion), and do not parallel work tasks as precisely. This means that GBAs may be seen as less job-related than other selection tools. Job-relatedness factors highly into judgments about how fair the selection process is (Gilliland, 1993) so there is some danger in using tools that are not so obviously job-relevant to candidates, regardless of their empirical connection to job performance.

In total, some work on fidelity supports the use of GBAs because applicants can feel the assessment is more face valid, more realistic, and more enjoyable than traditional assessments. Other work suggests just the opposite. It also may be the case that these perceptions are game-specific and candidate-specific; that is, two GBAs with a clear workplace context (e.g., retail store environment) might differ in perceived job relatedness even if assessing the same KSAOs, and two candidates taking the same GBA may differ in how job related they see it based on their own level of work experiences in that environment. There are few studies that can be used to make these extrapolations, but it is clear that further work is needed to derive more substantial implications about how the fidelity of GBAs affects reactions.

DISADVANTAGES

Some of the potential disadvantages of GBA use in selection are the cost of development, the difficulty of including certain game elements in a tool used for decision-making about individuals, and the breadth of what has not been researched relative to typical selection methods.

Cost and Complexity of Development

A major consideration in the selection process is how much money the organization is expending per applicant. A recent benchmarking study by the Society for Human Resource Management indicated that the average cost per hire is $4,129 (Society for Human Resource Management [SHRM], 2016). Organizations may use vendor assessments that cost as little as $3 per applicant for a prescreen measure, to $500 per applicant for a simulation or battery of executive assessments (Hunt, 2003). While the market shows increasing demand for more complex assessments, GBAs can be some of the most costly to develop because they require sophisticated graphics and stimuli. The price tag that comes with developing these assessments may not be worth it unless there are significant hikes in engagement and validity, but it is difficult to evaluate whether this will be the case until after the assessment is close to completion (Collmus et al., 2016). Fortunately, costs for developing technologically-heavy tools like GBAs have come down in recent years, and will continue to become more accessible to researchers and organizations alike. Utilizers can also choose whether they need to build the GBA completely custom and from scratch, or if existing modules can be harnessed to meet needs; these two pathways are discussed in more detail below.

The first option is to build a customized assessment. This may be an attractive option for a larger organization that is looking to assess for specific competencies, and will use the GBA with a large candidate pool. The build process will be resource-intensive, but the organization may be able to use the assessment with a lower per candidate cost than a vendor could offer while still getting a highly tailored assessment of KSAs. The initial stages of assessment development, such as conducting job analyses, determining which KSAs to assess, and having subject matter experts generate the necessary content, are similar for a GBA and most other tools. However, early in this process game designers, animation specialists, and software engineers must be incorporated to help organizational psychologists and other HR professionals involved in development understand the possibilities and constraints of the game platform and the game's design. This requires either additional staffing or working with outside experts, and much more collaboration than if a low-fidelity assessment such as a personality or situational judgment test was being developed. To help illustrate, in the development of one serious game designed to teach students about simple machines, the team was composed of two science teachers, a computer programmer, a cognitive psychologist, an experienced game designer, and a physics subject matter expert (Johnson-Glenberg et al., 2015). This example illustrates the breadth of experience needed for these projects. Incorporating so many different kinds of specialists elongates development time, and requires more iterations of editing which adds cost. During and after the GBA is developed, there are technical considerations such as coding and compatibility issues that have to be resolved (Blow, 2004). Game-based selection tools need to be beta tested the same way as their recreational counterparts, which requires time and resources (Bethke, 2003). In these scenarios, organizations also need to be prepared to update content to keep pace with the rate of change in both technology and modern jobs (Boyce, Corbet, & Adler, 2013), so flexible systems are preferred.

The second option is to repurpose an existing game, and either harness or add features to evaluate the constructs of interest. This has some obvious advantages: the work of building the base of the assessment is done, so a lot of time and money is saved on development. A GBA built from an existing game may have better sensory stimuli, like graphics and sounds, than what would be possible with limited resources had it been built from scratch. However, most games are not designed with the constraints of selection-specific assessments in mind. For example, in one paper, the authors describe the process of taking three existing games, and converting or using them for assessment purposes. For one of the games designed to measure problem solving and spatial skills, the researchers left the game untouched and intended to take the information they needed from the log files and score them using Bayesian networks (Wang, Shute, & Moore, 2015). Unfortunately, upon going into the log files the researchers could not develop a comprehensive scoring system because of the sheer amount of information the game collected over its course. Additional issues may include not being able to measure all the desired competencies, having a game that has extraneous modules or is too long, or including scenarios that are not work-appropriate, to name a few. Designers may also think the game assesses the constructs identified in the job analysis as being essential, and fail to do their due diligence of extensively validating to ensure those constructs are truly being measured. This can be an issue any time a GBA is not built from scratch. While repurposing existing games has been done in the educational literature (Buford & O'Leary, 2015; Dickey, 2005; Wang et al., 2015) there is virtually no work on doing this for a selection purpose. Therefore, there are likely many unexplored issues.

Related to the second option, organizations are able to use GBA vendors. Vendors have presumably already explored many of the challenges of GBAs and have developed solutions that are suitable to a hiring context. There are a limited number of vendors on the market currently, so the range of competencies and personalization is restricted. Organizations that use vendors would also need to deliberate on all the considerations that always come with choosing a vendor, such as psychometric support, cost, privacy, consistency of administration, etc.

Lastly, it may be useful to reiterate that developers can choose to add game elements to existing selection assessments (e.g., sensory stimuli can be part of an SJT or virtual assessment center; novelty can be part of what occurs in a simulation, Hawkes, 2013), but these assessments would be considered gamified rather than game-based. While this process is easier, more cost-effective, and less time-intensive, it may yield assessments that come across as pieced together or create unexpected psychometric issues that could require new validation, reliability, adverse impact, and/or applicant reactions studies to fully understand. Developers may make the folly of relying on evidence from before the assessment was gamified, not realizing that the introduction of new features can fundamentally change what is assessed and/or how well it is assessed.

GBAs are time and resource-intensive to develop, and pose a new challenge to the diverse team of specialists that are needed to build or modify them successfully. Organizations that wish to use GBAs have many decisions to make about how to choose the right tool in a relatively uncharted space.

Incorporating Game Elements for Selection

There are a few game elements that are likely easy to include and seem unlikely to alter the psychometric properties of the assessment, though they can have an effect on test perceptions. For example, one study found that incorporating a points system into the assessment caused the speed of response to increase though it did not change accuracy (Attali & Arieli-Attali, 2015). Other educational studies have found that points and levels increase engagement and motivation (Domínguez et al., 2013; Goehle, 2013). Elements like narratives can increase engagement (Dickey, 2005).

Other game elements can have a more significant impact on the assessment; avatars are an example of an element that can change test perceptions quite significantly. The Proteus Effect offers an explanation for why avatars are so influential: it posits that a user will conform to the behavioral expectations associated with the avatar's characteristics, either because of a change to the user's self-perceptions or a priming effect (Ratan & Dawson, 2016; Yee & Bailenson, 2007). The empirical support for the Proteus Effect is compelling. Some work has seen people who use a male avatar on math tasks perform better than people who use a female avatar, attributing the finding to stereotype threat (Lee, 2009). Other work has shown that users are more likely to seek and receive help when their avatars are female (Lehdonvirta, Nagashima, Lehdonvirta, & Baba, 2012). Users with taller avatars behaved more confidently in a negotiation task than those with shorter avatars in another study (Yee & Bailenson, 2007). There are some researchers that suggest women are more prone to the Proteus Effect, and that when they use male avatars they engage in more masculine behaviors (Huh & Williams, 2010; Ratan, Kennedy, & Williams, 2012). These findings imply that avatar use and customization can affect performance and perceptions of the assessment, and must be carefully considered. GBA avatars have the potential to ease stereotype threat and change in-game behaviors, so organizations that use them should be very deliberate about the ability to customize avatars and educate assesses about the effects of avatar characteristics. Those who utilize GBAs should systematically appraise the potential for adverse impact and bias when using avatars (a topic we discuss in more detail below).

We have illustrated that game elements are already incorporated into certain assessment methods, and that there is promise for adding other, less-explored elements. However, many of the game elements that are almost always present in compelling games like feedback, collaboration with others, or focused goals and rules, are rarely incorporated into selection tools and indeed run somewhat counter to the goals of hiring assessments. For example, collaborating with other assessment takers may provide some information about one's ability to work in a team, but can be antithetical to assessing individual aptitudes like cognitive ability. Feedback is another example of a game element with potential adverse effects. It is omnipresent and important in many gamified assessments used in other HRM applications because it helps with training and motivating (Killi, 2005; Ritterfeld & Weber, 2006). Feedback is also instilled into other game elements; points systems, leaderboards, and badges (game elements in their own respect) all contain feedback. However, providing feedback during an assessment for selection purposes can affect performance in ways that are construct-irrelevant (DuVernet & Popp, 2014), so feedback in GBAs for selection purposes has to be thoughtfully incorporated and considered. Another example is the game element of a leaderboard, which shows players' accomplishments relative to other players. These can be highly motivating in educational settings (Landers & Landers, 2015) but providing normative information during an assessment for selection can also introduce construct-irrelevant elements as well as negatively affect motivation and candidate perceptions. Legal ramifications are also possible as applicants may draw faulty conclusions about their overall performance compared to their peers, particularly when the GBA is only one component of a hiring process and the weighting of components is differential. Providing relative performance information can fuel legal battles if an applicant feels he or she was treated unfairly.

It is clear that GBA designers have to rethink the role of fundamental game elements because the needs and presses of a selection situation are so different than other arenas where games are used. This is troubling, because many of these contentious game elements are the ones that would be best-suited to weaving into the fabric of an assessment to accurately elicit behaviors of interest.

Lack of GBA-Specific Research

The last disadvantage of GBAs is the sheer breadth of the unknown. Very little research has been conducted specifically on GBAs in selection contexts, so most of the information we have is extrapolated from studies on high-fidelity simulations, serious games, and video games. While this provides a helpful surrounding context, it cannot replace a dedicated stream of research on GBAs in hiring contexts specifically. This means that when experts are designing and implementing GBAs they must draw primarily on judgment and previous experience in other HRM applications or outside of work settings, instead of more relevant empirical research. While we are optimistic that GBA research will burgeon in the coming years, it would be remiss to fail to acknowledge the constraints within which organizations currently have to work. Below, we discuss areas for future research so that the current gap can begin to shrink.

FUTURE RESEARCH

Throughout this review, it has been evident that there is little research dedicated specifically to GBAs in hiring situations. In the following section, we outline some of the most pressing areas of needed research; namely, on the reliability, validity, scoring, adverse impact, faking, cross-cultural use, and applicant perceptions of GBAs in selection contexts.

Validity and Reliability

One of these needed areas is how to best establish and measure the reliability and validity of GBAs. Measuring reliability of these tools can deviate from traditional assessments because there are not always multiple measurements of the same construct. However, there are often trials or rounds, and scores from these rounds can be grouped to evaluate Cronbach's alpha. For example, in one serious game for persistence the researchers settled on total time spent on quests and number of quest events completed as their indicators (DiCerbo, 2014). Reliability was then assessed across three different modules, resulting in six indicators with an overall alpha of .87. Evaluators can also use test-retest reliability or in the case of enough indicators, split-half reliability the way some serious game developers have (Buford & O'Leary, 2015). This initial work is promising, but there are still not well-developed guidelines for how to assess reliability, such as how many levels or scenarios should be used to get a stable estimate (Landers, 2015). Future work should determine how to best assess the reliability of measures of individual constructs, and whether GBAs face the same problems as SJTs in getting clear reliability estimates due to multidimensionality (McDaniel, Hartman, Whetzel, & Grubb, 2007).

In addition to reliability, research on the validity of inferences from GBAs is needed, although there is some work in which serious games have been successfully validated. Buford and O'Leary established the construct validity of their GBA cognitive ability measures by comparing them to widely accepted measures such as Raven's Progressive Matrices and the Shipley–2 assessment (2015; Raven, Raven, & Court, 2003; Shipley, Gruber, Martin, & Klein, 2012); this approach has been used by other studies too (Delgado, Uribe, Alonso, & Diaz, 2016; McPherson & Burns, 2008). Some researchers caution against relying too heavily on self-report measures to establish construct validity of GBAs, because of the influence of social desirability and lack of self-knowledge on those measures, which would not be an influence in more behaviorally-based GBA scores (Wang et al., 2015).

While some research has looked at the construct validity of GBAs, there is little to no research on content or criterion-related validity. Gathering validity evidence for GBAs may be fundamentally different than for other tools, so best practices are needed. To illustrate, to establish content validity job experts are often used to determine if the content of the test appropriately parallels the content of the job; while a job expert can look at the content of a GBA before it is built, it may be harder for him or her to identify job-relevance once that content is in as unfamiliar of a context as a game. Therefore, we suggest exploration of when to collect subject matter expert judgment and how collecting it at different times in the development process can change the conclusions regarding validity evidence that are drawn.

Missing almost entirely from this conversation is research that establishes criterion-related validity between GBAs and job-relevant outcomes. Because little published empirical research exists and vendor information is kept private, there is little direct evidence of the job-relatedness of GBAs as an assessment method. There is also little to no information about the potential for differential validity with protected subgroups. This should be remedied soon, as GBAs are currently being used to make selection decisions in organizations. We strongly urge researchers to focus on gathering criterion-related validity evidence, exploring how subgroups may be affected, and understanding the kinds of performance outcomes to which GBAs most strongly relate.

It also may be helpful to think of GBAs within the context of the distinction between assessment methods and predictor constructs (Arthur & Villado, 2008). Like situational judgment tests, biodata, and interviews, GBAs are methods that can be used to assess a range of potential predictor constructs, including cognitive abilities, skills, knowledge, and motivational and personality constructs. Thus, it is important that researchers recognize that any given GBA may be measuring very different things from another, and making comparisons about their reliability, validity, adverse impact, etc. can be akin to comparing apples and oranges. However, this capacity is also an attractive feature of the method as GBAs might be developed to assess a wide range of predictor constructs.

Finally, retesting policies with GBAs should take into account how novel they are and whether a no-retesting policy might put some candidates, like those who play more recreational games, at an advantage. Research has shown that repeated exposure to tests contributes to better performance (Hausknecht, Halpert, Di Paolo, & Gerrard, 2007), especially when, like in GBAs, the assessment items are heterogeneous or varied and the assessment itself is performance-based (Villado, Randall, & Zimmer, 2016). Administrators could consider exposing candidates to GBA content prior to testing to mitigate the construct-irrelevant noise of a new assessment method (Lievens, Reeve, & Heggestad, 2007) especially since familiarity with the speed and control mechanisms of a game may present a learning curve.

Scoring

There are several challenges in scoring GBAs. As one would expect, the constructs being assessed will drive what information from the game is scored; however, there are some issues related to scoring that are not as straight forward as with most traditional assessment tools. The first is what data points in the assessment are collected as scores. What can be collected depends on how the chosen constructs are being elicited and assessed. As mentioned in an earlier example, games are traditionally designed to generate hundreds of data points each minute. Imagine a GBA in which the candidate has a lot of freedom in how he or she navigates a virtual office, and who he or she speaks with to collect information before making strategic business decisions. In this case the GBA may not only be recording environmental variables (e.g., what other characters in the game were available to speak with, what room the player is in) and game status variables (how many points have been amassed, what special skills are available for the player to use in that moment), but also constantly tracking paradata, or auxiliary data, like how much time has passed from action to action, or how long the player spends reading dialogue and instructions (Kreuter, & Casas-Cordero, 2010). As part of this, the GBA may be assessing extraversion and informed decision-making through how many characters the player chooses to engage with, and impulsive risk-taking in how long the player takes to make decisions after collecting all the relevant information. Processing this amount of data can require machine learning or other methods that are not typically employed by organizational psychologists. In order to establish scoring parameters, meaningful data points need to be identified and isolated. There are often many trials in games, so creating a scoring system also means deciding when data should be treated as individual points, and when composites need to be used.

On a related point, what should be included in any score composite and how components might be weighted needs to be determined, either through empirical or rational methods. For example, suppose a GBA is designed to measure persistence. The applicant is presented with a task, and unbeknownst to him or her, this task is unbeatable. After a few trials, the applicant is told he or she can exit the module at any time and move to the next one even if the task has not been successfully completed. It would make sense to use the amount of time spent in the module as part of the scoring criteria, but a designer would also need to decide if accuracy and effort during the module relate to persistence as well. Because there is so much data and so many small decisions, deciding what to include in scoring become much more complex. Further, one can assume that many organizations will be using GBAs as part of a battery of instruments or within a multi-hurdle process with other methods. As with any selection process, decisions must be made regarding the order, combination, and weighting of subscores in decision making (Johnson & Oswald, 2010). There is also the issue of score cut-offs. While traditional methods such as Angoff or contrasting groups can be used (Mueller, Norris, & Oppler, 2007), there are few recommendations on how to apply these methods to the novel game landscape even though there can be a high legal cost for poor implementation (e.g. the Uniform Guidelines on Employee Selection Procedures in U.S. Equal Opportunity Employment Commission, 1978).

Lastly, there are elements of GBAs that make comparing scoring across applicants difficult; one primary example is branching. When branching is included, previous decisions that the applicant has made affect future options that are shown. This can result in different paths being taken by applicants, and unless these paths are carefully calibrated to measure the same constructs to the same degree, not all applicants will be assessed equally. Of course other tools, such as multimedia SJTs and adaptive tests also feature branching (Sydell et al., 2013) and test developers have found adequate solutions to these issues so while this warrants consideration, it is by no means an insurmountable barrier.

Future research is sorely needed to understand how to score GBAs. Test developers need to understand what constitutes an item in GBAs, and how many of these items, scenarios, or data points are needed to reach a stable assessment. As previously mentioned, GBA designers need an increased awareness of what kind of information is predictive of criteria so that they can design scoring models that include relevant pieces. More work is needed to know which scoring strategies are best for GBAs, as well as when and if expert judgment should enter into the process (e.g., after content is developed but before it is placed in a game-based context, after the assessment is fully developed). This work should also cover whether the usual strategies for weighting different assessments or portions of assessments hold for GBAs, or if measuring multiple, overlapping constructs throughout the assessment introduces new considerations. Lastly, researchers should work to understand how to negotiate branching in GBAs to ensure that all applicants have scores that yield sufficient information for comparison, even if they have chosen different paths in the assessment.

Adverse Impact

Another unknown in the arena of GBAs is the possibility for adverse impact (AI). As meta-analytic work shows higher levels of AI based on ethnicity for cognitive ability measures (Ployhart & Holtz, 2008), one would expect that the risk of exhibiting this form of AI is positively correlated with the extent to which a GBA assesses cognitive elements. Studies that focus on assessment centers have found that score differences between Whites and African-Americans increase when more cognitively-loaded exercises are included (Hough, Oswald, & Ployhart, 2001). This means the content of the assessments matters more than the method, in which case GBAs can fare quite well with regard to AI depending upon what they are designed to assess. Additionally, assessments that rely less on verbal ability and reading requirements, such as those that use video and multimedia formats as GBAs do, are recommended for reducing AI against ethnic minorities in cognitive ability measures (Ployhart & Holtz, 2008).

However, as discussed previously GBAs may increase cognitive load, thus unintentionally increasing the measurement of cognitive abilities which can have a negative impact on AI for women and ethnic minorities (Linn & Petersen, 1985; Roth, Bevier, Bobko, Switzer, & Tyler, 2001). On the other hand, GBAs may provide a method of measuring constructs while reducing cognitive load by eliminating language and prior knowledge requirements. One example of this is working memory tasks, which often require replicating patterns and are inherently game-like in nature (Aon, 2017). Future research should explore these issues definitively. We should better understand the extent to which GBAs as an assessment method exhibit AI against different subgroups and how GBA design can contribute to or diminish cognitive load on those assessed, regardless of what the GBA is measuring. Research should also illuminate how to tackle the validity-adverse impact dilemma so that developers understand how this balance operates in a game-based setting.

Faking and Socially Desirable Responding

As briefly mentioned earlier, GBAs may have some implications for faking and socially desirable responding on assessments. Socially desirable responding can be attributed to intentional self-enhancement to appear a more desirable candidate, or unintended self-enhancement based on an overly positive view of one's own self (Paulhus, 1984). GBAs may be able to partially remedy both of these issues. Intentional score inflations are less possible in game-based conditions because it is less clear what is being measured. Because GBAs can measure several constructs at once and are more complex than traditional measures, the ideal personality traits will be less transparent. While transparency can be positive for validity (Kleinmann, Kuptsch, & Koller, 1996), a lack of transparency makes faking much harder. Therefore, in cases where GBAs are measuring personality or other self-reported constructs, faking may be decreased. GBAs can also help with unintentional self-enhancement because there are few self-report items or scenarios. Behaviors are assessed more often, and applicants are pressed to perform instead of self-reflect on their tendencies and behaviors. However, research is needed to validate these assumptions and demonstrate that applicants or assessment-takers cannot fake on GBAs, even when explicitly directed.

Cross Cultural Applications

Some aspects of the human experience are universal, and a love of games seems to be one of them. The use of games dates back at least 5,000 years with early civilizations creating dice (Attia, 2016). Games are meant to be comprehensive in their ability to capture human interest, and are used all around the globe. While the immersion and motivational aspects of games may be shared, other aspects need to be localized by country or culture. This localization requires translation, but it may also require altering content so that it is culturally appropriate and understandable (Chandler, 2005). From an organizational side, designers must look at issues that are common to using any type of assessment cross-culturally; legal differences, technology requirements, the use of global versus local norms in establishing scoring, cross-cultural equivalence of measures, and applicant reactions just to name a few (Ryan & Tippins, 2009). From a game design perspective, there may be game elements or designs that have more global appeal than others (by way of illustration, Japanese gaming audiences prefer fantasy and a lot of instruction whereas American audiences prefer realism and less instruction) (Kent, 2004). Designers may also want to consider experience differences. For example, Japanese children have more experience playing video games so when a Japanese game is released in the United States, the game is made slower and easier so that it is not so challenging as to decrease the fun for American children (Carlson & Corliss, 2011). Clearly, there are a number of considerations from both a work context and an enjoyment perspective that shape how GBAs will look across cultures. The science of GBAs would benefit from an exploration of how to best design, translate, and alter GBAs for use in global selection.

Applicant Reactions

Lastly, there is limited work on how applicants will respond to GBAs in a selection context, some of which was referenced earlier in the recent Hamari and Keronen meta-analysis (2017). While there is ample evidence that games and game elements induce immersion, enjoyment, and motivation, most of the cited studies looked at games conducted in recreational or educational settings. These settings are not nearly as high cost as hiring scenarios, where someone's earnings and career trajectory are at stake. Researchers need to dedicate much more attention to understanding how applicants react to GBAs, specifically from the lens of job-relatedness and justice as these are some of the most important perceptions in predicting outcomes like offer acceptance intentions (Hausknecht et al., 2004). Further attention should also be dedicated to some of the issues touched upon earlier, such as feelings of test anxiety, perceived difficulty, and perceived test length. Finally, it would also be fruitful to understand how using a GBA in one's selection battery affects perceptions of the organization's attractiveness and fit as a place of employment, as organizations use these tools under the untested assumption that they promote a positive brand.

On a related note, there is no information about how stakeholders, such as hiring managers, will react to GBAs. The same concerns that applicants have can extend to these stakeholders; they may be skeptical about the relatedness of GBAs to the job, or about their appropriateness for the organization's image. Hiring managers may then be reluctant to use the scores from GBAs in making hiring decisions. Researchers should understand how GBAs are viewed by stakeholders, and whether there are characteristics that can be altered or education that can be shared to improve the perceptions of these tools.

There is also a philosophical issue at hand of how important it is that the selection process be fun and entertaining for candidates. While there is certainly demand, both from candidates and employing organizations, to attract young talent in a way that is appealing to them, one could argue that the chief purpose of assessments should be to evaluate the relevant KSAs. Skeptics could argue that any trade-offs in validity and reliability are not worth the small increase in applicant reactions. While it is yet to be seen if these tradeoffs do indeed exist, it is worth noting that selection decision-making contexts may not be the place to take these risks.

Another potential concern is how different demographic groups will respond to GBAs. Two prominent demographic groups that may react less positively are women and older applicants. Quite a bit of work suggests that women play fewer video games than men do (Entertainment Software Association, n.d.; Greenberg, Sherry, Lachlan, Lucas, & Holmstrom, 2010; Ivory, 2006; Ratan, Taylor, Hogan, Kennedy, & Williams, 2015). There are several reasons for this: many games are violent and competitive, which does not appeal to women the same way as it does men (Hartmann & Klimmt, 2006). A majority of games either leave out female characters or portray them in oversexualized ways, which can be unappealing to female players (Dill, Gentile, Richter & Dill, 2005; Ivory, 2006; Williams, Martins, Consalvo, & Ivory, 2009). We can also attribute some of the differences to the stereotype that men like video games more than women, which consequently leads women to be less willing or encouraged to get involved with games (Margolis & Fisher, 2002; Ratan et al., 2015). While there is certainly debate about the reason for and strength of these findings (Hayes, 2005), all of these factors contribute to lower interest and skill with games, which may then translate to more negative reactions and abilities when interfacing with GBAs.

However, recent trends show increased numbers of women in gaming; researchers have shown that there are aspects of games, such as rich social interaction (Hartmann & Klimmt, 2006) and realism (Kafai, 1996, 1998), which are very appealing to women. Other studies find many game elements are equally attractive to both genders (Kafai, 1998; Malone & Lepper, 1987). It is then incumbent upon GBA designers to understand how GBAs are perceived differently by gender, and whether there are any likely performance differences as a result of previous game-playing experience (Shen, Ratan, Cai, & Leavitt, 2016; Terlecki, Newcombe, & Little, 2008). Researchers should also explore what game elements are appealing to both men and women, and how to ensure that GBAs do not trigger stereotype threat or other feelings of being unwanted or unskilled.

In addition to the role of gender, age is important when it comes to gaming. Some work suggests that older populations use less technology and consequently are less comfortable with it (Czaja & Sharit, 1998; Zickuhr, 2011). This means that they may find GBAs less engaging and attractive than younger applicants. Older adults' lack of use and discomfort can have other implications too; they may be more skeptical about using game-based measures for hiring purposes. They may feel that games are frivolous and inappropriate for such a serious endeavor (Washburn, 2003) resulting in negative fairness and justice perceptions which have a host of other detrimental outcomes (Hausknecht et al., 2004). Older applicant populations may also worry about their performance on processing speed and reaction time measures and rightfully so, as empirical differences do exist (Der & Deary, 2006; Salthouse, 1996). Before GBAs are further used, empirical work should illuminate the effect of age on the reception of these tools, and similarly to gender, understand potential performance differences that could result in adverse impact.

Lastly, there needs to be consideration of how applicants with disabilities interact with GBAs. The Americans with Disabilities Act (ADA) protects the rights of those with disabilities when they are applying for jobs; these applicants must be provided reasonable accommodation during the hiring process so as to allow equal participation in the job application process as someone without a disability. Guidelines for how to appropriately accommodate can be found in federal, state, and local laws as well as The Standards for Educational and Psychological Testing (AERA, APA, & NCME, 2014), but GBAs pose somewhat of a unique challenge because of their novel test format. GBAs can vary widely in their content and requirements, and may assess constructs in different ways than traditional formats. Applicants with disabilities may have trouble anticipating what accommodation is needed. Organizations then need guidelines and best practices on how to establish accommodations (e.g., providing a sample test or test preview so applicants can request appropriate accommodations).

CONCLUSION

GBAs offer exciting promise; they hold great potential for assessing and immersing applicants during the hiring process. This assessment method takes the emerging trend of incorporating game elements into organizational tools to provide a uniquely absorptive experience. GBAs will likely continue to blossom in the selection space as organizations demand assessments that are cutting edge, technologically-friendly, and engaging. However, there need to be substantial gains in evidence-based guidelines and best practices so that GBAs can be valid, reliable, fair, and effective in addition to interesting. Because there is so much yet to explore, they offer an area ripe for exploration by eHRM researchers.

REFERENCES

AERA, APA, NCME. (2014). *Standards for educational and psychological testing*. Washington, DC: American Educational Research Assn. Publications.

Anderson, J. Q., & Rainie, H. (2012). Gamification: Experts expect 'game layers' to expand in the future, with positive and negative results. *Pew Internet & American Life Project*. Retrieved from http://www.pewinternet.org/files/old-media/Files/Reports/2012/PIP_Future_of_Internet_2012_Gamification.pdf

Aon. (2017). G.A.M.E: Global adaptive memory evaluation. Retrieved from http://www.aon.com/human-capital-consulting/talent/assessment-selection-game.jsp

Armstrong, M., Ferrell, J., Collmus, A., & Landers, R. (2016). Correcting misconceptions about gamification of assessment: More than SJTs and badges. *Industrial and Organizational Psychology, 9*(03), 671–677.

Arthur Jr, W., & Villado, A. J. (2008). The importance of distinguishing between constructs and methods when comparing predictors in personnel selection research and practice. *Journal of Applied Psychology, 93*(2), 435–442.

Arvey, R. D., Strickland, W., Drauden, G., & Martin, C. (1990). Motivational components of test taking. *Personnel Psychology, 43*(4), 695–711.

Attali, Y., & Arieli-Attali, M. (2015). Gamification in assessment: Do points affect test performance? *Computers & Education, 83*, 57–63.

Attia, P. (2016, Jan 21). The full history of board games. *Medium: The startup*. Retrieved from https://medium.com/swlh/the-full-history-of-board-games–5e622811ce89

Badger, J. M., Kaminsky, S. E., & Behrend, T. S. (2014). Media richness and information acquisition in internet recruitment. *Journal of Managerial Psychology, 29*, 866–883.

Bauer, T. N., Truxillo, D. M., Sanchez, R. J., Craig, J. M., Ferrara, P., & Campion, M. A. (2001). Applicant reactions to selection: Development of the selection procedural justice scale (SPJS). *Personnel Psychology, 54*(2), 387–419.

Bethke, E. (2003). *Game development and production.* Plano, TX: Wordware Publishing.

Blow, J. (2004). Game development: Harder than you think. *Queue, 1*(10), 28–37.

Bolch, M. (2007). Lights, camera… interview! *HR Magazine.* Retrieved from https://www.shrm.org/hr-today/news/hr-magazine/Pages/0307aganda_empstaff.aspx

Bowman, R. F. (1982). A "Pac-Man" theory of motivation: Tactical implications for classroom instruction. *Educational Technology, 22*(9), 14–17.

Boyce, A. S, Corbet, C. E., & Adler, S. (2013). Simulations in the selection context: Considerations, challenges, and opportunities. In M. Fetzer & K. Tuzinski (Eds.), *Simulations for personnel selection* (pp. 17–41). New York: Springer.

Bruk-Lee, V., Lanz, J., Drew, E. N., Coughlin, C., Levine, P., Tuzinski, K., & Wrenn, K. (2016). Examining applicant reactions to different media types in character-based simulations for employee selection. *International Journal of Selection and Assessment, 24*(1), 77–91.

Buford, C. C., & O'Leary, B. J. (2015). Assessment of fluid intelligence utilizing a computer simulated game. *International Journal of Gaming and Computer-Mediated Simulations, 7*(4), 1–17.

Carlson, R., & Corliss, J. (2011). Imagined commodities: Video game localization and mythologies of cultural difference. *Games and Culture, 6*(1), 61–82.

Chan, D., & Schmitt, N. (1997). Video-based versus paper-and-pencil method of assessment in situational judgment tests: Subgroup differences in test performance and face validity perceptions. *Journal of Applied Psychology, 82*(1), 143–159.

Chandler, H. M. (2005). *The game localization handbook.* Hingham, MA: Charles River Media.

Chiang, Y. -T., Lin, S. S. J., Cheng, C. -Y., & Liu, E. Z.-F. (2011). Exploring online game players' flow experiences and positive affect. *Turkish Online Journal of Educational Technology, 10*(1), 106–114.

Chin, J., Dukes, R., & Gamson, W. (2009). Assessment in simulation and gaming: A review of the last 40 years. *Simulation & Gaming, 40*(4), 553–568.

Chou, T.-J., & Ting, C.-C. (2003). The role of flow experience in cyber-game addiction. *CyberPsychology & Behavior, 6*(6), 663–675.

Chou, Y. K. (2015). *Actionable gamification: Beyond points, badges, and leaderboards.* Octalysis Media.

Collins, C. J., & Stevens, C. K. (2002). The relationship between early recruitment-related activities and the application decisions of new labor-market entrants: A brand equity approach to recruitment. *Journal of Applied Psychology, 87*(6), 1121–1133.

Collmus, A. (2016). *Game-framing cognitive assessments to improve applicant perceptions.* Retrieved from ProQuest Digital.

Collmus, A. B., Armstrong, M. B., & Landers, R. N. (2016). Game thinking within social media to recruit and select job candidates. In R. L. Landers & G. B. Schmidt (Eds.), *Social media in employee selection and recruitment: Theory, practice, and current challenges* (pp. 103–126). Cham, Switzerland: Springer.

Cortina, J. M. (1993). What is coefficient alpha? An examination of theory and applications. *Journal of Applied Psychology, 78*(1), 98–104.

Csikszentmihalyi, M. (1990). *Flow: The psychology of optimal experience.* New York: Harper & Row.

Czaja, S. J., & Sharit, J. (1998). Age differences in attitudes toward computers. *The Journals of Gerontology Series B: Psychological Sciences and Social Sciences, 53*(5), 329–340.

Delgado, M. T., Uribe, P. A., Alonso, A. A., & Diaz, R. R. (2016). TENI: A comprehensive battery for cognitive assessment based on games and technology. *Child Neuropsychology, 22,* 276–291.

Der, G., & Deary, I. J. (2006). Age and sex differences in reaction time in adulthood: Results from the United Kingdom Health and Lifestyle Survey. *Psychology and Aging, 21*(1), 62–73.

Deterding, S., Dixon, D., Khaled, R., & Nacke, L. (2011). From game design elements to gamefulness: Defining gamification. Proceedings from the 15th international academic MindTrek conference: *Envisioning future media environments.* Tampere: Finland. Retrieved from http://dl.acm.org/citation.cfm?id=2181040

DiCerbo, K. E. (2014). Game-based assessment of persistence. *Journal of Educational Technology & Society, 17*(1), 17–28.

Dickey, M. D. (2005). Engaging by design: How engagement strategies in popular computer and video games can inform instructional design. *Educational Technology Research and Development, 53*(2), 67–83.

Dill, K.E., Gentile, D.A., Richter, W.A., & Dill, J.C. (2005). Violence, sex, race, and age in popular video games: A content analysis. In E. Cole & D.J. Henderson (Eds.), *Featuring females: Feminist analyses of the media,* (pp. 115–130). Washington, DC: American Psychological Association.

Domínguez, A., Saenz-de-Navarrete, J., de-Marcos, L., Fernández-Sanz, L., Pagés, C., & Martínez-Herráiz, J.-J. (2013). Gamifying learning experiences: Practical implications and outcomes. *Computers & Education, 63,* 380–392.

DuVernet, A. M., & Popp, E. (2014). Gamification and workplace practices. *The Industrial–Organizational Psychologist, 52,* 39–43.

Entertainment Software Association. (n.d.). Distribution of computer and video gamers in the United States from 2006 to 2016, by gender. *In Statista—The Statistics Portal.* Retrieved from https://www.statista.com/statistics/232383/gender-split-of-us-computer-and-video-gamers/

Floryan, M. (2009). A literature review of the field of serious games. *Computer Science Department of University of Massachusetts, Amherst.*

Garris, R., Ahlers, R., & Driskell, J. E. (2002). Games, motivation and learning: A research and practice model. *Simulation & Gaming, 33*(4), 441–467.

Gee, J. P. (2009). Deep learning properties of good digital games: How far can they go? In U. Ritterfeld, M. Cody, & P. Vorderer (Eds.), *Serious games: Mechanisms and effects* (pp. 65–80). New York: Routledge.

Gilliland, S. W. (1993). The perceived fairness of selection systems: An organizational justice perspective. *The Academy of Management Review, 18*(4), 694–734.

Goehle, G. (2013). Gamification and web-based homework. *Primus, 23,* 234–246.

Goldstein, I. L., Zedeck, S., & Schneider, B. (1993). An exploration of the job analysis-content validity process. In N. Schmitt & W. Borman (Eds.), *Personnel selection in organizations* (pp. 2–34). San Francisco: Jossey-Bass.

Goth, G. (2017, June 6). Next-generation incentives: Interactive engagement promotes healthy behavior. *SHRM Benefits*. Retrieved from https://www.shrm.org/resourcesandtools/hr-topics/benefits/pages/next-generation-health-incentives.aspx

Greenberg, B. S., Sherry, J., Lachlan, K., Lucas, K., & Holmstrom, A. (2010). Orientations to video games among gender and age groups. *Simulation & Gaming, 41*(2), 238–259.

Hamari, J., & Keronen, L. (2017). Why do people play games? A meta-analysis. *International Journal of Information Management, 37*(3), 125–141.

Hamari, J., Shernoff, D. J., Rowe, E., Coller, B., Asbell-Clarke, J., & Edwards, T. (2016). Challenging games help students learn: An empirical study on engagement, flow and immersion in game-based learning. *Computers in Human Behavior, 54*, 170–179.

Hardy, J. H., Gibson, C., Sloan, M., & Carr, A. (2017). Are applicants more likely to quit longer assessments? Examining the effect of assessment length on applicant attrition behavior. *The Journal of Applied Psychology, 102*(7), 1148–1158.

Hartmann, T., & Klimmt, C. (2006). Gender and computer games: Exploring females' dislikes. *Journal of Computer-Mediated Communication, 11*(4), 910–931.

Hausknecht, J. P., Day, D. V., & Thomas, S. C. (2004). Applicant reactions to selection procedures: An updated model and meta-analysis. *Personnel Psychology, 57*(3), 639–683.

Hausknecht, J. P., Halpert, J. A., Di Paolo, N. T., & Gerrard, M. O. M. (2007). Retesting in selection: A meta-analysis of coaching and practice effects for tests of cognitive ability. *Journal of Applied Psychology, 92*, 373–385.

Hawkes, B. (2013). Simulation technologies. In M. Fetzer & K. Tuzinski (Eds.), *Simulations for personnel selection* (pp. 61–82). New York: Springer.

Hayes, E. (2005). Women, video gaming and learning: Beyond stereotypes. *TechTrends, 49*(5), 23–28.

Hough, L. M., Oswald, F. L., & Ployhart, R. E. (2001). Determinants, detection and amelioration of adverse impact in personnel selection procedures: Issues, evidence and lessons learned. *International Journal of Selection and Assessment, 9*(1-2), 152–194.

Howardson, G. N., & Behrend, T. S. (2014). Using the Internet to recruit employees: Comparing the effects of usability expectations and objective technological characteristics on Internet recruitment outcomes. *Computers in Human Behavior, 31*, 334–342.

Hsu, C. L., & Lu, H. P. (2004). Why do people play on-line games? An extended TAM with social influences and flow experience. *Information & Management, 41*(7), 853–868.

Huh, S., & Williams, D. (2010). "Dude looks like a lady": Online game gender swapping. In W. Bainbridge (Ed.), *Online worlds: Convergence of the real and the virtual*. New York: Springer.

Hunt. (2003, Feb 27). Estimating the financial value of staffing-assessment tools. *Workforce*. Retrieved from http://www.workforce.com/2003/02/27/estimating-the-financial-value-of-staffing-assessment-tools/

Ivory, J. D. (2006). Still a man's game: gender representation in online reviews of video games. *Mass Communication and Society, 9*(1), 103–114.

Johnson, J. W., & Oswald, F. L. (2010). Test administration and the use of test scores. In J. L. Farr, & N. T. Tippins (Eds.), *Handbook of employee selection; handbook of employee selection* (pp. 151–169). Routledge/Taylor & Francis Group: New York, NY.

Johnson-Glenberg, M. C., Birchfield, D. A., Megowan-Romanowicz, C., & Snow, E. L. (2015). If the gear fits, spin it!: Embodied education and in-game assessments. *International Journal of Gaming and Computer-Mediated Simulations*, 7(4), 40–65.

Kafai, Y. B. (1996). Gender differences in children's constructions of video games. In P. M. Greenfield & R. R. Cocking (Eds.), *Interacting with video* (pp. 39–66). Norwood, NJ: Ablex.

Kafai, Y. B. (1998). Video game designs by girls and boys: Variability and consistency of gender differences. In J. Cassell & H. Jenkins (Eds.), *From Barbie to Mortal Kombat. Gender and computer games* (pp. 90–111). Cambridge, MA: MIT.

Kanning, U. P., Grewe, K., Hollenberg, S., & Hadouch, M. (2006), From the subjects' point of view: Reactions to different types of situational judgment items. *European Journal of Psychological Assessment*, 22(3), 168–176.

Kantrowitz, T. M. (2014) Global assessment trends of 2014. *CEB Report*. Retrieved from https://www.cebglobal.com/talent-management/talent-assessment/resources/forms/global-assessment-trends-report.html

Kent, S. (2004, April 28). Video games that get lost in translation. *NBC News*. Retrieved from http://www.nbcnews.com/id/4780423/ns/technology_and_science-games/t/video-games-get-lost-translation/#.WVfgR4TyvX4

Killi, K. (2005). Digital game-based learning: Towards an experiential gaming model. *Internet and Higher Education, 8*, 13–24.

King, D., Delfabbro, P., & Griffiths, M. (2010). Video game structural characteristics: A new psychological taxonomy. *International Journal of Mental Health & Addiction, 8*(1), 90–106.

Kleinmann, M., Kuptsch, C., & Köller, O. (1996). Transparency: A necessary requirement for the construct validity of assessment centres. *Applied Psychology*, 45(1), 67–84.

Kozlowski, S. W. J., & DeShon, R. P. (2004). A psychological fidelity approach to simulation-based training: Theory, research, and principles. In E. Salas, L. R. Elliott, S. G. Schflett, & M. D. Coovert (Eds.), *Scaled Worlds: Development, validation, and applications* (pp. 75–99). Burlington, VT: Ashgate Publishing.

Kreuter, F., & Casas-Cordero, C. (2010). *Paradata*. RatSWD Working Paper Series. Working paper. Berlin, Germany: German Council for Social and Economic Data (RatSWD).

Lahey, Z. (2014, March). Trending now: Social learning. *Aberdeen Group*. Retrieved from https://www.skillsoft.com/assets/research/research_aberdeen_hcm_sociallearning.pdf

Landers, R. N. (2015). An introduction to game-based assessment: Frameworks for the measurement of knowledge, skills, abilities and other human characteristics using behaviors observed within videogames. *International Journal of Gaming and Computer-Mediation Simulations, 7*(4), iv-viii.

Landers, R. N., & Landers, A. K. (2015). An empirical test of the theory of gamified learning the effect of leaderboards on time-on-task and academic performance. *Simulation & Gaming, 45*(6), 769–785.

Lee, J. R. (2009). A threat on the net: Stereotype threat in avatar-represented online groups (Unpublished doctoral dissertation). Stanford University, CA.

Lehdonvirta, M., Nagashima, Y., Lehdonvirta, V., & Baba, A. (2012). The stoic male: How avatar gender affects help-seeking behavior in an online game. *Games and Culture, 7*(1), 29–47.

Lievens, F., & Sackett, P. R. (2006). Video-based versus written situational judgment tests: A comparison in terms of predictive validity. *Journal of Applied Psychology, 91*(5), 1181–1188.

Lievens, F., Reeve, C. L., & Heggestad, E. D. (2007). An examination of psychometric bias due to retesting on cognitive ability tests in selection settings. *Journal of Applied Psychology, 92*, 1672–1682.

Linn, M. C., & Petersen, A. C. (1985). Emergence and characterization of sex differences in spatial ability: A meta-analysis. *Child Development*, 1479–1498.

Locke, E. A., & Latham, G. P. (2002). Building a practically useful theory of goal setting and task motivation: A 35-year odyssey. *American Psychologist, 57*(9), 705–717.

Malone, T. W., & Lepper, M. R. (1987). Making learning fun: A taxonomy of intrinsic motivations for learning. In R. E. Snow & M. J. Farr (Eds.), *Aptitude, learning and instruction: Vol. 3. Cognitive and affective process analysis* (pp. 223–253). Hillsdale, NJ: Erlbaum.

Manly, L. (2015, Nov 19). A virtual reality revolution, come to a head set near you. *New York Times*. Retrieved from https://www.nytimes.com/2015/11/22/arts/a-virtual-reality-revolution-coming-to-a-headset-near-you.html

Margolis, J., & Fisher, A. (2002). *Unlocking the clubhouse: Women in computing*. Cambridge, MA: The MIT Press.

McDaniel, M. A., Hartman, N. S., Whetzel, D. L., & Grubb, W. (2007). Situational judgment tests, response instructions, and validity: A meta-analysis. *Personnel Psychology, 60*(1), 63–91.

McDonald, A. S. (2001). The prevalence and effects of test anxiety in school children. *Educational Psychology, 21*(1), 89–101.

McPherson, J., & Burns, N. R. (2008). Assessing the validity of computer-game-like tests of processing speed and working memory. *Behavior Research Methods, 40*(4), 969–981.

Meister, J. C. (2013, Jan 3). How Deloitte made learning a game. *Harvard Business Review*. Retrieved from https://hbr.org/2013/01/how-deloitte-made-learning-a-g

Meister, J. C. (2015, March 30). Future of work: Using gamification for human resources. *Forbes*. Retrieved from https://www.forbes.com/sites/jeannemeister/2015/03/30/future-of-work-using-gamification-for-human-resources/#404f40ef24b7

Messick, S. (1995). Validity of psychological assessment: Validation of inferences from persons' responses and performances as scientific inquiry into score meaning. *American Psychologist, 50*, 741–749.

Mislevy, R. J., Oranje, A., Bauer, M., von Davier, A. A., Hao, J., Corrigan, S., et al. (2014). *Psychometric considerations in game-based assessment*. New York, NY: Institute of Play.

Mueller, L., Norris, D., & Oppler, S. (2007). Implementation based on alternative validation procedures: Ranking, cut scores, banding, and compensatory models. In S. M. McPhail (Ed.), *Alternative validation strategies: Developing new and leveraging existing validity evidence* (pp. 349–405). John Wiley.

Paulhus, D. L. (1984). Two-component models of socially desirable responding. *Journal of Personality and Social Psychology, 46*(3), 598–609.

Ployhart, R. E., & Holtz, B. C. (2008). The diversity–validity dilemma: Strategies for reducing racioethnic and sex subgroup differences and adverse impact in selection. *Personnel Psychology, 61*(1), 153–172.

Ployhart, R. E., & Ryan, A. M. (1998). Applicants' reactions to the fairness of selection procedures: The effects of positive rule violations and time of measurement. *Journal of Applied Psychology, 83*(1), 3–16.

Potosky, D., & Bobko, P. (2004). Selection testing via the internet: Practical considerations and exploratory empirical findings. *Personnel Psychology, 57*(4), 1003–1034.

Prensky, M. (2001). *Digital game-based learning.* New York: McGraw-Hill.

Ratan, R., Kennedy, T., & Williams, D. (2012). League of gendered game play behaviors: Examining instrumental vs identity-relevant avatar choices. *Meaningful play, 13.* Retrieved December 13, 2013, from http://meaningfulplay.msu.edu/proceedings2012/mp2012_submission_143.pdf

Ratan, R. A., & Dawson, M. (2016). When mii is me: A psychophysiological examination of avatar self-relevance. *Communication Research, 43*(8), 1065–1093.

Ratan, R. A., Taylor, N., Hogan, J., Kennedy, T., & Williams, D. (2015). Stand by your man: An examination of gender disparity in League of Legends. *Games and Culture, 10*(5), 438–462.

Raven, J., Raven, J. C., & Court, J. H. (2003). *Manual for Raven's progressive matrices and vocabulary scales.* Harcourt: Harcourt Assessment.

Reeves, B., & Read, L. J. (2009). *Total engagement. Using games and virtual worlds to change the way people work and businesses compete.* Boston, MA: Harvard Business School Press.

Richman-Hirsch, W. L., Olson-Buchanan, J. B., & Drasgow, F. (2000). Examining the impact of administration medium on examinee perceptions and attitudes. *Journal of Applied Psychology, 85*(6), 880–887.

Ritterfeld, U., & Weber, R. (2006). Video games for entertainment and education. In P. V. J. Bryant (Ed.), *Playing video games: Motives, responses, and consequences* (pp. 399– 413). Mahwah, NJ: Lawrence Erlbaum Associates Publishers.

Roth, P. L., Bevier, C. A., Bobko, P., Switzer, F. S., & Tyler, P. (2001). Ethnic group differences in cognitive ability in employment and educational settings: A meta-analysis. *Personnel Psychology, 54*(2), 297–330.

Ryan, A. M., & Ployhart, R. E. (2000). Applicants' perceptions of selection procedures and decisions: A critical review and agenda for the future. *Journal of Management, 26*(3), 565–606.

Ryan, A. M., & Tippins, N. (2009). *Designing and implementing global selection systems.* West Sussex, UK: Wiley-Blackwell.

Ryan, R. M., Rigby, C. S., & Przybylski, A. (2006). The motivational pull of video games: A self-determination theory approach. *Motivation and Emotion, 30*(4), 344–360.

Salthouse, T. A. (1996). The processing-speed theory of adult age differences in cognition. *Psychological Review, 103*(3), 403–428.

Shen, C., Ratan, R., Cai, Y. D., & Leavitt, A. (2016). Do men advance faster than women? Debunking the gender performance gap in two massively multiplayer online games. *Journal of Computer-Mediated Communication, 21*(4), 312–329.

Shipley, W. C., Gruber, C. P., Martin, T. A., & Klein, A. M. (2012). *Shipley–2 manual.* Western Psychological Services.

Shute, V. J. (2011). Stealth assessment in computer-based games to support learning. In S. Tobias & J. D. Fletcher (Eds.), *Computer games and instruction* (pp. 503–524). Charlotte, NC: Information Age.

Shute, V.J. & Ke, F. (2012). Games, learning, and assessment. In D. Ifenthaler, D. Eseryel, & X. Ge (Eds.), *Assessment in game-based learning: Foundations, innovations, and perspectives* (pp. 43–58). New York, NY: Springer.

Smits, J., & Charlier, N. (2011). Game-based assessment and the effect on test anxiety: A case study. In *European Conference on Games Based Learning* (pp. 562–566). Reading, United Kingdom: Academic Conferences International Limited. Retrieved from http://search.proquest.com.proxy1.cl.msu.edu/docview/1009900796/abstract/5A10ADB0159D427BPQ/1

Society for Human Resource Management. (2016). 2016 human capital benchmarking report. *Society for Human Resource Management.* Retrieved from https://www.shrm.org/hr-today/trends-and-forecasting/research-and-surveys/Documents/2016-Human-Capital-Report.pdf

Steele, C. M., & Aronson, J. (1995). Stereotype threat and the intellectual test performance of African Americans. *Journal of Personality and Social Psychology, 69*(5), 797–811.

Sweetser, P., & Wyeth, P. (2005). GameFlow: A model for evaluating player enjoyment in games. *ACM Computers in Entertainment, 3*(3), 1–24.

Sydell, E., Ferrell, J., Carpenter, J., Frost, C., & Brodbeck, C. C. (2013). Simulation scoring. In M. S. Fetzer & K. A. Tuzinski (Eds.), *Simulations for personnel selection* (pp. 83–107). New York: Springer.

Terlecki, M. S., Newcombe, N. S., & Little, M. (2008). Durable and generalized effects of spatial experience on mental rotation: gender differences in growth patterns. *Applied Cognitive Psychology, 22*(7), 996–1013.

Tims, A. (2010, June 11). L'Oreal hopes recruitment game will attract top graduates. *The Guardian.* Retrieved from https://www.theguardian.com/money/2010/jun/12/loreal-recruitment-game-top-graduates

Tippins, N. T. (2015). Technology and assessment in selection. *Annual Review of Organizational Psychology and Organizational Behavior, 2,* 551–582.

Truxillo, D. M., Bauer, T. N., Campion, M. A., & Paronto, M. E. (2002). Selection fairness information and applicant reactions: A longitudinal field study. *Journal of Applied Psychology, 87*(6), 1020–1031.

Truxillo, D. M., Donahue, L. S., & Kuang, D. (2004). Work samples, performance tests, and competency testing. In M. Hersen (Ed.), *Comprehensive handbook of psychological assessment* (pp. 345–370). Hoboken, NJ: Wiley.

Truxillo, D. M., & Hunthausen, J. M. (1999). Reactions of African-American and White applicants to written and video-based police selection tests. *Journal of Social Behavior and Personality, 14*(1), 101–112.

Tuzinski, K. (2013). Simulations for personnel selection: An introduction. In M. Fetzer & K. Tuzinski (Eds.), *Simulations for personnel selection* (pp. 1–13). New York: Springer.

U.S. Equal Opportunity Employment Commission, U.S. Civil Service Commission, U.S. Department of Labor, & U.S. Department of Justice. (1978). Uniform guidelines on employee selection procedures. *Federal Register*, 43: 38295–38309.

Villado, A. J., Randall, J. G., & Zimmer, C. U. (2016). The effect of method characteristics on retest score gains and criterion-related validity. *Journal of Business and Psychology, 31*(2), 233–248.

Walker, H. J., Feild, H. S., Giles, W. F., Bernerth, J. B., & Short, J. C. (2011). So what do you think of the organization? A contextual priming explanation for recruitment Web site characteristics as antecedents of job seekers' organizational image perceptions. *Organizational Behavior and Human Decision Processes, 114*(2), 165–178.

Wang, L., Shute, V., & Moore, G. R. (2015). Lessons learned and best practices of stealth assessment. *International Journal of Gaming and Computer-Mediated Simulations, 7*(4), 66–87.

Washburn, D. A. (2003). The games psychologists play (and the data they provide). *Behavior Research Methods, 35*(2), 185–193.

Weibel, D., Wissmath, B., Habegger, S., Steiner, Y., & Groner, R. (2008). Playing online games against computer-vs. human-controlled opponents: Effects on presence, flow, and enjoyment. *Computers in Human Behavior, 24*(5), 2274–2291.

Wiechmann, D., & Ryan, A. M. (2003). Reactions to computerized testing in selection contexts. *International Journal of Selection and Assessment, 11*(2-3), 215–229.

Williams, D., Martins, N., Consalvo, M., & Ivory, J. D. (2009). The virtual census: Representations of gender, race and age in video games. *New Media & Society, 11*(5), 815–834.

Wilson, K. A., Bedwell, W. L., Lazzara, E. H., Salas, E., Burke, C. S., Estock, J. L., … Conkey, C. (2009). Relationships between game attributes and learning outcomes: Review and research proposals. *Simulation & Gaming, 40*(2), 217–266.

Winkler, C. (2006). HR technology: Job tryouts go virtual. *HR Magazine.* Retrieved from https://www.shrm.org/hr-today/news/hr-magazine/pages/0906hrtech.aspx

Wood, R. T., Griffiths, M. D., Chappell, D., & Davies, M. N. (2004). The structural characteristics of video games: A psycho-structural analysis. *CyberPsychology & Behavior, 7*(1), 1–10.

Yee, N., & Bailenson, J. (2007). The Proteus Effect: The effect of transformed self-representation on behavior. *Human Communication Research, 33*(3), 271–290.

Zickuhr, K. (2011, February 3). Generations and their gadgets. *Pew Research Center.* Retrieved from http://www.pewinternet.org/2011/02/03/generations-and-their-gadgets/

Zielinski, D. (2015, Nov 1). The gamification of recruitment. *HR Magazine.* Retrieved from https://www.shrm.org/hr-today/news/hr-magazine/pages/1115-gamification-recruitment.aspx

CHAPTER 5

E-SOCIALIZATION

The Problems and the Promise of Socializing Newcomers in the Digital Age

Jamie A. Gruman and Alan M. Saks

ABSTRACT

Socialization is the process during which newcomers develop the skills, knowledge and attitudes necessary to fit into an organization and adjust to their jobs and roles. This chapter introduces e-socialization - the process of facilitating newcomer adjustment through the use of information and communication technologies. We specify some of the main challenges and opportunities presented by e-socialization and structure our discussion around the organization-initiated socialization practices that are most widely discussed in the socialization literature as well as newcomer-initiated behaviors: e-orientation, e-training, e-socialization agents, e-socialization tactics, and e-proactive behaviors. We conclude that there are a number of important ways in which e-socialization differs from traditional socialization that can have both positive and negative consequences for the human capital, social capital, adjustment, and socialization of newcomers and that the effect of e-socialization practices on these outcomes will be moderated by the degree of virtuality. Based on these

The Brave New World of eHRM 2.0, pages 111–139.
Copyright © 2018 by Information Age Publishing
All rights of reproduction in any form reserved.

conclusions we offer a number of recommendations for future research and practice on e-socialization.

Keywords: socialization; e-socialization; technology; digital; virtual; e-HRM; electronic human resources.

Organizational socialization is the process through which new employees learn about and adjust to their new jobs and roles in organizations. It is "a learning and adjustment process that enables an individual to assume an organizational role that fits both organizational and individual needs" (Chao, 2012, p. 582). This often involves formal orientation and training sessions as well as informal interactions with other newcomers and members of the organization. Information and communication technologies (ICTs) present new methods for socializing newcomers, however, we know very little about how such technologies can help or hinder the socialization process. The present chapter addresses this issue by presenting a conceptually grounded overview of the problems and possibilities associated with socializing newcomers through electronic means.

The ICTs of the digital world are changing many human resource practices. For example, it is now commonplace for organizations to use online recruitment and selection procedures to hire new employees (Sylva & Mol, 2009). Web-based training is increasingly common with over a third of all learning activities performed through e-learning (Watson et al., 2013). Organizations have also begun to move from traditional group-based orientation sessions to computer-based sessions, a process that is likely to increase in the future (Wesson & Gogus, 2005). However, we know very little about how ICTs affect human resource management practices in general and socialization in particular. Electronic human resource management (e-HRM) is still a relatively new area of study in which there is a paucity of theory and research (Marler & Fisher, 2013; Stone & Dulebohn, 2013). Therefore, although digital technologies present new methods by which socialization can be accomplished, many questions exist about the effectiveness of incorporating ICTs into the socialization of newcomers, a process we call e-socialization.

Specifically, *e-socialization* is the process of leveraging ICTs to help newcomers adjust to their new work surroundings and learn the attitudes, behaviors, and skills required to fulfil their new roles and function effectively in organizations (c.f., Fisher, 1986; Van Maanen, 1976). As organizations continue to leverage the apparent advantages of ICTs it is important to consider how technology may affect the socialization of newcomers (Bartel, Wrzesniewski, & Wiesenfeld, 2007). The present chapter focuses on e-socialization and discusses the challenges and opportunities digital technologies present for the effective socialization of employees who are new to their role and/or organization.

SOCIALIZATION AND E-SOCIALIZATION

When individuals join organizations, they find themselves in a state of unfamiliarity and uncertainty. They are unsure of their roles and they don't understand the behavioral norms of the organization. They also have little sense of how well they will perform their jobs. They must learn how to think, behave, and interact with new colleagues if they are to become accepted and effective members of the organization. Not only do newcomers need to learn the technical requirements of their job, they must also learn appropriate social behaviors and organizational attitudes (Katz, 1980). The period and process in which this transformation occurs is known as organizational socialization.

Specifically, organizational socialization refers to the "introductory events and activities by which individuals come to know and make sense out of their newfound work experiences" (Katz, 1980, p. 88). It is generally considered to be a learning process during which new hires must learn new attitudes, behaviors, and ways of thinking (Klein & Weaver, 2000). Much of what newcomers learn about their new job, role, and organization comes from information obtained through observation and from co-workers and supervisors (Ostroff & Kozlowski, 1992).

Socialization is important not only because it facilitates newcomers' short-term adjustment, but because it has long term consequences for employee and organization success (Ashforth, Sluss, & Harrision, 2007). In the modern economy, with its elastic employee needs and greater employee mobility, socialization is more important than ever before. As noted by Bauer, Bodner, Erdogan, Truxillo, and Tucker (2007), employees today undergo socialization more frequently in their careers and, as a result, organizations must socialize newcomers more often and more effectively given the increased concerns regarding employee engagement and retention.

The various ICTs of the digital age create opportunities to change how newcomers are socialized. These opportunities present important, new questions about how easily and effectively employees can be socialized through electronic means. For example, can using asynchronous online multimedia presentations as part of the socialization process hasten the internalization of organizational values among newcomers? Can newcomers obtain quality information from co-workers and supervisors through e-socialization practices? Does the lack of face-to-face interaction in virtual organizations create role ambiguity (Stone, Stone-Romero, & Lukaszewski, 2006) and compromise newcomers' time to task proficiency? Does e-socialization increase or decrease adjustment and socialization outcomes such as fit perceptions, stress, and job satisfaction?

The potential issues associated with socializing newcomers who may not be physically co-located and who may be socialized through electronic means were first noted by Bauer, Morrison and Callister (1998) who suggested that "[s]ocialization may be a particularly great challenge for telecommuters, because they lack regular contact with coworkers. To our knowledge, this is an unexplored research area and one that poses great potential" (p. 170). In the many years since this

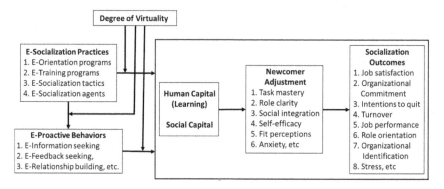

FIGURE 5.1.   A Model of E-socialization

observation was made, however, this great potential has not been exploited by researchers. Nor has the socialization of workers in other types of work arrangements which have been on the rise (e.g., part-time, temporary, seasonal, contract work) even though e-socialization is likely to be particularly relevant and even necessary for these types of workers and work arrangements.

To better understand the potential effects of e-socialization practices, we have developed a model (see Figure 5.1) based on socialization research in which e-socialization practices lead to three sets of outcomes in a sequential process: newcomer capital (human and social capital), newcomer adjustment (e.g., task mastery), and socialization outcomes (e.g., organizational commitment). While human capital involves resources associated with knowledge, skills, and ability, social capital refers to the resources within a social structure that can be accessed and leveraged to achieve desired ends (Fang, Duffy & Shaw, 2011; Seibert, Kraimer, & Liden, 2001).

As shown in Figure 5.1, e-socialization practices first lead to human and social capital which then lead to newcomer adjustment or proximal outcomes, that in turn lead to distal socialization outcomes (e.g., Ashforth, Sluss, & Saks, 2007; Bauer & Erdogan, 2012; Fang, Duffy, & Shaw, 2011; Klein & Heuser, 2008; Saks & Ashforth, 1997). This model is consistent with research that has found that human and social capital mediate the relationship between socialization practices (e.g., orientation, socialization tactics, mentoring, socialization agent helpfulness) and socialization outcomes (Allen, McManus, & Russell, 1999; Ashforth, Sluss, & Saks, 2007; Cooper-Thomas & Anderson, 2002; Klein, Fan, & Preacher, 2006; Klein & Weaver, 2000; Korte & Lin, 2013; Lapointe, Vandenberghe & Boudrais, 2014).

Because the ICTs that comprise e-HR systems can alter information flows, communication processes, and patterns of social interaction (Stone & Lukaszewski, 2009; Stone et al., 2006), the effect of e-socialization on human and social capital, newcomer adjustment, and socialization outcomes might differ from traditional socialization practices. Compared to traditional socialization, e-socialization might change socialization practices and experiences, modify what newcomers learn and the relationships they develop at work, alter levels of newcomer adjustment (e.g., anxiety), and produce different socialization outcomes (e.g., intentions to quit and turnover).

Specifically, we suggest that the extent to which the effects of e-socialization will differ from traditional methods of socialization will depend on the degree to which e-socialization alters the information acquisition, sensemaking, and relationship-building processes possible in traditional socialization. Such processes will be affected further by the degree of virtuality of e-socialization which, as shown in Figure 5.1, will moderate the effects of e-socialization practices.

The box surrounding human and social capital, newcomer adjustment, and socialization outcomes in Figure 1 indicates that virtuality will moderate the effect of e-socialization practices on all of these components given that they have all been shown to be directly influenced by socialization practices. Thus, virtuality plays a key role in determining the effect of e-socialization practices on human and social capital as well as newcomer adjustment and socialization outcomes. But what exactly is virtuality?

Virtuality

Virtuality is a ubiquitous feature of the contemporary workplace, but it is a complex construct that is difficult to define (Griffith & Neale, 1991). In their review of the literature on virtuality and teams, Foster, Abbey, Callow, Zu, and Wilbon (2015) identified almost 30 unique conceptualizations of virtuality noting that most are multidimensional. Despite this variety, a commonly identified theme is that virtuality involves communication and coordination across boundaries (e.g., Espinosa, Cummings, Wilson, & Pearce, 2003). For example, Dulebohn, and Hoch (2017) suggest that virtuality involves relying on technology-mediated communication to interact across multiple boundaries, such as organizational or geographic. The more organizational members interact through communication technologies across boundaries, the greater the level of virtuality (Griffith & Neale, 1991).

Groups can, but are not required to, be geographically dispersed to demonstrate virtuality (Gibson & Gibbs, 2006; Kirkman & Mathieu, 2005). For example, a manager and a newcomer may interact via email despite working in the same office. Co-workers who interact across boundaries using mediating technologies despite being co-located demonstrate virtuality. This is an important detail as many e-socialization practices may be implemented despite the relative physical proximity of newcomers to each other and organizational incumbents.

Early work on virtuality focused on media richness, the ability of a medium to reduce equivocality and enhance the processing of subjective, complicated messages (Daft & Lengel, 1986). Most research on media richness has explored people's choice of specific media (Dennis, Fuller, & Valacich, 2008). However, what is more informative from the perspective of e-socialization is the ability of a medium to support communication and coordination among employees interacting across boundaries.

One feature of virtuality is that it varies in degree. For example, individuals and groups vary in terms of the percentage of time they interact through the boundaries of time and space, and the level of technology-assisted communication used to support that interaction (Griffith & Neale, 1991). As described later in the chapter and shown in Figure 5.1, we consider virtuality to be a key factor in the e-socialization process that will moderate the effect of e-socialization practices on human and social capital as well as newcomer adjustment and socialization outcomes. In effect, we suggest that e-socialization will be more effective when virtuality is lower rather than higher. In other words, effective e-socialization programs should not require newcomers to interact exclusively across multiple technology-mediated boundaries. Instead, they should include some face-to-face interactions due to the additive value of such exchanges. We suggest that this is the case for all newcomers, regardless of whether their jobs involve predominantly virtual work (e.g., telework, virtual teams) or work that is conducted mostly face-to-face. As shown in Figure 5.1, virtuality will moderate the effects of a number of socialization practices.

Socialization Practices

Because socialization practices represent a significant focus of socialization research, and because they are the primary leverage points through which organizations can engineer successful adjustment and socialization, we structure the chapter around these practices. Specifically, our discussion is structured around what Saks and Gruman (2012) identified as the most studied organization-initiated antecedents in the socialization literature (*orientation programs*, *training programs*, *socialization agents*, and *socialization tactics*), as well as newcomer proactive behaviors that have also been recognized to play a key role in newcomer adjustment and socialization (Gruman, Saks, & Zweig, 2006). As shown in Figure 1, organization-initiated socialization practices such as socialization tactics have been found to influence the extent to which newcomers engage in proactive behaviors (Gruman et al., 2006). We provide a brief overview of research on these practices and discuss how e-socialization might affect them and their impact on newcomer human and social capital, adjustment, and socialization outcomes. Based on this discussion, we present recommendations for future research and practice on e-socialization.

The present chapter makes a number of contributions to both socialization theory and practice. First, by reviewing the ways that e-socialization might influence traditional socialization practices, we suggest numerous opportunities for new research. Second, based on our review, we offer specific, testable research propositions on the effects of e-socialization practices. Third, we draw on a number of literatures outside of the socialization area and thus present socialization researchers with new conceptual bases for grounding their research. Fourth, our review presents managers and HR practitioners with specific questions that should be considered to make e-socialization practices most effective.

In the remainder of the chapter, we consider each socialization practice in turn and discuss how it, and associated outcomes, may be affected during e-socialization. We begin with the two most common and formal socialization practices: orientation and training programs.

E-ORIENTATION PROGRAMS

For most newcomers, formal socialization begins with an orientation program. Orientation programs occur the first day or week on the job during which newcomers are introduced to the job, their colleagues, and the larger organization (Klein & Weaver, 2000) and have been shown to be an effective socialization practice.

In a classic experiment designed to help new employees overcome anxieties, Gomersall and Myers (1966) found that compared to a group that received a standard orientation, a group that received an orientation session that included material designed to reduce anxiety was more productive, had better job attendance, and reached higher levels of competence much sooner.

Saks (1994a) found that the accuracy and completeness of the information employees received from an orientation program was positively related to organizational commitment, met expectations, and ability to cope, which were subsequently related to job satisfaction, intention to quit, and job survival. Klein and Weaver (2000) found that employees who attended a voluntary orientation program had higher scores on several socialization content dimensions (human capital/learning) and also reported higher affective organizational commitment. The socialization content or learning mediated the relationship between orientation and organizational commitment.

There is considerable evidence that orientation is beneficial for newcomers, but what would happen if these socialization activities occurred through ICTs? As shown in Figure 5.1, e-orientation programs can have direct effects on human and social capital, newcomer adjustment, and socialization outcomes. However, the effects might not be as positive as those produced by traditional orientation programs.

In one of the few studies on computer-based orientation, Wesson and Gogus (2005) compared a traditional, face-to-face (social-based) orientation to a computer-based orientation program on learning socialization content and distal socialization outcomes in a sample of 261 newcomers from a large, technology-based consulting firm. The computer-based orientation was a self-guided, two- to three-day program that covered all of the same material as the traditional orientation through the use of multimedia technologies. The learning outcomes, assessed two months after starting the job, included six content areas of organizational socialization: self-assessed performance proficiency, politics, language, people, organizational goals/values, and history (Chao, O'Leary-Kelly, Wolf, Klein, & Gardner, 1994). The outcomes, assessed four months after starting the job, included job satisfaction, organizational commitment, and supervisory ratings of organizational goal and value socialization, performance proficiency, and role understanding.

The results indicated that newcomers who participated in the computer-based orientation scored significantly lower in the socially-oriented socialization content areas of organizational goals/values, people, and politics. Wesson and Gogus (2005) also found that participation in the computer-based orientation had a significant negative effect on job satisfaction and organizational commitment, and that the socially-oriented content dimensions fully mediated these relationships.

The deleterious effects of the computer-based orientation were not limited to self-report measures. Results also demonstrated that orientation via computer was significantly negatively associated with supervisor ratings of organizational goals and values socialization, and role understanding. Again, the socially-oriented content dimensions fully mediated these relationships.

These results suggest that computer-based orientation programs may hinder the socialization of newcomers. Specifically, preliminary research on this topic suggests that this hindrance occurs with respect to learning the socially-oriented content areas of socialization, not information-based content areas such as organizational history and language. This may be due to the fact that whereas technical information can be easily transmitted via ICTs, such technologies compromise the ability to transmit social information that is more subtle and often tacit. This is of particular relevance for e-socialization because a number of authors have suggested that socialization practices, and orientation programs in particular, are overly narrow in that they focus too much on information (Saks & Gruman, 2011; Wanous & Reichers, 2000), despite the fact that social phenomena such as those represented by the socially-oriented content areas, are a vital avenue to the successful socialization of newcomers (Fang, Duffy, & Shaw, 2011; Morrison, 2002).

For example, Morrision (2002) found that the structure of newcomers' informational and friendship networks was related to adjustment and socialization outcomes including knowledge, task mastery, role clarity, commitment, and social integration. Similarly, in their social capital model of socialization, Fang et al. (2011) suggest that access to social capital, comprised of newcomers' network structure and network resources, and the mobilization of that capital lead to newcomer adjustment and career success.

Nahapiet and Ghoshal (1998) suggested that social capital has three dimensions. The *structural* dimension refers to the pattern of connections or network ties among individuals. The *relational* dimension refers to the quality of those ties in terms of friendship, respect, trust, and obligations. Strong relational ties can provide informational, emotional, and instrumental assistance to newcomers in addition to offering other advantages such as a sense of role-based purpose and self-esteem (Thoits,

2011). The *cognitive* dimension refers to shared representations and mental models. E-socialization programs that involve exclusive or extensive online orientation processes may exacerbate existing problems noted in the socialization literature in that they may impair the social integration of newcomers by further minimizing social learning and development, compromising the formation of social capital, particularly the relational and cognitive dimensions.

The available theory and research suggest that e-socialization programs that include an online orientation (e-orientation) may benefit from including more face-to-face orientation components when possible. This suggestion is consistent with the literature on virtual teams that suggests that the success of such teams is enhanced when they include face-to-face contact (Powell, Piccoli, & Ives, 2004). Indeed, face-to-face contact has been found to foster socialization among virtual team members (Powell et al., 2004). Face-to-face contact may serve to enhance the social learning that appears to be compromised through online orientations. A lack of face-to-face contact and greater virtuality is likely to reduce the effectiveness of e-orientation programs in general and for social integration in particular.

Based on the preceding discussion on e-orientation, we offer the following research propositions:

Proposition 1. Relative to traditional orientation programs, e-socialization that involves electronically-mediated orientation (e-orientation) will result in newcomers learning less social and normative content (e.g., values, politics, norms, etc.).

Proposition 2. Relative to traditional orientation programs, e-socialization that involves electronically-mediated orientation (e-orientation) will result in lower levels of newcomer adjustment (e.g., social integration, fit perceptions) and socialization outcomes (e.g., job satisfaction, commitment, performance etc).

Proposition 3. The relationship between electronically-mediated orientation practices or e-orientation and the amount of newcomer social and normative learning, adjustment, and socialization outcomes will be moderated by the degree of virtuality such that e-orientation will be more strongly related to newcomer human and social capital, newcomer adjustment, and socialization outcomes when vituality is lower rather than greater.

Proposition 4. Deleterious outcomes associated with e-orientation will be reduced to the extent that such practices co-occur with traditional, non-electronically-mediated face-to-face orientation practices.

E-SOCIALIZATION TRAINING PROGRAMS

A highly formal and planned socialization practice, training is often one of the first experiences a newcomer has with an organization following orientation (Saks, 1996). Whereas orientation programs focus on organizational issues that are relevant to all newcomers, training programs focus on knowledge and skills that are job-specific. Training therefore helps newcomers get up to speed quickly (Saks, 1996). Relatively few studies in the socialization literature have focused on training, but it represents an important socialization practice because it can have a major influence on the development of norms, attitudes toward the job and organization, and learning about appropriate behavior (Saks & Gruman, 2012). As noted by Feldman (1989), training "plays a major role in how individuals make sense of and adjust to their new job settings" (p. 399).

Saks (1994b) compared the effects of formal training and tutorial (self-study) training on the anxiety and stress reactions of newly-hired entry-level accountants. He found that formal training was related to lower anxiety for newcomers with low technical self-efficacy while tutorial training was related to higher anxiety for newcomers with low academic self-efficacy. In another study, Saks (1995) found that the amount of training received was positively related to post-training self-efficacy, ability to cope, job satisfaction, organizational and professional commitment, and negatively related to intention to quit the organization and profession.

In a study of the socialization of military personnel, Delobbe, Cooper-Thomas, and De Hoe (2016) found that newcomers' perceptions of training utility positively predicted role clarity and organizational values understanding, reflecting the degree of congruence between the values of the recently enlisted personnel and the organization. However, training was not related to group integration.

As shown in Figure 5.1, e-training programs are also expected to influence human and social capital, newcomer adjustment, and socialization outcomes. However, e-socialization that involves virtual training methods (e.g., online, distance, or distributed training) might impact these outcomes in a manner different from traditional socialization training methods. In general, research comparing face-to-face and virtual training reveals no important differences on common training outcomes, such as reactions and learning (Bell, Tannenbaum, Ford, Noe, & Kraiger, 2017; Brown & Charlier, 2013; Brown & Van Buren, 2007). However, research has generally not examined socialization outcomes such as trainees' attitudes towards the organization and the quality of their relationships (Brown & Van Buren, 2007).

Brown and Van Buren (2007) suggest that online training may compromise the social capital trainees develop. With respect to the structural dimension of social capital, they suggest that technology-mediated training may make it easier to connect with more people, but that building and maintaining relationships with those people is more difficult. This is problematic because building and maintaining relationships helps to promote social integration which is an important indicator of newcomer adjustment (Morrison, 1993b). With respect to the relational dimension, they argue that online training environments are less likely to generate trust among trainees, or produce common norms of conduct, such as reciprocity norms, which are a key aspect of successful socialization. As for the cognitive dimension, they suggest that online training is less likely to generate a common, shared vision for the organization among employees. Shared visions or shared mental models are important because they can impact adjustment and socialization outcomes such as self-efficacy, satisfaction, and task performance (Cannon-Bowers & Salas, 2001).

In their review of the literature on virtual teams, Powell et al. (2004) noted that training among virtual team members improves performance and fosters cohesiveness and satisfaction. This is partly due to the common perspectives and approaches to work that training provides. In face-to-face socialization both technical and social information can be absorbed by newcomers through tacit means, facilitating the alignment of newcomers and incumbents. However, with e-socialization training social information, such as norms and cues regarding appropriate behavior, are less likely to be identified and internalized by newcomers, compromising the development of shared mental models (Maynard & Gilson, 2014). Nor are newcomers likely to inquire about such matters. In a study investigating the forms of information newcomers seek when socialized in virtual groups, Ahuja and Galvin (2003) found that normative information focused on values and expectations was by far the least sought. Therefore, it is advisable that e-socialization training include explicit communication and training about organizational norms, requirements, and expectations (Ahuja & Galvin, 2003).

In their review of the training literature, Bell et al. (2017) suggest that the effectiveness of technology-based training is determined by the design of the instruction and support provided to learners, not by the medium employed. We submit that this conclusion may be limited to the effectiveness of learning declarative and procedural knowledge and may not apply to more socially-oriented outcomes. Training can focus on social phenomena such as interpersonal relations (Salas, Rozell, Mullen, & Driskell, 1999) that influence the development of social capital. Because technology-based training may significantly compromise newcomers' ability to build social capital, and because such training is best used to teach explicit knowledge, whereas face-to-face training is best used to teach tacit knowledge characterizing interpersonal matters (Salas, DeRouin, & Littrell, 2005), a blended approach to e-socialization training may be most effective at promoting adjustment and socialization outcomes.

Salas and Cannon-Bowers (2001) suggest that research is needed to develop empirically validated principles for the design of distance learning, and that it is of particular importance to determine the necessary degree of interaction between instructors and learners. Given the significance of social capital for the effective adjustment of newcomers, in the context of e-socialization training it is additionally important to determine the necessary degree of interaction among newcomers themselves, something likely to be compromised through virtual training (Welsh, Wanberg, Brown, & Simmering, 2003), in addition to various incumbents, such as coworkers and managers.

Based on the preceding discussion, we offer the following propositions:

Proposition 5. E-socialization training will result in the development of less social capital than traditional socialization training.

Proposition 6. The degree of virtuality will moderate the relationship between e-socialization training and the development of social capital such that e-socialization training will be more strongly related to social capital when virtuality is lower rather than greater.

Also, consistent with the propositions advanced by Brown and Van Buren (2007), we offer the following propositions on e-socialization training:

Proposition 7. E-socialization training will result in lower levels and greater difficulty in establishing norms of conduct among newcomers than traditional socialization training.

Proposition 8. E-socialization training will compromise newcomers' common understanding of the organization compared to traditional socialization training.

Proposition 9. The degree of virtuality will moderate the relationship between e-socialization training and norm development and common understanding among newcomers such that the effect of e-socialization training on norm development and common understanding among newcomers will be stronger when virtuality is lower rather than higher.

Proposition 10. A blended approach to e-socialization training will be more effective than exclusively virtual training for the development of social capital as well as norm development and common understanding of the organization. Therefore, some traditional face-to-face training should be incorporated when these outcomes are important.

E-SOCIALIZATION AGENTS

In addition to formal orientation and training programs, members of the organization, or *socialization agents*, play an integral and often informal role in the socialization of newcomers (Bauer et al., 1998). Socialization agents are individuals who help to facilitate the adjustment of newcomers through various actions such as providing information, feedback, resources, and so on (Klein & Heuser, 2008). Recent models of socialization underscore socialization agents and social capital as fundamental to successful socialization (Fang et al., 2011; Jokisaari & Nurmi, 2013).

Louis, Posner, and Powell (1983) found that newcomers reported that the most helpful socialization practices were interactions with peers, buddy relationships with senior co-workers, and supervisor interactions followed by a mentor/sponsor and new recruits. As a set, the availability of the socialization practices was positively related to job satisfaction, organizational commitment, and tenure intention. Louis et al. (1983) concluded that the most important factor for making newcomers feel effective was daily interactions with peers while working.

Nelson and Quick (1991) examined the helpfulness of the same socialization practices as Louis et al. (1983) and found that daily interactions with peers, one's supervisor, and having a buddy/senior worker were rated as the most helpful practices.

Unlike other socialization practices, socialization agents tend to perform an informal role in the socialization of newcomers. As noted by Feldman (1989), "A great deal of what new recruits learn is learned through informal interactions with peers, supervisors, and mentors outside the context of formal training" (p. 386). In fact, the frequency of interactions with insiders has been described as the primary mechanism through which socialization occurs (Reichers, 1987). Indeed, Korte (2010) found that developing relationships with co-workers and managers and the quality of interactions was the primary mechanism for learning and successful socialization. Rollag, Parise, and Cross (2005) found that newcomers who were most quickly adjusted had developed a broad network of relationships with co-workers and concluded that what matters most for successful adjustment and socialization is how quickly newcomers develop relationships with a variety of co-workers.

As shown in Figure 5.1, e-socialization agents can have an effect on human and social capital, adjustment, and socialization outcomes. However, as suggested by Driskell, Radtke and Salas (2003), "interaction that is mediated by technology may lead to less intimacy and difficulty in establishing relationships" (p. 303). We suggest that e-socialization is likely to interfere with the development of newcomers' social capital and the impact of socialization agents for a number of reasons.

First, opportunities for informal social interaction are likely to be reduced in e-socialization. As suggested by Bartel et al (2007), social interactions are essential to cultivating a strong sense of organizational membership that is part of successful socialization, and this is likely to be compromised when newcomers and incumbents have fewer reasons to interact.

Second, e-socialization is likely to produce communication difficulties similar to those experienced in virtual teams such as delays in receiving feedback, a lack of contextual cues, and a lack of a common frame of reference (Powell et al., 2004). This is likely to be particularly challenging for newcomers. The difficulties produced by technologically-mediated interactions are likely to be more acute for newcomers because they lack experience and are not acquainted with their new work contexts (Bartel et al., 2007).

Third, the nature of communication among newcomers during e-socialization is likely to be similar to that of virtual teams and may be more task-focused than socially-focused (Powell et al., 2004), which can compromise the development of relationships. All of these issues are likely to reduce newcomers' social capital and socialization outcomes such as affective commitment, a finding that has been observed among people regularly engaged in computer-mediated communication (Johnson, Bettenhausen, & Gibbons, 2009). We suspect that these changes may additionally impact learning as well as proximal and distal socialization outcomes. For example, Bauer and Erdogan (2012) suggest that one reason online orientations produce less learning is that they are less social.

However, the impact of e-socialization on social capital may not be completely negative. Powell et al. (2004) note that compared to traditional teams, members of virtual teams tend to have weaker relational ties to their teammates. This is likely to also be the case among newcomers socialized through electronic media. In their social capital model of organizational socialization, Fang et al. (2011) explain that having many weak ties and structural holes (connections with unconnected others) can be beneficial in that they allow newcomers to access a wider network of information. However, this may only occur if newcomers are provided with structured opportunities to develop such networks. Such structured opportunities are included in *Socialization Resources Theory* (Saks & Gruman, 2012) which suggests that social events (e.g., office parties) and relationship development (e.g., introductions) are important resources that foster effective socialization. These resources may be particularly important in the context of e-socialization. Organizations can also leverage the social networking features of enterprise collaboration platforms to build "virtual water coolers" that facilitate the development of social capital among newcomers (Watkins, 2013). Research is needed to test how e-socialization impacts the access and mobilization of social capital (Fang et al., 2011) available to newcomers and their impact on human capital, proximal, and distal socialization outcomes.

The ways in which e-socialization changes newcomers' interactions with socialization agents might also affect outcomes not typically considered in socialization research. For example, e-socialization may affect newcomers' identity. Identity in general and organizational identity in particular is socially constructed (Ashforth & Mael, 1989). Because e-socialization alters the social interaction between newcomers and incumbents, organizational identity formation may be compromised. As noted by Cerulo (1997), new communication technologies have "altered the backdrop against which identity is constructed" (p. 397). Specifically, the difficulties newcomers experience in connecting with socialization agents, exacerbated by the weaker relationships accompanying compromised social e-socialization tactics (discussed below), may interfere with the development of newcomers' work identities and identification with the organization. However, as noted by Ashforth and Mael (1989), although an individual's self-definition develops through interaction, this interaction does not have to be personal. It can occur through any transmission of symbols, such as orientation sessions. Nonetheless, we contend that the more limited social interaction newcomers have during e-socialization may delay the formation of their organizational identities, and result in organizational identities that are less identified with the organization. More generally, the limited social interaction newcomers have during e-socialization may interfere with the production of emergent states and conditions such as trust (Kirkman, Rosen, Gibson, Tesluk, & McPherson, 2002), shared mental models (Marlow, Lacerenza, & Salas, 2017), and cohesion (Driskell, Radtke, & Salas, 2003), all of which may influence adjustment and socialization outcomes.

The relative difficulties of establishing high-quality relationships in e-socialization and any associated potential detrimental effects on outcomes may be mitigated by proactively reaching out to newcomers (Kirkman et al., 2002) and by assigning them a buddy or mentor. Several studies have found that having a buddy or mentor can facilitate the adjustment and socialization of newcomers. For example, Rollag et al. (2005) found that newcomers who had a "buddy" were more quickly adjusted compared to those who did not. Blau (1988) found that the quality of interns' relationship with their assignment manager (mentor) was positively related to interns' role clarity, organizational commitment, and performance. Similarly, Chatman (1991) found that spending time with a mentor was positively related to newcomers' person-organization fit. Ostroff and Kozlowski (1993) found that newcomers who had mentors learned more about their organizations than those without a mentor.

We suggest that the importance of a buddy and mentors during e-socialization may be even greater than during traditional socialization. During traditional socialization the predominant way newcomers obtain all types of information, except technical information, is through monitoring (Morrison 1993a). However, in e-socialization it may be difficult or impossible to engage in monitoring, and newcomers may need to take a more active approach to acquiring information (Ahuja & Galvin, 2003). Thus, having a buddy or mentor available to answer questions and provide feedback may be a particularly crucial resource during e-socialization.

The relationships that newcomers form with mentors or buddies during e-socialization may develop through the same ICTs that characterize traditional socialization. This form of mentoring is called electronic mentoring, or e-mentoring. Although there is an extensive literature on mentoring, e-mentoring has not been the subject of much research (DiRenzo, Linnehan, Shao, & Rosenberg, 2010). Nonetheless, the literature on e-mentoring suggests a number of factors that are likely to hasten the adjustment of newcomers such as the frequency of interaction between protégé and mentor (DiRenzo, et al., 2010), speaking on the phone, and occasional face-to-face meetings (Marcinkus Murphy, 2011).

ICTs also facilitate the use of mentoring models that are more difficult to implement without such technologies, such as network mentoring, multiple mentoring, and team mentoring (Hamilton & Scandura, 2003). The implementation of these mentoring models offers a means to help newcomers adjust more quickly and effectively. Research on the form, nature, and quality of e-mentoring relationships will aid in our understanding of how mentors can hasten the e-socialization of newcomers.

Based on the preceding discussion we offer the following propositions with respect to e-socialization agents:

Proposition 11. Compared to traditional socialization, e-socialization will make it more difficult for newcomers to establish relationships with socialization agents and other newcomers and will therefore result in lower social capital.

Proposition 12. Compared to traditional socialization agents, e-socialization agents will result in weaker work identities that take longer to develop and demonstrate less identification with the organization.

Proposition 13. The degree of virtuality will moderate the relationship between e-socialization agents and outcomes such that e-socialization will be more effective for newcomers who establish relationships with insiders and develop social capital, and will result in stronger work identities and greater organizational identification when virtuality is lower rather than greater.

Proposition 14. E-socialization agents can be more effective and more likely to result in positive socialization outcomes when newcomers are paired with a mentor and buddy.

E-SOCIALIZATION TACTICS

Socialization tactics refer to "the ways in which the experiences of individuals in transition from one role to another are structured for them by others in the organization" (Van Maanen & Schein, 1979, p. 230). Van Maanen and Schein (1979) identified six bipolar tactics and described how they influence newcomers' role orientations. Building on their work, Jones (1986) suggested that *institutionalized* tactics (collective, formal, sequential, fixed, serial, and investiture) represent a structured socialization process that reduces uncertainty and encourages newcomers to passively accept pre-set roles, thus reproducing the organizational status quo. Conversely, *individualized* tactics (individual, informal, random, variable, disjunctive, and divestiture) encourage newcomers to question the status quo and to develop their own unique approach to their roles. Individualized tactics may increase the uncertainty as well as anxiety of early work experiences (Jones, 1986).

Jones (1986) also suggested that the six tactics represent three broad factors. The *social* tactics consist of the investiture and serial dimensions and are considered to be the most important "because they provide the social cues and facilitation necessary during learning processes" (Jones, 1986, p. 266). The *content* tactics (sequential and fixed) have to do with the content of the information given to newcomers. The *context* tactics (collective and formal) concern the way in which organizations provide information to newcomers.

Two meta-analyses found that institutionalized socialization tactics are negatively related to role ambiguity, role conflict, and intentions to quit, and positively related to fit perceptions, self-efficacy, social acceptance, job satisfaction, organizational commitment, and job performance (Bauer et al., 2007; Saks, Uggerslev, & Fassina, 2007). In addition, the social tactics were most strongly related to socialization outcomes. Also, according to both meta-analyses, socialization tactics lead to traditional socialization outcomes (e.g., job satisfaction) through more proximal outcomes (e.g., fit perceptions). Institutionalized socialization tactics have also been found to be positively related to newcomer learning (Ashforth, Sluss, & Saks, 2007) and social capital (Lapointe et al., 2014).

These results have important implications for e-socialization. As shown in Figure 5.1, e-socialization tactics can have direct effects on human and social capital, newcomer adjustment, and socialization outcomes, however, the effects might not always be positive for a number of reasons.

First, a defining feature of new work systems is self-management (Gephart, 2002). Given that one of the major advantages of e-HRM is to allow employees to pursue HR activities (such as training) individually and at their own pace, online socialization tactics are likely to be more individualized than institutionalized. However, as noted above, the research evidence strongly suggests that individualized tactics are less likely to produce learning, social capital, proximal, and distal socialization outcomes than institutionalized tactics. In line with this argument, and noted in the Weeson and Gogus (2005) study discussed earlier, the computer-based orientation that produced inferior learning outcomes employed more individualized tactics than the social-based orientation. As noted by Weeson and Gogus, the social-based orientation was an established, week-long program in which newcomers were flown to a central location and secluded with other new hires in a process designed to create a sense of community. By contrast, the computer-based orientation was a self-guided process that didn't include the other institutionalized aspects of the social-based orientation.

Therefore, despite the flexibility and personalization provided by digital technologies, human capital, social capital, as well as positive proximal and distal socialization outcomes, may be more likely to be achieved by strategically implementing more institutionalized e-socialization tactics. Such tactics can include ensuring that all newcomers cover the same training materials and discuss them collectively, including a fixed schedule and deadlines by which newcomers must complete components of socialization, and providing newcomers with online mentors who can coach them and affirm their individual identities. These institutionalized tactics can help to promote the development of social capital (Fang et al., 2011) in addition to a common set of attitudes and values (Jones, 1986) that may be particularly important in e-socialization. As noted by Gephart (2002), in the brave new world of electronic workplaces, employees are motivated and their consent is obtained through cultural tactics, such as value and attitude internalization, as opposed to structural tactics. Tactics that emphasize the development of appropriate organizational values and attitudes may prove especially valuable in promoting newcomer e-socialization.

The second, related implication pertains to the way in which specific socialization tactics are likely to be affected by e-socialization. As suggested, institutionalized content tactics may be compromised in e-socialization due to the personalization and customization e-socialization permits. In the absence of more formal e-socialization tactics that establish timelines and deadlines by which socialization must occur, new employees may elect to learn and adapt capriciously. This may retard socialization and compromise all steps in the socialization process.

Context tactics are likely to become more individualized because in a virtual environment it is less likely for newcomers to be socialized as a group and go through common learning experiences. E-socialization doesn't require newcomers to be physically together so it is less likely for newcomers to share the same or even similar socialization experiences. This is likely to undermine the social capital newcomers are able to build.

Institutionalized social tactics are likely to be the most compromised during e-socialization because having access to role models who can model appropriate behavior and support newcomers' identities will be diminished. This is problematic because not only do social tactics predict both proximal and distal outcomes, they are the strongest predictors (Saks et al., 2007). Social tactics are most important for helping newcomers build the social capital that facilitates successful adjustment (Fang et al., 2011).

Based on the preceding discussion of e-socialization tactics, we offer the following propositions:

Proposition 15. E-socialization tactics will be more individualized than traditional socialization tactics.

Proposition 16. The context, content, and social e-socialization tactics dimensions will be more individualized than traditional socialization tactics dimensions.

Proposition 17. Compared to traditional socialization tactics, e-socialization tactics will result in lower human and social capital, adjustment, and socialization outcomes.

Proposition 18. The degree of virtuality will moderate the relationships between e-socialization tactics and outcomes such that the effect of e-socialization on human and social capital, adjustment, and socialization outcomes will be stronger when virtuality is lower rather than greater.

Proposition 19. Designing e-socialization programs to include more institutionalized tactics (especially social) will result in more human and social capital, and more positive adjustment and socialization outcomes.

E-PROACTIVE BEHAVIORS

Socialization researchers have come to recognize that newcomers play an active role in their own socialization by engaging in proactive behaviors, which can be defined as "anticipatory action that employees take to impact themselves and/ or their environments" (Grant & Ashford, 2008, p. 8). For example, Morrison (1993a) found that the frequency with which newcomers proactively sought specific information about their work positively affected their task mastery, role clarity and social integration 6 months after being hired. Research has investigated a number of other proactive behaviors, such as feedback seeking, relationship building, and job-change negotiation, and produced a relatively consistent pattern of results demonstrating that newcomer proactivity is positively related to newcomer adjustment and socialization outcomes (Ashford & Black, 1996; Morrison 1993a; Ostroff & Kozlowski, 1992; Wanberg & Kammeyer-Mueller, 2000).

As shown in Figure 5.1, e-socialization practices are likely to influence e-proactive behaviors which can then lead to improvements in human and social capital, newcomer adjustment, and socialization outcomes. However, the way in which proactive behavior manifests itself in e-socialization, and the nature of the relationships between proactive behaviors, human capital, social capital, and both proximal and distal outcomes during e-socialization, is virtually unexplored. Also, the way in which e-socialization tactics may affect proactive behavior is an open question. For example, by expanding the number of communication channels available, ICTs may increase newcomers' ability and tendency to proactively seek information about an organization (Flanagin & Waldeck, 2004). Alternatively, the compromised relationships that we have argued are likely to characterize e-socialization may make it less probable that newcomers will proactively seek feedback on assignments or try to build relationships.

Gruman et al. (2006) examined the relationship between socialization tactics and six proactive behaviors and found that institutionalized tactics were significantly positively associated with all but one proactive behavior. They also found that after controlling for socialization tactics and self-efficacy, the proactive behaviors incrementally predicted all of the adjustment and socialization outcomes. Additionally, they found that the proactive behaviors mediated the relationship between self-efficacy and tactics on the one hand and adjustment and socialization outcomes on the other hand. Gruman et al. (2006) concluded that newcomers are most likely to demonstrate proactive behavior when their socialization is institutionalized. Given that e-socialization tactics are likely to be more individualized, a corollary is that e-socialization is likely to reduce the types of proactive behaviors that newcomers will engage in and the frequency of proactive socialization behavior.

Bartel et al. (2007) provided evidence for this in their investigation of the socialization of newly hired employees at a large technology firm. Specifically, Bartel et al. examined the extent to which newly-hired remote workers sought to claim membership in the organization by proactively participating in, contributing to, and making known their participation in assorted work-related activities. They also examined the effect of these proactive behaviors on perceived membership granting (actions that signal inclusion to the newcomers) by incumbent employees, and newcomers' organizational identification. Their results demonstrated that the degree of newcomer remoteness was negatively associated with proactive membership claiming, however, the relationship did not reach conventional levels of significance. Remoteness was significantly negatively related to perceived membership granting and organizational identification. They also found that membership claiming and granting fully mediated the relationship between remoteness and organizational identification. These results support the contention that newcomers socialized through ICTs will engage in less proactive behavior, that will, in turn, have a deleterious effect on adjustment and socialization outcomes.

Based on the preceding discussion, we offer the following propositions with respect to e-proactive socialization behaviors:

> **Proposition 20.** E-socialization will reduce and limit the number of e-proactive behaviors that newcomers engage in as well as the frequency that they engage in e-proactive behaviors.
>
> **Proposition 21.** The degree of virtuality will moderate the relationship between e-socialization practices and the extent that newcomers engage in e-proactive behaviors such that newcomers will engage in more e-proactive behaviors and will do so more frequently when virtuality is lower rather than greater.
>
> **Proposition 22.** The degree of virtuality will moderate the relationships between e-proactive behaviors and human capital, social capital, adjustment, and socialization outcomes such that e-proactive behavior will be more strongly related to human capital, social capital, adjustment, and socialization outcomes when virtuality is lower rather than greater.
>
> **Proposition 23.** Designing e-socialization programs to include more institutionalized e-socialization tactics will increase the likelihood that newcomers will engage in more types of e-proactive behaviors and will do so more frequently.

THE FUTURE OF E-SOCIALIZATION

Despite the fact that technology is having a substantial effect on human resource management practices, there is very little theory and research on e-HRM (Stone & Dulebohn, 2013). As noted by Orlikowsli and Scott (2008), technology has become an integral part of most business operations, yet technology remains virtually absent from the world of management research. Socialization research is no exception. ICTs present new opportunities and challenges for the way organizations help new employees "learn the ropes". Although researchers have recognized this since the last millennium (e.g., Bauer et al., 1998), very little research has been conducted on how ICTs influence organizational socialization. Given the increasing prevalence of ICTs in organizations, and the growing frequency that newcomers are socialized and organizations must socialize newcomers, it seems important to reiterate the call for greater research attention to this issue. In line with Ashforth, Sluss and Harrison (2007), we contend that "research should continue to explore the use of technology in socialization" (p. 50).

E-socialization is becoming ever more popular and may soon become the norm. Given the changes in the nature of work and the increasing use of technology in the workplace, e-socialization is likely to become increasingly more feasible and practical than traditional socialization programs for many organizations. However, the various ways that ICTs affect socialization are not clear-cut or simple. The organizational outcomes that follow from the implementation of technology are often emergent and unpredictable (Orlikowsli & Scott, 2008). Our ability to socialize newcomers effectively and efficiently requires that we better appreciate how ICTs influence the way that newcomers develop human and social capital, and become adjusted and socialized in organizations.

E-socialization is likely to result in both problems and opportunities for newcomers and organizations. Some of the problems we have noted in this chapter are that e-orientation and e-socialization training are likely to hinder the learning of social content which can impair the social integration of newcomers and the development of shared mental models; e-socialization agents will make it more difficult for newcomers to develop high-quality relationships with insiders and weaken the development of social capital, strong work identities, and organizational identification; e-socialization tactics are more likely to be individualized than institutionalized which can reduce human and social capital as well as adjustment and socialization outcomes; and e-socialization is likely to limit the types and frequency of proactive behaviors that newcomers engage in and to reduce the effectiveness of e-proactive behaviors for newcomer human and social capital, adjustment, and socialization.

This does not mean that organizations should refrain from using technology to socialize newcomers. Rather, they need to be aware of the opportunities and challenges of e-socialization and understand how to design e-socialization programs to be most effective. Among the opportunities presented by e-socialization are having a greater number of weak relationship ties and drawing on non-traditional mentoring models. These opportunities may help organizations e-socialize new employees faster and better compared to traditional socialization methods. Among the challenges of e-socialization are communication difficulties, compromised relationships, changes in social capital, and a propensity towards implementing unstructured, individualized e-socialization tactics. These challenges may hinder the effectiveness of e-socialization.

In the present chapter, we presented questions and propositions about research and practice that we believe characterize e-socialization. However, we recognize that these ideas are speculations based on a limited amount of prior research. Research is needed to test the propositions outlined in this chapter and determine which e-socialization methods best help newcomers learn, build relationships, adjust to new jobs and roles and produce desirable outcomes.

Using various measures of virtuality, researchers and practitioners can assess the virtuality of e-socialization efforts and examine how they may differ from traditional socialization methods. For example, newcomers who interact with a mentor over email must contend with more of a boundary producing e-socialization experience that is likely to differ significantly, in terms of both process and outcomes, from face-to-face mentoring.

As shown in Figure 5.1, the degree of virtuality is expected to moderate the relationships between e-socialization and outcomes. We suggest that socialization researchers assess and explicitly note the degree of virtuality present in the various e-socialization practices they study so that differences in processes and outcomes between e-socialization and traditional socialization can be more thoroughly understood. Assessment of virtuality may also allow researchers to determine if there is a specific point along the dimensions of virtuality beyond which deleterious effects of e-socialization are observed. For example, Johnson et al. (2009) found that the negative effects of computer-mediated communication on group outcomes occurred only among groups that engaged in computer-mediated communication more than 90 percent of the time.

Organizations should carefully monitor the degree of virtuality of e-socialization programs and be sure to include some face-to-face communication. A reliance on communication and integration mechanisms that create or fail to overcome boundaries is likely to negatively affect the quality and types of information that newcomers receive and will fall short of achieving newcomers' goals of learning, integration, acceptance, and adjustment. E-socialization programs that are high on virtuality can be expected to be less likely to be accepted by newcomers and to be less effective than traditional socialization programs (Stone et al., 2006).

However, e-socialization programs can be designed to be as effective if not more effective than traditional socialization programs. For example, organizations should consider combining e-socialization programs with traditional socialization programs or what Stone et al. (2006) have referred to as "blended" HR systems or in this case, blended socialization programs. This is particularly important with respect to e-orientation and e-training both of which will benefit from some face-to-face contact and interaction between newcomers and organizational members. One way to accomplish this is through the use of a pre-training socialization program which is an introductory socialization period to provide newcomers with opportunities to interact and get to know other newcomers and members of the organization, develop relationships with co-workers, and develop a sense of trust with organizational members (Yanson & Johnson, 2016). A study by Yanson and Johnson (2016) showed that an e-learning program was more effective for learning when participants received face-to-face socialization before the training. Thus, it is possible that a similar intervention will improve the effectiveness of e-socialization programs.

Another issue that will affect the outcomes associated with e-socialization practices is the reason the practices are implemented. The primary reason organizations implement e-HR technologies is cost reduction (Marler, 2009), which can have deleterious effects on employee attitudes (Stone & Lukaszewski, 2009). However, Marler (2009) notes that this non-strategic goal can be supplanted by the HR goals of creating alignment with business strategy, or building internal resources, goals reflecting two dominant approaches to strategic human resource management. The success of e-socialization in producing adjustment and socialization outcomes may depend on the degree to which specific e-socialization practices reflect strategic design considerations that go beyond cost containment, or the superficial and non-strategic objective of implementing practices simply because other organizations have done the same. However, recent research suggests that non-strategic issues such as cost-containment and the mere availability of technology are the dominant drivers of e-HR implementation decisions (Schalk, Timmerman, & van den Heuvel, 2013). Socialization is an important component of strategic human resources management (Saks & Gruman, 2014). We suggest that research on e-socialization identify the extent to which e-socialization practices reflect and support the strategic goals of an organization. This may serve as a boundary condition for producing desirable e-socialization outcomes.

CONCLUSION

Although research has begun to consider the effects of e-learning, e-recruiting, e-selection, and e-compensation, there has been relatively little attention on the use and effectiveness of e-socialization programs. Our review of the most studied socialization practices through the lens of e-socialization suggests that like other eHRM functions, e-socialization can result in both functional and dysfunctional consequences for newcomers and organizations (Stone et al., 2006) and this is likely to be influenced in part by the degree of virtuality associated with e-socialization programs.

Based on our review, we suggest that organizations should not completely abandon traditional socialization programs in favor of strictly electronic programs. Doing so is likely to restrain the positive effects of orientation and training programs on human and social capital and social-oriented adjustment and socialization outcomes, and to overemphasize the use of individualized socialization tactics. It might also limit newcomers' access to socialization agents and restrict the use and frequency of newcomer proactive behaviors. Rather, we suggest that organizations use a blended approach to socialization that includes some face-to-face interaction as well as a pre-socialization program that provides newcomers with opportunities to interact and begin to develop relationships with each other and other members of the organization.

In conclusion, there is evidence to suggest that e-socialization may affect the nature of socialization practices, human and social capital, newcomer adjustment, and socialization outcomes. As ICTs continue to evolve and proliferate we encourage research that will advance our understanding of the best ways to exploit technology to e-socialize organizational newcomers quickly and effectively and ensure that it is acceptable, beneficial, and effective for employees and organizations.

REFERENCES

Ahuja, M. K., & Galvin, J. E. (2003). Socialization in virtual groups. *Journal of Management, 29,* 161–185.

Allen, T. D., McManus, S. E., & Russell, J. E. A. (1999). Newcomer socialization and stress: Formal peer relationships as a source of support. *Journal of Vocational Behavior, 54,* 453–470.

Ashford, S. J., & Black, J. S. (1996). Proactivity during organizational entry: The role of desire for control. *Journal of Applied Psychology, 81*(2), 199–214.

Ashforth, B. E., & Mael, F. (1989). Social identity theory and the organization. *Academy of Management Review, 14,* 20–39.

Ashforth, B. E., Sluss, D. M., & Harrison, S. H. (2007). Socialization in organizational contexts. In G. P. Hodgkinsion & J. K. Ford (Eds.), *International review of industrial and organizational psychology.* Chichester, UK: Wiley

Ashforth, B. E., Sluss, D. M., & Saks, A. M. (2007). Socialization tactics, proactive behavior, and newcomer learning: Integrating socialization models. *Journal of Vocational Behavior, 70,* 447–462.

Bartel, C. A., Wrzesniewski, A., & Wiesenfeld, B. (2007). The struggle to establish organizational membership and identification in remote work contexts. In C. Bartel, S. Blader & A. Wrzesniewski (Eds.), *Identity and the modern organization* (pp. 119–133. Mahwah, NJ: Lawrence Erlbaum Associates.

Bauer, T. N., Bodner, T., Erdogan, B., Truxillo, D. M., & Tucker, J. S. (2007). Newcomer adjustment during organizational socialization: A meta-analytic review of antecedents, outcomes, and methods. *Journal of Applied Psychology, 92,* 707–721.

Bauer, T., & Erdogan, B. (2012). Organizational socialization outcomes: Now and into the future. In C. R. Wanberg (Ed.), *The Oxford handbook of organizational socialization* (pp. 97–112). New York: Oxford University Press.

Bauer, T. N., Morrison, E. W., & Callister, R. R. (1998). Organizational socialization: A review and directions for future research. In G. R. Ferris (Ed.), *Research in personnel and human resources management* (vol. 16, pp. 149–214). Greenwich CT: JAI Press.

Bell, B. S., Tannenbaum, S. I., Ford, J. K., Noe, R. A., & Kraiger, K. (2017). 100 years of training and development research: What we know and where we should go. *Journal of Applied Psychology, 102,* 305–323.

Blau, G. (1988). An investigation of the apprenticeship organizational socialization strategy. *Journal of Vocational Behavior, 32,* 176–195.

Brown, K. G., & Charlier, S. D. (2013). An integrative model of e-learning use: Leveraging theory to understand and increase usage. *Human Resource Management Review, 23,* 37–49.

Brown, K. G., & Van Buren, M. E. (2007). Applying a social capital perspective to the evaluation of distance training. In S. M. Fiore & E. Salas (Eds.), *Toward a science of distributed learning* (pp. 41–63). Washington, DC. American Psychological Association.

Cannon-Bowers, J. A., & Salas, E. (2001). Reflections on shared cognition. *Journal of Organizational Behavior, 22,* 195–202.

Cerulo, K. A. (1997). Identity construction: New issues, new directions. *Annual Review of Sociology, 23,* 385–409.

Chao, G. T. (2012). Organizational socialization: Background, basics, and a blueprint for adjustment at work. In S. W. J. Kozlowski (Ed.), *The Oxford handbook of organizational psychology* (pp. 579–614). New York: Oxford University Press.

Chao, G. T., O'Leary-Kelly, A. M., Wolf, S., Klein, H. J., & Gardner, P. D. (1994). Organizational socialization: Its content and consequences. *Journal of Applied Psychology, 79,* 730–743.

Chatman, J. A. (1991). Matching people and organizations: Selection and socialization in public accounting firms. *Administrative Science Quarterly, 36,* 459–484.

Cooper-Thomas, H., & Anderson, N. (2002). Newcomer adjustment: The relationship between organizational socialization tactics, information acquisition and attitudes. *Journal of Occupational and Organizational Psychology, 75,* 423–437.

Daft, R. D., & Lengel, R. H. (1986). Organizational information requirements, media richness and structural design. *Management Science, 32,* 554–571.

Dennis, A. R., Fuller, R. M., & Valacich, J. S. (2008). Media, tasks, and communication processes: A theory of media synchronicity. *MIS Quarterly, 32,* 575–600.

Delobbe, N., Cooper-Thomas, H. D., & De Hoe, R. (2016). A new look at the psychological contract during organizational socialization: The role of newcomers' obligations at entry. *Journal of Organizational Behavior, 37,* 845–867.

DiRenzo, M. S., Linnehan, F., Shao, P., & Rosenberg, W. L. (2010). A moderated mediation model of e-mentoring. *Journal of Vocational Behavior, 76,* 292–305.

Driskell, J. E., Radtke, P. H., & Salas, E. (2003). Virtual teams: Effects of technological mediation on team performance. *Group Dynamics: Theory, Research, and Practice, 7,* 297–323.

Dulebohn, J. H., & Hoch, J. E. (2017). Virtual teams in organizations. *Human Resource Management Review.* Advance online publication. doi: http://dx.doi.org/10.1016/j.hrmr.2016.12.004

Espinosa, J. A., Cummings, J. N., Wilson, J. M., & Pearce, B. M. (2003). Team boundary issues across multiple global firms. *Journal of Management Information Systems, 19,* 157–190.

Fang, R., Duffy, M. K., & Shaw, J. D. (2011). The organizational socialization process: Review and development of a social capital model. *Journal of Management, 37,* 127–152.

Feldman, D. C. (1989). Socialization, resocialization, and training: Reframing the research agenda. In I. L. Goldstein (Ed.), *Training and development in organizations* (pp. 376–416). San Francisco: Jossey-Bass.

Flanagin, A. J., & Waldeck, J. H. (2004). Technology use and organizational newcomer socialization. *Journal of Business Communication, 41,* 137–165.

Fisher, C. D. (1986). Organizational socialization: An integrative review. In K. M. Rowland & G. R. Ferris (Eds.), *Research in personnel and human resources management* (vol. 4), 101–145. Greenwich, CT: JAI Press.

Foster, M. K., Abbey, A., Callow, M. A., Zu, X., & Wilbon, A. D. (2015). Rethinking virtuality and its impact on teams. *Small Group Research, 46,* 267–299.

Gephart, R. P. (2002). Introduction to the brave new workplace: organizational behavior in the electronic age. *Journal of Organizational Behavior, 23*, 327–344.

Gibson, C., & Gibbs, J. L. (2006). Unpacking the concept of virtuality: The effect of geographic dispersion, electronic dependence, dynamic structure, and national diversity on team innovation. *Administrative Science Quarterly, 51*, 451–495.

Gomersall, E. R., & Myers, M. S. (1966). Breakthrough in on-the-job training. *Harvard Business Review*, 44, 62–72.

Grant, A. M., & Ashford, S. J. (2008). The dynamics of proactivity at work. *Research in Organizational Behavior, 28*, 3–34.

Griffith, T. L., & Neale, M. A. (1991). Traditional, hybrid, and virtual teams: from nascent knowledge to transactive memory. *Research in Organizational Behavior, 23*, 379–421.

Gruman, J. A., Saks, A. M., & Zweig, D. I. (2006). Organizational socialization tactics and newcomer proactive behaviors: An integrative study. *Journal of Vocational Behavior, 69*, 90–104.

Hamilton, B. A., & Scandura, T. A. (2003). E-mentoring: Implications for organizational learning and development in a wired world. *Organizational Dynamics, 31*, 388–402.

Johnson, S. K., Bettenhausen, K., & Gibbons, E. (2009). Realities of working in virtual teams: Affective and attitudinal outcomes of using computer-mediated communication. *Small Group Research, 40*, 623–649.

Jokisaari, M., & Nurmi, J-E. (2013). Getting the right connections? The consequences and antecedents of social networks in newcomer socialization. In C. R. Wanberg (Ed.), *The Oxford handbook of organizational socialization* (pp. 78–96). New York: Oxford University Press.

Jones, G. R. (1986). Socialization tactics, self-efficacy, and newcomers' adjustments to organizations. *Academy of Management Journal, 29*, 262–279.

Katz, R. (1980). Time and work: Toward an integrative perspective. In B. Staw & L. L. Cummings (Eds.), *Research in organizational behavior* (vol. 2, pp. 81–127). Greenwich CT: JAI Press.

Kirkman, B. L., & Mathieu, J. E. (2005). The dimensions and antecedents of team virtuality. *Journal of Management, 31*, 700–718.

Kirkman, B., Rosen, B., Gibson, C. B., Tesluk, P. E., & McPherson, S. O. (2002). Five challenges to virtual team success: Lessons from Sabre, Inc. *Academy of Management Executive, 16*, 67–79.

Klein, H. J., Fan, J., & Preacher, K. J. (2006). The effects of early socialization experiences on content mastery and outcomes: A mediational approach. *Journal of Vocational Behavior, 68*, 96–115.

Klein, H. J., & Heuser, A. E. (2008). The learning of socialization content: A framework for researching orientating practices. *Research in Personnel and Human Resources Management, 27*, 279–336.

Klein, H. J., & Weaver, N. A. (2000). The effectiveness of an organizational-level orientation training program in the socialization of new hires. *Personnel Psychology, 53*, 47–66.

Korte, R. (2010). "First get to know them": A relational view of organizational socialization. *Human Resource Development International, 13*, 27–43.

Korte, R., & Lin, S. (2013). Getting on board: Organizational socialization and the contribution of social capital. *Human Relations, 66*, 407–428.

Lapointe, E., Vandenberghe C., & Boudrais, J-S. (2014). Organizational socialization tactics and newcomer adjustment: The mediating role of role clarity and affect-based trust relationships. *Journal of Occupational and Organizational Psychology, 87,* 599–624,

Louis, M. R., Posner, B. Z., & Powell, G. N. (1983). The availability and helpfulness of socialization practices. *Personnel Psychology, 36,* 857–866.

Marcinkus Murphy, W. (2011). From e-mentoring to blended mentoring: Increasing students' developmental initiation and mentors' satisfaction. *Academy of Management Learning and Education, 10,* 606–622.

Marler, J. H. (2009). Making human resources strategic by going to the Net: Reality or myth? *The International Journal of Human Resource Management, 20,* 515–527.

Marler, J. H., & Fisher, S. L. (2013). An evidence-based review of e-HRM and strategic human resource management. *Human Resource Management Review, 23,* 18–36.

Marlow, S. L., Lacerenza, C. N., & Salas, E. (2017). Communication in virtual teams: A conceptual framework and research agenda. *Human Resource Management Review, 27,* 575–589.

Maynard, M. T., & Gilson, L. L. (2014). The role of shared mental model development in understanding virtual team effectiveness. *Group & Organization Management, 39,* 3–32.

Morrison, E. W. (1993a). Newcomer information seeking: Exploring types, modes, sources, and outcomes. *Academy of Management Journal, 36,* 557–589.

Morrison, E. W. (1993b). Longitudinal study of the effects of information seeking on newcomer socialization. *Journal of Applied Psychology, 78,* 173–183.

Morrison, E. W. (2002). Newcomers' relationships: The role of social network ties during socialization. *Academy of Management Journal, 45,* 1149–1160.

Nahapiet, J., & Ghoshal, S. (1998). Social capital, intellectual capital, and the organizational advantage. *Academy of Management Review, 23,* 242–266.

Nelson, D. L., & Quick, J. C. (1991). Social support and newcomer adjustment in organizations: Attachment theory at work? *Journal of Organizational Behavior, 12,* 543–554.

Orlikowski, W. J., & Scott, S. V. (2008). Sociomateriality: Challenging the separation of technology, work, and organization. *The Academy of Management Annals, 2,* 433–474.

Ostroff, C., & Kozlowski, S. W. J. (1992). Organizational socialization as a learning process: The role of information acquisition. *Personnel Psychology, 45*(4), 849–874

Ostroff, C., & Kozlowski, S. W. J. (1993). The role of mentoring in the information gathering processes of newcomers during early organizational socialization. *Journal of Vocational Behavior, 42,* 170–183.

Powell, A., Piccoli, G., & Ives, B. (2004). Virtual teams: A review of current literature and directions for future research. *The DATA BASE for Advances in Information Systems, 35,* 6–23.

Reichers, A. E. (1987). An interactionist perspective on newcomer socialization rates. *Academy of Management Review, 12,* 278–287.

Rollag, K., Parise, S., & Cross, R. (2005). Getting new hires up to speed quickly. *MIT Sloan Management Review, 46,* 35–41.

Saks, A. M. (1994a). A psychological process investigation for the effects of recruitment source and organization information on job survival. *Journal of Organizational Behavior, 15,* 225–244.

Saks, A. M. (1994b). Moderating effects of self-efficacy for the relationship between training method and anxiety and stress reactions of newcomers. *Journal of Organizational Behavior, 15,* 639–654.

Saks, A. M. (1995). Longitudinal field investigation of the moderating and mediating effects of self-efficacy on the relationship between training and newcomer adjustment. *Journal of Applied Psychology, 80,* 211–225.

Saks, A. M. (1996). The relationship between the amount and helpfulness of entry training and work outcomes. *Human Relations, 49,* 429–451.

Saks, A. M., & Ashforth, B. E. (1997). Organizational socialization: Making sense of the past and present as a prologue for the future. *Journal of Vocational Behavior, 51,* 234–279.

Saks, A. M., & Gruman, J. A. (2011). Organizational socialization and positive organizational behavior: Implications for theory, research and practice. *Canadian Journal of Administrative Science, 28,* 4–16.

Saks, A. M. & Gruman, J. A. (2012). Getting newcomers on board: A review of socialization practices and introduction to socialization resources theory. In C. Wanberg (Ed.), *The Oxford handbook of organizational socialization* (pp. 27 – 55). New York: Oxford University Press.

Saks, A, M. & Gruman, J. A. (2014). Making organizations more effective through organizational socialization. *Journal of Organizational Effectiveness: People and Performance, 1,* 261–280.

Saks, A. M., Uggerslev, K. L., & Fassina, N. E. (2007). Socialization tactics and newcomer adjustment: A meta-analytic review and test of a model. *Journal of Vocational Behavior, 70,* 413–446.

Salas, E., & Cannon-Bowers, J. A. (2001). The science of training: A decade of progress. *Annual review of Psychology, 52,* 471–499.

Salas, E., DeRouin, R. E., & Littrell, L. N. (2005). Research-based guidelines for designing distance learning. In H. G. Gueutal & D. L. Stone (Eds.), *The brave new world of eHR* (pp. 104–137). San Francisco, CA: Jossey-Bass.

Salas, E., Rozell, D., Mullen, B., & Driskell, J. E. (1999). The effect of team building on performance: An integration. *Small Group Research, 30,* 309–329.

Schalk, R., Timmerman, V., & van den Heuvel, S. (2013). How strategic considerations influence decision making on e-HRM applications. *Human Resource Management Review, 23,* 84–92.

Seibert, S. E., Kraimer, M. L., & Liden, R. C. (2001). A social capital theory of career success. *Academy of Management Journal, 44,* 219–237.

Stone, D. L., & Dulebohn, J. H. (2013). Emerging issues in theory and research on electronic human resource management (eHR). *Human Resource Management Review, 23,* 1–5.

Stone, D. L., & Lukaszewski, K. M. (2009). An expanded model of the factors affecting the acceptance and effectiveness of electronic human resource management systems. *Human Resource Management Review, 19,* 134–143.

Stone, D. L., Stone-Romero, E. F., & Lukaszewski, K. (2006). Factors affecting the acceptance and effectiveness of electronic human resource management systems. *Human Resource Management Review, 16,* 229–244.

Sylva, H., & Mol, S. T. (2009). E-recruitment: A study into applicant perceptions of an online application system. *International Journal of Selection and Assessment, 17(3),* 311–323.

Thoits, P. A. (2011). Mechanisms linking social ties and support to physical and mental health. *Journal of Health and Social Behavior, 52,* 145–161.

Van Maanen, J. (1976). Breaking in: Socialization to work. In R. Dubin (Ed.), *Handbook of work, organization, and society* (pp. 67–130). Chicago: Rand McNally.

Van Maanen, J., & Schein, E. H. (1979). Toward a theory of organizational socialization, In B. M Staw (Ed.), *Research in organizational behaviour*, (Vol. 1, pp. 209–264). Greenwich, CT: JAI Press.

Wanberg, C. R., & Kammeyer-Mueller, J. D. (2000). Predictors and outcomes of proactivity in the socialization process. *Journal of Applied Psychology, 85*(3). 373–385.

Wanous, J. P., & Reichers, A. E. (2000). New employee orientation programs. *Human Resource Management Review, 10,* 435–451.

Watkins, M. D. (2013, June 27). Making virtual teams work: Ten basic principles. *Harvard Business Review*. Retrieved from https://hbr.org/2013/06/making-virtual-teams-work-ten

Watson, A. M., Thompson, L. F., Rudolph, J. V., Whelan, T. J., Behrend, T. S., & Gissel, A. L. (2013). When big brother is watching: goal orientation shapes reactions to electronic monitoring during online training. *Journal of Applied Psychology, 98,* 642–657.

Welsh, E. T., Wanberg, C. R., Brown, K. G., & Simmering, M. J. (2003). E-learning: Emerging uses, empirical results and future directions. *International Journal of Training and Development, 7,* 245–258.

Wesson, M. J. & Gogus, C. I. (2005). Shaking hands with a computer: An examination of two methods of organizational newcomer orientation. *Journal of Applied Psychology, 90,* 1018–1026.

Yanson, R., & Johnson, R. D. (2016). An empirical examination of e-learning design: The role of trainee socialization and complexity in short term training. *Computers & Education, 101,* 43–54.

CHAPTER 6

A REVIEW OF DESIGN CONSIDERATIONS IN E-LEARNING

Richard D. Johnson and Jason G. Randall

ABSTRACT

Technology, especially technology that supports e-learning, has become central to organizations' training and development strategies. As such, a vast research literature has emerged in fields as diverse as education, human resources, information systems, I/O psychology, and management. Each of these fields has investigated e-learning from a number of different technology, design, motivation, and pedagogical perspectives that can inform organizations on how to most effectively design e-learning programs. Despite this vast literature, the findings from these multiple domains are not often integrated, and it is not always clear what steps organizations can undertake to improve e-learning outcomes.

In 2005, Salas, DeRouin, & Littrell (2005) published a review of e-learning design considerations and made a number of recommendations for e-learning design. Since that time though, technology has dramatically changed, and our knowledge of training and learning has evolved. Therefore, our goal in this chapter is to revisit and expand on previous design recommendations by investigating several technology

The Brave New World of eHRM 2.0, pages 141–188.
Copyright © 2018 by Information Age Publishing
141

and design considerations such as learner control, organization support, trainee interaction, and interface design. In addition, we review the research on how technology design can affect psychological learning processes and trainee engagement. The results of this review suggest that despite the dramatic advances in technology and the continued focus on e-learning, much more research is needed to understand the linkage between design considerations, learning processes, and learning outcomes.

Technology has become central to organizations' training and development strategy, especially technology that supports e-learning. Indeed, as of 2015, roughly half of the training conducted in the United States was delivered through a technology-based method, with over 25% of industry training occurring in an autonomous (i.e., not instructor-led) online environment (American Society for Training and Development, 2015). Estimates also indicate that over $50 billion is spent annually on e-learning (Piccioli, 2014). Despite the central role that technology plays in training and development, there has also been a great deal of debate surrounding its effectiveness, especially as it relates to learning outcomes. For example, e-learning has been argued to reduce training costs and time (Salas et al., 2005; Welsh, Wanberg, Brown, & Simmering, 2003) and to provide greater customization, control, and flexibility over learning processes (Kraiger, 2003; Long, Dubois, & Faley, 2009). However, others argue that e-learning is less effective than face-to-face (FTF) training because it isolates trainees, reduces communication, and decreases trainee satisfaction (Garrison & Arbaugh, 2007; Welsh et al., 2003). Ultimately, meta-analytic research on the efficacy of web-based versus classroom instruction found that web-based training can be as effective as FTF training when effectively designed (Sitzmann, Kraiger, Stewart, & Wisher, 2006). Therefore, in order to capitalize on the advantages of e-learning and avoid its disadvantages, considerable forethought has to be devoted to how online training programs are designed and delivered. Unfortunately, the pertinent design considerations in e-learning and their implications for learning outcomes are not yet well understood (Alavi & Leidner, 2001; Kraiger & Jerden, 2007). That is, training designers are faced with a wide array of design choices when developing online training initiatives (e.g., graphics options, technological and organizational supports, degrees of feedback and interaction, allowances for learner control, etc.) that all have the potential to influence the learning process and training outcomes. Unfortunately, although recent research in the e-learning and training fields is beginning to investigate such design issues, to our knowledge, there has not been a systematic review specifically focusing on design considerations to guide design decisions. Therefore, increased reliance on e-learning, because of its ease and advantages, may have, in some cases, outpaced the science of e-learning, with many such programs being reduced to an electronic version of traditional FTF training or, alternatively, a flashy user interface (e.g. display screens) with features that distract from or even impede the learning process.

Therefore, a key question facing organizations is how to effectively design e-learning initiatives that maximize trainee outcomes, yet still maintains cost-effectiveness. To address this question, a number of design factors must be considered. These factors include the appropriateness of training content for e-learning, how to best support psychological learning processes through design, the role of interface design, how to improve trainee engagement, how to support trainee interaction, how to incorporate learner control, and how to most effectively provide organizational support. Although some recommendations have been made by researchers (e.g. Salas et al., 2005), and a number of studies have been undertaken, there has yet to be a systematic review of the research on these important e-learning design considerations.

The most recent comprehensive review of design considerations in e-learning, by Salas et al. (2005), generated a valuable set of guidelines for e-learning design. However, these recommendations are now more than a decade old. Given the rapid pace of technological innovation in training design and the rise in popularity of e-learning, we attempt to update Salas et al.'s (2005) recommendations based upon research conducted since that review. In addition, we note where the research supports their conclusions, where there are differences between the recommendations and extant research, and where research findings suggest the need for additional guidelines. Such an update is necessary not just because of the gap in time since Salas et al.'s (2005) review, but more importantly, because e-learning programs that are not well-designed threaten training effectiveness by interfering with cognitive learning and harming other training outcomes such as reactions, engagement, and transfer.

Thus, the goal of this paper is to review the research and recommendations on e-learning design and inform scholars and designers on the course design factors that can affect e-learning outcomes. As with previous research in this area, we focus less on technology differences between classroom instruction and online instruction, and instead focus on how technology and other design features work together to improve e-learning outcomes. The paper is organized as follows. First, we briefly discuss and define e-learning and discuss the various literature reviews on the topic. Next, we organize the research on e-learning design considerations into seven broad streams and discuss the major research findings associated with each. For each stream, we finish with a brief discussion of important research questions that still need to be addressed. After this, we discuss five new technologies that can affect e-learning design and discuss how future research can address how to best utilize these technologies in e-learning.

DEFINITION OF E-LEARNING AND REVIEWS OF EFFECTIVENESS OF E-LEARNING

Defining e-Learning

Before discussing the factors that contribute to the effective design of e-learning initiatives, it is important to define precisely what is meant by e-learning. For example, scholars have used the following terms to describe e-learning: "distance learning," "Virtual Learning Environments," "Technology Mediated Learning," "online learning," "web-based training," and "computer-based instruction" (Alavi & Leidner, 2001; Gupta & Bostrom, 2009; Piccoli, Ahmad, & Ives, 2001; Welsh et al., 2003). In terms of actual definitions, e-learning has been defined as "training or educational initiatives which provide learning material in online repositories, where course interaction and communication and course delivery are technology mediated" (Johnson, Hornik, & Salas, 2008, p. 356). Alavi and Leidner (2001) define e-learning as "an environment in which the learner's interactions with learning materials, peers, and/or instructor are mediated through advanced information technology" (p. 2), a definition similar to Johnson et al.

Welsh et al. (2003) highlight the importance of computer networks in their definition, defining e-learning as "the use of computer network technology, primarily over an intranet or through the Internet, to deliver information and instruction to individuals" (Welsh et al., 2003, p. 246). Others though have taken a different approach. For example, Salas et al. note that the American Society for Training and Development (ASTD) defined distance learning (a term used synonymously with e-learning) as an "educational situation in which the instructor and student are separated by time, location, or both" (Salas et al., 2005, p. 106). Finally, Piccoli, Ahmed, and Ives (2001) note that e-learning environments differ from traditional classroom environments based upon time, place, and technology.

Together, these definitions highlight several key defining characteristics of e-learning. These are time, place, technology, and purpose. Unlike the traditional classroom, e-learning is often asynchronous and frequently occurs at a distance. That is, instructors and trainees often do not meet at the same time or same place. Second, all interactions between trainees and with the instructor are mediated via technology. Third, all course content is accessed and consumed via technology. This creates an additional barrier to communication and use with which the trainee has to contend, altering and potentially weakening the social context within which the trainees will learn (Johnson et al., 2008). In addition, technology can potentially enable increased and more diverse communications than a traditional classroom. However, this same benefit can bring with it a potential cost; that is, the more messages received, the harder it may be for individuals to process them effectively, and the reduced salience that each message may have for the trainee. Each of these defining characteristics of e-learning informs successful e-learning design—which is the focus of the current review. Specifically, in this paper, we refer to e-learning design as the selection of instructional techniques, training methods, and learning tools and technology that will be harnessed to help trainees achieve desired learning objectives (Goldstein & Ford, 2002).

e-Learning Outcomes

The next important consideration in e-learning is defining success. Not surprisingly, e-learning researchers typically operationalize success similar to how it is operationalized in the training literature: affective reactions (e.g. satisfaction &

utility judgments) to the training, actual training performance or knowledge gain, and training transfer (Kirkpatrick, 1976). However, some differences exist in the importance of certain outcomes in e-learning relative to traditional training, and how frequently different outcomes are evaluated in e-learning. The primary difference in outcome importance centers on affective reactions.

Researchers have suggested satisfaction and utility judgments are lower order factors reflective of overall satisfaction (Brown, 2005). As such, each has been found to affect e-learning outcomes, but in unique ways. Within the e-learning context, satisfaction is often assessed as a trainee's positive or negative reaction to the training or the environment (Johnson et al., 2008). Satisfaction is particularly important in e-learning environments because it can affect intentions to take more e-learning courses (Carswell & Venkatesh, 2002), and can influence learning through the mediating role of engagement (Brown, 2005; Orvis, Fisher, & Wasserman, 2009). In contrast to satisfaction, rather than focusing on the course and the environment itself, utility judgments focus on the value of the training itself and the extent to which it provides individuals with relevant knowledge and skills. Utility judgments have been shown to predict training transfer as well as, if not better than actual learning (Alliger, Tannenbaum, Bennett Jr., Traver, & Shotland, 1997; Sitzmann, Brown, Casper, Ely, & Zimmerman, 2008). Thus, affective reactions, including satisfaction and utility judgments appear to be particularly important when defining successful e-learning.

Beyond trainee reactions, e-learning success has also been assessed at deeper levels of learning, including knowledge gained, skills learned, and behavioral transfer. As noted by Kraiger, Ford and Salas (1993) trainees can have improved cognitive outcomes, such as improved knowledge, mental models, or learning strategies (e.g. Kraiger & Jerden, 2007; Orvis et al., 2009). Meta-analytic evidence suggests e-learning is equally effective to traditional classroom-based instruction when training is evaluated using procedural (skill-based) knowledge or reactions as outcomes, but e-learning showed a slight advantage when declarative (factual) knowledge was assessed (Sitzmann et al., 2006). This advantage was attributed to the increased likelihood that e-learning programs would use multiple instructional methods and encourage active participation through more required practice rather than to the technology itself. In addition, training can lead to improved skills and expertise, where learned behaviors become quicker and more fluid, and trainees become more flexible and adaptable (e.g.Hughes et al., 2013; Keith & Frese, 2005). Additionally, more behavioral, on-the-job outcomes such as training transfer, including adaptive transfer—the flexible application of learned knowledge or skill into a new context—have also been evaluated as important e-learning outcomes (Bell & Kozlowski, 2008; Carolan, Hutchins, Wickens, & Cumming, 2014; Keith & Frese, 2008). Therefore, e-learning success should extend beyond affective reactions to cognitive and skill-based learning, and transfer of learning.

Although other outcomes have been studied in training, including motivational indicators such as self-efficacy, and more distal outcomes such as productivity or organizational performance, they have not often been studied in the e-learning context (Johnson & Brown, 2017). In our review, our goal is to attempt to highlight the projected influence of design features on as many of these outcomes as the length permits.

Existing e-Learning Reviews

Although a number of different reviews have been undertaken in the area of e-learning, none has yet to explicitly focus on key design issues in e-learning. For example, Welsh et al. (2003) conducted a literature review and focused on how e-leaning outcomes compared to traditional training outcomes, highlighting the value of e-learning, along with its risks. In addition, Sitzmann et al. (2006) conducted a meta-analysis on the difference in effectiveness of web-based learning compared to FTF, or classroom, instruction. The results of this meta-analysis found that web-based instruction can be as effective as FTF instruction, and that technology is not the reason for these differences. Instead, the differences in outcomes could be explained by pedagogical design differences and the fit between the technology and class design.

Other e-learning research has focused on university use of e-learning and blended learning in the business disciplines, the types of topics investigated by researchers, and the preferred publication outlets (Arbaugh, 2010; Arbaugh, Desai, Rau, & Sridhar, 2010). In 2012, Brown, Charlier, and Pierotti (2012) investigated the research on the use of e-learning at work, specifically focusing on those studies published within the Industrial and Organizational Psychology discipline. They organized their findings around three broad themes: learner motivation, reactions to training, and training effectiveness. Each of the above studies approaches e-learning through the lens of employee training, focusing on learning outcomes and inputs such as learner motivation to review the research in the field. Finally, Towler and Mitchell (2015) reviewed research on the role of the trainer/ instructor in facilitating e-learning.

Other reviews, though, have focused more on technology issues within e-learning. For example, Brown and Charlier (2013) reviewed the literature to create a model of the factors that affect the use of e-learning and discuss how organizations can increase its use. In addition, Wan, Fang, and Neufeld (2007) utilized the Piccoli et al. (2001) framework to review the research on Technology Mediated Learning (TML), and Gurtner (2015) conducted a review of the research on Virtual Learning Environments (VLE). Both of these reviews, however, only dealt with a subset of the literature that explicitly focused on either TML or VLE research rather than considering the whole scope of e-learning research.

Two reviews have partially focused on some e-learning design issues. First, in their recent review, Johnson and Brown (2017) drew on several models of e-learning effectiveness and reviewed research from management, psychology, education, and information systems that focused on adult learners' use of e-learning. Although their goal was not specifically geared toward an investigation of design issues, their review did touch on several design related issues including trainee interaction, learner control, and pedagogical issues in e-learning. Second, one of the earliest, and most influential, reviews of e-learning by Salas et al. (2005) made a number of recommendations based on a review of the literature of distance education and offered a set of guidelines to industry in regards to how to most effectively design e-learning. Although this study provided a number of important recommendations to both researchers and practitioners, at the time of its publication, the research on distance learning was still fairly new. Since this review was published in 2005, there have been many advancements made in both technology and research, so our review will account for these changes and evaluate the extent to which the recommendations made by Salas et al. (2005) still hold true today.

DESIGN CONSIDERATIONS IN E-LEARNING

At the heart of Salas et al.'s (2005) recommendations is the idea of e-learning design. In their recommendations, the authors focus on a number of important design issues. These include how technology limitations may affect the types of content appropriate for e-learning and how technology and training design can affect learning processes, trainee engagement, and learning outcomes. Their chapter further begins to look at how the design of the user interface (e.g., how the trainee will interact with the e-learning system) may play a role in how trainees respond to e-learning and how they learn. Finally, they conclude with a discussion of how to enhance e-learning success by placing more control in the hands of trainees and how organizations can help support trainees in exercising this control. In the following sections, we review the extant research, shaping our discussion around the questions and guidelines developed by Salas et al. (2005). At the core of this review is the idea that the most successful e-learning initiatives will exhibit a strong fit between trainee needs, learning content, course pedagogy and technology.

When is e-Learning Appropriate?

One of the first questions facing organizations is whether there are times where e-learning is not an effective way to deliver some types of training. The basic assumption behind this is that no design considerations may overcome the shortcomings of e-learning for specific types of training. For example, Salas et al. (2005) made two recommendations in regards to the use of e-learning in organizations. These were:

- "Only provide distance learning when you are sure it meets the organization's needs." (p. 107)

- "Provide distance learning for hard skill training but supplement it with other forms of training for soft skill training and for training on such abstract topics as workplace ethics" (p. 120)

Surprisingly, very little research has systematically investigated whether certain types of training may be more appropriate for e-learning than for FTF learning. For example, Welsh et al. (2003) in their interviews with subject matter experts suggested that e-learning may be less appropriate for soft skill acquisition in areas such as leadership and teamwork development. Additional empirical studies also suggest that e-learning may present challenges for complex training (Granger & Levine, 2010; Yanson & Johnson, 2016). Research has also found that university courses with more algorithmic paradigms (e.g., chemistry) had higher e-learning outcomes than courses with lower algorithmic paradigms (e.g., sociology) (Hornik, Saunders, Li, Moskal, & Dzuiban, 2008).

There are several potential reasons that researchers have argued that certain types of training are less appropriate for e-learning than FTF learning. First, the technology itself can add a layer of complexity to the training, which can take cognitive resources away from the training itself (Hillman, Willis, & Gunawardena, 1994). For topics that are already more complex, a technology mediated learning context can reduce the cognitive resources available to learners (Yanson & Johnson, 2016). Second, technology often lacks the richness and ability to convey non-verbal communication cues and other non-structured information needed for more complex and abstract topics (Salas et al., 2005; Welsh et al., 2003). Early theories on the use of media argued that certain types of technology are less rich in their ability to convey contextual and non-verbal communication cues (Daft & Lengel, 1986). Therefore, some have argued that the messages received in e-learning may be less rich and less salient to those involved due to the communications barrier and lack of connections (Johnson et al., 2008).

At the same time, though, research has found that when organizations provide higher levels of support to trainees, e-learning outcomes are improved (Sawang, Newton, & Jamieson, 2013). This suggests that, contrary to the recommendations of Salas et al. (2005), the relationship between type of content and outcomes may be more complex than previously thought. It also suggests that rather than researchers questioning the appropriateness of certain types of training for e-learning, they should focus instead on how to best deploy technology to maximize the creation of a shared learning environment. The creation of a shared and collaborative learning environment is thought to be central to effective training and learning both in FTF learning as well as in e-learning (Leidner & Jarvenpaa, 1995; Vygotsky, 1978). Although Media Richness Theory (Daft & Lengel, 1986) suggests that a technology mediated environment will lack the richness necessary for the support of a shared learning environment, other research suggests that communications in a technology mediated environment can support rich connections and communications necessary for a shared learning environment (Gunawardena & Zittle, 1997; Zack & McKinney, 1995).

Moreover, in a meta-analysis comparing the effectiveness of e-learning to more traditional classroom-based instruction, Sitzmann et al. (2006) evaluated whether technology enhances learning, as has been argued by others (Goldstein & Ford, 2002; Welsh et al., 2003). The totality of the empirical evidence they analyzed suggested e-learning was comparable to classroom-based instruction when satisfaction or procedural "how-to" knowledge was assessed, and they found a slight advantage for e-learning on declarative (factual) knowledge (Sitzmann et al., 2006). Although this might suggest e-learning is better than FTF instruction when used to primarily present facts and principles to be memorized, the authors dug deeper to determine if there were technology or design characteristics that might account for this difference in declarative knowledge outcomes. Interestingly, they found that e-learning tended to employ multiple instructional techniques and allowed for more practice than FTF training. In addition, they found that e-learning courses that did not provide learner control, practice, and feedback to learners actually demonstrated lower declarative knowledge levels than learners in a traditional classroom setting. Thus, their conclusion was that the technology medium itself may not drive differences in training outcomes, but instead, such differences might be attributed to design characteristics specifically (e.g., learner control, opportunities for practice, feedback, varied instructional methods).

In summary, there has been limited work on the appropriateness of e-learning for different types of training content, and the results of existing studies are mixed with respect to Salas et al.'s recommendations. Thus, we believe that rather than focusing on the types of courses best suited to e-learning, there is value in understanding how key design considerations can encourage the development of a shared learning environment and shared context through improving engagement, interaction, and connections between trainees. In conclusion, with respect to the question, "When is e-learning appropriate?" very little research has been undertaken to specifically address this issue. However, we also think that as technology has advanced and more is known about electronic communication, technology design, and deployment of e-learning, the question of when is e-learning appropriate is more appropriately updated to, "How can design factors improve e-learning processes and outcomes?" In the following sections, we address this question by focusing on the extant e-learning design research.

Psychological Learning Processes

The second section of design considerations in our paper centers on the criticality of designing e-learning with psychological learning processes in mind. Psychological learning processes are learning processes that revolve around a learner's cognitive and information processing, their metacognitive processes, their motivation, and their interest in the course material (Alavi & Leidner, 2001; Johnson & Brown, 2017). Specifically, Alavi and Leidner (2001, p. 4) define cognitive learning processes as "states within the learner that are involved in learning. They include the learner's cognitive and information processing activities, motivation, interest, and cognitive structures (memory)." Salas et al. (2005) note the importance of one aspect of the psychological learning processes, cognitive processes. Specifically they recommend that designers:

- Take into consideration human cognitive processes when designing distance learning programs.

With respect to cognitive processes, Clark and Mayer (2003) identify four steps for successful information processing and comprehension. These steps include:

1. recognition of critical information,
2. clearing of working memory in order to rehearse the new information,
3. consolidation of information and integration with existing knowledge through rehearsal, and
4. recall of information once stored in long-term memory.

One of the challenges facing e-learners is that the technology mediation of communication and learning adds a layer of complexity that can negatively influence cognitive processes. For example, learners will need to allocate a portion of their cognitive resources to communicating and navigating the technology mediated environment that may have fewer learning cues and connections than a traditional classroom (Dennis, Fuller, & Valacich, 2008; Hillman et al., 1994).

Based upon these cognitive learning processes, researchers have recommended presenting critical information as a list of learning objectives and removing irrelevant or distracting information and visuals to improve recognition of critical information (Mayer, 2008; Salas et al., 2005). Similarly, presenting information using visuals, audio, text and activities that reinforce important points assist in processes of rehearsal, thereby increasing the likelihood of learning and long-term storage (Mayer, 2008). Finally, the use of job-relevant examples in the training assist in processes of integration and facilitate future retrieval when situational cues on the job ignite recall of the previously learned information and can improve engagement (Orvis et al., 2009; Randall, 2015; Salas & Cannon-Bowers, 2000). Reducing extraneous material, highlighting essential material, reducing redundancy, and displaying temporal and spatial contiguity of words and graphics can also help reduce cognitive load and processing (Mayer, 2008). Research also suggests that segmenting training into smaller sections, or "chunks" can reduce cognitive overload, allowing learners to focus on shorter, more focused content before moving on to other material (Sweller, 1988; van Merrienboer & Sweller, 2005; Yanson & Johnson, 2016). Third, using multiple media methods (e.g., words *and* pictures) and presenting new information in a more conversational (i.e., less formal) manner helps individuals make sense of the incoming material and integrate it with existing knowledge (Mayer, 2008; Salas et al., 2005).

A few studies have begun to investigate how technology and design considerations surrounding its use can potentially impact e-learning outcomes. For example, research has found that when trainees find that the technology capabilities are not matched to their learning style, they communicated less, felt less part of a learning community, were less satisfied with the course, and had lower learning outcomes (Hornik, Johnson, & Wu, 2007). In addition, Yanson and Johnson (2016) found that designing an initial FTF socialization experience into an online course before the training increased trainee motivation to learn and was positively related to course performance.

However, more research directly demonstrating how to apply sound training principles through technology is needed. Some specific areas include differentiating between short and long-term learning goals, accounting for differences between novice versus expert learners, and acknowledging the limits of cognitive resources.

First, training researchers have noted the need to distinguish short-term gains and subjective feelings of success during training from the deeper, more important job-relevant changes in behavior, knowledge, and skills (e.g., training transfer; Bjork, Dunlosky, & Kornell, 2013; Hesketh, 1997; Schmidt & Bjork, 1992). Specifically, to train for cognitive learning and transfer, researchers recommend that training should introduce a level of *desirable difficulty* that encourages exploration and more effortful processing in order to facilitate cognitive learning through processes of rehearsal, integration, and long-term storage (Bjork, 1994; Schmidt & Bjork, 1992). One way to do this is to use tests as learning tools. Advances in technology can help designers to more effectively target training to specific learners within the overall course. For example, content and pace can be adjusted based upon achieved knowledge and skills of trainees rather than being applied to all learners globally. Evidence suggests that testing individuals multiple times on new information can increase learning beyond increased time devoted to personal study or guided instruction (Roediger III & Karpicke, 2006). Therefore, e-learning software can push multiple testing opportunities to students based upon prior performance and experience so that the tests may be used not merely as post-training assessments, but also as learning tools to facilitate knowledge gain and recall (Dunlosky, Rawson, Marsh, Nathan, & Willingham, 2013; Randall & Villado, 2017; Schmidt & Bjork, 1992). However, research is needed to assess how this will affect trainee reactions and different types of learning outcomes before specific recommendations can be made.

Second, research shows that novices and experts learn differently and have different needs (Beier, Villado, & Randall, 2017). Those with prior knowledge can learn similar content more quickly than those with low or no prior knowledge (Beilock, Bertenthal, Hoerger, & Carr, 2008; Smith, Ford, & Kozlowski, 1997). Existing expertise provides a pre-established framework to build upon in order to integrate new knowledge. Just as computer adaptive testing can improve selection efficiency (Alkhadher, Anderson, & Clarke, 1994), it may be possible to utilize software to help create an adaptive learning environment for learners. No longer would all learners have to complete the same training and content; instead, the software can adapt to learners' knowledge on pre-training assessments and based upon their in-training performance. Pre-training assessments may allow individuals with prior knowledge to filter out irrelevant content (Beier et al., 2017; Mayer, 2008). Technology can also support the use of different features for novices such as additional study aids or providing more guidance for learners lacking prior knowledge or expertise (e.g., increased practice time, additional test items).

Third, understanding and accounting for the limits of individuals' cognitive capacities is important. Our cognitive capacities are finite pool of regulatory resources we use to stay focused and learn (Kanfer & Ackerman, 1989) and can be impacted by external stimuli or other distractions. Distractions are particularly important in e-learning because irrelevant stimuli diverting are just a click away (Randall, 2015; Sitzmann & Ely, 2010). Research has found that increased distractions can impair learning outcomes (Bell & Kozlowski, 2002; Brown, 2001; Fisher & Ford, 1998; Orvis et al., 2009). Therefore, research is needed to determine how e-learning programs and software can be designed to keep learners cognitive resources focused and engaged on learning tasks. For example, as noted above, learning tasks can be broken into moderate- to small-sized modules, and altering training delivery methods (e.g., text, video, audio) decreases the likelihood of information overload leading to distraction (Mayer, 2008). Additionally, training research has demonstrated the importance of taking breaks in order to recharge learners' cognitive capacities (Randall, 2015; Trougakos, Beal, Green, & Weiss, 2008), and to encourage long-term storage and retrieval through distributing practice (Schmidt & Bjork, 1992). The ability for learners to self-regulate their cognitive, affective, and behavioral processes are important to e-learning success (A. M. Schmidt & Ford, 2003; Sitzmann, Bell, Kraiger, & Kanar, 2009; Sitzmann & Ely, 2010; Sitzmann & Johnson, 2012), and it may be possible to design e-learning software to prompt effective self-regulation by encouraging learners to review content, set goals and track progress, utilize learning tools (e.g., note-taking, highlighting, outlines), and take breaks

One final aspect of the psychological learning process is the importance of metacognitive processes and learning motivation. Metacognitive processes are learning processes representing a learner's awareness and regulation of his or her cognitive processes (Flavell, 1979). These include activities such as monitoring learning processes and adjusting behavior when problems occur (Ford, Smith, Weissbein, Gully, & Salas, 1998). Metacognitive processes are particularly important to e-learning, because e-learning is often designed in ways that grants more control to the learner. Learners with more metacognitive skill should be able to better utilize e-learning tools and features that help them assess and adapt to the learning environment. Many of the design strategies associated with improving metacognitive processes are focused on helping learners leverage control and are discussed in later sections. Finally, motivation to learn is another factor that is of critical importance to learning (Colquitt, LePine, & Noe, 2000). Motivation to learn reflects the desire of the trainee to learn the content of the training. Despite the importance of motivation to learn, only limited research has focused on it, as well has how design may improve learner motivation. For example, Johnson and Brown (2017) suggested that the use of online knowledge repositories could increase learners' motivation because they can extend the learning classroom, especially with tools such as video repositories with annotation capabilities.

In summary, designing e-learning without considering how learning occurs at a cognitive level is akin to designing a new car without an understanding of how automobiles operate—you might end up removing the alternator in a mistaken attempt to save space. Understanding mental processes of attention, organization, and integration provide necessary direction for how to design e-learning in a way that supports the learning process. Nonetheless, the call to investigate the particular design features of e-learning that enhance technology-mediated learning processes still stands (Alavi & Leidner, 2001), as the link between specific features and learning is still poorly understood. Thus, future research would benefit from investigating the influence of specific e-learning design features on the processes involved in cognitive learning, especially as it relates to creating desirable difficulties, adapting training as expertise develops, accounting for the limits of attentional capacity, and incorporating metacognition and learning motivation into e-learning. This section has focused on the cognitive aspects of psychological learning processes. The next section focuses more on the broad motivational and engagement aspects of these psychological learning processes.

Trainee Engagement

Salas et al. (2005) also developed recommendations focused on how to most effectively design e-learning to support trainee engagement. Engagement is a multidimensional motivational construct, including affective, behavioral, and cognitive components (Kahn, 1990; Rich, Lepine, & Crawford, 2010). Despite some confusion in construct definition, engagement is often a blanket term covering various motivational processes characterized by effort, attention, and persistence directed towards completion of learning goals (see Noe, Tews, & Dachner, 2010; Sitzmann & Weinhardt, 2015). Engagement is particularly important in e-learning settings that tend to be more discretionary, flexible, and self-directed than traditional face-to-face training (Brown, 2005; Orvis et al., 2009; Randall, 2015; Sitzmann & Ely, 2011). Failing to engage learners can produce individual and organizational problems such as high attrition rates and skill deficiencies (Moshinskie, 2001; Sitzmann & Weinhardt, 2015). For this reason, Salas et al. (2005) made two recommendations regarding trainee engagement:

1. "Include learning games" (p. 114)
2. " Keep learners engaged" (p. 115)

As noted earlier, one of the major challenges in e-learning is its isolating nature, which can lead to higher attrition. Salas et al. (2005) suggest that one of the major benefits of engagement is that it can reduce these high attrition rates. Researchers have suggested that engagement in e-learning can be improved by making training material and objectives job relevant (Orvis et al., 2009; Randall, 2015; Salas & Cannon-Bowers, 2000), and by having learners produce a tangible product (e.g., action plan, computer program) that can later be used on the job (Horton, 2000). Other methods to promote engagement include designing more learner-centric training, encouraging active learner involvement and control, and facilitating social interaction (Noe et al., 2010). As these concepts overlap with trainee interaction and learner control, we address these suggestions in more detail in those sections of this paper. Additionally, Sitzmann and colleagues have made a number of recommendations of process changes that can improve engagement and reduce attrition. For example, e-learning should incorporate self-regulation prompts to make sure trainees are paying attention to what they are learning (Sitzmann & Ely, 2010). In addition, e-learning courses should support learners to set plans for when, where, and how long they will devote to different training segments (Sitzmann & Johnson, 2012), and promoting commitment and self-efficacy among learners (Sitzmann, 2012). Each of these suggestions help focus the learner on the learning tasks and can help them engage more fully in the learning processes.

Associated with this, is the recommendation to include learning games as part of the e-learning experience. Games can support learning by

a. Making training more appealing,
b. Reducing the anxiety of testing,
c. Facilitating more exploratory, self-guided learning, and
d. Offering more substantial amounts of practice by engaging in the training content (Horton, 2002).

Indeed, games can serve as a method to facilitate cognitive learning by enabling learners to practice and apply newly learned material, thereby organizing new information and skills into existing scaffolds of knowledge and experience. From their early appeal and extensive application in military settings, learning games are becoming increasingly common in educational and workplace training as a motivational tool to capitalize on what learners from younger generations find inherently enjoyable and motivating: playing video games (Hamari & Keronen, 2017; Shute, Ventura, Bauer, & Zapata-Rivera, 2009).

Recommendations have been made that the successful use of games will be based on the following principles (Horton, 2002; Salas & Cannon-Bowers, 2000), some of which have received empirical support:

• Incorporate the game directly into the training to reduce distraction

- Use games that increase in difficulty over time so learners remain engaged, but not so difficult that learners give up on the training program altogether (Hamari et al., 2016; Wang & Chen, 2010).
- Games should provide continuous and useful feedback to allow learners to try new things and learn from their mistakes.
- Games should be flexible and adaptable to training context and needs (e.g., new content, new technology, individual vs team) (Vogel, Greenwood-Ericksen, Cannon-Bowers, & Bowers, 2006).

Recent advances in the use of games in organization has brought a number of new design opportunities, specifically around the idea of gamification. Gamification is defined as the introduction of game-like design characteristics to non-game settings through various technological tools (computers, mobile devices, etc.) in order to improve individual engagement and reactions (Deterding, Sicart, Nacke, O'Hara, & Dixon, 2011; Hamari & Koivisto, 2014; Hamari, Koivisto, & Sarsa, 2014). Gamified activities involve the use of game elements, such as accrual of points or badges, tracking progress competitively with scores and leaderboards, communicating with others in an online community, and immersive storylines or virtual reality scenarios, among others, in an effort to produce desired psychological or behavioral outcomes (Hamari et al., 2014). Thus advances in technology supported games broadens the types of design features that can be implemented into online training to include additional game elements not originally considered in other reviews on e-learning.

In e-learning, games can go beyond use as learning tools in a course, and can be embedded into the learning processes and environment of the organization. Gamification can improve participation in training (Snyder & Hartig, 2013), learner motivation (Dominguez et al., 2013), and learning performance (Snyder & Hartig, 2013) and learning (Foster, Sheridan, Irish, & Frost, 2012; McDaniel, Lindgren, & Friskics, 2012). In addition, gamified activities can facilitate engagement and flow by providing opportunities for exploration, practice, and transfer (Chang, Wu, Weng, & Sung, 2012; Davidson, 2008; Hamari et al., 2016; Horton, 2002). In addition, playing games can improve learner's reaction to training, specifically perceived training utility (Hamari & Keronen, 2017).

Despite these benefits, there are risks to gamifying e-learning elements. Some studies have suggested that gamification may improve skills-based outcomes, although having a detriment on cognitive outcomes (Dominguez et al., 2013). Another challenge is that not all trainees will like the perceived competition inherent in some types of gamified activities. Finally, poorly designed gamified activities have been show to actually reduce learner engagement (Foster et al., 2012). Ultimately one of the challenges faced by researchers is that rather than developing theoretically driven models about how we can utilize gamification in e-learning, many studies are simply comparing the relative effectiveness of gamified environments versus non-gamified environments (Johnson & Brown, 2017). Cannon-

Bowers (2006), quoted in Shute et al. (2009, p. 300) summarizes it well, noting that "we are charging head-long into game-based learning without knowing if it works or not. We need studies."

Interface Design

Another important question facing e-learning is how to design the user interface to make e-learning more effective. The user interface is the point at which an individual trainee will interact with the e-learning system. This can includes features such as the display screen, as well as the methods through which the trainee would interact with the software (e.g., a keyboard, mouse, smartphone, tablet, touch screen, etc.). It has long been suggested that poor design can contribute to high attrition rates (Mullich, 2004), but the challenge is that the specific technologies and interface design capabilities continue to evolve. The recommendations made by Salas et al. (2005) illustrate this issue:

- "Enhance the learning experience by including both graphics and text in the presentation of learning topics" (p. 113)
- "Make the e-learning program user friendly." (p. 127)

Consider the recommendation to include both graphics and text in e-learning. In developing this recommendation, Salas et al. draw on training and learning research that suggests that individuals will learn better when text-based material are supplemented with visual, or graphical, representations of content (Clark & Mayer, 2003; Mayer & Anderson, 1991). These recommendations were important to the advancement of the field of e-learning, because designers would often simply take existing training content and place the text online as a means of making e-learning possible. The challenge is that the capabilities of e-learning have long surpassed the use of graphics. For example, organizations are now using video, advanced simulations, and augmented and virtual reality to deliver more effective training. In addition, rather than learners utilizing PCs as they consume learning material, today's e-learning designs must consider that learners may access training material over PCs, laptops, and mobile devices. In addition, they may access learning over many different types of networks. Finally, technological capabilities are advancing at an ever-increasing rate, suggesting that within a few years, organizations will be utilizing technologies not even being considered today. Therefore, to best understand how interface design influences the effectiveness of e-learning, scholars must identify key lasting design principles, as well as the role that advanced tools and technologies have in improving e-learning outcomes. In this section, we start with broader design principles and close with a discussion of some newer technologies and the interface design issues that must be considered for each.

Two major design principles drawn from the information systems literature have informed the design of e-learning interfaces. Specifically, researchers have investigated the role of perceived usefulness (PU) and perceived ease of use (EOU). Perceived usefulness is the extent to which using a system would improve performance, and perceived ease of use is defined as the extent to which using a system is free from effort (Davis, Bagozzi, & Warshaw, 1989). Although some studies have found that PU and EOU are positively related to e-learning outcomes (e.g., affective reactions and performance) (Arbaugh, 2005, 2014; Balakrishnan, 2014; Capece & Campisi, 2013; Galy, Downey, & Johnson, 2011; Johnson et al., 2008), others have found mixed or non-significant results (Arbaugh, 2000b, 2002; Arbaugh & Duray, 2002; Carswell & Venkatesh, 2002). Ultimately, as with broader information systems, PU and EOU are important, but "it is difficult to discern whether or not usefulness and ease of use play an important role or if they are a reflection of the organizational context and the design choices made by trainees and designers." (Johnson & Brown, 2017, p. 14). We discuss a number of these design choices contributing to accessibility and utility that have been investigated by e-learning researchers.

The first of these issues to be discussed is how the interface design can support a rich communication environment. Media synchronicity theory suggests that technologies differ in their ability to

a. Provide immediate feedback,
b. Allow the trainee to rehearse or edit messages,
c. Allow for communication parallelism (e.g. multiple simultaneous conversations),
d. Allow for message reprocessing (e.g. storing of information so that it can be recalled for future use), and
e. Support symbol variety (e.g., voice inflection, "body language") (Dennis et al., 2008).

Research has found that trainees are able to differentiate between the richness of different communication tools (Lan & Sie, 2010), and in general, richer and more interactive learning tools should lead to better learning outcomes and affective reactions (Hsieh & Cho, 2011; Johnson, Gueutal, & Falbe, 2009).

However, organizations cannot assume that providing rich, sophisticated communication tools will automatically lead to stronger outcomes. For example, Alavi, Marakas, and Yoo (2002) found that a less rich communication medium was associated with better training outcomes than a more rich medium. One of the potential reasons for this is that within an e-learning environment it is not simply the application of the most sophisticated tools that will improve outcomes. Instead, research suggests that for e-learning processes and outcomes to be stronger, there should be a fit between the design of the technology and the preferred learning style of the learner (Hornik et al., 2007). Therefore, it may be beneficial for e-learning programs to offer multiple communication tool options (e.g., message boards, chat functionality, video recorded messages) to be flexible to learners' needs.

Two recent trends in technology design are already beginning to attract e-learning scholars. These are the use of mobile devices in training (e.g. mobile learning) and the use of virtual reality technology. Mobile learning, also called mLearning is the use of smaller, portable, and mobile devices in the delivery of training content. Organizations are increasingly turning to mLearning to meet the needs for flexible delivery and timing of training. Estimates suggest expenditures in this growing segment of the e-learning market will approach $15 billion by 2019 (Ambient Insight, 2015). MLearning is argued to improve learning motivation by providing training in smaller, more consumable chunks where learners can remotely access files at their convenience, can annotate and share files, and can quickly search on keywords to find annotations or content (Chao & Chen, 2009; Zhang, Zhao, Zhou, & Nunamaker Jr., 2004). However, despite signs of growing interest in mLearning, research suggests that organizations should view the move to mobile with caution, and may need to rethink the delivery and display of content. Specifically, in a recent study by Kaganer, Giordano, Brion, and Tortoriello (2013), the researchers found that students using tablets were less satisfied with course materials, communicated less, and felt less connected to their peers than those who did not use tablets. In addition, those using tablets found it harder to read, comprehend, and conduct analysis on more complex financial data than those accessing these materials over more traditional technology (e.g., the PC). Additional research is needed to evaluate how to effectively design and deliver mLearning, and whether these considerations differ from those developed here to inform e-learning.

The second advance in technology that has design implications for e-learning is virtual reality. Virtual reality is a "technology that enables users to view or 'immerse' themselves in an alternate world" (Aguinis, Henle, & Beaty Jr, 2001, p. 70). To some extent, the virtualization of training has been around since the earliest days of computerized training, with flight simulators mimicking the look and feel of a cockpit. However, recent advances in technology are allowing organizations to create virtual environments where the learner can interact within a three-dimensional learning space, and where they can interact with objects as if they were real (Mujber, Szecsi, & Hashimi, 2004). Research on virtual, or augmented, reality in training has found that its use can improve training outcomes in a number of different fields (Bowman & McMahan, 2007; Brasil et al., 2011; Larsen, Oestergaard, Ottesen, & Soerensen, 2012).

Related to virtual reality, organizations are starting to utilize virtual worlds in training. A virtual world is a three-dimensional representation of a physical space on earth where individuals are represented by simulated bodies (called avatars) that interact with objects and each other through voice and text (deNoyelles, Hornik, & Johnson, 2014). One of the argued benefits of virtual worlds are that they should increase engagement (Mennecke, Triplett, Hassall, Conde, & Heer,

2011; Stone, Deadrick, Lukaszewski, & Johnson, 2015). Although more research is needed before fully understanding how virtual worlds can be used to enhance e-learning, existing research has found that virtual worlds can improve learner engagement (Hearrington, 2010), interaction (Merchant et al., 2012), and learning outcomes (Hornik & Thornburg, 2010). At the same time, though researchers have cautioned that communication and navigation can be more challenging in virtual worlds (deNoyelles, 2012; Mennecke, Hassall, & Triplett, 2008).

In summary, multiple communication and information sharing technologies exist that vary in richness, ease of use, and perceptions of utility, these technologies vary in how they can be most effectively be incorporated into e-learning. Effective e-learning will capitalize on the benefits of various technological tools by matching technologies to training purpose, and by providing options to allow for personal preferences in communication. One of the challenges facing researchers in this area is that the technology is changing faster than researchers, and even course designers, can keep up with. For this reason, it is important that designers look for broad themes about how technology design can affect learning processes. Themes and theories from information systems such as task-technology fit (Goodhue & Thompson, 1995), media synchronicity theory (Dennis et al., 2008), and other theories focusing on how interface design can affect behavior (Dickson, Senn, & Chervany, 1977; Todd & Benbasat, 1991) can inform e-learning designers as they design classes that maximize learner outcomes.

Trainee Interaction

The ability of peers and instructors to interact is important to any training and e-learning initiative. Although interaction can mean many things, in the context of e-learning research, it has often been defined as "the exchange of information between the various stakeholders in the course" (Johnson et al., 2008, p. 360). It has been argued that e-learning initiatives should be designed to support interaction because it is the most natural and effective way to learn (Benbunan-Fich & Arbaugh, 2006; Gunawardena, 1995; Hiltz, 1994). Not surprisingly, Salas et al. (2005) made the following recommendation with respect to interaction:

- Allow for interaction between trainees and for communication between trainees and facilitators. (p. 117)

One of the major challenges within e-learning environments is that interactions are mediated via technology, which can reduce the effectiveness of the communication (Stone & Lukaszewski, 2009). Specifically, according to the Yale Model of Communication and Persuasion (Hovland, Janis, & Kelley, 1953), for effective communication to occur, the targets of the message must attend to the message, comprehend its meaning and accept it. The effectiveness of these processes can be reduced when communication is online. For example, when communication is electronic, there are many cues that are not available to those in the environment, such as voice inflection, mannerisms, and eye contact. In addition, e-learning interactions often occur in the form of email, which is a one to one communication tool, or in group discussion boards or chats, which are easy for trainees to ignore. In fact, Stone and Lukaszewski (2009) stress that with electronic messages, the target of these messages will be less likely to attend to these messages than with traditional face-to-face communication. In addition, electronic communication can be harder to comprehend than face-to-face communication, and less likely to change attitudes and behaviors.

Finally, one of the hallmarks of effective learning and training is the development of a shared learning environment where learning occurs as trainees work together to create and share knowledge (Liedner & Jarvenpaa, 1995). In fact, Kraiger (2008) has argued that contemporary e-learning places a new emphasis on social interaction, as the learning process can potentially be more social in nature—with learners creating shared meaning based on their online interactions with instructors and peers. The challenge is that many e-learning programs are designed as electronic repositories of information where communication is one way, where trainees interact with course content in online audio, video, and text repositories rather than with peers and instructors. This one-way communication can reduce learning effectiveness. A number of studies have demonstrated the benefits of designing e-learning environments that support and encourage interaction, including greater information processing and attention to communication during e-learning, stronger feedback, and increased learning (Johnson et al., 2008; Piccoli et al., 2001). The review of the research in this area is organized by instructor interaction and peer interaction.

Instructors. The instructor can play a very important role in supporting communication and interaction in e-learning. First, although many e-learning initiatives are done independently, and in isolation, research has found that trainees who had an instructor present during an e-learning course were more satisfied than those who received only computer simulations (Gupta & Bostrom, 2013). In addition, Arbaugh (2001) argues that instructor communication, his or her encouragement of peer interaction, using student names, and providing feedback can reduce the social and psychological distance between learners. For example, research has found that adult vocational students felt that instructor feedback was positively related to their learning (Inayat, Amin, Inayat, & Salim, 2013). In addition, with respect to affective reactions to the training, one research study found that increased interaction with the course instructor was positively related to both course satisfaction, and utility judgments (Arbaugh & Rau, 2007). One of the strongest findings in this area is that the more that an instructor is actively engaged with trainees and learners (e.g. more immediacy in communication), the better the e-learning outcomes (e.g. satisfaction, utility judgments, and performance (Arbaugh, 2014; Marks, Sibley, & Arbaugh, 2005; Yang & Durrington, 2010).

Peers. The second type of interaction that is important is that between the peers in the online environment. Scholars have long argued that learning best occurs when peers are able to interact with each other, share ideas, and provide feedback (Bransford, Brown, & Cocking, 1999; Kraiger, 2008; Leidner & Jarvenpaa, 1995; Salas et al., 2005). "When trainees interact more and process information more deeply, they should be more likely to see the value in the training content. Further, when they interact with peers, they should feel more connected and should be more positive and satisfied with their learning experiences." (Johnson & Brown, 2017, p. 33). It is interesting that beyond actual interactions, trainee perceptions of how much they are interacting also matters (Arbaugh, 2005).

Researchers have argued that peer interaction can improve peer connections, can encourage deeper peer feedback, can support deeper information processing, and can lead to greater learning (Garrett, 2011; Johnson et al., 2008; Piccoli et al., 2001). In addition, it can improve trainee self-efficacy (Gupta & Bostrom, 2013). Research has also found that peer interaction affects both reactions to training as well as actual performance. (Alavi et al., 2002; Benbunan-Fich & Arbaugh, 2006; Gunawardena, Lowe, Constance, & Anderson, 1997; A. M. Schmidt & Ford, 2003). Specifically, research has found that both the amount of interaction and the centrality of a learner to a communication network were both positively related to learning performance (Hwang & Arbaugh, 2006; Johnson et al., 2009; Johnson et al., 2008; Lin, Huang, & Chuang, 2015; Strang, 2011). In addition, research has found that higher levels of peer interaction were associated with greater course satisfaction (Arbaugh, 2000a, 2002; Arbaugh & Hornik, 2006; Arbaugh & Rau, 2007; Johnson et al., 2009; Johnson et al., 2008). Surprisingly, the results with respect to utility judgments are mixed, with some studies finding a statistically significant relation between peer interaction and utility judgments (Arbaugh, 2000b, 2002; Arbaugh & Benbunan-Fich, 2007; Arbaugh & Rau, 2007; Yang & Durrington, 2010) and some finding no relation (Johnson et al., 2009; Johnson et al., 2008).

Another positive aspect of peer interactions is that they can reduce isolation and increase the richness of social connections. Social connections are critical to the creation of a shared learning environment and social presence. Social presence is a feeling or perception of being connected to others and the salience of the interpersonal connections with these others (Marks et al., 2005; Short, Williams, & Christie, 1976). With respect to e-learning, it has been defined as "the extent to which the technology enables students to create a warm, personal, sociable, and active environment and allows them to be connected in a shared learning space" (Johnson & Brown, 2017, p. 34).

Although the technology mediation of e-learning may suggest that a rich social environment and high social presence may be lacking, research has found that a rich communication environment with a shared social context can be created in technology-mediated environments (Kraiger, 2008; Markus, 1994; Zack & McKinney, 1995). In e-learning, this is done as students structure the learning environment through their technology-mediated interactions (Hillman et al., 1994). In addition, as illustrated in the work on computer mediated groups, a shared environment can lead to greater and more complex interactions (McGrath, Arrow, Grunfeld, Hollingshead, & O'Connor, 1993), can increase the likelihood that peers will pay attention to electronic messages (Mackie, Worth, & Asuncion, 1990), and may help learners better judge the quality of peer contributions (Lowry, Roberts, Romano, Cheney, & Hightower, 2006). Ultimately, research has argued that social connections and the development of a shared learning environment will improve e-learning outcomes (Gunawardena, 1995; Gunawardena & Zittle, 1997; Richardson & Swan, 2003).

Interestingly, the results of research on social connections regarding e-learning outcomes is mixed. Specifically, research has not found a statistically significant relationship between social presence and e-learning performance (Baturay, 2011; Johnson et al., 2009; Johnson et al., 2008). However, social presence has consistently found a positive relation between social presence and utility judgments and satisfaction (Arbaugh, 2001, 2002, 2008, 2014; Arbaugh & Hornik, 2006; Gunawardena & Zittle, 1997; Johnson et al., 2009; Johnson et al., 2008). Finally, some recent research suggests that by simply designing an introductory FTF socialization period into an online learning program can improve learning performance (Yanson & Johnson, 2016).This suggests that enabling peers to connect may not lead to better immediate performance outcomes, but may instead affect trainee perceptions of the environment.

In summary, it is clear that both instructor and peer interaction are important design considerations in e-learning. Greater interactions with both instructors and peers can create richer learning environments with a greater sense of social presence. In turn, this increase in social presence can contribute to better trainee reactions to training. Finally, although interaction has been shown to improve learning performance, the social presence enabled by this interaction has not.

Learner Control

The role of learner control has long been of interest to e-learning researchers (Johnson & Brown, 2017), and has been emphasized as one of the major benefits of e-learning and other technology-based training methods (Bell & Kozlowski, 2008; Brown, 2001; Brown, Howardson, & Fisher, 2016). Learner control is defined as the degree of discretion or responsibility an individual is granted to make important decisions about their own learning environment (DeRouin, Fritzsche, & Salas, 2004; Johnson & Brown, 2017; Reeves, 1993). These decisions often revolve around questions of pace, content, and structure of the training environment (Fisher, Howardson, Wasserman, & Orvis, 2017; Fisher, Wasserman, & Orvis, 2010). In their review of the literature, Salas et al. (2005) made the following suggestions in regards to the use of learner control in e-learning:

- "Offer trainees control over certain aspects of instruction" (p. 121)
- "Guide trainees through the distance learning program" (p. 126)

- "When offering trainees control over instruction, make sure that trainee preparation, system design, and workplace conditions facilitate successful use of that control" (p. 122).

Research has identified a number of important benefits to the use of learner control in e-learning. These include improved cognitive outcomes, such as skill and knowledge development (Bell & Kozlowski, 2002, 2008; Hughes et al., 2013; Kraiger & Jerden, 2007), affective outcomes, such as higher trainee satisfaction and enhanced emotion control (Bell & Kozlowski, 2008; Orvis et al., 2009), and behavioral outcomes such as adaptive performance and training transfer (e.g., Carolan et al., 2014; Hughes et al., 2013; Keith & Frese, 2005; Ross, Morrison, & O'Dell, 1989)

However, increasing learner control does not always lead to favorable results, and not every learner is prepared to take advantage of the capabilities associated with learner control (Brown, 2001; DeRouin et al., 2004; Mayer, 2004; Steinberg, 1989). Learner control adds additional complexity to the learning process, which can negatively affect training, especially when training is shorter in length or more complex (DeRouin et al., 2004; Granger & Levine, 2010). In addition, higher learner control can lead to changes in off-task attention compared to traditional training. Some scholars have found that it reduced off-task attention (Orvis et al., 2009), but others found that it led to higher off-task attention and lower performance (Karim & Behrend, 2014). Finally, two recent meta-analyses (Carolan et al., 2014; Kraiger & Jerden, 2007) suggest that learner control design features that allow learners to set their own pace can improve learning, but allowing learners to establish their own sequence or select their own content can yield mixed to negative effects on learning. Additionally, the findings suggest that learner control may be more beneficial when learning outcomes are skill-based or procedural rather than cognitive (e.g., knowledge-based), and when learners have no prior experience (Kraiger & Jerden, 2007). Together the findings suggest that care must be taken when designing learner control into the e-learning environment, and that organizations should provide certain types of learner control under certain conditions to enhance learning and transfer (Carolan et al., 2014; Kraiger & Jerden, 2007).

In addition to the specific design considerations outlined above, it is important to understand that individual characteristics of the learner may also influence how effective learner control is. Specifically, research suggests that younger trainees with higher levels of ability, self-efficacy, prior experience, openness to experience, extraversion, and learning goal orientation may benefit more from learner control than those who do have these same characteristics (Bell & Kozlowski, 2008; Carter & Beier, 2010; Hughes et al., 2013; Kanfer & Ackerman, 1989; Orvis, Brusso, Wasserman, & Fisher, 2010; Orvis et al., 2009). Ultimately, not only are certain types of learner control more effective than others, but certain types of people benefit more from this control more than others.

Therefore, an important question to consider is how can organizations best realize the benefits of learner control at the same time as reducing its risks? In this section, we highlight three general suggestions for learner control that include several specific design recommendations.

First, research suggests that learner control should be limited to a shallow surface-level training features (e.g., pace, practice context). By doing this the risk of overburdening trainees' limited attentional capacities is reduced (Brown et al., 2016; Freitag & Sullivan, 1995). For example, allowing trainees to choose the context of their examples and practice in training, such as in the context of their specific industry or profession, may promote control and transfer (Ross et al., 1989). Additionally, and somewhat counter-intuitively, presenting extra or optional material in a way that allows trainees to skip rather than add can increase the likelihood of learners completing optional material (Hicken, Sullivan, & Klein, 1992). Importantly, when granting control, designers should provide enough hierarchical structure and smooth transitions between modules to help trainees navigate through the course in a way that facilitates coherent mental models (e.g., by using footprints, return arrows, and landmark links) (El-Tigi & Branch, 1997; Nielsen, 1990; Park, 1991).

Second, greater degrees of control for either surface-level or deep-level features may be granted as trainee experience and skill increases. Research findings suggest that only after learners can demonstrate the ability to leverage control should they be given more control of deep-level control features such as content and difficulty compared to learners who are less experienced (Brown et al., 2016; Hughes et al., 2013). This can help accommodate learner differences in the rate of skill acquisition (Brown et al., 2016; Wickens, Hutchins, Carolan, & Cumming, 2012). Additionally, allowing learners to be responsible for their own level of control can improve satisfaction (Fisher et al., 2010; Orvis et al., 2009). In other words, providing flexibility to learners and providing control options with varying degrees may be beneficial. One way to determine learner readiness for increased control is to offer help resources and self-testing to assist trainees in diagnosing their development, thereby facilitating self-regulated learning (Brown & Ford, 2002; Sitzmann et al., 2009), and preparing learners to better control themselves.

Third, learner control in should be complemented with adequate supports. Research has long supported the view that some type of training and guidance should be provided to learners so that they are better prepared to navigate a learning environment with expanded control (DeRouin et al., 2004; Freitag & Sullivan, 1995; Gray, 1987; Reeves, 1993). Applying the principles of guided exploration and error management can also support e-learners who are granted learner control, especially when training material is complex or adaptive transfer is required. This includes variable practice and opportunities to explore tasks without step-by-step instructions (Bell & Kozlowski, 2008; Keith & Frese, 2005). This also includes clearly communicated messages that frame errors in a positive light, and that support learners' emotion control. These messages might be delivered as reminders in the training environment or might come from the external organizational environment (DeRouin et al., 2004). Nonetheless, their main purpose should be to help reduce the anxiety that can arise from autonomous learning, thereby allowing learners to maintain their focus on the training (Bell & Kozlowski, 2008; Kanfer & Ackerman, 1989, 1996).

Additionally, a related concept of adaptive guidance suggests that in order to support learner control, training should be supplemented by individualized diagnostic feedback of trainees' progress that builds sequentially, so learners know how to self-regulate their own learning (Bell & Kozlowski, 2002). This can be facilitated by presenting training material in groups of similar topics that increase in difficulty, and then by providing intermittent evaluations (e.g., tests), so trainees learn to effectively control pace and sequencing. Finally, beyond how the specific e-learning modules are deployed, training research suggests that developing a positive and supporting learning culture that values training and helps learners focus on framing errors as learning opportunities should lead to better overall learning outcomes (Baldwin & Ford, 1988; Egan, Yang, & Bartlett, 2004; Salas & Cannon-Bowers, 2000; Salas & Cannon-Bowers, 2001; Tannenbaum & Yukl, 1992).

In summary it is clear from the research that learner controlled e-learning environments are an important part of organizational e-learning. In addition, the research supports the value of providing certain types of control to learners within the e-learning environment. However, this control may come at a cost, with less experienced, less prepared, and lower performing individuals potentially being at a disadvantage when more control is given. To combat this, instructional and organizational supports should be put in place to help learners successfully utilize control features. Finally, the results support the recommendations of Salas et al. (2005), but go deeper, suggesting that control can be given in steps, starting with surface level control and adding more deep-level control as learners develop and demonstrate proficiency. Finally, we believe that additional research should be undertaken to better understand how and when each type of learner control can affect learning processes and outcomes, and how such design considerations interact with the individual differences highlighted that moderate the effectiveness of control in e-learning.

Organizational Support

The last area of design is organizational support. This is less of an issue of the design of a specific e-learning course, or how to use technology to support learning, but more broadly reflective of the design of e-learning initiatives. One of the challenges facing organizations is that not everyone has the confidence to use technology effectively in the e-learning environment (Brown, 2001; Salas et al., 2005). For this reason, Salas et al. (2005) recommended:

- Offer computer-based, distance learning methods to computer savvy trainees or train learners on computer basics before offering computer-based training (p. 119).

There is strong research supporting this recommendation. Specifically, a number of studies suggest that both computer self-efficacy (CSE) and computer anxiety (CA) affect e-learning outcomes. CSE is an individual's belief in her ability to complete computer related tasks (Marakas, Yi, & Johnson, 1998) and CA is an affective state where individuals are fearful and apprehensive regarding the use of computers (Thatcher & Perrewe, 2002). Each of these are reflective of an individual's sense of confidence and comfort in an e-learning environment. A recent review of the e-learning research suggests that CSE and CA can affect both learning processes and outcomes (Johnson & Brown, 2017). This suggests that employees entering e-learning should have a basic comfort level with computing before starting training. This way learners can focus on the content to be learned rather than focusing on learning both the technology to be mastered and the content (Schelin & Smarte, 2002).

In addition, other scholars have noted that factors such as age may also play a role in how comfortable learners are with e-learning, how they respond to different types of e-learning technology, and the time and effort it takes to complete training (Becker, Fleming, & Keijsers, 2012; Brown, 2001; Kubeck, Delp, Haslett, & McDaniel, 1996). As people age, experientially-based knowledge typically increases (or at least remains stable), whereas cognitive abilities important for learning (e.g., working memory capacity) decline across the lifespan (Beier & Ackerman, 2005). As a result, older workers tend to take longer and learn less in training than younger adults (Kubeck et al., 1996). Extant research, though, suggests this may be more of a design issue than an age issue. For example, research has found that older learners were more satisfied with e-learning (Hashim, Ahmad, & Abdullah, 2010) and were more motived to participate in self-directed e-learning courses (Kim & Frick, 2011) than were younger employees.

In other words, these recommendations suggest the importance of developing organizational policies that maximize trainee's chances for success. One way to do this is to ensure that e-learning design is supported within a broader organizational climate that supports learning and training. When training programs are designed to support employees, employees will be more likely to participate in them (Colquitt et al., 2000; Noe & Schmitt, 1986). In addition, the training climate and organizational support have been shown to affect learning and transfer (Holton, Bates, Seyler, & Carvalho, 1997; Rouiller & Goldstein, 1993; Tracey, Tannenbaum, & Kavanagh, 1995).

Thus, to overcome any potential issues associated with age or computer experience, the training climate of an organization should provide the financial resources, technology, support, and opportunities necessary for them to succeed (Hurtz & Williams, 2009; Maurer, Pierce, & Shore, 2002; Noe & Schmitt, 1986).

Specifically, certain design features such as self-pacing, providing multiple instructional methods (e.g., lecture, modeling), encouraging active participation, and facilitating exploratory learning with adequate structure may be utilized to support older workers and those with less computer experience (Callahan, Kiker, & Cross, 2003; Carter & Beier, 2010). Another design component, closely related to learner control, is that the nature of e-learning design may need to be flexible enough to provide high structure for low-ability trainees and low structure for high-ability trainees (Bell & Kozlowski, 2008). This finding also extends to age, with older employees performing better with more structure (regardless of ability) and younger employees performing better with less structure (Carter & Beier, 2010). Research also suggests that when organizations provide greater support for e-learning, learners will react more positively to the training (Byun & Mills, 2011; Cheng, Wang, Moormann, Olaniran, & Chen, 2012), and will be more likely to transfer what they have learned to the workplace (Park, Sim, & Roh, 2010).

In summary, based upon the research, we concur with Salas et al.'s (2005) recommendation that effective pre e-learning computer training be provided to those with lower computer skills, and extend the recommendation to those who may be at risk of lower performance (e.g. older trainees, lower ability employees). This can take the form of basic pre-training to introduce computer and e-learning basics. However, it also extends to training design considerations: enhanced training structure, allowing trainees to set their own pace, supporting active learning opportunities with encouragement in making errors in the learning process, and providing adequate structure in the training to help guide learners through the material (Bell & Kozlowski, 2008; Callahan et al., 2003; Carter & Beier, 2010). Ultimately, though, organizations need to understand that successful e-learning initiatives, just like successful training programs, are enabled by a broader organizational training design that provides material support to trainees and a strong learning climate.

DISCUSSION

As technology continues to rapidly evolve, and fundamentally alters the way we live and work, it also has changed the way we conduct employee training. To most effectively deploy e-learning programs, organizations must have a stronger understanding of how the technological and pedagogical design of these programs can maximize e-learning outcomes. In looking at Salas et al.'s (2005) guidelines it is clear that there is a growing interest in and support for them (see Table 6.1). More importantly, these recommendations support the idea of Task Technology Fit (TTF), or "the correspondence between task requirements, individual abilities, and the functionality of technology" (Goodhue & Thompson, 1995, p. 218). Essentially TTF argues that when there is a fit between the individual, the task, and the technology, outcomes will be improved. Research from e-learning also suggests the importance of fit (Hornik, Johnson, & Wu, 2007) for improving e-learning outcomes.

TABLE 6.1. Revised Guidelines for e-Learning

Guideline	Representative References	Summary of Findings	Potential Research Questions
1. Only provide distance learning when you are sure it meets the organization's needs	Goodhue & Thompson, 1995; Welsh et al., 2003	More of a philosophical recommendation than an empirically testable recommendation. All training should be based on a needs analysis, and should be built around the fit between instructional objectives and methods (see #9 below).	How can organizations best determine what form of training and what specific training features are best for different types of training content?
2. Take into consideration human cognitive processes when designing distance learning programs	Mayer, 2008; Kraiger & Mattingly, 2017; Orvis et al., 2009; Yanson & Johnson, 2016	Strongly supported. Well-designed e-learning helps learners attend to, organize, and integrate learning material with existing knowledge and skill without overwhelming learners' limited capacities. Technologies allowing customization can facilitate metacognition in the learning process.	What features of virtual worlds and communication tools enhance e-learning most effectively? How do content filters based on trainee expertise levels influence e-learning outcomes?
3. Enhance the learning experience by including multiple media methods (e.g., graphics, text, audio, video, etc.) in the presentation of learning topics	Alavi et al., 2002; Hornik et al., 2007; Mayer, 2008	Recommendation is dated. Today's e-learning initiatives, include texts, graphics, audio, video, and more to enhance the learning experience. To avoid information overload, simple delivery and communication methods should reinforce key learning points.	How can different media be deployed to maximize learning outcomes for a variety of learners? Are certain media better than others for communicating different types of learning content?
4. Incorporate learning games and game elements into e-learning design, where appropriate	Snyder & Hartig, 2013; Foster et al., 2012; Hamari et al., 2016	Strongly supported. Games and simulations can enhance engagement, affective reactions, and learning. Gamification, or the incorporation of game elements (e.g., leaderboards, badges) into e-learning can be used when games are less appropriate.	How and where can gamified techniques help or hinder e-learning processes and outcomes? How do individual characteristics (e.g., personality, disability) influence gamification effectiveness?

#	Guideline	References	Evidence	Research Questions
5.	Keep learners engaged	Noe et al., 2010; Orvis et al., 2009; Sitzmann & Weinhardt, 2015	Strongly supported. Failing to engage learners leads to attrition and can harm learning, motivation, and trainee reactions. Recent research has expanded the focus of engagement in e-learning to include self-regulated learning (see #14 below), learner control (#10 below), and trainee interaction (#7 below).	What learning prompts can best improve engagement in e-learning, and what is their optimal timing? To what extent can engaging design make up for deficiencies in trainee motivation and skill?
6.	Offer a blended approach	Arbaugh et al., 2010; Yanson & Johnson, 2016	Strongly supported. However, no strong evidence for the extent to which organizations are employing blended learning. As methods for online interaction increase, it is uncertain if organizations will opt for hybrid approaches over the convenience of solely online training.	What is the utility of blended learning, and is it a cost-effective delivery mechanism for global organizations? Is there an optimal mix of face-to-face and online learning?
7.	Allow for interaction between trainees and for communication between trainees and facilitators	Arbaugh, 2001; Inayat et al., 2013; Johnson et al., 2008; Piccoli et al., 2001; Yanson & Johnson, 2016	Strongly supported. Recent research details the mechanisms by which this takes place, and highlights the benefit of an introductory face-to-face socialization period prior to online interactions.	What type of interaction is most effective during different learning phases? Should instructors guide trainees to communicate differently during different phases of learning process?
8.	Offer computer-based, distance learning methods to computer-savvy trainees or train learners on computer basics before offering computer-based training	Carter & Beier, 2008; Johnson et al., 2008; Eom, 2011; deNoyelles et al., 2014	Strongly supported. Extra support should go beyond a basic computer skill training, but should also focus on aspects of the training such as self-pacing, self-regulation, seeking training support, etc. to reduce concerns of older, lower-ability, and lower self-efficacy learners (see #15 below).	How can technology be utilized during e-learning to help less prepared individuals learn more effectively? To what extent do individuals elect to take advantage of basic or remedial training supports?

(continues)

TABLE 6.1. Continued

Guideline	Representative References	Summary of Findings	Potential Research Questions
9. Match e-learning design technology and pedagogy to the type of training occurring (e.g. hard-skill vs. soft-skill training)	Granger & Levine, 2010; Hornik et al., 2008; Sitzmann et al., 2006; Yanson & Johnson, 2016	Evidence shows a variety of topics and content can be supported in e-learning (i.e., both hard and soft skills) given adequate pedagogical support. Different, and richer, communication (including in-depth interactions, videos, etc.) may be needed for effective soft-skills training.	Where and how can technology be utilized to enhance the richness and validity of interaction and community to improve soft-skill learning?
10. Offer trainees control of certain aspects of instruction	Brown et al., 2016; Bell & Kozlowski, 2002, 2008; Fisher et al., 2017; Kraiger & Jerden, 2007; Orvis et al., 2009	Strongly supported. However, increasing learner control may not always improve learning outcomes. Recent research suggests the benefits of learner control depend on control type (better for shallow than deep features), training type (better for skill-based than knowledge-based), and certain individual characteristics indicative of readiness for control.	How can e-learning be designed to allow different trainees to be able exert more control over learning compared to others? To what extent should organizations account for preferences in learner control, and how might this affect e-learning outcomes?
11. When offering trainees control over instruction, make sure that trainee preparation, system design, and workplace conditions facilitate successful use of that control	Bell & Kozlowski, 2008; Brown et al., 2016; Carter & Beier, 2010; Fisher et al., 2010; Orvis et al., 2009	Strongly supported. Research suggests the importance of enabling learner control over time as learners demonstrate capability. Framing errors positively, prompting self-regulation, variable practice, guided exploration, and system and organizational support help facilitate learner control.	How can organizations determine when trainees are ready to have more control over learning? How can we help learners more accurately self-diagnose training progress and success?
12. Guide the trainees through the distance learning program	Bell & Kozlowski, 2002; Brown & Ford, 2002; El-Tigi & Branch, 1997; Salas & Cannon-Bowers, 2001	Strongly supported. Well-designed, well-supported e-learning will support comprehension, acceptance, motivation, self-evaluation, learning, and transfer.	How can technology and organizational members provide adequate guidance and support, yet also encourage exploratory learning?

Recommendation	Summary of support	Future research questions	References
13. Make the program user-friendly	Fairly strong support that the easier an e-learning system is to use and the more valuable it is to the trainees, the stronger the learning and affective outcomes.	How do the display capabilities on different types of devices affect learning comprehension? How should organizations reconcile benefits of user-friendliness vs. desirable difficulties in e-learning?	Arbaugh 2014; Carswell & Venkatesh, 2002; Galy et al., 2011
New Recommendations			
Promote self-regulated learning	Designing for self-regulation (e.g., metacognitive prompts, setting goals and tracking progress, encouraging exploration) enhances learning outcomes by facilitating engagement, deeper information processing, and efficient use of time and resources.	What are the most effective methods for technology to promote self-regulated learning? To what extent should self-regulation techniques be determined by individual preference vs. system requirements?	Bell & Kozlowski, 2008; Brown & Ford, 2002; Randall, 2015; Sitzmann & Ely, 2010, 2011
Provide additional resources for learners who are less able and less prepared to take advantage of e-learning design features and learner control opportunities	Individuals who are older, have lower levels of ability, self-efficacy, prior experience, openness, extraversion, and learning goal orientation tend to perform worse and have more negative affective reactions to e-learning than those not lacking these characteristics. Increased structure, limited control options, and additional sources of support (e.g., technology, instructional, organizational) may be needed to assist learners most at-risk to struggle in e-learning settings.	How does pre-training help those with lower e-learning readiness perform better during e-learning? What are the individual and organizational consequences of designing e-learning differently for individuals who differ in e-learning readiness?	Brown et al., 2016; Callahan et al., 2003; Carter & Beier, 2008; Hughes et al., 2013; Orvis et al., 2010

Note. Italics represent updates to Salas et al.'s (2004) original recommendations.

TTF provides an excellent way of integrating the findings from the literature with the guidelines developed by Salas et al. (2005). When reviewing their guidelines, it is clear that these guidelines consider technology, pedagogy (e.g. learning task), the individual, and their interaction when developing their guidelines. In assessing and updating these guidelines, we briefly discuss the support (or lack thereof) for Salas et al.'s recommendations, and set an agenda for future research with the goal of understanding how new technology might facilitate or hinder the fit between technology, pedagogy and the trainee. Moreover, as research within certain areas of e-learning matures, we are beginning to see more detailed mechanisms and theories (e.g., trainee interaction, psychological learning processes), and more nuanced understandings (e.g., aptitude-treatment interactions in learner control) of fit that extend beyond previous recommendations.

Updating Salas' et al's (2005) Guidelines

Several conclusions emerge from our review on e-learning. The first of these builds on the theme of task-technology fit introduced above, and led us to revise or qualify two of Salas et al.'s (2005) original recommendations. Guideline #1 suggested that organizations not assume that e-learning will improve training and development programs. Instead, a decision to implement e-learning should be based upon a thorough needs analysis. As a more strategic decision, not much research has been undertaken to better understand when to implement e-learning. However, advances in technology that permit the presentation of rich forms of information and more interactive tools have enabled many more types of training content to be delivered in an e-learning format than was previously available, even just a decade ago. Thus, we believe that the research suggests that guideline #9, which originally restricted e-learning to hard skills and warned against e-learning for soft skills and abstract topics, should be updated as well.

Instead of determining what types of learning are more or less appropriate for e-learning, we believe these guidelines should be updated to emphasize the need to match e-learning design technology and instructional techniques to the type of training undertaken (e.g., hard vs. soft skills; declarative knowledge vs. procedural skill), and the context in which it occurs (e.g. existing teams, onboarding, individuals who do not know each other, etc.). For example, instructional methods such as recorded lectures, step-by-step instructional lists, and multiple-choice tests may be more suitable for e-learning programs designed to present factual information and ideas (e.g., company policies) than for e-learning programs designed to teach soft skills (e.g., communication). These types of training might require more video examples and opportunities for trainee practice and interaction. Therefore, given the growing dependence on and versatility of e-learning, the focus has shifted from "when is e-learning appropriate?" to "how can we design e-learning to be most effective given our specific training needs?"

A second conclusion is that advances in technology since Salas et al. (2005) first conducted their review require a rethinking of how to deploy e-learning. For example, one of their recommendations was to utilize a blended approach for e-learning that mixes e-learning with face-to-face instruction. Although there are numerous theoretical reasons supporting a blended approach, it seems to be more heavily utilized in educational learning than in corporate training (Arbaugh, 2010; Arbaugh et al., 2010). Thus, the number of research studies investigating blended learning is limited. For this reason, given the evolution of the richness of technology capabilities, it is important to assess how newer technologies might overcome the communication and interaction limitations of previous technology generations. Thus, the value and role of blended learning may be evolving, and research should investigate how to most effectively utilize the face-to-face and online aspects of e-learning.

Another guideline related to e-learning delivery suggests that e-learning should be enhanced by "including both graphics and text in the presentation of learning topics" (p. 113). Although research strongly supports the value of presenting graphics and text together (referred to as the "multimedia principle"; Mayer, 2008), advances in technology now allow for a variety of rich media methods, including video and audio in addition to text and graphics. Therefore, we updated Guideline #3 to acknowledge the increased number and richness of available media methods and their ability to deliver training content.

On the last point related to changes in e-learning delivery, we expanded Salas et al.'s (2005) fourth guideline to include utilizing game elements to improve e-learning outcomes. Growing interest and recent research in gamification, or the introduction of game-like elements or features, such as leaderboards, accrual of badges or points, immersive storylines, etc., into e-learning has demonstrated positive effects for motivation and performance (e.g., Hamari et al., 2016). Gamification allows more of a hybrid approach to the use of learning games where training designers can choose to implement one or more game elements into e-learning without introducing full-blown learning games or simulations. We acknowledge that future research in the area of e-learning design and delivery is needed to address when and how to incorporate media within e-learning, including how specific design choices and game elements are linked to psychological learning processes and outcomes.

A third conclusion from our review is that, in addition to revising Salas et al.'s (2005) original recommendations, research conducted since their review supports two additional recommendations. Specifically, recommendation #14 is to *"promote self-regulated learning"*. This goes beyond Salas et al.'s (2005) original recommendation #5 ("keep learners engaged"), because it moves the emphasis from avoiding attrition in e-learning to promoting motivation, individual accountability, and the strategic use of resources. Designing for self-regulation includes implementing features that allow individuals to set learning goals, track progress, receive feedback, set their own schedule, explore new areas, and prompt reminders for self-evaluation and self-control, among others. Recent research demonstrates the learning, affective, and motivational benefits of e-learning programs that promote self-regulated learning (e.g., Bell & Kozlowski, 2008; Randall, 2015; Sitzmann & Ely, 2010), and underscores the need for self-regulation to be a separate recommendation for successful e-learning.

Likewise, recommendation #15 is added, *"Provide additional resources for learners who are less able and less prepared to take advantage of e-learning design features and learner control opportunities."* Recent research highlights the possibility for aptitude-treatment interactions in e-learning, such that some learners may be expected to respond worse than others in e-learning settings. Specifically, research has demonstrated that individuals who are older, and have lower levels of ability, experience, and computer self-efficacy tend to perform worse in e-learning and enjoy it less than their younger, more capable counterparts (e.g., Callahan et al., 2003; Carter & Beier, 2008; Hughes et al., 2013). Additionally, these same individuals (in addition to those who have lower levels of openness to experience, extraversion, and learning goal orientation), might also be less likely to capitalize on the benefits of learner control (Brown et al., 2016; Fisher et al., 2010; Orvis et al., 2009). Consequently, in order to ameliorate the additional challenges at-risk e-learners may face, research suggests increasing training structure, limiting more advanced learner control options, allowing individuals to self-pace, and providing multiple sources of support (e.g., from the system and the organization) for technology use and training content (Brown et al., 2016; Carter & Beier, 2008). This new recommendation expands beyond offering training for computer basics (guideline #8) and guiding trainees through the program (#12) by acknowledging that certain individuals may be more in need of help, and that ensuring their success in e-learning requires both design considerations and bigger changes in climate and organizational support.

Fourth, the fact that many of Salas et al.'s (2005) original recommendations for e-learning design have received strong support speaks to their success in identifying broad themes of importance. However, we also wish to highlight several areas where empirical research and theory have added a deeper level of understanding and richness to the original recommendations. First, as researchers learn more about the cognitive and neural underpinnings of the learning process, the recommendation to design with human cognitive processes in mind is more relevant than ever. Based on the research reviewed here, it is evident that organizations can and should leverage technological advances to design features that create desirable difficulties, customize and adapt training for learners of different levels, help direct learners' attention, although not overtaxing it, and encourage metacognition.

Additionally, recommendations to offer blended approaches to e-learning and to allow for trainee interaction have been reinforced as tools and techniques to encourage interaction have advanced. The issue of interaction and communication is particularly important as more and more organizations are moving away from traditional instructor-led e-learning, and turning more to on-demand training supported by videos and knowledge repositories. Given that research emphasizes the importance of interaction to facilitate stronger learning outcomes, organizations need to determine if the reduction in costs associated with computer-based learning outweighs the potential loss in performance and satisfaction when interaction is removed. In other words, it actually may be in an organization's best interest to have a higher cost, but more effective e-learning program.

Furthermore, recent research in the area of learner control has provided more specificity to the guideline that control is a valuable e-learning tool. In order to maximize the potential for success, learner control should be provided with adequate support to learners and it should be released in steps, as learners master the various control features. Finally, in order to promote successful e-learning, especially for at-risk learners, well-designed training that provides adequate structure, self-pacing, and active learning opportunities, should be complemented by organizational support and a strong learning climate.

Future Research

Despite strong support for many of Salas et al.'s (2005) recommendations for well-designed e-learning, and the updates and additions of our own, we recognize that a significant challenge facing designers is the shifting technological landscape. More research is needed to understand how advanced technologies such as virtual worlds, virtual reality, and mobile technologies can best be leveraged to improve learning outcomes. For example, as noted earlier, some mobile learners found it challenging to access and interpret data displayed on tablets. Therefore, future research needs to look more closely at how to best design and display content across multiple technological platforms and devices to maximize learning for multiple learners within the same course (i.e., see guideline #13 for user-friendly programs).

In addition to the more targeted future research directions presented throughout our review, we detected a common theme: that relatively little is known about the link between specific technology design choices and e-learning outcomes. This is perhaps due, in part, to the rapid increase in the number of tools available to e-learning designers, allowing them to experiment and implement innovative methods without scientific evidence. In addition, given the importance of fit to e-learning success, we believe that researchers should look more closely at technology features and functionality as well as learning processes to determine how communications technology, content delivery, and other aspects of the training may affect learning processes and outcomes. For example, scholars could draw from work on groups (McGrath et al., 1993) and group support systems (Dennis, 1996; Dennis et al., 2008) to better understand how to apply these technologies in different parts of the learning process. In addition, e-learning scholars could draw from work on human-computer interaction to better understand how technology platforms, devices, and interface design can affect how learners will use the technology, how they will process information, and ultimately their knowledge and skill gains as well as their reactions to training. Additional specific examples for future research questions, highlighting these directions in the field, are included in the Potential Research Questions column of Table 6.1.

CONCLUSION

Based on our review of the available empirical evidence on e-learning, we evaluated and refined Salas et al.'s (2005) guidelines for e-learning design put forth more than a decade ago to promote evidence-based practices for effective e-learning. Given its increasing popularity in today's workforce, e-learning has spurred research interest that, although providing useful guidelines for the design and delivery of e-learning, still faces many unknowns. Ultimately, rather than chasing the latest technology to transform e-learning initiatives, it is clear that, as specified in the literature on Task Technology Fit, researchers need to consider the correspondence between technology, training tasks, and individuals with e-learning. Organizations cannot assume that the application of any specific technological tool, no matter how sophisticated, will necessarily improve e-learning outcomes. Instead, the research clearly shows that it is the application of technology, or a suite of technologies, applied to a specific training context with a specific set of individuals that will lead to the best outcomes. Therefore, we hope this review illustrates the need for scholars from multiple disciplines to come together and undertake studies that explicitly connect technology capabilities with sound training and learning design principles to deliver e-learning which will most effectively meet the needs of all learners.

REFERENCES

Aguinis, H., Henle, C. A., & Beaty Jr., J. C. (2001). Virtual reality technology: A new tool for personnel selection. *International Journal of Selection and Assessment, 9*(1–2), 70–83.

Alavi, M., & Leidner, D. E. (2001). Research commentary: Technology-meediated learning - A call for greater depth and breadth of research. *Information Systems Research, 12*(1), 1–10.

Alavi, M., Marakas, G. M., & Yoo, Y. (2002). A comparative study of distributed learning environments on learning outcomes. *Information Systems Research, 13*(4), 404–415.

Alkhadher, O., Anderson, N., & Clarke, D. (1994). Computer-based testing: A review of recent developments in research and practice. *European Work and Organizational Psychologist, 4*(2), 169–189.

Alliger, G. M., Tannenbaum, S. I., Bennett Jr., W., Traver, H., & Shotland, A. (1997). A meta analysis of the relations among training criteria. *Personnel psychology, 50,* 341–358.

Ambient Insight. (2015). *The 2014–2019 worldwide mobile learning market.* Retrieved from http://www.ambientinsight.com/Resources/Documents/AmbientInsight-2014-2019-Worldwide-Mobile-Learning-Market-Executive-Overview.pdf

American Society for Training and Development. (2015). *2015 State of the industry: ASTD's annual review of workplace learning and development data.* Alexandria, VA.

Arbaugh, J. B. (2000a). Virtual classroom characteristics and student satisfaction with internet-based MBA courses. *Journal of Management Education, 24*(1), 32–54.

Arbaugh, J. B. (2000b). Virtual classroom: An exploratory study of class discussion patterns and student learning in an asynchronous Internet-based MBA course. *Journal of Management Education, 24*(2), 213–233.

Arbaugh, J. B. (2001). How instructor immediacy behaviors affect student satisfaction and learning in web-based courses. *Business Communication Quarterly, 64*(4), 42–54.

Arbaugh, J. B. (2002). Managing the on-line classroom: A study of technological and behavioral characteristics of web-based MBA courses. *The Journal of High Technology Management Research, 13*(2), 203–223.

Arbaugh, J. B. (2005). Is there optimal design for on-line MBA courses? *Academy of Management Learning & Education, 4*(2), 135–149.

Arbaugh, J. B. (2008). Does the community of inquiry framework predict outcomes in online MBA courses? *The International Review of Research in Open and Distance Learning, 9*(2), 1–21.

Arbaugh, J. B. (2010). *Online and blended business education for the 21st century: Current research and future directions.* Oxford, UK: Woodhead Publishing.

Arbaugh, J. B. (2014). System, scholar or students? Which most influences online MBA course effectiveness? *Journal of Computer Assisted Learning,* 351–362.

Arbaugh, J. B., & Benbunan-Fich, R. (2007). The importance of participant interaction in online environments. *Decision Support Systems, 43*(3), 853–865.

Arbaugh, J. B., Desai, A., Rau, B., & Sridhar, B. S. (2010). A review of research on online and blended learning in the management disciplines: 1994–2009. *Organization Management Journal, 7*(1), 39–55.

Arbaugh, J. B., & Duray, R. (2002). Technological and structural characteristics, student learning and satisfaction with web-based courses an exploratory study of two online MBA programs. *Management Learning, 33*(3), 331–347.

Arbaugh, J. B., & Hornik, S. (2006). Do Chickering and Gamson's seven principles also apply to online MBAs. *The Journal of Educators Online, 3*(2), 1–18.

Arbaugh, J. B., & Rau, B. L. (2007). A study of disciplinary, structural, and behavioral effects on course outcomes in online MBA courses. *Decision Sciences Journal of Innovative Education, 5*(1), 65–95.

Balakrishnan, V. (2014). Using social networks to enhance teaching and learning experiences in higher learning institutions. *Innovations in Eduaction and Teaching International, 51*(6), 595–606.

Baldwin, T. T., & Ford, J. K. (1988). Transfer of training: A review and directions for future research. *Personnel psychology, 41*, 63–105.

Baturay, M. H. (2011). Relationships among sense of classroom community, perceived cognitive learning and satisfaction of students at an e-learning course. *Interactive Learning Environments, 19*(5), 563–575.

Becker, K., Fleming, J., & Keijsers, W. (2012). E-learning: Ageing workforce versus technology-savvy generation. *Education & Training, 54*(5), 385–400.

Beier, M. E., & Ackerman, P. L. (2005). Age, ability, and the role of prior knowledge on the acquisition of new domain knowledge: promising results in a real-world learning environment. *Psychology and Aging, 20*(2), 341–355.

Beier, M. E., Villado, A. J., & Randall, J. G. (2017). Cognitive ability and training: Practical implications from the science of learning. In K. G. Brown (Ed.), *Cambridge handbook of workplace training and employee development* (pp. 123–147). Cambridge, UK: Cambridge University Press.

Beilock, S. L., Bertenthal, B. I., Hoerger, M., & Carr, T. H. (2008). When does haste make waste? Speed-accuracy tradeoff, skill level, and the tools of the trade. *Journal of Experimental Psychology: Applied, 14*(4), 340–352.

Bell, B. S., & Kozlowski, S. W. J. (2002). Adaptive guidance: Enhancing self-regulation, knowledge, and performance in technology-based training. *Personnel psychology, 55*(2), 267–306.

Bell, B. S., & Kozlowski, S. W. J. (2008). Active learning: Effects of core training design elements on self-regulatory processes, learning, and adaptability. *Journal of Applied Psychology, 93*, 296–316.

Benbunan-Fich, R., & Arbaugh, J. B. (2006). Separating the effects of knowledge construction and group collaboration in learning outcomes of web-based courses. *Information & Management, 43*(6), 778–793.

Bjork, R. A. (1994). Memory and metamemory considerations in the training of human beings. In J. Metcalfe & A. Shimamura (Eds.), *Metacognition: Knowing about knowing.* Cambridge, MA: MIT Press.

Bjork, R. A., Dunlosky, J., & Kornell, N. (2013). Self-regulated learning: Beliefs, techniques, and illusions. *Annual Review of Psychology, 64*, 417–444.

Bowman, D. A., & McMahan, R. P. (2007). Virtual reality: How much immersion is enough? *IEEE Computer, 40*(7), 36–43.

Bransford, J. D., Brown, A. L., & Cocking, R. R. (1999). *How people learn: Brain, mind, experience and school.* Washington, DC: National Academy Press.

Brasil, I. S., Neto, F. M. M., Chagas, J. F. S., de Lima, R. M., Souza, D. F. L., Bonates, M. F., & Dantas, A. (2011). *An intelligent agent-based virtual game for oil drilling operators training.* Paper presented at the Virtual Reality (SVR), 2011 XIII Symposium on, Uberlandia.

Brown, K. G. (2001). Using computers to deliver training: Which employees learn and why? *Personnel Psychology, 54*(2), 271–296.

Brown, K. G. (2005). An examination of the structure and nomological network of trainee reactions: A closer look at "smile sheets." *Journal of Applied Psychology, 90*(5), 991–1001.

Brown, K. G., & Charlier, S. D. (2013). An integrative model of e-learning use: Leveraging theory to understand and increase usage. *Human Resource Management Review, 23*(1), 37–49.

Brown, K. G., Charlier, S. D., & Pierotti, A. (2012). E-Learning at work: Contributions of past research and suggestions for the future. *International Review of Industrial and Organizational Psychology, 27*, 89–114.

Brown, K. G., & Ford, J. K. (2002). Using computer technology in training: Building an infrastructure for active learning. In K. Kraiger (Ed.), *Creating, implementing, and managing effective training and development* (pp. 192–233). San Francisco, CA: Jossey-Bass.

Brown, K. G., Howardson, G., & Fisher, S. L. (2016). Learner control and e-learning: Taking stock and moving forward. *Annual Review of Organizational Psychology and Organizational Behavior, 3*, 267–291.

Byun, S., & Mills, P. J. (2011). Exploring the creation of learner-centered e-training environments among retail workers: A model development perspective. *Cyberpsychology, Behavior, and Social Networking, 14*(1–2), 66–69.

Callahan, J. S., Kiker, D. S., & Cross, T. (2003). Does method matter? A meta-analysis of the effects of training method on older learner training performance. *Journal of Management, 29*(5), 663–680.

Canon-Bowers, J. (2006). *The state of gaming and simulation.* Paper presented at the Training 2006 Conference and Expo, Orlando, FL.

Capece, G., & Campisi, D. (2013). User satisfaction affecting the acceptance of an e-learning platform as a mean for the development of the human capital. *Behaviour & Information Technology, 32*(4), 335–343.

Carolan, T. F., Hutchins, S. D., Wickens, C. D., & Cumming, J. M. (2014). Costs and benefits of more learner freedom: Meta-analyses of exploratory and learner control training methods. *Human Factors, 56*, 999–1014.

Carswell, A. D., & Venkatesh, V. (2002). Learner outcomes in an asynchronous distance education environment. *International Journal of Human-Computer Studies, 56*, 475–494.

Carter, M., & Beier, M. E. (2010). The effectiveness of error manageement training with working-aged adults. *Personnel psychology, 63*(3), 641–675.

Chang, K. E., Wu, L. J., Weng, S. E., & Sung, Y. T. (2012). Embedding game-based problem-solving phase into problem-posing system for mathematics learning. *Computers & Education, 58*(2), 775–786.

Chao, P. Y., & Chen, G. D. (2009). Augmenting paper-based learning with mobile phones. *Interacting with Computers, 21*(3), 173–185.

Cheng, B., Wang, M., Moormann, J., Olaniran, B., & Chen, N. (2012). The effects of organizational learning environment factors on e-learning acceptance. *Computers & Education, 58*, 885–899.

Clark, R. C., & Mayer, R. E. (2003). *e-Learning and the science of instruction: Proven guidelines for consumers and designers of multimedia learning.* San Francisco: Pfeiffer.

Colquitt, J. A., LePine, J. A., & Noe, R. A. (2000). Toward an integrative theory of training motivation: a meta-analytic path analysis of 20 years of research. *Journal of Applied Psychology, 85*(5), 678–707.

Daft, R. L., & Lengel, R. H. (1986). Organizational information requirements, media richness and structural design. *Management Science, 32*(5), 554–571.

Davidson, D. (2008). *Beyond fun: Serious games and media.* Pittsburgh, PA: ETC Press.

Davis, F. D., Bagozzi, R. P., & Warshaw, P. R. (1989). User acceptance of computer technology: A comparison of two theoretical models. *Management Science, 35*(8), 982–1003.

Dennis, A. R. (1996). Information exchange and use in group decision-making: You can lead a group to information but you can't make it think. *MIS Quarterly, 20*, 433–455.

Dennis, A. R., Fuller, R. M., & Valacich, J. S. (2008). Media, tasks, and communication processes: A theory of media synchronicity. *MIS Quarterly, 32*(3), 575–600.

deNoyelles, A. (2012). Analysis in virtual worlds: The influence of learner characteristics on instructional design. In K. Seo (Ed.), *Using social media effectively in the classroom: Blogs, wikis, Twitter, and more* (pp. 2–18). New York, NY: Routledge.

deNoyelles, A., Hornik, S. R., & Johnson, R. D. (2014). Exploring the dimensions of self-efficacy in virtual world learning: Environment, task, and content. *Journal of Online Learning and Teaching, 10*, 255–271.

DeRouin, R. E., Fritzsche, B. A., & Salas, E. (2004). Optimizing e-learning: Research-based guidelines for learner-controlled training. *Human Resource Management, 43*(2–3), 147–162.

Deterding, S., Sicart, M., Nacke, L., O'Hara, K., & Dixon, D. (2011). *Gamification. using game-design elements in non-gaming contexts.* Paper presented at the CHI 11, Vancouver, CA.

Dickson, G. W., Senn, J. A., & Chervany, N. L. (1977). Research in management information systems: The Minnesota experiments. *Management Science, 23*(9), 913–934.

Dominguez, A., Saenz-de-Navarrete, J., De-Marcos, L., Fernandez-Sanz, L., Pages, C., & Martinez-Herraiz, J. J. (2013). Gamifying learning experiences: Practical implications and outcomes. *Computers & Education, 63*, 380–392.

Dunlosky, J., Rawson, K. A., Marsh, E. J., Nathan, M. J., & Willingham, D. T. (2013). Improving students' learning with effective learning techniques: Promising directions from cognitive and educational psychology. *Psychological Science in the Public Interest, 14*(1), 4–58.

Egan, T. M., Yang, B., & Bartlett, K. R. (2004). The effects of organizational learning culture and job satisfaction on motivation to transfer learning and turnover intention. *Human Resource Development Quarterly, 15*(3), 279–301.

El-Tigi, M., & Branch, R. M. (1997). Designing for interaction, learner control, and feedback during web-based learning. *Educational Technology Research and Development, 37*(3), 23–29.

Fisher, S. L., & Ford, J. K. (1998). Differential effects of learner effort and goal orientation on two learning outcomes. *Personnel Psychology, 51*(2), 397–420.

Fisher, S. L., Howardson, G., Wasserman, M., & Orvis, K. (2017). How do learners interact with elearning? Examining patterns of learner control behaviors. *AIS Transactions on Human Computer Interaction, 9*(2), 75–98.

Fisher, S. L., Wasserman, M., & Orvis, K. (2010). Trainee reactions to learner control: An important link in the e-learning equation. *International Journal of Training and Development, 14*(3), 198–210.

Flavell, J. H. (1979). Metacognition and cognitive monitoring: A new area of cognitive–developmental inquiry. *American Psychologist, 34*(10), 906–911.

Ford, J. K., Smith, E. M., Weissbein, D. A., Gully, S. M., & Salas, E. (1998). Relationships of goal orientation, metacognitive activity, and practice strategies with learning outcomes and transfer. *Journal of Applied Psychology, 83*(2), 218–233.

Foster, J. A., Sheridan, P. K., Irish, R., & Frost, G. S. (2012). *Gamification as a strategy for promoting deeper investigation in a reverse engineering activity.* Paper presented at the 2012 American Society for Engineering Education Conference.

Freitag, E. T., & Sullivan, H. J. (1995). Matching learner preference to amount of instruction: An alternative form of learner control. *Educational Technology Research and Development, 43*(2), 5–14.

Galy, E., Downey, C., & Johnson, J. (2011). The effect of using e-learning tools in online and campus-based classrooms on student performance. *Journal of Information Technology Education, 10*, 209–230.

Garrett, N. (2011). An e-portfolio design supporting ownership, social learning, and ease of use. *Educational Technology & Society, 14*(1), 187–202.

Garrison, D. R., & Arbaugh, J. B. (2007). Researching the community of inquiry framework: Review, issues, and future directions. *The Internet and Higher Education, 10*(3), 157–172.

Goldstein, I. L., & Ford, J. K. (2002). *Training in organizations.* Belmont, CA: Wadsworth.

Goodhue, D. L., & Thompson, R. L. (1995). Task-technology fit and individual performance. *MIS Quarterly, 19*(2), 213–236.

Granger, B., & Levine, E. (2010). The perplexing role of learner control in e-learning: Will learning and the transfer benefit suffer? *International Journal of Training and Development, 14*(3), 180–197.

Gray, S. H. (1987). The effect of sequence control on computer assisted learning. *Journal of Computer-Based Instruction, 14*(54–56).

Gunawardena, C. N. (1995). Social presence theory and implications for interaction and collaborative learning in computer conferences. *International Journal of Educational telecommunications, 1*(2), 147–166.

Gunawardena, C. N., Lowe, X., Constance, A., & Anderson, T. (1997). Analysis of a global debate and the development of an interaction analysis model for examining social construction of knowledge in computer conferences. *Journal of Educational Computer Research, 17*(4), 397–431.

Gunawardena, C. N., & Zittle, F. J. (1997). Social presence as a predictor of satisfaction within a computer-mediated conferencing environment. *The American Journal of Distance Education, 11*(3), 8–26.

Gupta, S., & Bostrom, R. P. (2009). Technology-mediated learning: A comprehensive theoretical model. *Journal of the Association for Information Systems, 10*(9), 686–714.

Gupta, S., & Bostrom, R. P. (2013). An investigation of the appropriation of technology-mediated training methods: Incorporating enactive and collaborative learning. *Information Systems Research, 24*(2), 454–469.

Gurtner, J.-L. (2015). Effective virtual learning environments. In K. Kraiger, J. Passmore, N. R. d. Santos, & S. Malvezzi (Eds.), *The Wiley Blackwell handbook of the psychology of training, development, and performance improvement.* Chichester, West Sussex, UK: John Wiley & Sons.

Hamari, J., & Keronen, L. (2017). Why do people play games? A meta-analysis. *International Journal of Information Management, 37*(3), 125–141.

Hamari, J., & Koivisto, J. (2014). Measuring flow in gamification: Dispositional flow scale–2. *Computers in Human Behavior, 40*, 133–143.

Hamari, J., Koivisto, J., & Sarsa, H. (2014). *Does gamification work?—A literature review of empirical studies on gamification.* Paper presented at the 47th Hawaii International Conference on System Sciences, Waikola, HI.

Hamari, J., Shernoff, D. J., Rowe, E., Coller, B., Asbell-Clarke, J., & Edwards, T. (2016). Challenging games help students learn: An empirical study on engagement, flow and immersion in game-based learning. *Computers in Human Behavior, 54*, 170–179.

Hashim, R., Ahmad, H., & Abdullah, C. Z. (2010). Antecedents of ICT attitudes of distance education students. *The Turkish Online Journal of Educational Technology, 9*(1), 28–36.

Hearrington, D. (2010). Evaluation of learning efficiency and efficacy in a multi-user virtual environment. *Journal of Digital Learning in Teacher Education, 27*(2), 65–75.

Hesketh, B. (1997). Dilemmas in training for transfer and retention. *Applied Psychology, 46,* 317–339.

Hicken, S., Sullivan, H., & Klein, J. (1992). Learner control modes and incentive variations in computer-delivered instruction. *Educational Technology Research and Development, 40*(4), 15–26.

Hillman, D. C., Willis, D. J., & Gunawardena, C. N. (1994). Learner-interface interaction in distance education: An extension of contemporary models and strategies for practitioners. *American Journal of Distance Education, 8*(2), 30–42.

Hiltz, S. R. (1994). *The virtual classroom: Learning without limits via computer networks.* Norwood, NJ: Ablex Publishing Company.

Holton, E. F., Bates, R. A., Seyler, D. L., & Carvalho, M. B. (1997). Toward construct validation of a transfer climate instrument. *Human Resource Development Quarterly, 8*(2), 95–113.

Hornik, S., Johnson, R. D., & Wu, Y. (2007). When technology does not support learning: Conflicts between epistemological beliefs and technology support in virtual learning environments. *Journal of Organizational and End User Computing, 19*(2), 23–46.

Hornik, S., Saunders, C. S., Li, Y., Moskal, P. D., & Dzuiban, C. D. (2008). The impact of paradigm development and course level on performance in technology-mediated learning environments. *Informing Science: The International Journal of an Emerging Transdiscipline, 11,* 35–58.

Hornik, S., & Thornburg, S. (2010). Really Engaging Accounting: Second Life™ as a learning platform. *Issues in Accounting Education, 25*(3), 361–378.

Horton, W. K. (2000). *Designing web-based training: How to teach anyone anything anywhere anytime.* Hoboken, NJ: John Wiley & Sons.

Horton, W. K. (2002). Games that teach: Simple computer games for adults who want to learn. In A. Rossett (Ed.), *The ASTD e-learning handbook.* New York: McGraw Hill.

Hovland, C. I., Janis, I. L., & Kelley, H. H. (1953). *Communication and persuasion: Psychological studies of opinion change.* New Haven, CT: Yale University Press

Hsieh, P., & Cho, V. (2011). Comparing e-learning tools' success: The case of instructor-student interactive vs. self-paced tools. *Computers & Education, 57,* 2025–2038.

Hughes, M. G., Day, E. A., Wang, X., Schuelke, M. J., Arsenault, M. L., Harkrider, L. N., & Cooper, O. D. (2013). Learner-controlled practice difficulty in the training of a complex task: Cognitive and motivational mechanisms. *Journal of Applied Psychology, 98,* 80–98.

Hurtz, G. M., & Williams, K. J. (2009). Attitudinal and motivational antecedents of participation in voluntary employee development activities. *Journal of Applied Psychology, 94*(3), 635–653.

Hwang, A., & Arbaugh, J. B. (2006). Virtual and traditional feedback-seeking behaviors: Underlying competitive attitudes and consequent grade performance. *Decision Sciences Journal of Innovative Education, 4*(1), 1–28.

Inayat, I., Amin, R., Inayat, Z., & Salim, S. S. (2013). Effects of collaborative web based vocational education and training (VET) on learning outcomes. *Computers & Education, 68,* 153–166.

Johnson, R. D., & Brown, K. G. (2017). e-Learning. In G. Hertel, D. L. Stone, R. D. Johnson, & J. Passmore (Eds.), *The Wiley-Blackwell handbook of the psychology of the internet at work.* Chichester, UK: Wiley-Blackwell.

Johnson, R. D., Gueutal, H., & Falbe, C. M. (2009). Technology, trainees, metacognitive activity and e-learning effectiveness. *Journal of Managerial Psychology, 24*(6), 545–566.

Johnson, R. D., Hornik, S., & Salas, E. (2008). An empirical examination of factors contributing to the creation of successful e-learning environments. *international Journal of Human-Computer Studies, 66*(5), 356–369.

Kaganer, E., Giordano, G. A., Brion, S., & Tortoriello, M. (2013). Media tablets for mobile learning. *Communications of the ACM, 56*(11), 68–75.

Kahn, W. A. (1990). Psychological conditions of personal engagement and disengagement at work. *Academy of Management Journal, 33*, 692–724.

Kanfer, R., & Ackerman, P. L. (1989). Motivation and cognitive abilities: An integrative/aptitude-treatment interaction approach to skill acquisition. *Journal of Applied Psychology, 74*(4), 657–690.

Kanfer, R., & Ackerman, P. L. (1996). A self-regulatory skills perspective to reducing cognitive interference. In I. G. Sarason, B. R. Sarason, & G. R. Pierce (Eds.), *Cognitive interference: Theories, methods, and findings* (pp. 153–171). Mahwah, NJ: Erlbaum.

Karim, M. N., & Behrend, T. S. (2014). Reexamining the nature of learner control: Dimensionality and effects on learning and training reactions. *Journal of Business and Psychology, 29*(1), 87–99.

Keith, N., & Frese, M. (2005). Self-regulation in error management training: Emotion control and metacognition as mediators of performance effects. *Journal of Applied Psychology, 90*, 677–691.

Keith, N., & Frese, M. (2008). Effectiveness of error management training: A meta-analysis. *Journal of Applied Psychology, 93*, 59–69.

Kim, K., & Frick, T. W. (2011). Changes in student motivation during online learning. *Jounal of Educational Computing Research, 44*(1), 1–23.

Kirkpatrick D. L. (1976). Evaluation of training. In R. L. Craig (Ed.), *Training and development handbook* (2nd ed.). New York: McGraw-Hill.

Kraiger, K. (2003). Perspectives on training and development. *Handbook of Psychology*, 171–192.

Kraiger, K. (2008). Transforming our models of learning and development: Web-based instruction as enabler of third-generation instruction. *Industrial and Organizational Psychology: Perspectives on Science and Practice, 1*, 454–457.

Kraiger, K., Ford, J. K., & Salas, E. (1993). Application of cognitive, skill-based, and affective theories of learning outcomes to new methods of training evaluation. *Journal of Applied Psychology, 78*(2), 311–328.

Kraiger, K., & Jerden, E. (2007). A meta-analytic investigation of learner control: Old findings and new directions. In S. M. Fiore & E. Salas (Eds.), *Toward a science of distributed learning* (pp. 65–90). Washington, DC: American Psychological Association.

Kraiger, K., & Mattingly, V. P. (2017). Cognitive and neural foundations of learning. In K. G. Brown (Ed.), *Cambridge handbook of workplace training and employee development*, (pp. 11–37). Cambridge, UK: Cambridge University Press.

Kubeck, J. E., Delp, N. D., Haslett, T. K., & McDaniel, M. A. (1996). Does job-related training performance decline with age? *Psychology and Aging, 11*(1), 92–107.

Lan, Y., & Sie, Y. (2010). Using RSS to support mobile learning based on media richness theory. *Computers & Education, 55*, 723–732.

Larsen, C. R., Oestergaard, J., Ottesen, B. S., & Soerensen, J. L. (2012). The efficacy of virtual reality simulation training in laparoscopy: a systematic review of randomized trials. *Acta obstetricia et gynecologica Scandinavica, 91*(9), 1015–1028.

Leidner, D. E., & Jarvenpaa, S. L. (1995). The use of information technology to enhance management school education: A theoretical view. *MIS Quarterly, 19*(3), 265–291.

Lin, J., Huang, H., & Chuang, Y. (2015). The impacts of network centrality and self-regulation on an e-learning environment with the support of social network awareness. *British Journal of Educational Technology, 46*(1), 32–44.

Long, L. K., Dubois, C., & Faley, R. (2009). A case study analysis of factors that influence attrition rates in voluntary online training programs. *International Journal of E-learning, 8*(3), 347–359.

Lowry, P. B., Roberts, T. L., Romano, N. C. J., Cheney, P. D., & Hightower, R. T. (2006). The impact of group size and social presence on small group communication: does computer-mediated communication make a difference. *Small Group Research, 37,* 631–661.

Mackie, D. M., Worth, L. T., & Asuncion, A. G. (1990). Processing of persuasive in-group messages. *Journal of Personality and Social Psychology, 58,* 812–822.

Marakas, G. M., Yi, M. Y., & Johnson, R. D. (1998). The multilevel and multifaceted character of computer self-efficacy: Toward clarification of the construct and an integrative framework for research. *Information Systems Research, 9*(2), 126–163.

Marks, R. B., Sibley, S. D., & Arbaugh, J. B. (2005). A structural equation model of predictors for effective online learning. *Journal of Management Education, 29*(4), 531–563.

Markus, M. L. (1994). Electronic mail as the medium of managerial choice. *Organization Science, 5*(4), 502–527.

Maurer, T. J., Pierce, H., & Shore, L. (2002). Perceived beneficiary of employee development activity: A three-dimensional social exchange model. *Academy of Management Review, 27*(3), 432–444.

Mayer, R. E. (2004). Should there be a three-strikes rule against pure discovery learning? The case for guided methods of instruction. *American Psychologist, 59,* 14–19.

Mayer, R. E. (2008). Applying the science of learning: Evidence-based principles for the design of multimedia instruction. *American Psychologist, 63,* 760–769.

Mayer, R. E., & Anderson, R. B. (1991). Animations need narrations: An expereimental test of a dual-processing system in working memory. *Journal of Educational Psychology, 90,* 312–320.

McDaniel, R., Lindgren, R., & Friskics, J. (2012). *Using badges for shaping interactions in online learning environments.* Paper presented at the 2012 IEEE International Professional Communication Conference, Orlando, FL.

McGrath, J. E., Arrow, H., Grunfeld, D. H., Hollingshead, A. B., & O'Connor, K. M. (1993). Groups, tasks, and technology: The effects of experience and change. *Small Group Research, 24,* 406–420.

Mennecke, B. E., Hassall, L. M., & Triplett, J. (2008). The mean business of Second Life: Teaching entrepreneurship, technology and e-commerce in immersive environments. *MERLOT Journal of Online Learning and Teaching, 4*(3), 339–348.

Mennecke, B. E., Triplett, J. L., Hassall, L. M., Conde, Z. J., & Heer, R. (2011). An examination of a theory of embodied social presence in virtual worlds. *Decision Sciences, 42*(2), 413–450.

Merchant, Z., Goetz, E. T., Keeney-Kennicutt, W., Kwok, O., Cifuentes, L., & Davis, T. J. (2012). The learner characteristics, features of desktop 3D virtual reality environments, and college chemistry instruction: A structural equation modeling analysis. *Computers & Education, 59*(2), 551–568.

Moshinskie, J. (2001). How to keep e-learners from e-scaping. *Performance Improvement, 40*(6), 30–37.

Mujber, T. S., Szecsi, T., & Hashimi, M. S. (2004). Virtual reality applications in manufacturing process simulation. *Journal of materials processing technology, 155,* 1834–1838.

Mullich, J. (2004). A second act for e-learning. *Workforce Management, 83,* 51–55.

Nielsen, J. (1990). The art of navigating through hypertext. *Communications of the ACM, 33,* 296–310.

Noe, R. A., & Schmitt, N. (1986). The influence of trainee attitudes on training effectiveness: Test of a model. *Personnel psychology, 39*(3), 497–523.

Noe, R. A., Tews, M. J., & Dachner, A. M. (2010). Learner engagement: A new perspective for enhancing our understanding of learner motivation and workplace learning. *Academy of Management Annals, 4,* 279–315.

Orvis, K. A., Brusso, R. C., Wasserman, M. E., & Fisher, S. L. (2010). E-nabled for e-learning? The moderating role of personality in determining the optimal degree of learner control in an e-learning environment. *Human Performance, 24*(1), 60–78.

Orvis, K. A., Fisher, S. L., & Wasserman, M. E. (2009). Power to the people: Using learner control to improve trainee reactions and learning in web-based instructional environments. *Journal of Applied Psychology, 94,* 960–971.

Park, O. (1991). Hypermedia: Functional features and research issues. *Educational Technology, 31,* 24–31.

Park, S., Sim, H., & Roh, H. (2010). The analysis of effectiveness on "transfer" through e-learning courses in industry and technology. *British Journal of Educational Technology, 41*(6), 32–34.

Piccoli, G., Ahmad, R., & Ives, B. (2001). Web-based virtual learning environments: A research framework and a preliminary assessment of effectiveness in basic IT skills training. *MIS Quarterly, 25*(4), 401–426.

Piccioli, V. (2014). *E-learning market trends & forecast 2014–2016 report.* Retrieved from https://www.docebo.com/landing/contactform/elearning-market-trends-and-forecast-2014-2016-docebo-report.pdf

Randall, J. G. (2015). *Mind wandering and self-directed learning: Testing the efficacy of self-regulation interventions to reduce mind wandering and enhance online training* (Unpubished Doctoral Dissertation). Rice University, Houston, TX.

Randall, J. G., & Villado, A. J. (2017). Take two: Sources and deterrents of score change in employment retesting. *Human Resource Management Review, 27,* 536–553.

Reeves, T. C. (1993). Pseudoscience in computer-based instruction: The case of learner control research. *Journal of Computer-Based Instruction, 20,* 39–46.

Rich, B. L., Lepine, J. A., & Crawford, E. R. (2010). Job engagement: Antecedents and effects on job performance. *Academy of Management Journal, 53*(3), 617–635.

Richardson, J. C., & Swan, K. (2003). Examining social presence in online courses in relation to students' perceived learning and satisfaction. *Journal of Asynchronous Learning Networks, 7*(1), 68–88.

Roediger III, H. L., & Karpicke, J. D. (2006). The power of testing memory: Basic research and implications for educational practice. *Psychological Science, 1*, 181–210.

Ross, S. M., Morrison, G. R., & O'Dell, J. K. (1989). Uses and effects of learner control of context and instructional support in computer-based instruction. *Educational Technology Research and Development, 37*(4), 29–39.

Rouiller, J. Z., & Goldstein, I. L. (1993). The relationship between organizational transfer climate and positive transfer of training *Human Resource Development Quarterly, 4*(4), 377–390.

Salas, E., & Cannon-Bowers, J. A. (2000). Design training systematically. In E. A. Locke (Ed.), *The Blackwell handbook of principles of organizational behavior*. Oxford, UK: Blackwell Publishers Ltd. .

Salas, E., & Cannon-Bowers, J. A. (2001). The science of training: A decade of progress. *Annual Review of Psychology, 52*(1), 471–499.

Salas, E., DeRouin, R., & Littrell, L. (2005). Research-based guidlines for designing distance learning: What we know so far. In H. Gueutal & D. L. Stone (Eds.), *The brave new world of eHr* (pp. 104–137): Jossey Bass.

Sawang, S., Newton, C., & Jamieson, K. (2013). Increasing learners's satisfaction/intention to adopt more e-learning. *Education & Training, 55*(1), 83–105.

Schelin, E., & Smarte, G. (2002). Recognizing the champions. *E-Learning, 3*(4), 12–19.

Schmidt, A. M., & Ford, J. K. (2003). Learning within a learner control training environment: The interactive effects of goal orientation and metacognitive instruction on learning outcomes. *Personnel psychology, 56*, 405–429.

Schmidt, R. A., & Bjork, R. A. (1992). New conceptualizations of practice: Common principles in three paradigms suggest new concepts for training. *Psychological Science, 3*(4), 207–217.

Short, J., Williams, E., & Christie, B. (1976). *The social psychology of telecommunications*. New York: Wiley.

Shute, V. J., Ventura, M., Bauer, M., & Zapata-Rivera, D. (2009). Melding the power of serious games and embedded assessment to monitor and foster learning. *Serious Games: Mechanisms and Effects, 2*, 295–321.

Sitzmann, T. (2012). A theoretical model and analysis of the effect of self-regulation on attrition from voluntary online training. *Learning and Individual Differences, 22*, 46–54.

Sitzmann, T., Bell, B. S., Kraiger, K., & Kanar, A. M. (2009). A multilevel analysis of the effect of prompting self-regulation in technology-delivered instruction. *Personnel Psychology, 62*(4), 697–734.

Sitzmann, T., Brown, K. G., Casper, W. J., Ely, K., & Zimmerman, R. D. (2008). A review and meta-analysis of the nomological network of trainee reactions. *Journal of Applied Psychology, 93*(2), 280–295.

Sitzmann, T., & Ely, K. (2010). Sometimes you need a reminder: The effects of self-regulation on regulatory processes, learning and attrition. *Journal of Applied Psychology, 95*(1), 132–144.

Sitzmann, T., & Ely, K. (2011). A meta-analysis of self-regulated learning in work-related training and educational attainment: What we know and where we need to go. *Psychological Bulletin, 137*, 421–442.

Sitzmann, T., & Johnson, S. K. (2012). The best laid plans: Examining the conditions under which a planning intervention improves learning and reduces attrition. *Journal of Applied Psychology, 97*(5), 967–981.

Sitzmann, T., Kraiger, K., Stewart, D., & Wisher, R. (2006). The comparative effectiveness of web-based and classroom instruction: A meta-analysis. *Personnel Psychology, 59*(3), 623–664.

Sitzmann, T., & Weinhardt, J. M. (2015). Training engagement theory: A multilevel perspective on the effectiveness of work-related training. *Journal of Management, Advanced Online Publication.*

Smith, E. M., Ford, J. K., & Kozlowski, S. W. J. (1997). Building adaptive expertise: Implications for training design. In M. A. Quinones & A. Ehrenstein (Eds.), *Training for a rapidly changing workplace: Applications of psychological research* (pp. 89–118). Washington, DC: APA Books.

Snyder, E., & Hartig, J. R. (2013). Gamification of board review: A residency curricular innovation. *Medical Education, 47*(5), 524–525.

Steinberg, E. R. (1989). Cognition and learner control: A literature review, 1977–1988. *Journal of Computer-Based Instruction, 16*, 117–121.

Stone, D. L., Deadrick, D. L., Lukaszewski, K. M., & Johnson, R. (2015). The influence of technology on the future of human resource management. *Human Resource Management Review, 25*(2), 216–231.

Stone, D. L., & Lukaszewski, K. M. (2009). An expanded model of the factors affecting the acceptance and effectiveness of electronic human resource management systems. *Human Resource Management Review, 19*(2), 134–143.

Strang, K. D. (2011). How can discussion forum questions be effective in online MBA courses? *Campus-Wide Information Systems, 28*(2), 80–92.

Sweller, J. (1988). Cognitive load during problem solving: effects on learning. *Cognitive Science, 12*, 257–285.

Tannenbaum, S. I., & Yukl, G. (1992). Training and development in work organizations. *Annual Review of Psychology, 43*(1), 399–441.

Thatcher, J. B., & Perrewe, P. L. (2002). An empirical examination of individual traits as antecedents to computer anxiety and computer self-efficacy. *MIS Quarterly, 26*(4), 381–396.

Todd, P., & Benbasat, I. (1991). An experimental investigation of the impact of computer based decision aids on decision making strategies. *Information Systems Research, 2*(2), 87–115.

Towler, A., & Mitchell, T. (2015). Facilitation in E-Learning. In K. Kraiger, J. Passmore, N. R. d. Santos, & S. Malvezzi (Eds.), *The Wiley Blackwell handbook of the psychology of training, development, and performance improvement* (pp. 171–187): Wiley Blackwell.

Tracey, J. B., Tannenbaum, S. I., & Kavanagh, M. J. (1995). Applying trained skills on the job: The importance of the work environment. . *Journal of Applied Psychology, 80*(2), 239–252.

Trougakos, J. P., Beal, D. J., Green, S. G., & Weiss, H. M. (2008). Making the break count: An episodic examination of recovery activities, emotional experiences, and positive affective displays. *Academy of Management Journal, 51*(1), 131–146.

van Merrienboer, J. J. G., & Sweller, J. (2005). Cognitive load theory and complex learning: recent developments and future directions. *Educational Psychology Review, 17*, 147–177.

Vogel, J. J., Greenwood-Ericksen, A., Cannon-Bowers, J., & Bowers, C. A. (2006). Using virtual reality with and without gaming attributes for academic achievement. *Journal of Research on Teaching in Education, 39*(1), 105–118.

Vygotsky, L. (1978). *Mind in society*. Cambridge, MA: Harvard University Press.

Wan, Z., Fang, Y., & Neufeld, D. J. (2007). The role of information technology in technology-mediated learning: A review of the past for the future. *Journal of Information Systems Education, 18*(2), 183–192.

Wang, L. C., & Chen, M. P. (2010). The effects of game strategy and preference-matching on flow experience and programming performance in game-based learning. *Innovations in Eduaction and Teaching International, 47*(1), 39–52.

Welsh, E. T., Wanberg, C. R., Brown, K. G., & Simmering, M. J. (2003). E-learning: emerging uses, emperical results and future directions. *International Journal of Training and Development, 7*(4), 245–258.

Wickens, C. D., Hutchins, S., Carolan, T., & Cumming, J. (2012). Effectiveness of part-task training and increasing difficulty training strategies: A meta-analysis approach. *Human Factors, 55*, 461–470.

Yang, Y., & Durrington, V. (2010). Investigation of students' perceptions of online course. *International Journal on E-Learning, 9*(3), 341–361.

Yanson, R., & Johnson, R. D. (2016). An empirical examination of e-learning design: The role of trainee socialization and complexity in short term training. *Computers & Education, 101*, 43–54.

Zack, M. H., & McKinney, J. L. (1995). Social context and interaction in ongoing computer-supported management group. *Organization Science, 6*(4), 394–422.

Zhang, D., Zhao, J. L., Zhou, L., & Nunamaker Jr., J. F. (2004). Can e-learning replace classroom learning? *Communications of the ACM, 47*(5), 75–79.

CHAPTER 7

ELECTRONIC PERFORMANCE MANAGEMENT

Does Altering the Process Improve the Outcome?

Stephanie C. Payne, Anjelica M. Mendoza, and Margaret T. Horner

ABSTRACT

Electronic performance management (ePM) systems have flourished and are now used by a large percentage of US Organizations (Sierra-Cedar, 2016). Considering the fast-paced growth of adoption, it is important to determine if these changes are helping or hurting corresponding human resource management processes. In the meantime, another workforce trend is a growing dissatisfaction with the traditional performance appraisal process (Aguinis, Joo, & Gottfredson, 2011; Pulakos & O'Leary, 2011). Although the formal annual evaluation has traditionally been the cornerstone of performance management, there is a growing perception in practice that performance ratings are of little value to organizations (Adler et al., 2016). In light of these issues, many organizations claim to have stopped gathering performance ratings entirely (Culbert, 2008; Resker, 2017; Rock, Davis & Jones, 2014; Rock & Jones, 2015). The purpose of this chapter is to describe how technology

The Brave New World of eHRM 2.0, pages 189–215.

impacts the performance management process and can potentially address some of the concerns raised about traditional performance appraisal. We propose that technology influences the performance management process in the following five ways. It (1) automates, (2) documents, (3) integrates, (4) structures, and (5) makes the process more accessible and these changes can in turn result in altered employee outcomes. We summarize the limited research on ePM, describe how ePM has the potential to address various age-old performance appraisal problems, and put forward 15 propositions and research questions in order to inspire new research-based insights and empirical evidence to support corresponding practice.

The union of human resources (HR) processes and technology has created transformative changes in Human Resource Management (HRM; Gueutal, 2003; Stone & Dulebohn, 2013). In Sierra-Cedar's most recent (2016–2017) survey on the adoption and utilization of eHRM, the "HRM application journey" begins with administrative applications like payroll and benefit administration. They report that 98% of their 3,544 survey respondents representing 1,528 organizations have a payroll solution/software system and 92% use an eHRM system. eHRM systems are more likely to be used by large organizations due to their size and complexity. Many small organizations use standalone software products for particular HR functions (e.g., applicant tracking, OSHA reporting) or report plans to implement an eHRM system in the next year.

eHRM is a standardized platform to support multiple HR functions. Some of the functions include administrative applications (payroll, profile management, benefits, and human resource analytics), workforce management (time keeping and labor tracking systems, absence and leave management, and scheduling), and talent management (recruiting, training, performance management, and compensation). eHRM systems typically contain self-service elements in which the employees can access information and make updates without needing assistance from the HR department. Manager self-service allows managers to review applicant resumes; evaluate employees; and approve merit bonuses, incentives, and training. In general, eHRM streamlines HR processes.

A trend within the adoption of eHRM is the movement to the cloud and to mobile-enabled technology. A cloud-based HRM system is fully supported by an external provider and usually subscription-based with or without an upfront license fee. All updates and technology-related problems are handled by the external provider. Over half of core HRM systems are cloud-based solutions, which are accessed online by employees and supervisors and standardized across the company (Mercer, 2016). Of the organizations surveyed by Sierra-Cedar (2016), 40% have adopted mobile-enabled eHRM. There is also the hybrid option of cloud and local software in which some HR functions are embedded in the cloud and others are accessed via local software. Considering the fast-paced growth of these movements, is it important to determine if these changes are helping, hurting, or having no effect on HR processes like performance management (PM).

WORKFORCE TREND #1: ADOPTION OF ELECTRONIC PERFORMANCE MANAGEMENT

Within eHRM systems, there are often suites of functions that are dedicated to specific HR purposes such as "Talent Management." Whereas other eHRM suites were developed for the administration of HR processes like payroll, talent management suites tend to focus on the management of human capital including employee careers and skill development in order to satisfy organizational goals and needs. As with other eHRM applications, supervisors and employees can access and utilize these systems; however, supervisors are likely to have additional permissions and capabilities. Within a talent management suite, one is likely to find what some have labeled the four pillars of talent management, which are recruitment, PM, professional development, and compensation management (TechTarget, n.d.)

Software companies use different terms to refer to the electronic performance management (ePM) module or application. For example, PeopleFluent and Ultimate Software, refer to their ePM module simply as "Performance Management," whereas SAP SuccessFactors' ePM is embedded within the "Performance and Goals" module. Additionally, ePM modules can be sold as a stand-alone product (e.g., Frontier Software's "e-Performance") or as part of a larger eHRM system (e.g., Oracle, Workday, and Ceridian).

Likewise, in the research literature, ePM has been referred to by many different names including Business Performance Management (BPM; Neely, 1999), Electronic Performance Support Systems (EPSS; Raybould, 1990), technology-based performance management systems (Pulakos, 2009), and Electronic Performance Measurement Systems (EPMS; Keong Choong, 2014). It is also important to note that *electronic performance monitoring* is also sometimes abbreviated as "EPM" in the literature (McNall & Roch, 2009). This is particularly problematic as electronic performance monitoring is *not* the same as an electronic performance management system. Electronic performance monitoring systems are designed to continually observe, record, and analyze information related to an employee's performance (Stanton, 2000). While some providers like Workday offer both performance monitoring and ePM applications, others do not. When performance monitoring data are linked to ePM, raters can easily consider these data when generating ratings.

Whereas there is very limited research on ePM, there is considerable research on electronic performance monitoring and because elements of this can be included or incorporated into an ePM system, we very briefly review some of the research on this sensitive and somewhat controversial topic. Electronic performance monitoring systems have been implemented in a number of large organizations. For example, in 2013, the Bank of America implemented "sociometric solutions" which are sensors in their employee ID badges that gather real time information about the customer-facing employees' tone of voice, movement, and posture (Giang, 2013). Likewise, Amazon uses wearable monitors to document the number of boxes each employee packs in an hour (Streitfield, 2015). Studies have shown that performance monitoring is positively associated with higher levels of task performance (Aiello & Kolb, 1995; Bhave, 2014; Goomas & Ludwig, 2009). However, controversy surrounds the efficacy and ethicacy of constantly monitoring the movements and actions of employees (Perkins, 2013), given its negative association with job satisfaction and health outcomes (Smith, Carayon, Sanders, Lim, & LeGrande, 1992). The extent to which ePM may prompt more utilization of performance monitoring software is unknown, however the two are clearly related and research on the combination of the two is needed.

It is clear that these ePM systems have grown considerably in popularity. In their annual HR systems survey of small, medium, and large organizations across a wide array of industries, Sierra-Cedar (2016) reported that 92% of the responding organizations use ePM systems. Fifty-six percent of the organizations that use ePM systems are small (2,500 employees or fewer) which highlights the growing prevalence of these systems. There is also a trend to adopt mobile-enabled systems. Indeed, of the organizations that had adopted ePM systems, 28% have adopted mobile-enabled PM systems and another 10% planned to adopt these systems within the next year. The fast rate at which ePM technology is advancing (Vasudeva, Good, & Eerrenstein, n.d.) suggests that these systems will continue to evolve, presenting an opportunity for HRM researchers to shape decisions embedded within the process using rigorous research.

Aguinis (2013) defines PM as a "continuous process of identifying, measuring and developing the performance of individuals and teams, and aligning performance with the strategic goals of the organization" (p. 2). Broadly speaking, most ePM systems consist of *three sub-processes*: (1) setting goals and tracking performance relative to these goals, (2) evaluating employee performance, and (3) generating and distributing performance feedback. Appropriately, a Capterra survey of HR professionals from over 500 organizations found that performance appraisal, goal management, and 360-degree feedback were among the primary ePM functions used across industries (Wille, 2016).

When part of a broader eHRM system, ePM can retrieve and populate relevant data (e.g., position description, duties, task statements, goals, definitions) from other modules so as to customize screens for individual employees and to give the rater easy access to applicable information. For example, rather than rating employees on a generic set of performance dimensions, each employee could be evaluated on the task statements listed in his/her position description. When ePM is a part of a bigger eHRM system, data can be linked across HR processes, allowing for an endless number of HR analytics. For instance, performance ratings could be aggregated by recruitment sources or pre-employment test scores (ClearCompany, 2017) allowing for an analysis of the quality of hires or validation of selection tools. Within the Workday Talent Management System, each employee has a professional profile that details his/her job description, ratings of performance, proficiencies, and work experience. Managers can use these profiles to help develop their talent, to track performance across the employee's tenure, and to do some workforce planning, as well as succession planning. This is especially helpful in really large, global organizations where employees are located all over the world.

Each software system has its own structure and features that make it unique. For example, some mobile-focused ePM providers create applications similar to social media and fitness trackers where everyone in the company has the opportunity to leave real-time anonymous feedback to foster a climate for feedback (HighGround; Impraise), which is believed to increase the likelihood that employees will accept feedback (Cleveland & Murphy, 2016).

WORKFORCE TREND #2: DISSATISFACTION WITH THE TRADITIONAL PA PROCESS

There is a long-held and growing perception in practice that performance appraisal (PA) is of little value to organizations, it is ineffective, and/or has a negative impact on engagement and organizational culture (Adler et al., 2016; Aguinis, Joo, & Gottfredson, 2011; Deming, 1982; Murphy & Cleveland, 1995; Pettijohn, Parker, Pettijohn, & Kent, 2001). A *traditional PA* is characterized by an annual or biannual evaluation whereby the supervisor delivers feedback about employee performance by generating ratings on a standardized form. These ratings are then shown to the employee who must sign the form to acknowledge his/her supervisor's assessment of his/her performance and then the forms are placed in an employee's personnel file.

Managers spend hours completing evaluations which they feel are not effective and employees are rated on a system that has been described as frustrating, bureaucratic, and irrelevant to their jobs (Adler et al., 2016). As a result, PA skeptics have encouraged organizations to cease conducting PAs entirely (Culbert, 2008; Resker, 2017; Rock, Davis & Jones, 2014; Rock & Jones, 2015). Some organizations such as GE, Deloitte, and Adobe have followed suit eliminating the traditional annual rating process (Baer, 2014; Baldassarre & Finken, 2015; Buckingham & Goodall, 2015), despite discouragement by PA scholars (e.g., Adler et al., 2016; Cleveland & Murphy, 2016).

One of the core issues underlying many of the criticisms about PA is the use of performance ratings for multiple purposes. Cleveland, Murphy, and Williams (1989) identified four primary PA purposes demonstrating its potential versatility and importance to organizations:

1. to make decisions between employees,
2. to make decisions within employees,
3. to make system maintenance decisions, and
4. to document actions and decisions for legal requirements.

In a classic PA article, Meyer, Kay, and French (1965) noted that when supervisors conduct PAs for multiple purposes, they are faced with conflicting roles of both coach and a judge. As a coach, managers guide employees through feedback to improve their performance (Ellinger, Beattie, & Hamlin, 2010). As a judge, managers decide whether employees perform satisfactorily and determine whether they have earned a raise or promotion or should experience punitive actions (Moberg, 2003). Despite the potential versatility and efficiency of using one assessment for multiple purposes, PA scholars strongly oppose using one assessment for more than one purpose (Cleveland & Murphy, 2016).

Despite the dissatisfaction or perhaps because of it, there is a strong desire to fix it (e.g., Pulakos, Hanson, Arad, & Moye, 2014; Smither, 2015) and/or identify alternatives. The reality is organizations continue to need to evaluate and manage employee performance in order to justify or back-up administrative decisions (e.g., pay raises) and provide employees with feedback. In a recent poll of the Society for Industrial and Organizational Psychology (SIOP) membership, the highest rated workplace trend for 2017 was Performance Management (Society for Industrial and Organizational Psychology, 2016). Within PM, there has been a movement away from once-a-year PAs to more frequent and real-time feedback. Instead of focusing on evaluation, there is an emphasis on improvement (i.e. PM rather than PA). Correspondingly, there is also a need to ensure managers have the resources and skills to provide more frequent coaching and feedback. Informal feedback methods, like coaching, encourage managers to regularly guide employee success through conversations about goal progress, skill development, and well-being (Grant, 2017). HRM scholars need to empirically determine the right balance between feedback for the purpose of coaching and more formal feedback for organization-wide processes to critically assess the efficacy of new PM systems including ePM (cf. SIOP, 2016).

CAN ePM FIX PA?

The effectiveness of an e-HRM system can be evaluated a number of different ways. For example, Stone and her colleagues (2003) articulated both functional and dysfunctional consequences of eHRM for both employees and their organizations. Alternatively, Strohmeier (2007) examined micro and macro-level consequences. Micro-level consequences are impacts on the user like acceptance and satisfaction which can be predicted based on the technology acceptance model (e.g., Marler & Dulebohn, 2005). Macro-level consequences are impacts at a higher level of analysis. They include relational consequences between the employee and others (e.g., supervisor), operational consequences like reducing costs or alleviating administrative burdens for the supervisor or HR department, as well as transformational consequences such as the generation of HR analytics that can be used to contribute to overall organizational performance (Snell, Stueber, & Lepak, 2002).

As we examine the role that technology can play in PM systems, we propose that the majority of the immediate consequences (or direct outcomes) are operational or procedural. In fact, Krauss and Snyder (2009 identify a number of elements that can be automated and ways that technology can potentially enhance the process and make it less labor-intensive for the supervisor. To the extent that ePM is associated with *relational* consequences (e.g., improvements in communication or interpersonal relationships), technology could address age-old challenges to PA. At the same time, it is critical to point out that technology is not a panacea. It will not correct a poor supervisor-employee relationship, inappropriate supervi- sor behaviors, or a poorly implemented process. As Pulakos and O'Leary (2011) noted, "Done effectively, performance management communicates what is important to the organization, drives employees to achieve results, and implements the organization's strategy. Done poorly, performance management not only fails to achieve these benefits but can also undermine employee confidence and damage relationships" (p. 147). Furthermore, Farr, Fairchild, and Cassidy (2013) point out that technology is simply a tool to facilitate the process and "should not be the driving force behind the process" (p. 83).

In an effort to reduce the science-practice gap on the topic of PM (Banks & Murphy, 1985), PA research is needed to inform the way that ePM is designed and implemented. The *purpose* of this chapter is to describe how the movement to ePM has the potential to address some PA challenges. We summarize the very limited research on ePM and put forth a number of propositions that we hope will provide new research-based insights and empirical evidence to support corresponding practice.

HOW DOES TECHNOLOGY AFFECT PERFORMANCE MANAGEMENT?

We propose that technology indirectly addresses some of the challenges raised about PA by altering various aspects of the PM process. Specifically, we propose that technology

a. automates,
b. documents,
c. integrates,
d. structures, and
e. makes the process more accessible.

We depict both the proximal and distal influences of technology on the PM process in Figure 7.1.

Briefly, within an ePM system, communication, data analyses, and reporting tasks can be automated reducing the amount of time and effort devoted to these tasks (Krauss & Snyder, 2009). ePM systems also serve as repositories of data concerning various PM-related processes and outcomes; thus, to a certain extent

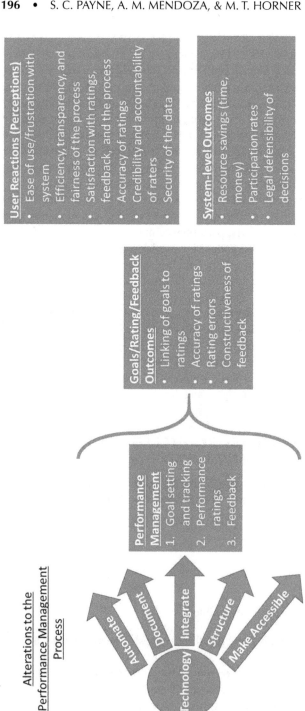

FIGURE 7.1. Impact of Technology on the Performance Management Process

ePM systems document, store, and archive an extensive amount of performance-related data (Farr et al., 2013). As noted earlier, ePM systems are often integrated into a broader eHRM system and some interface with other systems (e.g., performance monitoring) allowing for data to be retrieved from these systems. ePM systems impose structure on the process which can and should be customized to how managers within the organization have decided the various related procedures should be implemented, but it also likely facilitates standardization of the process within the organization. Finally, ePM systems make it easy to access performance-related data and to conduct PM-related tasks.

In order for ePM to address the concerns previously raised about PA, it will need to improve or enhance traditional PM outcomes (e.g., ratings), user reactions, and system-level outcomes. It will have a significant impact if it affects these outcomes as they are considered the most important (Cleveland & Murphy, 2016). Consistent with how ePM providers market the capabilities of ePM systems, we propose that technology directly influences the PM process (Oracle, 2009), which may, in turn, influence the distal individual and organizational outcomes depicted in Figure 7.1. However, rigorous research studies are needed to determine if such improvements do occur. Next, we elaborate on the various ways that technology directly affects the PM process. Along the way, we offer propositions about how ePM influences the distal outcomes. Table 7.1 summarizes all of the research propositions and research questions put forth.

Automate

The most fundamental change that technology brings to PM is to automate some aspects of the process which should, in turn, enhance the speed and efficiency of the process (Krauss & Snyder, 2009). Overall, ePM systems can reduce the resources expended by automating many of the tedious PM tasks that involve communication, analyses, and documentation.

Various forms of communication like notifications, alerts, and reminders can be sent out automatically based on calendar dates (e.g., an employee's anniversary date), relative to the last evaluation or submission of feedback (e.g., every six months), upon completion of a task or project, or in response to a request. Communications can be sent to employees at all levels of the organization, as well as stakeholders outside the organization (e.g., clients). Ideally, any reminders would automatically cease upon completion of the requested task. Likewise, employees can be automatically prompted to set goals and log performance progress to date.

In addition to automated communications, some data could automatically populate based on organizational records or who was logged into the system (e.g., name of supervisor, date of evaluation). Some quality-control elements could be automated as well. For example, the system could be structured so that a rater cannot submit his/her ratings unless they are complete or a rating of "needs improvement" requires a meaningful comment before the system will allow the rater to proceed, possibly enhancing the quality of the ratings provided.

TABLE 7.1.   PA Challenges, ePM Features, and Research Propositions and Questions

Traditional PA Challenge	Alteration to PM Process	Research Proposition/Question
Rating errors	Automate	*Proposition 1:* ePM ratings screened for rater errors and corrected will have fewer rater errors than traditional PA ratings.
Employee dissatisfaction	Automate	*Proposition 2:* Employees who receive ePM ratings screened for rater errors will be more satisfied with their ratings than ratings not screened for errors.
Employee dissatisfaction	Automate	*Proposition 3:* When ePM prompts supervisors and employees to share their PM goals with each other, employees are less dissatisfied with the process.
Quantity of supervisor feedback	Automate	*Proposition 4:* Employees evaluated using ePM report significantly more feedback than employees evaluated using traditional PA.
Timeliness of feedback	Automate	*Proposition 5:* Employees evaluated using ePM report more timely feedback than employees evaluated using traditional PA.
Accountability	Document	*Proposition 6:* Employees are significantly more likely to perceive supervisors as accountable for the completion and accuracy of ePM ratings than traditional PA ratings.
Accountability	Document	*Proposition 7:* Supervisors are significantly more likely to report feeling accountable for completing timely and accurate ePM ratings than traditional PA ratings.
Compliance and bias	Document	*Proposition 8:* ePM screened data (ratings and comments) are more legally defensible than traditional PA data.
Fair, accurate, and legally defensible ratings	Integrate	*Proposition 9:* ePM ratings generated when consulting additional data are perceived as more fair, accurate, and are more legally defensible than traditional PA ratings.
Relationship between ratings and objective performance data	Integrate	*Proposition 10:* Objective performance data will be more strongly related to subjective performance ratings when raters have objective data readily available to them within ePM when making ratings.
Interrater reliability	Integrate	*Proposition 11:* ePM self-evaluations will have a stronger relationship with ePM supervisor ratings than traditional self-evaluations have with traditional PA supervisor ratings.
Conflicting supervisor roles	Standardize	*Proposition 12:* Supervisors will report feeling fewer conflicting PA roles when using ePM that separates developmental and evaluative ratings compared to traditional PA.
Quantity of peer feedback	Standardize	*Proposition 13:* Employees evaluated using ePM report receiving more peer feedback than employees evaluated using traditional PA.
Quantity and frequency of feedback from multiple sources	Automate	*Research Question 1:* What is the optimal amount of work-related feedback and how frequently should it be delivered?
Security of personnel data	Access	*Research Question 2:* Are ePM data less secure than traditional PA data?

Various data analyses, comparisons, and reporting could be automatically conducted such as correlations across data sources, interrater reliabilities, changes in ratings over time, rating trends by rater or level of the rater (e.g., subordinates) and automatically populated into a pre-formatted report. Performance could be tracked over time using graphs which make it easier to see change. Additionally, between-person comparisons of ratings could facilitate employment-related decisions (e.g., raises, promotions).

Rater errors. Automating data screening and analyses can directly address the long-standing issue of rater errors among the ratings (Borman & Dunnette, 1975). When ratings take on predetermined patterns (e.g., negative skew, halo, central tendency), raters can be alerted to these potential errors in real time. They could then be prompted to make corrections or adjustments ideally reducing the number of errors present in the data, potentially making them more accurate. However, thresholds for these patterns need to be established and agreed upon in advance.

Proposition 1: ePM ratings screened for rater errors and corrected will have fewer rater errors than traditional PA ratings.

Proposition 2: Employees who receive ePM ratings screened for rater errors will be more satisfied with their ratings than ratings not screened for errors.

Rater goals. It has been proposed that supervisors lack the motivation to evaluate accurately and they have multiple, sometimes conflicting, goals (e.g., Murphy, Cleveland, Skattebo, & Kinney, 2004). Thus, ePM is more likely to be effective if it encourages supervisors to be motivated to provide accurate ratings and meaningful feedback. One way that automation within ePM systems could address rater goals is to prompt supervisors and employees at the beginning of any ePM feedback report to list or check-off their primary goal for a given feedback session. Typically, goal-setting in a PM context focuses on performance goals. Here goals would be oriented on objectives desired from the ratings and/ or feedback session. Murphy et al. (2004) identified four kinds of rater goals: task performance, interpersonal, strategic, and internalized goals. Additionally, we propose that there are organizational compliance goals as federal and state-funded organizations are required to comply with various rules including having an evaluation for each employee every year or they will be fined by auditors for failing to comply. For example, an employee may report the following personal strategic goal "to learn what I need to do to be eligible to be promoted to the next level," whereas a supervisor might report the following organizational compliance goal "to complete this task that I am required to do." Inevitably, this would give supervisors and employees something to reflect on and to discuss. At a minimum, sharing goals could promote more communication about perceptions of these processes and ideally over time, they could work together to ensure both of their goals are met.

Proposition 3: When ePM prompts supervisors and employees to share their PM goals with each other, they are more likely to discuss them which could, in turn, result in employees who are more satisfied with the PM process.

Feedback. PA scholars point out that PA is predicated on the unsubstantiated assumptions that (1) employees want to receive feedback, (2) raters can generate accurate feedback, and (3) employees are motivated to respond to that feedback (e.g., Adler et al., 2016). This is further complicated by the issue that PAs are frequently conducted annually, which is not often enough, assuming there are reasons to give employees feedback more frequently than that. It is quite likely that employees will complete tasks or projects, perform exceptionally well, or perform less than perfectly multiple times within a year. Correspondingly, they deserve feedback more than frequently than once a year.

ePM has the potential to promote more frequent feedback simply by automatically prompting for it. It would be relatively easy to embed more opportunities for evaluations and feedback into the system. Rather than annual reviews, supervisors could be prompted to submit quarterly reviews. However, quantity is not quality. So, we are skeptical if more is better as others have noted the excessive feedback can be perceived as harassment (Cleveland & Murphy, 2016). Instead, the frequency of reviews could be tied to the completion of projects and thus be presented "real-time" or at least relatively closely (e.g., within one week) of project completion, rather than numerous months later. Ideally, the recommended timeframe for the immediacy of feedback would be scientifically determined. Behaviorism theory supports the superiority of immediate feedback over delayed feedback. Research is needed to determine if ePM actually results in the delivery of more frequent feedback and the perception of more feedback.

Organizations may want to set a cap or maximum number of times an employee can request feedback to ensure that supervisors are not overburdened by such requests. Likewise, the organization may want to also set minimum and maximum numbers of feedback delivery options as well to ensure employees receive a minimum amount of feedback but also do not feel harassed (cf, Cleveland & Murphy, 2016). What is the optimal amount of feedback and how frequently should it be delivered are empirical questions that remain to be tested and ePM presents a unique opportunity to manipulate and test it.

Proposition 4: Employees evaluated using ePM report significantly more feedback than employees evaluated using traditional PA.

Proposition 5: Employees evaluated using ePM report more timely feedback than employees evaluated using traditional PA.

Research Question 1: What is the optimal amount of work-related feedback and how frequently should it be delivered?

Document

The second way that the PM process is enhanced by technology is documentation and archiving of the process and the information contained therein. Historically, most PA data would concern the content of the evaluation and a little bit of the process such as who submitted the ratings and when. These data would traditionally be archived in an employee's paper personnel file which are usually organized by employees' last names. ePM presents the opportunity to relatively easily capture data on various aspects of the process in addition to the content. The range of process-oriented data is endless including but not limited to: who completed what ratings when, how many reminders were necessary, how long it took to complete the ratings, who did not complete ratings, who provided constructive comments, characteristics of those who provide the most timely and/or constructive feedback, etc. Additional process-related data include the time and date of all notifications, alerts, and actions within the software application. This facilitates oversight and the ability to track progress on all of the PM sub-processes.

Rater accountability. PM process-related data could automatically be generated and populated into reports that may be informative to supervisor evaluations, addressing a long held concern about the lack of supervisor accountability in PA (Church & Bracken, 1997; Lewis, 2011). This feature could improve the timeliness and overall rate of completion, thus potentially enhancing the overall experience for both employees and supervisors. Together with the previously noted automation enhancements, these data could be automatically recorded, tracked, and summarized without extensive additional effort.

On the other hand, the embedded identification information within technology makes it difficult to gather anonymous 360-degree ratings. Even if the identity of the raters is masked, it is likely that someone has access to who generated what ratings, which is likely to make some employees apprehensive about providing honest ratings and feedback.

Rating accuracy/quality. PA researchers have lamented the lack of criteria available for evaluating the accuracy of performance ratings. ePM systems may facilitate the collection and analysis of additional types of data to check and improve the accuracy of ratings. For example, qualitative comments, video recordings, and transcripts of dialogue could be analyzed and evaluated for correspondence with ratings generated. For example, following extensive coding of transcripts of PA interviews (i.e., feedback sessions), Meinecke, Lehmann-Willenbrock, and Kauffeld (2017) revealed that successful interviews were associated with both task- and relation-oriented communications by the supervisor. Theoretically, using a similar coding scheme, ePM systems could scan supervisor comments and/or video-recorded interviews for corresponding communications, provide feedback to supervisors about the nature of these communications, and prompt for corrections when deficiencies are detected.

Proposition 6: Employees are significantly more likely to perceive supervisors as accountable for the completion and accuracy of ePM ratings than traditional PA ratings.

Proposition 7: Supervisors are significantly more likely to report feeling accountable for completing timely and accurate ePM ratings than traditional PA ratings.

Technology may also indirectly enhance the legal defensibility of PM by automatically screening and integrating additional data into the process. For example, ratings and comments could be screened for alignment with one another and with organizational goals (an issue lamented in the research literature, Pulakos et al., 2014). Further, ePM systems can screen for aspects of the evaluation that have appeared in litigation. For example, supervisor comments could be screened for inappropriate words (Cardy & Miller, 2005). SAP SuccessFactors advertises that their ePM application includes built-in writing assistants that aid the user by providing templates and reviewing the content to offer suggestions to improve the quality of the evaluations (SAP SuccessFactors, n.d). One of the review functions SAP SuccessFactors offers is a legal-scan that identifies words that are legally sensitive. Upon finding such words, the program flags the words and explains the legal context under which the words may be inappropriate. The program then suggests alternative wording that can replace the flagged language. Additionally, the integration of more objective data sources (performance monitoring, timeliness of task completion, number of goals accomplished) should make it easier for supervisors to use this information when they complete their evaluations which should result in more accurate ratings and thus more legally defensible ratings.

Proposition 8: ePM screened data (ratings and comments) are more legally defensible than traditional PA data.

Integrate

As noted earlier, ePM is frequently one application or module embedded or integrated within a broader eHRM software system. Thus, it is a part of a centralized system that houses multiple HR functions. Beyond being integrated with other HRM practices, technology can facilitate the formatting of information and integration of data from other sources as well. ePM systems can make it easy to see and compare data from multiple sources at the same time (e.g., on the same screen). Ideally, the integration of other data extends the amount of data available for raters to consider when generating ratings. Some examples of these data include but are not limited to performance monitoring data, attendance records, hours worked, sales, injuries, compensation, physiological data from wearables (e.g., average number of steps taken each day), as well as employee and customer survey data. Integrating additional data into the PM process should reduce the subjectivity of the ratings resulting in ratings that are perceived to be more accurate and fair. Personnel decisions (e.g., termination, promotion) based on multiple sources of data should also be more legally defensible than ratings without these additional data. For instance, performance monitoring data concerning the amount of time an employee spends "off-task" would support a low rating and in turn, a termination decision.

> *Proposition 9:* ePM ratings generated when consulting additional data are perceived as more fair, accurate, and are more legally defensible than traditional PA ratings.

PM sub-processes (goal setting, performance ratings, and feedback) are also integrated within the ePM system. For example, ratings can be scheduled to follow time-sensitive goals, so that employees receive timely feedback. Performance data can be graphed relative to goals to reflect how well performance met expectations. Employees can be prompted to set new goals following the completion of earlier goals and/or receiving ratings and feedback from others. Ideally, this integration improves the quality of the ratings generated, feedback provided, and overall experience for the employee and the raters.

Misaligned ratings. Another challenge faced in PA practice is the misalignment between employee performance and the ratings they receive. ePM systems have the potential to address this concern by presenting the supervisor with data from other sources. Previous research has shown that objective performance data are not very strongly related to subjective performance data ($\rho = .39$; Bommer, Johnson, Rich, Podsakoff, & MacKenzie, 1995). In an ePM context where subjective ratings can be informed by objective data, it seems inevitable that objective and subjective data will be more highly related than they have been in the past.

> *Proposition 10: Objective performance data will be more strongly related to subjective performance ratings when raters have objective data readily available to them within ePM when making ratings.*

Structure

Fundamentally, technology imposes structure and boundaries and by doing so, this results in standardization. Thus, ePM helps to standardize the PM process to ensure some similarities in the way that it is completed across employees within the organization. ePM systems could also standardize the PM process across organizations if organizations simply buy the software off the shelf and do not alter it in any way (i.e., accept the default settings). However, it is more likely that an organization will be involved in contributing to the decisions embedded within the system and have some influence on the process (Johnson & Gueutal, 2011), thus *customizing* the content and process to their given organization, but within that structure, the system should facilitate some standardization (e.g., all entry-level employees are evaluated by their immediate supervisor every six months starting at the beginning of the fiscal year).

The standardization of the PM process is a place where ideally science has contributed to practice and where we believe HR researchers can further contribute. For example, it is well-established that it is better and more legally defensible to evaluate employees on behaviors rather than traits (Malos, 1998); correspondingly, ePM systems should be structured so that raters are asked to evaluate behaviors. Although there are a handful of best practices and recommendations about how to design a good PM system (e.g., Mohrman, Resnick-West, & Lawler, 1989; Smither & London, 2009), there is room for considerably more research (Farr et al., 2013).

Numerous decisions are embedded into ePM systems including who is rated and by whom, what they are rated on, how frequently they are rated, how the ratings are used, etc. Further, there are a number of process-related decisions that are embedded as well including how long will raters be given to complete the task, when will notifications be sent, the nature of these notifications, how many reminders will be sent, will raters be allowed to submit ratings after a deadline and if so for how long after the deadline, are ratings approved by anyone and if so who approves and how long are they given to do so, how much archival performance data and ratings will be stored and easily retrievable and by whom, will self-ratings be collected and if so, will they evaluate the same dimensions as other raters, will self-ratings be made available to the supervisor and if so, when? The list is endless. Additionally, as noted earlier, the inclusion of performance monitoring data presents additional customization decisions (who, what, where, when, and how performance is monitored) that should be grounded in scientific data and the integration of these two systems presents all kinds of new research questions that have yet to be answered.

Rater disagreement. Another problem with PA ratings is that raters disagree when evaluating the same performance (Adler et al., 2016; Harris & Schaubroeck, 1988; Heidemeier & Moser, 2009). Theoretically, rater disagreement has been attributed to meaningful variance due to different rater roles, perspectives, and observations (e.g., supervisor vs. customer; Murphy & DeShon, 2000). Disagreement has also been interpreted as error (Ones, Viswesvaran, & Schmidt, 2008). Despite the disagreement over what the discrepancy among raters can be attributed to, researchers tend to agree that low rates of interrater reliability and agreement are concerning.

ePM systems have the potential to facilitate the identification of rating discrepancies and to prompt raters to address these discrepancies before feedback is given to the focal employee. Just prompting raters to explain why they rated the way they did could be illuminating to the science that has tried to explain rater discrepancies (e.g., Harris & Schaubroeck, 1988; Heidemeier & Moser, 2009) and insightful to both the raters and ratees. This information could clarify expectations about performance, reveal information about the relative importance of various tasks and major work behaviors or duties, and reveal other differences related to the rating process like how performance dimensions and rating anchors are interpreted across raters.

Many ePM systems include an opportunity for the employee to generate self-ratings. If this information is readily available and possibly even prepopulates into the supervisor's evaluation, we propose there will be fewer discrepancies between self and supervisor ratings. It may also result in shorter feedback meetings following assessments as the supervisor and employee may only need to focus on the dimensions about which they disagree. On the other hand, if the supervisor accepts all of the employee's self-ratings as his/her own, the employee might feel like he or she has done the supervisor's job and resent that the supervisor did not have to expend much effort. ePM is not likely to resolve rater discrepancies, but it can bring discrepancies to various stakeholders' attention and indirectly promote communication about them before moving the evaluation to the next step in the process.

> *Proposition 11: ePM self-evaluations will have a stronger relationship with ePM supervisor ratings than traditional self-evaluations have with traditional PA supervisor ratings.*

Multiple uses. Recognizing the well-established influence of the purpose or use of the appraisal on the ratings (Jawarahar & Williams, 1997), some researchers have proposed that the resolution to this conflict is to *separate* evaluation for development in time from evaluation for administrative decisions (Meyer et al., 1965) although the efficacy of this solution does not appear to have been empirically tested. Alternatively, the supervisor can be tasked with only generating developmental feedback and serving as a coach, and ratings from others (e.g., subordinates, peers, and customers) could be averaged for administrative decision making.

Thus, in contrast to technology integrating the PM process, ePM could facilitate the separation of developmental and administrative PM purposes by being structured so that each has a separate module and ratings are not easily accessible when generating developmental feedback. To further substantiate the separation, the tasks or statements evaluated for developmental purposes could be customized to the employee's position description and populated directly from that document; whereas the items or dimensions evaluated for administrative reasons could be standardized across all employees so everyone is rated on the same dimensions, facilitating perceptions of procedural justice. Ratings for administrative decisions could populate to other modules designed for approving merit raises or bonuses or directly to compensation/payroll modules. Further, the coaching relationship between employees and their supervisors might be improved by structuring the ePM system so that employees are encouraged to provide feedback to their supervisors as well.

> *Proposition 12: Supervisors will report feeling fewer conflicting PA roles when using ePM that separates developmental and evaluative ratings compared to traditional PA.*

Multi-source feedback. ePM systems can serve as the backbone for 360-degree assessments (Farr et al., 2013) so that anyone can provide feedback to anyone else, promoting a more complete view and perspective of the employees' performance. Logistically, the collection and comparison of these ratings are likely to be much easier due to the automation features embedded in ePM. Further, statistical calculations could be pre-programmed, so that various descriptive statistics could be calculated instantaneously upon entering the ratings. Some research suggests that 360-degree evaluations are most useful when they are anonymous and used for developmental purposes rather than evaluative purposes (Balzer, Greguras, & Raymark, 2004; Tornow, 1993). Correspondingly, ePM systems should be structured accordingly (e.g., the identity of raters disassociated with the ratings).

> *Proposition 13: Employees evaluated using ePM report receiving more peer feedback than employees evaluated using traditional PA.*

Make Accessible

Finally, technology affects access to the process and data therein. The ability to conduct PM sub-processes from anywhere and at any time is a great benefit of technology. This removes any restrictions on when and where PM sub-processes were previously conducted (e.g., 8 am–5 pm, Monday through Friday in the office), making it more convenient for all parties involved. ePM vendors boast both cloud and mobile-enabled platforms to increase accessibility beyond the office (SAP SuccessFactors News Center, 2017), using multiple mediums (e.g., tablets and mobile devices). As a result, employees have some discretion over when they access it and may receive more timely feedback (Proposition 5). Further, some vendors' software programs integrate with wearables (e.g., Apple Watch) which allow employees to access goal and task tracking information from these devices (Betterworks). This increase in access may make sensitive data less secure which is another empirical question.

> *Research Question 2: Are ePM data less secure than traditional PA data?*

Goals/Ratings/Feedback Outcomes

Perhaps the ultimate test of the value of ePM is the extent to which it positively impacts the focal outcomes of the sub-processes: goals, ratings, and feedback. Ideally, goals are linked to ratings, ratings are accurate and free of the previously discussed rater errors, and feedback is constructive.

User Reactions

As indicated by the various research propositions put forth, technology-induced alterations to the PM process are expected to result in positive user reactions. Users include all potential stakeholders but particularly employees, supervisors, and HR personnel. There are a wide-range of user reactions that are likely to be affected including but not limited to those listed in Figure 7.1. These include traditional reactions associated with new technology/software systems like the ease of use and frustration with the system itself.

Theoretically, ePM is a part of a user-friendly interface that supervisors are comfortable using on a regular basis. Ideally, all of the information that an employee and supervisor need to set goals, complete an evaluation or provide feedback should be available in one place, thus ePM has the potential to streamline the process and reduce the amount of time it takes to complete the evaluations. However, this is most likely to be the case after supervisors have learned how to use the program and can easily navigate through it with relatively efficiency. Thus, any new program is likely to involve a bit of a learning curve and if employees and supervisors do not access it routinely, invariably they will need some re-familiarity time.

Whereas electronic systems are intended to make life easier, sometimes technology can over-complicate a process, take a long time to learn, or be too structured and rigid (Stone et al., 2003), especially for those with less technology-related experience (Farr et al., 2013). Given its anticipated influence on processes, ePM is also expected to influence user perceptions of how efficient, transparent, and fair the process is. Traditional PA-related user reactions (Keeping & Levy, 2000) like satisfaction with the ratings and process, perceived credibility of the raters and accountability to provide accurate ratings, as well as perceptions about the security of the data will also remain relevant.

System-Level Outcomes

Ideally, ePM results in organization or system level improvements in the PM process. As depicted in Figure 7.1, this includes the amount of organizational resources allocated to the process including personnel time and money. Other system-level outcomes include but are not limited to participation rates across multiple constituents including managers, supervisors, employees, customers, etc. It could also include the legal defensibility of employment-related decisions. It is particularly informative to consider how these outcomes change when moving from a traditional PA system to an ePM system.

As technology evolves, new advancements may extend the ways in which the PM process is altered. There are also likely to be other outcomes and user reactions to monitor and consider. Correspondingly, we anticipate the model depicted in Figure 7.1 is a preliminary version that will likely evolve over time and with new information. It would also be helpful to determine which specific alterations have the biggest impact on the various outcomes, although it may be difficult to determine this as most ePM systems include all of the process-related alterations to some extent –integration may be the one exception.

THE SCIENCE BEHIND EPM

The implementation of ePM can be conceptualized as an experimental intervention, and the only way to know if it is effective and to be able to make causal inferences about it is to conduct rigorous tests using a sound scientific method and internally valid experimental methodology (cf., Marler & Fisher, 2013). To us, the focal comparator is non-electronic PM; however, to date, no studies have made such a comparison. For example, a quasi-experimental study could be structured in which one geographical site or location of a company adopts ePM for a year while another site maintains its current approach (non-electronic PM). Ideally, data from employees, managers, and HR personnel are gathered from both sites before the adoption of ePM. Similar data are gathered midway through the year and then again at the end of the year. Process-related data like time to complete ratings, generate feedback, and deliver feedback could be assessed, as well as the some of the more distal outcomes depicted in Figure 7.1.

It is important to note that the adoption of ePM has facilitated organizations moving from PA to PM. As noted earlier, a *traditional PA* is characterized by an annual or biannual evaluation in which the supervisor delivers feedback about employee performance by generating ratings on a standardized form, shares the form with the employee in a performance appraisal interview, and then files it away in the employee's personnel file. *Non-electronic PM* involves more frequent goal setting and feedback sessions between the employee and his/her supervisor without the interface of a software program to facilitate this. PM also involves aligning employee goals with the strategic goals of the organization. The ePM sub-processes identified earlier (1) setting goals and tracking performance relative to these goals, (2) evaluating employee performance, and (3) generating and distributing performance feedback are important to examine particularly when considering the capabilities of ePM and the potential advantages and disadvantages it has to offer.

Despite all the potential advantages, the science behind ePM is lacking. With a few exceptions, we were only able to locate a handful of empirical studies that have examined the effectiveness of ePM or something similar. While the move to using ePM systems is increasing (Sierra-Cedar, 2016), it seems precipitous to do so without knowing that ePM benefits the organization and its employees. Next, we briefly summarize ePM-related research to date.

In 2002, Neary presented a case study of the implementation of a company-wide ePM developed in house. Previously, this 100,000+ employee company on five continents used a paper-based system that was specific to each of the many different units within the organization. No empirical data were collected during the ePM implementation, but consistent with the idea that ePM automates and integrates PM process, the author reported a "dramatic improvement in efficiency and efficacy of the entire employee performance appraisal, professional development, and succession management process for the company" (Neary, 2002, p. 491).

In 2005, Kurtzberg, Naquin, and Belkin conducted a series of three studies aimed at examining the differences between raters using a traditional paper-and-pencil performance appraisal and raters completing the same performance appraisal by email. We should note that completing and delivering an appraisal over email is not the same as ePM. However, it is similar in that it involves electronic media. Based on previous research indicating that people give more negative appraisals via a computer than face-to-face (Herbert & Vorauer, 2003; Siegel, Dubrovsky, Kiesler, & McGuire, 1986). Kurtzberg et al. proposed and found that in all three studies that raters would deliver more harsh ratings over email than on paper. The authors confirmed that social obligation (feeling of pressure or responsibility to give more positive ratings and/or comments) mediated the relationship between the communication mode of the performance review and the ratings made. In conclusion, Kurtzberg et al.'s (2005) three studies demonstrated that individuals generate lower ratings when submitting them by e-mail than on paper and the authors attributed the lower ratings to lower social obligations.

In a quasi-experimental study, Payne, Horner, Boswell, Schroeder, and Stine-Cheyne (2009) examined employee reactions to the implementation of an online PA system at a large university. Participating departments were assigned to either complete their annual performance appraisal using paper-and-pencil or by using the new online system. All participants were asked to complete a survey of their reactions to the PA process. After receiving responses from 83 individuals who completed a paper-and-pencil appraisal and 152 responses from individuals who completed an electronic appraisal, Payne et al. (2009) found that that perceptions of both rater accountability and employee participation were higher and that perceptions of the quality of the ratings were lower with the electronic PA. The two groups did not differ significantly on perceived security of the ratings, the utility of the ratings, or satisfaction with the PA.

In summary, the research we could locate to date has examined a variety of outcomes including the efficiency of the process and efficacy of the system (Neary, 2002) and inflation in the ratings (Kurtzburg et al., 2005). One study explored rater accountability; employee participation; and quality, security, utility, and satisfaction with ratings (Payne et al., 2009). All of these studies were conducted at least a decade ago and technology has certainly advanced in that time. In short, there is plenty of room for more research to inform the use of ePM.

CONCLUSION

The adoption of ePM systems are on the rise (Sierra-Cedar, 2016) and the capabilities have progressed well-beyond any science to back up all the decisions embedded in this practice. We identify five ways that technology alters the PM process: (1) automates, (2) documents, (3) integrates, (4) structures, and (5) makes it more accessible. We propose that these enhancements can, in turn, have positive influences on traditional PA outcomes, user reactions, and system-level outcomes, possibly addressing some age-old problems with traditional PA. To date, there is a dearth of research on this topic. Correspondingly, it appears to be an area ripe for scientifically-sound research to substantiate all of the various ePM design characteristics. ePM also presents an opportunity to salvage the fundamental goals of PA: set performance goals, evaluate performance, and provide feedback to employees.

REFERENCES

Adler, S., Campion, M., Colquitt, A., Grubb, A., Murphy, K., Ollander-Krane, R., & Pulakos, E. D. (2016). Getting rid of performance ratings: Genius or folly? A debate. *Industrial and Organizational Psychology: Perspectives on Science and Practice, 9*, 219–252. doi:10.1017/iop.2015.106

Aguinis, H. (2013). *Performance management* (3rd ed.). Upper Saddle River, NJ: Pearson/ Prentice Hall.

Aguinis, H., Joo, H., & Gottfredson, R. K. (2011). Why we hate performance management—And why we should love it. *Business Horizons, 54*(6), 503–507. doi:10.1016/j.bushor.2011.06.001

Aiello, J. R., & Kolb, K. J. (1995). Electronic performance monitoring and social context: Impact on productivity and stress. *Journal of Applied Psychology, 80*, 339. doi:10.1037//0021–9010.80.3.339

Baer, D. (2014, April 10). *Adobe abolished annual performance review.* Retrieved from http://www.businessinsider.com/adobe-abolished-annual-performance-review–2014-4

Baldassarre, J., & Finken, B. (2015, August 12). *GE's real-time performance development.* Retrieved from https://hbr.org/2015/08/ges-real-time-performance-development

Balzer, W., K., Greguras, G. J., & Raymark, P. H. (2004). In J. C. Thomas (Ed.), *Comprehensive handbook of psychological assessments* (Vol. 4, pp. 390–411). Hoboken, NJ: Wiley.

Banks, C., & Murphy, K. (1985). Toward narrowing the research-practice gap in performance appraisal. *Personnel Psychology, 38*, 335–345.

BetterWorks. (n.d.). *Get it while it's hot: The BetterWorks Apple Watch app is now live.* Retrieved from https://blog.betterworks.com/betterworks-apple-watch-app-is-live/

Bhave, D. P. (2014). The invisible eye? Electronic performance monitoring and employee job performance. *Personnel Psychology, 67*, 605–635. doi:10.1111/peps.12046

Bommer, W. H., Johnson, J. L., Rich, G. A., Podsakoff, P. M., & MacKenzie, S. B. (1995). On the interchangeability of objective and subjective measures of employee performance: A meta-analysis. *Personnel Psychology, 48*, 587–605. doi:10.1111/j.1744–6570.1995.tb01772.x

Borman, W. C., & Dunnette, M. D. (1975). Behavior-based versus trait-oriented performance ratings: An empirical study. *Journal of Applied Psychology, 60*, 561–565. doi:10.1037//0021–9010.60.5.561

Buckingham, M., & Goodall, A. (2015, April). *Reinventing performance management.* Retrieved from https://hbr.org/2015/04/reinventing-performance-management

Cardy, R. L., & Miller, J. S. (2005). eHR and performance management: A consideration of positive potential and the dark side. In H. G. Gueutal & D. L. Stone (Eds.), *The brave new world eHR: Human resources management in the digital age* (pp. 138–165). San Francisco: Jossey-Bass.

Church, A. H., & Bracken, D. W. (1997). Advancing the state of the art of 360-degree feedback. *Group & Organization Management, 22*, 149–161. doi:10.1177/1059601197222002

ClearCompany (2017, July 31). *Performance Management System.* http://www.clearcompany.com/performance-management

Cleveland, J. N. & Murphy, K. R. (2016). Organizations want to abandon performance appraisal: Can they? Should they? In D. L. Stone & J. H. Dulebohn (Eds.), *Human resource management theory and research on new employment relationships* (pp. 15–46). Charlotte, NC: Information Age.

Cleveland, J. N., Murphy, K. R., & Williams, R. (1989). Multiple uses of performance appraisal: Prevalence and correlates. *Journal of Applied Psychology, 74*, 130–135. doi:10.1037//0021–9010.74.1.130

Culbert, S. A. (2008, October 20). *Get rid of the performance review!* Retrieved from https://www.wsj.com/articles/SB122426318874844933

Deming, W. E. (1982). *Out of the crisis.* Cambridge, MA: Massachusetts Institute of Technology.

Ellinger, A. D., Beattie, R. S., & Hamlin, R. G. (2010). The manager as coach. In E. Cox & T. Bachkirova (Eds.), *The complete handbook of coaching* (2nd ed., pp. 257–270). Los Angeles, CA: Sage.

Farr, J. L., Fairchild, & Cassidy, S. E. (2013). Technology and performance appraisal. In M. D. Coovert & L. F. Thompson (Eds.), *The psychology of workplace technology* (pp. 76–98). London: Taylor and Francis.

Frontier Software. (n.d.). *Performance management (e-Performance).* Retrieved from https://www.frontiersoftware.com/products/EPM21-human-resource-management-e-performance

Giang, V. (2013, March 14). *Companies are putting sensors on employees to track their every move.* Retrieved April 10, 2017, from http://www.businessinsider.com/tracking-employees-with-productivity-sensors–2013–3

Goomas, D. T., & Ludwig, T. D. (2009). Standardized goals and performance feedback aggregated beyond the work unit: Optimizing the use of engineered labor standards and electronic performance monitoring. *Journal of Applied Social Psychology, 39*(10), 2425–2437. doi:10.1111/j.1559–1816.2009.00532.x

Grant, A. M. (2017). The third 'generation' of workplace coaching: Creating a culture of quality conversations. *Coaching: An International Journal of Theory, Research and Practice, 10*(1), 37–53. doi:10.1080/17521882.2016.1266005

Gueutal, H. G. (2003). The brave new world of eHR. *Advances in Human Performance and Cognitive Engineering Research, 3*, 13–36. doi:10.1016/s1479–3601(02)03002–3

Harris, M. M., & Schaubroeck, J. (1988). A meta-analysis of self-supervisor, self-peer, and peer-supervisor ratings. *Personnel Psychology, 41*, 43–62. doi: 10.1111/j.1744–6570.1988.tb00631.x

Heidemeier, H., & Moser, K. (2009). Self-other agreement in job performance ratings: A meta-analytic test of a process model. *Journal of Applied Psychology, 94*, 353–370. doi: 10.1037/0021–9010.94.2.353.

Herbert, B. G., & Vorauer, J. D. (2003). Seeing through the screen: Is evaluative feedback communicated more effectively in face-to-face or computer-mediated exchanges. *Computers in Human Behavior, 19,* 25–38. doi:10.1016/s0747–5632(02)00031–6

HighGround. (n.d.). *Employee performance management & development.* Retrieved from http://www.highground.com/employee-engagement/employee-development

Impraise. (n.d.). *Employee-driven performance management and coaching software — Real-time 360 degree feedback and performance review software.* Retrieved from https://www.impraise.com/product/

Jawarahar, I. M., & Williams, C. R., (1997). Where all the children are above average: The performance appraisal purpose effect. *Personnel Psychology, 50,* 905–925. doi:10.1111/j.1744–6570.1997.tb01487.x

Johnson, R. D., & Gueutal, H. G. (2011). Transforming HR through technology: The use of E-HR and HRIS in organizations. In *Society for human resource management effective practice guidelines series.* Alexandria, VA: SHRM Foundation.

Keeping, L. M., & Levy, P. E. (2000). Performance appraisal reaction: Measurement, modeling, and method bias. *Journal of Applied Psychology, 85,* 708–723. doi:10.1037//0021–9010.85.5.708

Keong Choong, K. (2014). The fundamentals of performance measurement systems: A systematic approach to theory and a research agenda. *International Journal of Productivity and Performance Management, 63*(7), 879–922. doi:10.1108/ijppm-01–2013-0015

Krauss, A. D., & Snyder, L. A. (2009). Technology and performance management. In J.W. Smither & M. London (Eds.), *Performance management: Putting research into practice* (pp. 445–491). San Francisco: Jossey-Bass.

Kurtzberg, T. R., Naquin, C. E., & Belkin, L. Y. (2005). Electronic performance appraisals: The effects of e-mail communication on peer ratings in actual and simulated environments. *Organizational Behavior and Human Decision Processes, 98,* 216–226. doi:10.1016/j.obhdp.2005.07.001

Lewis, R. E. (2011). Accountability is key to effective performance appraisal systems. *Industrial and Organizational Psychology: Perspectives on Science and Practice, 4*(02), 173–175. doi:10.1111/j.1754–9434.2011.01318.x

Malos, S. B. (1998). Current legal issues in performance appraisal. In J. W. Smither (Ed.), *Performance appraisal: State of the art in practice* (pp. 49–94). San Francisco: Jossey-Bass.

Marler, J. H., & Dulebohn, J. (2005). A model of self-service technology acceptance. *Research in personnel and human resources management, 24,* 139–182. doi:10.1016/s0742–7301(05)24004–5

Marler, J. H., & Fisher, S. L. (2013). An evidence-based review of e-HRM and strategic human resource management. *Human Resource Management Review, 23,* 18–36. doi:10.1016/j.hrmr.2012.06.002

McNall, L. A., & Roch, S. G. (2009). A social exchange model of employee reactions to electronic performance monitoring. *Human Performance, 22*(3), 204–224. doi:10.1080/08959280902970385

Meinecke, A. L., Lehmann-Willenbrock, N., & Kauffeld, S. (2017). What happens during annual appraisal interviews? How leader–follower interactions unfold and impact interview outcomes. *Journal of Applied Psychology, 102,* 1054–1074.. doi: 10/1037/ap10000219

Mercer. (2016). *HR transformation: Cloud based HR systems.* Retrieved April 10, 2017, from https://www.mercer.com/our-thinking/hrt-cloud-based-hr-systems.html

Meyer, H. H., Kay, E., & French, Jr., J.R.P. (1965). Split roles in performance appraisal. *Harvard Business Review, 43,* 123–129. doi:10.1007/978–1–349-04809-0_6

Moberg, D. J. (2003). Managers as judges in employee disputes: An occasion for moral imagination. *Business Ethics Quarterly, 13,* 453–477. doi:10.5840/beq200313432

Mohrman, A. M., Resnick-West, S. M., & Lawler, E. E. (1989). *Designing performance appraisal systems.* San Francisco: Jossey-Bass.

Murphy, K. R., & Cleveland, J. N. (1995). *Understanding performance appraisal: Social, organizational, and goal-oriented perspectives.* Newbury Park, CA: Sage.

Murphy, K. R., Cleveland, J. N., Skattebo, A. L., & Kinney, T. B. (2004). Raters who pursue different goals give different ratings. *Journal of Applied Psychology, 89,* 158–164. doi:10.1037/0021–9010.89.1.158

Murphy, K. R., & DeShon, R. (2000). Interrater correlations do not estimate the reliability of job performance ratings. *Personnel Psychology, 53,* 873–900. doi:10.1111/j.1744–6570.2000.tb02421.x

Neary, D. B. (2002). Creating a company-wide, on-line, performance management system: A case study at TRW Inc. *Human Resource Management, 41,* 491–498. doi:10.1002/hrm.10056

Neely, A. (1999). The performance measurement revolution: Why now and what next? *International Journal of Operations & Production Management, 19*(2), 205–228. doi:10.1108/01443579910247437

Ones, D. S., Viswesvaran, C., & Schmidt, F. L., (2008). No new terrain: Reliability and construct validity of job performance ratings. *Industrial and Organizational Psychology: Perspectives on Science and Practice, 1,* 174–179. doi:10.1111/j.1754–9434.2008.00033.x

Oracle. (2009, September). *BI & EPM: The Oracle guide to management excellence.* Retrieved from http://www.oracle.com/us/solutions/business-intelligence/064045.pdf

Payne, S. C., Horner, M. T., Boswell, W. R., Schroeder, A. N., & Stine-Cheyne, K. J. (2009). Comparison of online and traditional performance appraisal systems. *Journal of Managerial Psychology, 24,* 526–544. doi:10.1037/e518442013–821

Perkins, D. (2013). Electronic performance monitoring in call centers: An ethical decision model. *Electronic Journal of Business Ethics and Organization Studies, 18,* 4–14.

PeopleFluent. (n.d.). *Performance management software and appraisal.* Retrieved from http://www.peoplefluent.com/products/performance

Pettijohn, L. S., Parker, R. S., Pettijohn, C. E. & Kent, J. L. (2001). Performance appraisals: Usage, criteria and observations. *Journal of Management Development, 20,* 754–772. doi:10.1108/eum0000000006159

Pulakos, E. D. (2009). *Performance management: A new approach for driving business results.* Chichester, UK: Wiley-Blackwell.

Pulakos, E. D., Hanson, R. M., Arad, S., & Moye, N. (2014). Performance management can be fixed: An on-the-job experiential learning approach for complex behavior change, *Industrial and Organizational Psychology: Perspectives on Science and Practice, 8,* 51–76. doi:10.1017/iop.2014.2

Pulakos, E. D., & O'Leary, R. S. (2011). Why is performance management broken? *Industrial and Organizational Psychology: Perspectives on Science and Practice, 4,* 146–164. doi:10.1111/j.1754–9434.2011.01315.x

Raybould, B. (1990). Solving human performance problems with computers a case study: Building an electronic performance support system. *Performance Improvement, 29*(10), 4–14. doi:10.1002/pfi.4160291004

Resker, J. (2017, March 28). *Why eliminating performance reviews isn't just another trend.* Retrieved from http://www.hrexaminer.com/why-eliminating-performance-reviews-isnt-just-another-trend/

Rock, D., Davis, J., & Jones, B. (2014, August 8). *Kill your performance ratings.* Retrieved from https://www.strategy-business.com/article/00275

Rock, D., & Jones, B. (2015, September). Why more and more companies are ditching performance ratings. *Harvard Business Review.* Retrieved from https://hbr.org/2015/09/why-more-and-more-companies-are-ditching-performance-ratings.

SAP SuccessFactors. (n.d.). *How online performance appraisals can make your life easier.* Retrieved from https://www.successfactors.com/en_us/lp/articles/online-performance-appraisals.html

SAP SuccessFactors News Center. (2017, June 14). *Reinvented SAP SuccessFactors mobile delivers unmatched employee experience.* Retrieved from http://news.sap.com/reinvented-sap-successfactors-mobile-delivers-unmatched-employee-experience/

Sierra-Cedar (2016). *2016–2017 HR systems survey white paper* (19th annual ed.). Alpharetta, GA: Sierra-Cedar.

Siegel, J., Dubrovsky, V., Kiesler, S., & McGuire, T. W. (1986). Group processes in computer mediated communication. *Organizational Behavior and Human Decision Processes, 37,* 241–262. doi:10.1016/0749–5978(86)90050–6

Smith, M. J., Carayon, P., Sanders, K. J., Lim, S. Y., & LeGrande, D. (1992). Employee stress and health complaints in jobs with and without electronic performance monitoring. *Applied Ergonomics, 23*(1), 17–27. doi:10.1016/0003–6870(92)90006-h

Smither, J. W. (2015). The fate of performance ratings: Don't write the obituary yet. *Industrial and Organizational Psychology, 8,* 77–80. doi: 10.1017/iop.2015.1

Smither, J. W., & London, M. (2009). *Performance management: Putting research into action.* John Wiley & Sons.

Snell, S. A., Stuebner, D., & Lepak, D. P. (2002). Virtual HR departments: Getting out of the middle (pp. 81–101). In R. L. Henneman & D. B. Greenberger (Eds.), *Human resource management in virtual organizations.* Greenwich, CT: Information Age Publishing.

Society for Industrial and Organizational Psychology. (2016, December 20). *Top ten workforce trends 2017.* Retrieved from http://www.siop.org/article_view.aspx?article=1610

Stanton, J. M. (2000). Reactions to employee performance monitoring: Framework, review, and research directions. *Human Performance, 13*(1), 85–113. doi:10.1207/s15327043hup1301_4

Stone, D. L., & Dulebohn, J. H. (2013). Emerging issues in theory and research on electronic human resource management (eHRM). *Human Resource Management Review, 23,* 1–5. doi:10.1016/j.hrmr.2012.06.001

Stone, D. L., Stone-Romero, E. F., & Lukaszewski, K. (2003). The functional and dysfunctional consequences of human resource information technology for organizations and their employees. *Advances in Human Performance and Cognitive Engineering Research, 3,* 37–38. doi:10.1016/s1479–3601(02)03003–5

Streitfeld, J. K. (2015, August 15). *Inside Amazon: Wrestling big ideas in a bruising workplace.* Retrieved from https://www.nytimes.com/2015/08/16/technology/inside-amazon-wrestling-big-ideas-in-a-bruising-workplace.html

Strohmeier, S. (2007). Research in e-HRM: Review and implications. *Human Resource Management Review, 17,* 19–37. doi: 10.1016/j.hrmr.2006.11.002.

TechTarget. (n.d.). *The four pillars of talent management systems: A solid HR foundation.* Retrieved from http://searchfinancialapplications.techtarget.com/essentialguide/The-four-pillars-of-talent-management-systems-A-solid-HR-foundation

Tornow, W. W. (1993). Perceptions or reality: Is multiperspective measurement a means or an end? *Human Resource Management, 32,* 221–230. doi:10.1002/hrm.3930320203

Vasudeva, P., Good, T., & Eerrenstein, J. (n.d.). *Technology reinvents performance management.* Retrieved from https://www.accenture.com/us-en/insight-technology-reinvents-performance-management

Wille, R. (2016, December 19). Talent management industry user research report. Retrieved from http://www.capterra.com/talent-management-software/user-research

Workday Talent Management (2017). Retrieved from https://www.workday.com/content/dam/web/en-us/documents/datasheets/datasheet-workday-talent-management.pdf

CHAPTER 8

USING EHRM TO MANAGE WORKERS IN THE PLATFORM ECONOMY

Elizabeth A. Cassady, Sandra L. Fisher, and Shawnee Olsen[1]

ABSTRACT

This paper explores how electronic human resource management (eHRM) could be used to manage task workers, a relatively new type of contingent worker that utilizes online platforms to complete short-term tasks for a variety of clients. We define the differences between task workers, independent contractors, and permanent workers to better understand the existing work relationships and attachments between task workers and their clients. Task workers are likely to form transactional psychological contracts with the client organizations, which may seem ideal from the contractual perspective but could reduce overall work effectiveness. We then analyze four different triangular relationships that result from the relationships between task workers, platform providers, and clients. Using the employee relationship management perspective, we argue that relational eHRM systems could be used to create more productive work relationships with task workers. We examine three differ-

[1] Note: The authors contributed equally to this paper and are listed in alphabetical order.

The Brave New World of eHRM 2.0, pages 217–246.
Copyright © 2018 by Information Age Publishing

ent types of relational eHRM systems, communication, performance management, and training and development, analyzing how they are currently used and how they could be used to enhance the task worker relationship. The paper concludes with future research directions for studying task worker relationships to determine which types of task workers would benefit most from the use of relational eHRM systems.

Contingent workers are not a new concept in the world of human resource management (HRM), with many firms utilizing them to complete projects or minor tasks. The concluding chapter in the 2005 edited book *The Brave New World of eHR* noted that the rising use of contingent work and how to effectively manage contingent workers will be critical concerns for organizations (Henson, 2005). Further, Henson noted that these contingent workers will come from all over the globe, and "work will occur from anywhere, any time—and from anybody." (p. 280). In 2016, twenty to thirty percent of the workforce in the United States and the EU–15 countries was engaged in independent work (McKinsey Institute, 2016), suggesting that Henson's prediction was correct. However, the HRM literature has provided only limited guidance for how companies can effectively manage this segment of the workforce. The goal of this paper is to explore how electronic human resource management (eHRM) could be used to manage one specific type of contingent worker; the task worker.

While there are many different types of contingent workers including agency temps, independent contractors, and consultants (Fisher & Connelly, 2017), this paper focuses on the *task worker*. Task workers are similar to concepts such as freelancers and eLancers (Aguinis & Lawal, 2013), where workers freely engage with companies to perform well defined tasks on a contractual basis. Examples of task workers include people who provide transportation through Uber and Lyft, rent out apartments and houses through Airbnb, and design websites or logos through marketplaces such as Fiverr or Upwork. All types of contingent workers offer potential advantages to organizations such as increasing staffing flexibility, providing access to specialized skills, and reducing direct costs. Contingent workers are paid wages but rarely receive benefits and typically have fixed contracts that end after a determined amount of time or the completion of certain tasks (Fisher & Connelly, 2017). We argue that task workers are a more extreme case of the existing contingent worker paradigm (Horney, 2016; Subasinghe, 2016). These workers may find work independently or through one of the many online platforms (such as Uber) or marketplaces (such as Fiverr) that help task workers and client firms find each other (Kenney & Zysman, 2016). Task workers have much more flexibility and may choose their own work hours in a way that may seem random to the organization (such as with Uber drivers) or complete a work task that only takes five minutes (such as with Fiverr). Workers at this far end of the contingency spectrum have typically not been included in research on contingent work. One notable exception is Aguinis and Lawal (2013) who analyzed the eLancer, or an individual who "from literally anywhere in the world can sign up and complete work using the Internet for an employer who literally can also be anywhere in the world" (p. 6) using online marketplaces. However, the market conditions for these workers have changed even in the few short years since Aguinis and Lawal's paper was published and we believe the broader concept of a *task worker* better addresses this type of worker.

The organizing structure for much of the task work being performed is known by various names including the gig economy, sharing economy, collaborative economy, and platform economy. Each term has slightly different implications for the work performed and how it is organized. For our examination of the task worker, we chose to focus on the *platform economy* as the organizing structure. The platform economy is defined as a way of finding workers through "the use of online platforms, which decreases the transaction costs of labour outsourcing and temporary access to goods and services" (Drahokoupil & Fabo, 2016, p. 2). Both work location and work time are often quite flexible, making the platform economy and task work attractive to many individual workers. It allows them to avoid office cubicles and unpleasant or overly demanding bosses and gives them the capability to manage their own time (McKinsey Institute, 2016). There are also potential disadvantages of engaging in task work through the platform economy, such as uncertainty of workload and compensation, lack of retirement and health care benefits, and the extra time and effort required to continually seek new tasks. In spite of the advantages listed above, for some workers, task work and the platform economy may be "just a positive spin put on last-resort precarious work" (Tomlinson, 2016, para. 2).

Little is known in the HRM literature about effective management of task workers. Much of the research about the platform economy and its workers has been centered around legal perspectives on the contractual relationship. For example, Brown (2016) discussed the "Uberdilemma" that characterizes the relationship between platforms and their workers. Platforms consistently maintain that task workers are not employees, although numerous task workers have sued companies such as Uber over perceived violations of labor law. Acevedo's (2016) research notes that while there might be an employment relationship present, it does not mean that it "reaches the level of employee-employer ties under current laws" (Acevedo, 2016, p. 35). Because task workers are not legally considered employees, they experience many challenges in dealing with self-employment issues such as taxes, and the platforms offer little assistance in this area (Oei & Ring, 2017). More broadly, Aguinis and Lawal (2013) laid out a detailed agenda for research on eLancing, examining eight different aspects of HR and how these might be impacted by eLancing. Unfortunately, there has been little published research following up on this agenda.

The purpose of the current paper is to examine how we might begin to resolve the "Uberdilemma" and other similar dilemmas within the platform economy by applying HRM techniques through HR technology. We assume that companies and consumers find value in utilizing task workers and wish to continue doing so (Horney, 2016). We also have evidence that task workers vary in their motivation for participating in task work. For decades we have known that contingent workers more generally are divided on their motivation for this type of work, with some preferring it more than others (Marler, Woodward Barringer, & Milkovich, 2002). A study conducted by the McKinsey Institute (2016) found that task workers vary on two important dimensions; motivation and financial status. Individuals who engaged in task work voluntarily were divided into *free agents*, who are task workers as their primary income, and *causal earners*, who use task work to earn a little extra money on the side. The remaining two groups of task workers engaged in this work out of financial necessity. The group called the *reluctants* would have preferred a more typical job but sought task work because they had no other alternative. The final group, the *financially strapped*, had another full time job but needed additional income and so pursued task work as a way to earn extra money. These different motivational profiles are likely to impact worker satisfaction, performance, and willingness to continue performing this type of work (Marler et al., 2002). Given these many differences, the question arises of how companies can interact with task workers to maximize performance and maintain a continued supply of qualified task workers.

Given the descriptions from the study done by McKinsey Institute (2016), these categories of task workers can include those who are self-employed or consultants who use platforms to conduct business. An example would be a self-employed graphic designer who can conduct business from any location. This graphic designer may have their own locally operated shop where they do business, but the platform offers them another revenue stream where individuals or organizations globally pay the graphic designer for his or her services. Another example would be a financial consultant who helps local individuals or organizations create a budget. With the use of a platform, the consultant is able to increase their potential customer reach without adding a large fixed cost such as renting a physical location in every city worldwide. These examples are just two of the many scenarios that can occur with the use of a platform.

We argue that eHRM can help organizations more effectively manage the relationship with task workers in the platform economy. Just as internet technology helped create this new class of task workers, it also offers great potential for helping to effectively manage this segment of the workforce. eHRM can be described as systems that "provide organizational stakeholders with access to HR information in specific HR functions via the Internet or Intranets" (Stone & Dulebohn, 2013, p. 1). Using eHRM to manage task workers challenges HR at all three levels of eHRM outcomes; operational, relational, and transformational (Parry & Tyson, 2011; Ruel, Bondarouk & Looise, 2004). Many existing systems for contingent worker management address the operational or efficiency goal of eHRM, with internal and external platforms that facilitate rapid and cost-effective recruitment of task workers and compensation processes that remain in compliance of tax law. This area seems fairly well covered. Therefore, we explore how eHRM can be used for more than just handling the contractual or procurement elements of the task worker relationship through the relational eHRM systems: communication, performance management, and training and development.

Specifically, we see opportunity for eHRM to also help address relational outcomes. The existing research literature clearly suggests that contingent workers can and do form emotional attachments and psychological contracts (PCs) with client organizations (Chambel, 2014; Liden, Wayne, Kraimer & Sparrowe, 2003). What is less clear is how task workers form attachments such as PCs with clients, and how these attachments impact their performance and other outcomes (Aguinis & Lawal, 2013). For example, within permanent employee populations, we know that organizational commitment can be increased in exchange for support received, but it is unknown if this holds true for contingent workers (Liden et al., 2003). Further, the contingent worker literature shows that it becomes more difficult to clearly evaluate a contingent worker's commitment to a client, as they may have multiple commitments with multiple parties. These relationships can become even more complicated with task workers, as they are likely to have multiple clients and work through multiple platforms. Some task workers and clients may wish to maintain an arm's length relationship and avoid forming attachments. However, task workers may form attachments to their clients in an effort to secure continued work assignments, or simply to engage in a more social work relationship that could be otherwise missing from the self-employment work context (McKinsey, 2016). From the client perspective, it may be useful to better understand the attachments, particularly the PCs, that task workers form with both platforms and clients to facilitate a steady supply of qualified task workers. Offering support to the task worker through eHRM could be both an efficient and effective way to meet relational goals.

Once companies are meeting relational goals with task workers more effectively, the transformational or strategic perspective can be addressed. For example, Horney (2016) noted the need for firms to get more strategic about managing the full talent portfolio, not just permanent employees. With appropriate data on permanent employees and the range of contingent workers, HR strategic partners can make sound decisions about where employees best fit, where task workers best fit, and keep the organization flexible and cost effective (Rousseau & Wade-Benzoni, 1995).

In order to begin addressing the lack of existing research on the application of eHRM to managing task workers, this paper explores approaches companies can use to more effectively engage with task workers. We compare practices currently used with permanent employees and longer-term independent contractors to ensure we address the full talent portfolio, but we use the concept of employee relationship management (ERM) to better understand and apply segmentation of HRM practices to specific subgroups. The remainder of the paper is organized as follows: First, we examine the ways in which employment relationships differ across task workers, independent contractors, and permanent workers. Next we review research examining social exchange and psychological contracts. We use the triangular employment relationship concept to analyze where we see potential for managing workers in a more engaged way, and then describe ways in which eHRM could be used to enhance relational outcomes for workers and companies. Finally, we identify future research directions that could help us better understand the effectiveness of using eHRM to enhance relational outcomes.

Continuum of Contingency

As noted above, we believe that task workers are an extreme example of the concept of contingency in the modern workplace. To more effectively identify the HRM issues associated with task workers, and potential solutions to these issues, we compare them to other types of workers on different places in a continuum of contingency (see Figure 8.1). To illustrate key differences along this continuum, we use Lewchuck and Clarke's (2011) model of characteristics of the employment relationship. They noted that contingent and permanent jobs vary on three primary dimensions; levels of uncertainty, effort, and support that are evident in the employment relationship. Uncertainty includes characteristics such as fragility, earnings uncertainty, and scheduling uncertainty. Fragility addresses differences in labor laws and legal protection available to different types of workers. Contingent workers in many countries receive less protection than permanent workers (Wears & Fisher, 2012). Earnings and scheduling uncertainty describe the level of consistency workers can expect in how much money they make and when they work. Here we also include expected duration of the work relationship as an indicator of uncertainty, with shorter work assignments generally representing greater levels of uncertainty on long-term employment prospects. Support consists of emotional and economic support from people in the worker's community. For example, a task worker may experience social isolation in his or her work

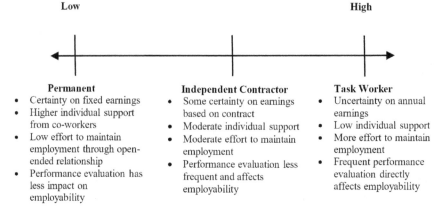

FIGURE 8.1.   Worker Contingency Continuum

because of the lack of co-workers. Permanent workers are more likely to have this individual level support. Finally, work relationships vary on the amount of effort required on the part of the worker. This attribute includes how much effort workers have to expend to stay employed, how often they have to look for work, and how frequently their performance is formally evaluated. In this category we also include intensity of the selection process.

Figure 8.1 illustrates the differences among workers along these dimensions. For purposes of this paper, we focus on three prototypical types of workers: permanent worker, IC, and task worker, recognizing that there are other types of workers that fit into this continuum. While these worker types are generally distinct, the lines between them may blur together and worker types can overlap on some dimensions. Below we discuss each of those three types in more detail.

Permanent Workers. Employment relationships may be shifting towards a more contingent workforce, but there is still a need for permanent employees (Wilkin, 2012). Permanent employees generally have lower levels of uncertainty and effort, and higher levels of relationship support. For example, permanent employment is characterized by an indefinite or open-ended employment term, lasting until one party chooses to terminate it. Permanent employees tend to perform their work, full-time, at the employer's location (Chambel & Castanheira, 2007). They receive consistent salary and benefits as compensation for performing the work required. Permanent workers tend to have higher direct labor costs, which is part of the motivation for organizations to use contingent workers.

Because lower uncertainty for the employee can lead to greater long-term risk for the employer, companies tend to be more cautious about hiring and gather more information during the selection process. Throughout the hiring process and after a permanent employee accepts an offer for a full-time position, the hiring company usually does a number of background checks. This can be done in the form of an application blank, reference checks, and interviews, to verifying social security numbers, credit information, driving records and criminal history. These selection processes help protect a company from negligent hiring or employment discrimination (Levashina & Campion, 2009).

Independent Contractors. ICs "can be broadly characterized as self-employed workers who offer their services to a 'client' organization on an hourly or per-project basis" (Fisher & Connelly, 2017, p. 6). They typically have clearly defined contracts of medium length, lasting more than a month but less than a year (Liden, et al., 2003; Wears & Fisher, 2012). Thus, ICs fall in the middle of the continuum, experiencing more uncertainty than permanent workers but less uncertainty than task workers. ICs generally work on larger and longer term contracts than task workers, reducing the effort required to stay employed and reducing earnings uncertainty. ICs often have more flexibility and autonomy than task workers to plan and manage their work activities (Davis-Blake & Uzzi, 1993). Scheduling certainty may be relatively high, as ICs may work on the site of the employer or from a different location, depending on the type of work. Direct wage costs tend to be higher than with permanent employees, but the client organization using the services typically does not pay benefits (Fisher & Connelly, 2017).

There are several prototypical ways in which ICs contract with client organizations, and levels of uncertainty may vary across these. For example, ICs may sign a contract directly with a client organization as an individual, with a consulting company that utilizes ICs, or through an "agent of record." In the direct hire situation, an organization may put out a call for proposals from individual ICs who would send in their bids for the contract at hand. Once bids have been submitted, the organization would select the best IC for the job. Alternatively, client organizations may request bids for larger projects from consulting companies who then subcontract with individual ICs. An agent of record acts much like a platform for a task worker and can conduct background checks or a compliance reviews during the selection process (Fisher & Connelly, 2017). Using an agent of record could reduce the effort the IC expends to stay employed, although that would come at some financial cost.

Task Workers. Task workers experience the greatest levels of uncertainty among these three types as they find short-term work tasks (also known as gigs) through a platform. This industry is changing at a fast pace, with platforms starting up, shutting down, or being acquired. The platforms we include are Work-Market, Upwork, Fiverr, Guru.com, Uber, Lyft and Airbnb. The tasks performed by task workers are generally shorter in duration compared to ICs and the work is rarely performed at the client work site. While tasks can have a variety of time frames, some platforms limit the contract duration to be no more than thirty days, although few tasks are intended to require that much time (Fiverr's Terms of Service, 2016). This may decrease uncertainty for a particular task, but increase earnings uncertainty and employment effort overall.

Task workers are paid by the specific task, for an amount generally agreed upon prior to accepting the assignment. Task workers must agree with the terms and conditions of each platform provider. These conditions normally include the fee (often a percentage of the total contract amount) charged by the platform provider for the service of connecting the client and task worker. For example, Fiverr charges a twenty percent commission fee, while WorkMarket's standard fee is ten percent (WorkMarket Terms of Use Agreement for Users, 2017). Task workers are paid only direct wages (no benefits) and are generally paid less than a permanent employee would be for the same task. Again, we see some certainty within a task, but overall task workers have high earnings uncertainty overall. Both task workers and ICs tend to have multiple clients at any one point in time, or within a calendar year, as is often required by law in North America in order to maintain status as a non-employee.

The effort required to stay employed can be quite high. Selection processes for potential task workers vary from platform to platform. Some of these selection procedures are basic checks performed by the platform to allow the worker to access the platform. Other selection procedures are intended for clients to use in determining which task worker to engage for a particular task. Access-oriented selection procedures, perhaps better described as simple screening checks, include checking for a valid I.D., a valid driver's license (e.g., for Uber), or signing a code of conduct. Many platforms provide additional selection resources that clients can use to identify a qualified task worker for a particular task. These can include rating systems, feedback sections, skill tests, and certification tests (Aguinis & Lawal, 2013; How It Works, 2015). Task workers also exposed to constant evaluation with these rating and feedback systems, and ratings are often critical to them being able to obtain additional work.

Thus, as workers vary in the degree of uncertainty and contingency they experience with their work, they have different expectations about the continuity of their work, how they will be paid, and where they will work, among other factors. These issues are related to another important way in which contingency affects different types of workers; their attachment patterns to the organization. In the next section we discuss psychological contracts, one important kind of attachment between a worker and an organization.

Psychological Contracts

Psychological contracts (PCs) are a specific construct developed from broader work examining the quality of relationships in the workplace (e.g., between line workers and supervisors) and how the quality of those relationships affects work outcomes (Rousseau, 2011). PCs are "an individual's system of beliefs, based on commitments expressed or implied, regarding an exchange agreement with another" (Rousseau, 2011, p. 191). These may be commitments about the type of work performed, the duration of the work, compensation for the work, and other inducements such as training that is offered, when promotions can be expected, and so on. PCs are often initially established during recruiting, but they can change over time. Technology, peer relationships, and business strategy can all have an effect on a worker's PC (Suazo & Stone-Romero, 2016). The content and nature of the PC have been shown to be related to many important outcomes including commitment, trust, organizational citizenship behaviors, and turnover intentions (Rousseau, 2011; Rousseau & Wade-Benzoni, 1995).

Two important attributes of PCs are the duration and the specificity of performance terms. Based on these factors, a PC can fall into one of four categories: transactional, transitional, relational, or balanced (Rousseau & Wade-Benzoni, 1995). Transactional contracts are short-term in length and include clearly specified work terms. They tend to focus on economic terms of the relationship. Transactional contracts typically result in low ambiguity for the worker but also a low commitment level. In contrast, relational contracts are long-term and have less specified work requirements. They address more socioemotional terms of the relationship. Relational contracts tend to produce more positive outcomes in terms of attachments, such as high levels of continuous and affective commitment from the individual, along with a feeling of integration or identification with the firm (Rousseau, 2011; Rousseau & Wade-Benzoni, 1995).

Two other contract types are transitional and balanced contracts (Rousseau & Wade-Benzoni, 1995). Transitional contracts are short-term in length but include unspecified performance terms, which can lead to higher levels of uncertainty and turnover rates. These contracts, due to their high ambiguity, are often confusing to all parties involved. Transitional contracts may be formed during a corporate acquisition or during a period of downsizing, and often represent change in the relationship between worker and organization. On the other hand, balanced contracts are long-term and specified. They reflect instances when both parties are contributing a great deal to the employment relationship, and result in high levels of commitment, integration, identification, learning, development, and support (Rousseau, 2011; Rousseau & Wade-Benzoni, 1995).

Individual worker attitudes are affected not only by the type and nature of the PC with the organization, but also by the extent to which they perceive the agreement is upheld. Psychological contract breaches can occur when the individual has certain expectations regarding the job they will be doing and the organization does not meet those expectations (Robinson & Morrison, 2000). If there is a disagreement between the worker and the company in their obligations to one another, this can indicate a breach (Tekleab & Taylor, 2003). Breaches can than result in negative attitudinal and behavioral reactions (Tekleab & Taylor, 2003). Breaches are inherently subjective, and are more difficult to evaluate (or even avoid) in the case of a less defined contract (such as with the transitional PC described above). According to Robinson and Morrison's (2000) research, individuals in organizations that had stricter socialization processes were less likely to experience contract breach. This, in addition to more communication between the worker and organization pre-hire, can lead to better understanding of obligations from each party.

Early work on PCs focused on the traditional, permanent employee. Rousseau and Wade-Benzoni (1995) were among the first to examine the concept of PCs within the context of contingent work. They argued that temporary workers (e.g., individuals finding work through agencies such as Manpower, Nurse Temps, and Accountemps) would by definition experience transactional PCs as the duration of the work assignment is short and the tasks are well defined. The relationship is focused on a clear economic exchange without expectation for high involvement from either side, or "a fair day's work for a fair day's pay" (Rousseau & Wade-Benzoni, 1995, p. 294). Empirical research has generally confirmed this, finding that temporary workers tend to form low obligation, transactional PCs (De Cuyper, Rigotti, Witte, & Mohr, 2008; Scheel, Rigotti & Mohr, 2013).

Subsequent research has examined the nature of the contingent worker PC in a broader range of situations. De Cuyper, et al. (2008) examined the degree of balance in PCs for both permanent and temporary workers. Permanent employees were more likely to experience high mutual obligations within their PC, and were not only more committed to the firm but also more satisfied with their jobs (De Cuyper et al., 2008). The PC between a temporary worker and the firm also tends to be more unbalanced, with the worker bearing the over-obligation. This situation can lead to weakened relationships and a negative impact on the worker's attitude. Interestingly, a much larger percentage of temps in their sample perceived a mutual high-obligation relationship (44.9%) than a mutual low-obligation relationship (7.1%). Thus, while contingent workers are more likely than permanent workers to have a transactional PC, there is evidence of substantial variation in practice (De Cuyper et al., 2008).

Chambel and colleagues (Chambel, 2014; Chambel, Lorente, Carvalho & Martinez, 2016) examined the PCs that temporary agency workers hold about the client firm. They found that these temps do indeed form PCs about the client organization, and that perceived fulfillment of these contracts can lead to positive outcomes such as higher job satisfaction and affective commitment toward the client. Once hired as a direct temporary worker, the temps formed PCs with both the client and the supervisor (Chambel, 2014). The supervisor-oriented PC was more important for temps than for permanent workers in predicting job satisfaction. Client supervisors can play an important role in the formation of productive relationships between the temp and the client through better communication practices (Chambel et al., 2016).

Core vs. Support

Attachments between the organization and the worker can also be affected by the worker's role within the organization. When the worker has a more central role, we expect stronger, more balanced attachments (Rousseau & Wade-Benzoni, 1995) as the company offers more inducements and the worker demonstrates loyalty. The more central workers, or core workers (Lepak, Taylor, Tekleab, Marrone, & Cohen, 2007) are defined as those who contribute directly towards meeting strategic organizational goals, performing the work that is directly related to production of goods or services. Support workers, in contrast, are those who perform tasks necessary to allow the core employees to do their work (Lepak et al., 2007). For example, a production worker would be considered a core worker for a manufacturing firm, while the maintenance or marketing employees would be considered support. The specific roles that fall into these categories would differ depending on the strategic intent of the firm. While a person who works as a web developer for a manufacturing firm would be considered support, a web developer working for a web development consulting firm would be considered core.

An alternative view on defining core human capital considers skill levels rather than the strategic nature of the work performed. Core workers in this context are those who have unique and valuable skills that would be difficult to replace (Cappelli & Neumark, 2004), while periphery workers have generic skills that are easy to replace. Combining the two ideas, Lepak and Snell (2002) argued that workers who have high strategic value and offer uniqueness specific to the firm will have the highest levels of human capital and be considered core.

Companies often invest more resources into their core workers. This can be through a high-investment human resource (HIHR) system (Lepak et al., 2007), such as investing in the human capital of the core workers through selective staffing practices or comprehensive training initiatives in hopes of reducing turnover (Lepak & Snell, 2002). Research by Lepak and colleagues (2007) suggests that organizations invest more into core workers than support workers. This is partially due to the fact that organizations generally profit less from support workers, and thus it is too costly to invest in them significantly. Therefore, HIHR systems, and other HR investments are applied and used differently by different employee groups (Lepak & Snell, 2002; Lepak et al., 2007). Extending this logic to PCs, companies will offer more inducements to core workers than to support workers, as they are expected to make a greater contribution to the firm (Lepak & Snell, 2002). This suggests that core workers may have more relational, balanced contracts while support workers would have more transactional contracts.

It is intuitively appealing to assume that task workers would all be support employees. When using the core-periphery distinction, quite often contingent workers are used for the periphery jobs and their numbers fluctuate according to work demands (Cappelli & Neumark, 2004). However, when looking at the definition of core work that focuses on what work is performed (Lepak et al., 2007), task workers can be found in both core and support categories. Task workers who perform the direct product or service production of the company are core workers. Those who perform more ancillary tasks are classified as support workers.

The task workers for companies such as Uber and Airbnb better match the description for core employees. The primary service provided by Uber is transportation.[2] In this case, we argue that the drivers are the core employees while the permanent employees (engineers, project managers, and so on) are actually the support employees who develop and maintain the platform that allows drivers to connect with riders. Uber without its drivers would be a company with no incoming revenue or purpose. The same circumstances arise for Airbnb, where without its task workers renting out their homes the company is unable to provide its core service. Airbnb encourages its hosts to follow a set of guidelines that go beyond simply renting a room or apartment to a customer, providing hospitality consistent with its organizational goals.

Task workers who work through marketplaces such as Fiverr, Upwork, and WorkMarket can be a mix of core and support workers. From the platform perspective, the task workers are similar to those working through Uber and Airbnb in that they are critical to the existence of the platform. However, the task workers are not performing work directly for Fiverr or Upwork. The core service activity

---

[2] We acknowledge that Uber often disagrees that it is a transportation company, arguing instead that it is an "information society services provider" (Brant, 2016).

of these platforms is clearly to facilitate matching of the task worker to a client organization that is offering a task. Consequently, with these platforms we consider the work being performed for the client in determining if the worker is doing core or support work. This adds more complexity to the analysis. For example, consider a task worker who is seeking task work digitally retouching photographs. If this worker is hired on Work Market by a large consumer goods company to retouch photos to be used in its annual report, that task worker is doing support work. In contrast, if the same worker is hired by a small photography company to retouch portraits that the company will then sell, the task worker would be doing core work. In the next section of the paper, we further examine the complexities of these relationships between the task worker, the platform, and the client to examine the impact of the core/support distinction on PCs and the potential need for eHRM.

Triangular Relationship

One defining aspect of the task worker environment is the more complex, multiple relationship with clients and platforms. Task workers are likely to work with multi-faceted platforms and multiple clients. Permanent workers typically will experience a relationship with one employer at a time, making the formation and evaluation of PCs more straightforward. In contrast, contingent workers are often part of a triangular relationship (Wears & Fisher, 2012), where the employment relationship involves three parties: the worker, an employment services agency of some kind (e.g., temporary agency), and a client who is purchasing the services. With task workers, the platform substitutes for the agency, providing workers with the technology to find clients and helping clients find task workers. These clients may be organizations or individuals who are contracting for the task. Further, the extent to which the worker is engaged in core versus support work also impacts the quality of the triangular relationship, as clients are likely to place higher value on relationships in which core work is performed. Below we review four prototypical triangular relationships (see Figure 8.2) and the implications for PC development in each.

To illustrate specific triangular relationships, we explore the relationships and interactions among platforms, the clients that are requesting services, and the task workers. In each triangle we assume the type of platform (i.e., Uber, Work Market, Fiverr) will not have an impact on the nature of the relationship. The two changing elements are the type of task performed (i.e., core or support) and the type of client (i.e., organization or individual). In the initial discussion of the triangles, we consider the relationships among task workers, platforms, and clients to be primarily transactional in nature. In the extant literature, contingent workers such as temporary agency workers have most commonly had transactional relationships with the client organizations (De Cuyper et al., 2008; Rousseau & Wade-Benzoni, 1995). As previously discussed, the research on task workers has not specifically addressed PCs.

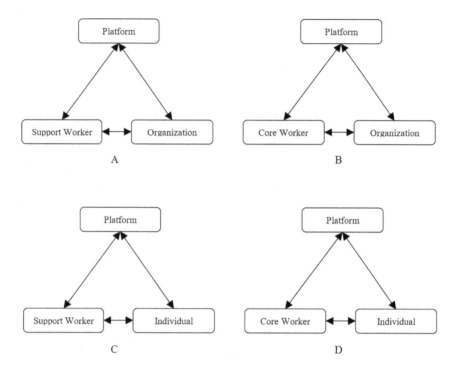

FIGURE 8.2. Triangular Task Worker Relationships

Support—Organization. Triangle A of Figure 8.2 is what we consider to be the most typical task worker relationship where the client is an organization and the worker is performing a support task that is not central to the main strategy of the organization. The organization uses the platform to find task workers. The worker registers through the platform in order to gain access to available tasks. For example, an organization might need a logo created, so it could post the task on the Fiverr platform. Workers can express interest in completing the task and the organizations will be able to select a qualified task worker using selection techniques as described above. Upon completion of the task, the organization can evaluate the task worker's performance. Evaluations are compiled into an overall rating that is visible to all future organizations.

Currently each PC relationship displayed here is transactional, but the platform provider should desire for workers and organizations to have a positive experience so they will return. The platform provider realizes financial benefits when organizations continue to complete transactions with task workers through the platform. If a work assignment goes well, workers will want to continue using the platform and possibly express interest in future tasks from the same organization.

Given a positive experience, the organization might be more inclined to choose the same task worker again.

Core—Organization. In triangle B of Figure 8.2, the organization is still using the platform to requests tasks to be completed. Now, however, the task is central to the main strategy of the organization. For example, a busy photography studio might need to request tasks on Fiverr such as photo retouching. The worker will still register through the platform to gain access to available tasks and could express interest in completing the photo retouching task. Similar to the situation in triangle A, the organization will select which task worker they believe to be most qualified. In addition, the organization can evaluate the work done by the task worker to make their overall rating.

Because the strategic importance of the task has changed, the client may specify more concrete performance terms or may wish to engage a talented task worker for similar tasks in the future. Thus, while the relationship between task worker and client is still transactional in this triangle, there is more potential for greater attachment to develop. With this potential situation in mind, platform providers also want to ensure that the platform itself is user-friendly so that organizations will continue to post tasks and workers will continue to check for available tasks.

Support—Individual. The relationship depicted in triangle C in Figure 8.2 between a support worker and client is very different than the others. Here, the client is an individual requesting a support task. The worker will register through the platform to gain access to tasks. Tasks that an individual might post on a platform such as Fiverr could be creating a dietary plan or personal training schedule. Similar to the previous situations, the task worker will express interest in completing the task. The main difference is that an individual is now responsible for selecting the most qualified task worker. Upon completion, the individual may evaluate the worker's performance. Evaluations will be compiled into an overall rating for the task worker that is visible on the platform.

In this situation we assume that the individual requesting the support task will not be repeatedly posting or requesting the same task. Therefore, there will not be a motivation to use the same task worker again in the future. With this situation in mind, the platform provider will need to be focused on consistently obtaining new individual clients to post work offers on the platform. Without task requests on the platform, task workers will not be motivated to use the platform to find potential work.

Core—Individual. Triangle D in Figure 8.2 depicts an entirely different relationship. Here the client is an individual requesting a task that is related to the platform provider's core business strategy. This relationship is best illustrated with Uber. For the task worker (the driver), signing up takes slightly longer than with other platforms. Not only does the identity of the driver need to be verified, but also proof of insurance and access to an appropriate vehicle. Once drivers are approved they can go online and begin searching for rides. Individual clients (riders) can download the app and begin requesting tasks (rides) in a matter of a few minutes. Unlike the other platforms, where clients were able to select which workers they wanted to use, in this case, drivers select which individuals they want to complete rides for. Upon completion of the ride, individuals can evaluate their ride experience. Then, like with other triangular relationships, the evaluations are compiled into an overall rating.

Though it may seem that the driver has complete control over selection of rides, Uber pre-screens the rides available to its drivers to maximize efficiency system-wide based on driver location, rider location, traffic patterns, and other variables. Therefore, drivers are only able to see a certain number of ride requests within a certain distance and decide which to accept. Thus, drivers and riders alike are unable to purposely select each other. This makes the PC between the driver and rider in this situation unique, nearly eliminating it. The rider has expectations for how a generic driver will perform, but cannot select the actual driver. This raises the importance of the PC between Uber and its drivers, as it is critical for Uber to have a large pool of skilled, knowledgeable drivers in every market where it competes.

The previous illustrations show how each triangular relationship can lead to different motivations and opportunities for relationship development depending on the type of client and work being done. In some situations, it makes sense for the platform provider or client to pursue a more relational PC with the task worker because there is potential for greater value. Table 8.1 summarizes which relationships we believe have the greatest potential for transformation and which party (platform provider or client) has resources to make that change. We assume that when clients are individuals, they will not have significant resources to utilize formal HR systems or eHRM to improve their relationship with the task worker. Therefore, in these cases the platform provider will have greater ability to affect the relationship. Utilizing eHRM can help workers improve their skills and develop commitment to the platform. On the flip side, when the client is an organization, they will have the ability to affect the relationship (Chambel et al., 2016). For this case we assume that organizations will want to continually use task workers with whom they have had positive interactions. Therefore, managing eHRM would be beneficial.

TABLE 8.1.   Potential Gains from Enhancing Worker Relationships

	Client Type	
Task Type	**Individual**	**Organization**
Core	High potential for impact	High potential for impact
	Managed by platform	Managed by client
Support	Low potential for impact	Low potential for impact
	Managed by platform	Managed by client

Thus, it appears that both platforms and clients are currently creating transactional relationships with task workers. This is aligned with existing ideas about PCs, where short term relationships are typically characterized by transactional PCs (Millward & Hopkins, 1998; Rousseau & Wade-Benzoni, 1995). However, some contingent workers do have relational, balanced PCs with the client firm, resulting in more positive work attitudes and motivations (De Cuyper et al., 2008). Shifting to a more relational approach may increase the value that task workers bring to the platform or client. Organizations may want to improve worker loyalty to decrease transaction costs and increase motivation, where higher motivation could lead to higher quality of work produced. To accomplish this, we believe that platform providers and clients should use eHRM to create more meaningful attachments with task workers. It may also be beneficial to consider the aspects of relational or balanced contracts, such as less specific tasks. Though this might not be possible given the inherent specific nature of task-based work, platform providers and clients could focus on better socialization or pre-hire communication practices, as these can improve expected obligations from each party and thus more fulfilled PCs (Robinson & Morrison, 2000).

USING eHRM TO MANAGE DIFFERENT TYPES OF WORKER RELATIONSHIPS

The variation in PCs among permanent and contingent workers suggests that organizations should approach effective management of these workers in different ways. As stated earlier, the purpose of this chapter is to examine the ways in which eHRM can be used to meet this goal. Many of the advances in eHRM and talent analytics have served the goals of the employer without providing much direct benefit to the workers (Barrette, 2017). For example, Uber uses sophisticated analytics based on psychological principles to motivate drivers to spend more time driving. These methods are intended to provide better service to customers in terms of reduced wait time and minimal surge pricing rather than to directly benefit the drivers (Scheiber, 2017), but may actually have negative effects on the long-term health of the drivers. In this section we build on the concept of employee relationship management (Strohmeier, 2013) to explore new avenues for using eHRM to add value for different types of workers.

Employee Relationship Management. Strohmeier (2013) introduced the concept of employee relationship management (ERM) into the eHRM literature. This concept is built on well-developed ideas about customer relationship management (CRM) from the marketing literature (Schweitzer & Lyons, 2008), suggesting that companies can and should do more to build high-quality relationships with their employees, much as they attempt to do with customers. CRM, or the relationship-based view of marketing, uses a relational view of the customer-organization relationship. Instead of trying to sell a product or service one time to many different customers, CRM seeks to identify ways to build customer loyalty over the long term. This is done through techniques such as targeted communication with customers, or giving them special status such as in frequent flyer programs. ERM looks at how companies can create a long term, mutually beneficial relationship with employees. This is similar to the idea of creating relational rather than transactional PCs, with the accompanying benefits of the relational contracts as discussed above. Just as with customers, ERM suggests that employees can be segmented into different categories that should be treated differently (Schweitzer & Lyons, 2008; Strohmeier, 2013). Thus, high-value, skilled permanent employees should be treated differently and offered more inducements than peripheral workers, who are likely to be ICs and task workers (Lepak & Snell, 2002). Similarly, core workers should receive more resources than support employees (Lepak et al., 2007).

While we acknowledge that companies should dedicate more resources to managing permanent employees, we argue that organizations will benefit from establishing relational contracts with many kinds of task workers to minimize transaction costs and improve overall performance. For example, consider a company that posts an opportunity on Work Market for translating a 50-page business report from English into German. The task worker who takes the assignment would likely have clearly established expectations about the nature of the work, the duration of the work, and the payment for the work. This would be a transactional PC. When the work is completed, that worker may again notice a posting from the same company for more translation work. The important question to consider is if either party would benefit from connecting for a second project. Depending on the type of work, there may be less of a learning curve for the task worker on her second assignment for the company (Fisher & Connelly, 2017). In the translation example, the task worker is likely to already be familiar with the quality standards the company has for the work. She may have already learned unique terminology that the company uses and figured out how to translate it. From the client perspective, working with the same translator again could result in higher quality work with less instruction required. Contingent workers are likely to perform better if they perceive the opportunity for future work from the same company. Thus, offering some kind of ERM inducement to task workers, and establishing a more relational PC, could ultimately benefit the client company.

Similarly, platform providers could also benefit from engaging in ERM with the goal of establishing longer term relationships with the task workers without crossing the boundary into full time employee. Uber is likely to benefit from retaining drivers over a longer period of time. These drivers would become more skilled and potentially offer better service to the riders. Further, the platform providers benefit financially whenever a task is completed through their marketplace. The platforms have an incentive to retain task workers and motivate them to use their service rather than spreading work across many different platforms.

Strohmeier (2013) argues that technology is an "enabler" of the ERM process. This is similar to arguments made by Boudreau (2017) who promotes the concept of *technological empowerment* in the context of the platform economy. Boudreau argues that technology allows task workers who are outside of the traditional boundary of the organization to participate in the work of the organization. While there are times when an organization may not want an ongoing relationship with a task worker, strategic use of HR technology could allow task workers to form and maintain a relationship with the company, perhaps creating a more balanced contract.

The Procurement View. In many large companies, contract management of contingent workers is currently handled through the procurement department rather than the HR department (Feffer, 2016). The main objectives of procurement are focused on driving down costs, avoiding legal issues, and complying with contract regulations. From this viewpoint, the purpose of a task worker or IC is to perform the job when they are told to do so, quickly and safely, and then separate from the company after performing their task. Engagement and talent management are not part of the discussion. Many of the existing technology solutions for managing contingent workers tend to be procurement oriented, focusing more on the transactional elements of the relationship (Bersin, 2017). For example, the SAP Fieldglass marketing messages on their website focus on efficiency, cost-effectiveness, and compliance, highlighting processes such as requisitions, invoicing, and payment. The pure procurement approach to engaging contingent workers has the risk of minimizing the connection the contingent has with the employer, and limiting any benefits that the worker might receive. Some of the marketplace platforms offer services specifically targeted to organizations managing a large number of task workers. For example, Guru has an Enterprise offering for companies in this situation. Work Market advertises full integration with HR information systems such as SAP, Workday, and Oracle. This suggests that some companies may be moving toward including ICs and task workers in their broader workforce planning efforts, with the data all in one place. Efficient and effective management of transactional worker data is important, of course, but is the minimum that needs to be offered (Bissola & Imperatori, 2014). Extending ERM to the more relational aspect of eHRM may provide an array of advantages to all three parties in the triangular relationship.

THREE TYPES OF RELATIONAL eHRM

Bissola and Imperatori (2013, 2014) defined relational eHRM as "electronic practices that allow the HR department to manage the relationships between the organisation and their employees." (Bissola & Imperatori, 2013, p. 453). They further identified three categories of relational e-HRM practices; communication, training and development, and performance management. In two samples of young Italian employees (all permanent, full-time employees), Bissola and Imperatori (2013, 2014) found that the use of relational eHRM practices was associated with stronger employee affective commitment and greater perceptions of procedural justice and trust in the organization. Although their studies focused on more traditional employees, they suggested that relational eHRM might be extended to contingent workers to help build stronger employment relationships (2014). For example, for a worker who is engaging in task work involuntarily, the option to engage more with the client organization via online communication or performance management could help enhance procedural justice perceptions and lead to other positive work outcomes. Thus, we use these three categories of relational eHRM to examine existing tools being used by organizations to manage workers more effectively, looking at how these are used for permanent employees and task workers. For task workers, we examine the use of eHRM from perspectives of both the platform providers and client organizations. We also explore how eHRM tools offered to employees might be extended to other worker groups. These eHRM functions/capabilities for permanent and task workers are summarized in Table 8.2.

Communication Systems. One type of relational eHRM is a communication system where organizations can push several different kinds of information out to workers, or make information more easily available to workers who seek it. Web-based recruiting can be also considered a communication practice (Bissola & Imperatori, 2014), although to external audiences rather than internal. Some communication systems can even assist workers with performance improvements simply by alerting them to environmental factors that may impact demand for their services. Another critical function of communication in eHRM is during the hiring process, as effective pre-hire communication can help prevent PC breach (Robinson & Morrison, 2000).

Permanent Workers. Employee self-service (ESS) is one common type of eHRM that allows companies to communicate more effectively with employees. Through ESS, employees can find information about company holiday schedules, how much vacation they have left, requirements for applying for family or medical leave, or benefits that are available to them (Johnson, Thatcher, & Burleson,

TABLE 8.2.   Relationship-enhancing eHRM Functionality

Relational eHRM System	Worker Type	
	Permanent	Task
Communication	• Employee self-service • Pre-hire communication	• Pre-registration communication • Information on upcoming tasks • Platform blog space to enhance communication
Performance Management	• Enhancing performance management through more regular feedback • Goal setting, social feedback	• Collecting feedback from clients (individual and organizational) • Performance monitoring • Two-way feedback allowing task worker to evaluate client
Training and Development	• E-learning systems for cost effective and tailored training • Recommendations for further training	• Minimal training for task workers • Platform blogs or discussion spaces function as informal learning tools

2016). Pre-hire communication is also regularly performed through eHRM channels (Johnson et al., 2016), allowing employers to have broader reach and customize messages to subgroups of potential recruits. The use of e-recruiting methods has been shown to promote more effective recruiting overall.

Platforms. While the nature of the hiring decision is different for task workers, many platforms do appear to include some element of pre-hire communication with task workers. In the cases of Uber and Airbnb, there are very clear directions for what is necessary to register with the platform to become a driver or host. The pre-hire communication is very straightforward and the requirements are minimal. Uber clearly states intended inducements and terms of the agreement to potential drivers. If drivers are reading the available communications before signing up, then their responsibilities should be just as clear. To strengthen this type of communication function and enhance the likelihood that people understand the information, platforms could require potential task workers to complete a short online assessment on the work requirements.[3]

Platform providers are using technology to communicate with task workers in other ways that serve eHRM functions. For example, Uber provides information to drivers about events in their cities and uses the driver app to communicate where the local "hot spots" are to direct drivers to waiting riders. Uber also sends drivers new requests as they approach their final destination, minimizing the downtime between rides. Another way for eHRM to facilitate communication is between workers. Guru provides functionality for members of work teams, regardless of location or organizational status, to communicate with one another. Thus, task workers and client employees can easily communicate about brainstorming, project schedules, or work quality. Several platforms offer blog space on their websites to facilitate communication among task workers or clients. For example, Upwork has a Community Discussion space with threads dedicated to new platform users, freelancers, clients, and even a "Coffee Break" page for random, fun discussions.

Clients. Clients can use platforms to communicate more effectively with potential task workers before hiring them for a task. They can clarify the nature of the task, performance expectations, and compensation. As with permanent workers, this type of pre-hire communication is expected to enhance the formation of an accurate PC and subsequently prevent breach. There are also options for using eHRM to communicate with task workers post-hire. Research has shown that effective communication between the client supervisor and the task worker helps form a more productive relationship (Chambel et al., 2016). For example, a project supervisor in the client organization could use the platform technology or other communication tools to check in periodically with the task worker on project status.

---

[3] We thank an anonymous reviewer for this suggestion,

Performance Management Systems. The second type of relational eHRM is the performance management system. This category includes all systems intended to provide performance feedback (e.g., online performance appraisals or 360-degree evaluations) and assist with performance improvement.

Permanent Workers. Research has demonstrated positive outcomes of e-performance management functions. Moving performance management to eHRM has allowed organizations to provide feedback more regularly, enhance participation and accountability for ratings, include peers in providing feedback, and enhance social functions of performance feedback (Ledford, Benson & Lawler, 2016; Payne, Horner, Boswell, Schroeder, & Stine-Cheyne, 2009). Real-time goal setting is often integrated into these tools, with clear linkages between individual goals, group goals, and organizational goals. Integration into eHRM or HRIS systems enhances organizational ability to analyze and use the performance data.

Platforms. Many task worker platforms include a performance evaluation function. The platform does not conduct the evaluation but collects and analyzes the data from clients for use by either clients or the platform itself. Most of the marketplace platforms such as Work Market, Upwork, and Fiverr have an integrated rating function. This constant evaluation and the impact it has on the task worker's ability to find future work can increase the relationship effort required of task workers (Lewchuck & Clarke, 2011).

Uber's performance ratings system is more extensive. Uber riders are offered the option to evaluate drivers at the end of each trip. Drivers can view the ratings and the associated comments to try and improve their performance. These ratings are also used to evaluate drivers for overall performance quality, and if they fall below a certain level drivers can be suspended from the system. The minimum rating level is determined on a city-by-city basis because "there are cultural differences in the way people in different cities rate each other," (Uber Community Guidelines, 2016, Quality). If a driver's rating drops below the approved level after multiple warnings, they will be officially suspended from the system and not allowed to use the Uber platform.

The extent to which these systems qualify as performance *management*, with a performance improvement function, is unclear. A true performance management system would provide real-time, constructive feedback to guide the worker about how to improve his or her performance (Adler, Campion, Colquitt, Grubb, Murphy, Ollander-Krane, & Pulakos, 2016). Uber drivers do receive warnings when they are approaching the suspension level. Uber then gives drivers the option to complete an approved third-party quality improvement course at the driver's expense. Upon proof of completion, drivers can be allowed back onto the system and continue driving. Uber is also exploring an appeals court option for those who feel they were wrongfully removed from the system. These options for reinstatement are likely to enhance drivers' sense of procedural justice and point to a more durable relationship. As suggested by Rousseau and Wade-Benzoni, with purely transactional contracts "incompetent employees are terminated and employees will quit untrustworthy organizations," (1995, p. 296). Instead, we see evidence that the relationship between the driver and Uber moves to a slightly more balanced PC. Uber is putting in effort towards the driver to facilitate long-run success. The relationship is characterized by mutual support on this facet of the relationship because both sides are contributing to long term maintenance. Uber offers drivers the opportunity to take a course in order to get back into the system, and drivers can invest in taking the courses because they want to begin driving again.

Another approach to platform performance management takes the form of performance monitoring. Upwork offers a function called Work Diary that takes periodic screen captures of the task worker's screen and posts them to the client's account. This allows the client to track what the task worker is actually doing and manage the performance process more closely, particularly for hourly jobs. However, the Work Diary appears to be purely a performance monitoring function and does not include any feedback or performance improvement functions. This level of monitoring also implies a strictly transactional relationship characterized by low trust.

Clients. As noted above, the client or end user is making the performance ratings and may use the ratings given by other clients to help make the task worker selection decision. If a client gives negative performance feedback to a task worker, it is unclear if that client would be interested in working with the task worker to improve his or her performance. In the traditional employment situation, the employer has sunk costs from selection and training that often motivate it to try and improve the employee's performance. With ICs and task workers, such sunk costs are much lower and the client may simply choose to move on and hire a different task worker for the next opportunity. Thus, performance management may not be a viable option from the client perspective. Within a contract or task, however, the client may have some motivation to provide feedback and attempt to improve the worker's performance rather than terminating the contract for poor performance and engaging a different worker to start over.

It appears that with many of the task worker platforms, the performance ratings are one-sided meaning that the client can rate the worker but the worker cannot formally rate the client. Airbnb and Uber are exceptions, as they allow the task worker to also rate the person who stays in their property or rides in their vehicle. The two-way feedback system is more similar to Etsy or Ebay, where both the buyer and seller have the opportunity to rate one another to enhance overall levels of trust in the system. Implementing a two-way rating system for task workers could help create more balanced relationships where the workers have more voice.

Training and Development Systems. The third type of relational eHRM system is training and development. These are technology mediated systems for improving knowledge and skills, and can include e-learning, e-coaching or e-mentoring, and formalized online career development planning (Imperatori, personal communication, April 3 2017; Johnson et al, 2016; Strohmeier, 2007).

Permanent Workers. Employers use eHRM technologies to make training more readily available, make it more cost effective, and make their training and development systems more responsive to individual employees' needs. Further, organizations can use existing eHRM analytic functionality to guide and provide training for employees. For example, eHRM can provide an "automated recommendation of an individualized set of successive training measures and job assignments for each employee" (Strohmeier, 2013, p. 99).

Platforms. We see some evidence of platforms providing informal training and development support to task workers. This support tends to be minimal and voluntary. For example, Airbnb provides online guidance to renters on how to maximize their earnings. Uber provides some self-directed learning resources for drivers, such as tips on how to get trips without waiting and how to provide a high quality rider experience. (Driver App, 2017). As noted above, Uber offers Quality Improvement classes (outsourced to a training provider) to help drivers with low ratings improve their performance. These classes are offered online and in-person in some cities, and focus more on customer service skills than actual driving skills. Guru has a blog on its website where it offers advice to both parties in the engagement, the freelancer and the client, to improve aspects of the work process. Upwork's Community Discussion space, mentioned in the communication section above, can also function as an informal learning tool. Work Market offers a more formal Learning Management System (How It Works, 2015), although it appears to be used more for selection purposes (i.e., to test a potential worker's skills) than for training.

Clients. Client organizations often hire ICs and task workers because they already have the needed skills and do not require training and development. Thus, training and development efforts for contingent workers are often limited to basic workplace orientation (Fisher & Connelly, 2017).

Other Relational Inducements. Platforms or clients may offer other kinds of inducements outside of these three eHRM categories to enhance the relationship with the task worker. Uber offers discounts on mobile phone service, gasoline, and car maintenance that may create a sense of continuance commitment among drivers. Some platforms have features intended to ease the payment process, allowing flexibility in when and how a task worker receives payment. Others such as Guru offer assistance with tax forms. Thus, while we focus on the categories of communication, performance management, and training and development (Bissola & Imperatori, 2014), there are certainly other ways to engage and retain task workers that may be unrelated to eHRM.

EXTERNAL THIRD PARTY eHRM SERVICES

It is interesting to note that external third parties are growing to fill this sparsely populated space and provide eHRM services to task workers. For example, the website SherpaShare markets itself as the "#1 support platform for OnDemand workers." (SherpaShare, 2016). This website allows task workers affiliated with a variety of platforms such as Uber, Lyft, and Airbnb to track metrics related to work performed and earnings, keep records for tax purposes, and connect and communicate with fellow task workers (SherpaShare, 2016). The website assists with transactional details of the task worker life, but also seeks to help workers optimize their performance and earnings. Further, it emphasizes that it allows workers to have voice and to develop relationships with peer task workers. It would be interesting to see if a similar functionality promoting communication among task workers would be useful for client organizations. SherpaShare appears to benefit from this communication functionality by using data from user postings to further develop their services. By listening to the workers they are better able to anticipate user needs. Other external websites such as Reddit are used for task worker communication, with specific forums dedicated to Uber drivers, Airbnb hosts, and Upwork workers. There is even a website with an associated Reddit page for Airbnb that serves a training and development function. Called "learnairbnb," this page offers tips on how to better promote listings and make more money hosting (Learnairbnb, 2017; We Can Make You A Smarter Airbnb Host, 2016).

External providers have also entered the training and development space for task workers. Beyond the informal learning resources offered on sites such as Reddit, there are many formal training programs available to help task workers navigate the various platforms such as Fiverr and learn how to build a successful business as a task worker. On the Udemy website, where several such training programs are listed, freelance instructors charge for these training programs. Thus, it appears that there is demand for eHRM services for task workers, and currently there is minimal supply for such services.

FUTURE RESEARCH DIRECTIONS

We believe this concept of using eHRM to strengthen attachments between task workers, platforms, and clients offers several avenues for future research. Most fundamentally, we need to conduct research on the extent to which the use of relational eHRM practices would change perceptions of task worker existing PCs or result in the formation of more relational PCs among new task workers. PCs can change over time at new milestones in the relationship or due to new technology (Suazo & Stone-Romero, 2016). There are already some platforms, and possibly some clients, that offer relational eHRM resources for task workers. One option for starting research in this area is to study task worker PCs with platforms that offer eHRM resources compared to other platforms that offer fewer inducements to see if there are differences. Longitudinal research that directly examines changes in PCs due to introduction of new relational eHRM would also be useful. It is important to keep in mind that different types of task workers may be differentially affected by eHRM resources depending on their motivation for being a task worker. A financially strapped (McKinsey Institute, 2016) task worker who feels forced to be a task worker may need more inducements to perceive a balanced PC.

In contrast, task workers who are motivated by their choices and their passions may increase their own contributions to the relationship if they receive additional inducements through eHRM.

We then need to investigate the extent to which relational eHRM practices impact outcomes for task workers. Bissola and Imperatori (2014) suggest that these practices lead to enhanced trust in HR for permanent workers through the mechanism of procedural justice. Future research should examine the extent to which a similar effect holds for task workers, and then for different types of task workers. For example, it is possible that people who are engaged in task work voluntarily (free agents or casual earners) may not appreciate the relational practices as much as someone who is doing task work involuntarily (reluctants or financially strapped; McKinsey, 2016). However, true free agents may have more alternatives for task work engagements and thus both platforms and clients may need to implement eHRM inducements to attract and retain these workers. Workers who experience higher levels of employment relationship uncertainty and effort and lower levels of support (Lewchuck & Clarke, 2011) may also benefit more from relational practices.

Further, we need research investigating each of the three types of relational eHRM practices. Are these equally effective in producing positive outcomes? One theoretical perspective that could be applied here is the high involvement HR practice (Lepak et al., 2007). Some relational eHRM practices are likely to be characterized as high involvement while others would be low involvement. For example, communication practices, self-directed learning, and automated performance feedback (e.g., aggregated client ratings) appear to be more low involvement. These practices would require less investment and be more appropriate for workers performing support tasks. In contrast, performance management and in-depth training would be more high involvement. These practices require more involvement from the organization and would be more appropriate for workers performing core tasks, or workers who have longer term relationships with the client or platform.

From the more practical perspective, it is important to further analyze the potential impact of relational eHRM on employment status of task workers. It is possible that the use of certain relational eHRM practices, and ERM more broadly, could lead to undesired employment or co-employment relationships between task workers and client organizations. As noted by Wears and Fisher (2012), the HR practices that facilitate closer relationships and better performance are often the same things that can lead to an assessment of an employment relationship rather than a contractor or task worker relationship. Considering the IRS control test often used to evaluate contractor status, platforms and clients would probably need to make use of the eHRM tools voluntary rather than mandatory.

CONCLUSION

The use of task workers can help organizations reduce direct labor costs, access specialized skills in the labor market, and enhance their labor flexibility. However, from the strategic supply chain perspective, firms also need to keep in mind the potential benefits of longer term task worker relationships and development of human capital, particularly for task workers performing core functions. The assumption in the HRM and OB literatures has generally been that contingent worker relationships with client organizations are, and should be, transactional. Based on a review of psychological contracts and the various triangular work relationships, we argue that taking a more relational approach may help firms better leverage segments of this on-demand workforce. Relational eHRM solutions offer promise for improving worker relations in a cost-effective way. As noted by Barrette (2017), "The new challenge is to expand talent analytics to help grow and develop employees, with the aim of building a thriving workforce that fuels organizational success" (para. 2).

REFERENCES

Acevedo, D. D. (2016). Regulating employment relationships in the sharing economy. *Employee Rights and Employment Policy Journal* 20(1), 1–35.

Adler, S., Campion, M., Colquitt, A., Grubb, A., Murphy, K., Ollander-Krane, R., & Pulakos, E. D. (2016). Getting rid of performance ratings: Genius or folly? A debate. *Industrial and Organizational Psychology, 9*(2), 219–252.

Aguinis, H., & Lawal, S. O. (2013). ELancing: A review and research agenda for bridging the science-practice gap. *Human Resource Management Review, 23*, 6–17. doi:10.1016/j.hrmr.2012/06.003

Barrette, J. (2017, February 14). Talent analytics that benefit employees. *LinkedIn.* Retrieved from https://www.linkedin.com/pulse/talent-analytics-benefit-employees-jamie-barrette?trk=hp-feed-article-title-like

Bersin, J. (2017, February). Top trends in HR technology. *HR Magazine.*

Bissola, R., & Imperatori, B. (2013). Facing e-HRM: the consequences on employee attitude towards the organisation and the HR department in Italian SMEs. *European Journal of International Management, 7*(4), 450–468.

Bissola, R., & Imperatori, B. (2014). The unexpected side of relational e-HRM: Developing trust in the HR department. *Employee Relations, 36*(4), 376–397.

Boudreau, J. (2017, January 10). How workforce changes and technology will affect organizations in the future. *SmartTalk HR Blog.* Retrieved from http://blog.risesmart. com/how-workforce-changes-and-technology-will-affect-organizations-in-the-future/#sthash.0ITvNbpe.dpuf

Brant, T. (2016, November 29). Uber to European court: We're not a transportation company. *PC Magazine.* Retrieved from http://www.pcmag.com/news/349940/uber-to-european-court-were-not-a-transportation-company

Brown, G. E. (2016, March 31). An Uberdilemma: Employees and independent contractors in the sharing economy. *Maryland Law Review Endnotes, 75*(15), 15–43.

Cappelli, P., & Neumark, D. (2004). External churning and internal flexibility: Evidence on the functional flexibility and core-periphery hypotheses. *Industrial Relations: A Journal of Economy and Society, 43*(1), 148–182.

Chambel, M. J. (2014). Does the fulfillment of supervisor psychological contract make a difference? *Leadership & Organization Development Journal, 35*(1), 20–37.

Chambel, M. J., & Castanheria, F. (2007). They don't want to be temporaries: Similarities between temps and core workers. *Journal of Organizational Behavior, 28,* 943—959.

Chambel, M. J., Lorente, L., Carvalho, V., & Martinez, I.M. (2016) Psychological contract profiles among permanent and temporary agency workers. *Journal of Managerial Psychology, 31*(1), 79–94.

Davis-Blake, A., & Uzzi, B. (1993). Determinants of employment externalization: A study of temporary workers and independent contractors. *Administrative Science Quarterly, 38*(2), 195–223.

De Cuyper, N. D., Rigotti, T., De Witte, H., & Mohr, G. (2008). Balancing psychological contracts: Validation of a typology. *The International Journal of Human Resource Management, 19*(4), 543–561.

Drahokoupil, J., & Fabo, B. (2016). *The platform economy and the disruption of the employment relationship.* European Trade Union Institute Policy Briefs Series. Retrieved from www.etui.org/publications.

Driver App. (2017). *Uber.* Retrieved from https://www.uber.com/drive/partner-app/

Feffer, M. (October 27, 2016). Easing contract labor pains. *HR Magazine, 61*(9), 72–73.

Fisher, S. L., & Connelly, C. E. (2017). Lower cost or just lower value? Modeling the organizational costs and benefits of contingent work. *Academy of Management Discoveries, 3*(2), 1–22.

Fiverr's Terms of Service. (2016, October). *Fiverr.* Retrieved from https://www.fiverr.com/terms_of_service

Henson. R. (2005). The next decade of HR: Trends, technologies, and recommendations. In H. G. Gueutal & D. L. Stone (Ed.), *The brave new world of eHR.* (pp. 255–292). San Francisco, CA: Jossey-Bass.

Horney, N. (2016). The gig economy: A disruptor for HR agility. *HR People & Strategy, 39*(3), 20–27.

How It Works. (2015). *Work Market.* Retrieved from https://www.workmarket.com/how-it-works

Johnson, R. D., Thatcher, J. B., & Burleson, J. (2016). A framework and research agenda for studying eHRM. In D. L. Stone & J. H. Dulebohn (Eds.), *Human resource management theory and research on new employment relationships* (pp. 227–256). Charlotte, NC: Information Age Publishing.

Kenney, M. & Zysman, J. (2016). The rise of the platform economy. *National Academies of Sciences, Engineering, and Medicine—The University of Texas at Dallas & Arizona State University.* Retrieved from http://www.brie.berkeley.edu/wp-content/uploads/2015/02/Kenney-Zysman-The-Rise-of-the-Platform-Economy-Spring–2016-ISTx.pdf

Learnairbnb. (2017). *Reddit.* Retrieved from https://www.reddit.com/r/learnairbnb/ on April 10, 2016.

Ledford, G. E., Benson, G., & Lawler, E. E. (2016). Aligning research and the current practice of performance management. *Industrial and Organizational Psychology, 9*(2), 253–260.

Lepak, D. P., & Snell, S.A. (2002). Examining the human resource architecture: The relationships among human capital, employment, and human resource configurations. *Journal of Management, 28*(4), 517–543.

Lepak, D. P., Taylor. S. M., Tekleab, A., Marrone, J. A., & Cohen, D. J. (2007). An examination of the use of high-investment human resource systems for core and support employees. *Human Resource Managemen, 46*(2), 223–246.

Levashina, J., & Campion, M. A. (2009). Expected practices in background checking: Review of the human resource management literature. *Employee Responsibilities and Rights Journal, 21*, 231–249.

Lewchuk, W., & Clarke, M. (2011). *Working without Commitments: The health effects of precarious employment.* McGill-Queen's Press-MQUP.

Liden, R. C., Wayne, S. J., Kraimer, M. L., Sparrowe, R. T. (2003). The dual commitments of contingent workers: An examination of contingents' commitment to the agency and the organization. *Journal of Organizational Behavior, 24*, 609—625.

Marler, J. H., Woodard Barringer, M., & Milkovich, G. T. (2002). Boundaryless and traditional contingent employees: Worlds apart. *Journal of Organizational Behavior, 23*(4), 425–453.

McKinsey Institute. (2016). *Independent work: Choice, necessity, and the gig economy.* Retrieved from http://www.mckinsey.com/global-themes/employment-and-growth/ Independent-work-choice-necessity-and-the-gig-economy

Millward, L. J., & Hopkins, L. J. (1998). Psychological contracts, organizational and job commitment. *Journal of Applied Social Psychology, 28*(16), 1530–1556.

Oei, S., & Ring, D. M. (2017). The tax lives of Uber drivers: Evidence from Internet discussion forums. *Columbia Journal of Tax Law, 8*(56), 58–112.

Parry, E., & Tyson, S. (2011). Desired goals and actual outcomes of e-HRM. *Human Resource Management Journal, 21*(3), 335–354.

Payne, S. C., Horner, M. T., Boswell, W. R., Schroeder, A. N., & Stine-Cheyne, K. J. (2009). Comparison of online and traditional performance appraisal systems. *Journal of Managerial Psychology, 24*(6), 526–544.

Robinson, S. L., & Morrison, E. W. (2000). The development of psychological contract breach and violation: A longitudinal study. *Journal of Organizational Behavior, 21*(5), 525–546.

Rousseau, D. M. (2011). The individual–organization relationship: The psychological contract. In S. Zedeck (Ed.), *APA handbook of industrial and organizational psychology, vol 3: Maintaining, expanding, and contracting the organization* (pp. 191–220). American Psychological Association: Washington, D.C.

Rousseau, D. M., & Wade-Benzoni, K. A. (1995). Changing individual–organization attachments: A two-way street. In A. Howard (Ed.), *The changing nature of work* (pp. 290–322). Jossey-Bass Publishers: San Francisco, CA.

Ruel, H., Bondarouk, T. & Looise, J. K. (2004), E-HRM: Innovation or irritation. An explorative empirical study in five large companies on web-based HRM. *Management Revue, 15*(3), 364–380.

Scheel, T. E., Rigotti, T. & Mohr, G. (2013). HR practices and their impact on the psychological contracts of temporary and permanent workers. *The International Journal of Human Resource Management, 24*(2), 285–307.

Scheiber, N. (April 2, 2017). How Uber uses psychological tricks to push its drivers' buttons. *New York Times.*

Schweitzer, L., & Lyons, S. (2008). The market within: A marketing approach to creating and developing high-value employment relationships. *Business Horizons, 51*(6), 555–565.

SherpaShare. (2016). *SherpaShare.* Retrieved from www.sherpashare.com

Stone, D., & Dulebohn, J. (2013). Emerging issues in theory and research on electronic human resource management (eHRM). *Human Resource Management Review, 23*, 1–5.

Strohmeier, S. (2013). Employee relationship management—Realizing competitive advantage through information technology? *Human Resource Management Review, 23*(1), 93–104.

Suazo, M. M., & Stone-Romero, E. F. (2016). A review of theory and research on psychological contracts in organizations. In D. L. Stone & J. H. Dulebohn (Eds.), *Human resource management theory and review on new employment relationships* (pp, 111–150). Charlotte, NC: Information Age Publishing.

Subasinghe, R. (October 20, 2016). The employment status of gig economy workers matters. *Equal Times.* Retrieved from https://www.equaltimes.org/the-employment-status-of-gig?lang=en#.WC4qC6IrJmA

Tekleab, A. G., & Taylor, S. M. (2003). Aren't there two parties in an employment relationship? Antecedents and consequences of organization-employee agreement on contract obligations and violations. *Journal of Organizational Behavior, 24*(5), 585–608.

Tomlinson, D. (October 2016). How can employers support well-being in the gig economy? *Employee Benefits.* Retrieved from https://www.employeebenefits.co.uk/issues/october–2016/daniel-tomlinson-how-can-employers-support-wellbeing-in-the-gig-economy/

Uber Community Guidelines (2016). *Community guidelines.* Retrieved from https://www.uber.com/legal/community-guidelines/us-en/

We Can Make You a Smarter Airbnb Host. (2016). *Learnairbnb.* Retrieved from http://learnairbnb.com/

Wears, K. H., & Fisher, S. L. (2012). Who is an employer in the triangular employment relationship? Sorting through the definitional confusion. *Employee Rights and Responsibilities Journal, 24*, 159–176. doi:10.1007/s10672-012–9189-3

Wilkin, C. L. (2012). I can't get no job satisfaction: Meta-analysis comparing permanent and contingent workers. *Journal of Organizational Behavior, 34*, 47–64.

WorkMarket terms of use agreement for users. (2017). *WorkMarket.* Retrieved from https://www.workmarket.com/tos

CHAPTER 9

UNPACKING THE "E" OF E-HRM

A Review and Reflection on Assumptions about Technology in e-HRM Research

Markus Ellmer and Astrid Reichel

ABSTRACT

For research in electronic Human Resource Management (e-HRM), the ongoing diffusion of sophisticated information technology (IT) in HRM invokes critical questions concerning the role and status of technology in theoretical contemplation and empirical analysis. Earlier research indicates that the domain treats technology solely as a general and generic entity. At the same time, scholars in kindred domains warn that analytically waiving technology can lead to puzzling results and one-sided contribution made to knowledge. Perspectives and conceptions applied in research are based on (often implicit) assumptions that profoundly shape the questions asked and conclusions drawn. To scrutinize prevailing assumptions about technology in e-HRM, we conduct a systematic literature review of 62 research papers. The review uncovers rich and manifold assumptions and conceptions on technology but confirms that technology is largely addressed only at a very general and generic level. We discuss potential consequences of this finding and call for more complex considerations of the "e" in e-HRM. To this end, we suggest avenues for theorizing technology in e-HRM contexts more extensively. We argue that these perspectives can bring fresh explanatory resources and open up the domain for new insights in future research.

The Brave New World of eHRM 2.0, pages 247–278.

247

Keywords: e-HRM, affordances, technological identities, Sociomateriality, Actor-Network Theory

For the past four decades, advancements in information technology (IT) have widely been integrated into Human Resource Management (HRM). Accordingly, electronic HRM (e-HRM), a domain dedicated to the integration mechanisms and interfaces between IT and HRM, rapidly emerged as a research field in its own right (Bondarouk, Parry, & Furtmueller, 2016; Bondarouk & Ruël, 2009; Gueutal & Stone, 2005; Lengnick-Hall & Moritz, 2003; Stone & Dulebohn, 2013; Strohmeier, 2007). Over time, different generations of IT became established in HRM. Besides the continuing dissemination of Human Resource Information Systems (HRIS) and HR modules in Enterprise Resource Planning (ERP) systems (Bondarouk, Parry, et al., 2016; Stone & Dulebohn, 2013), technologies and methods associated with HR analytics (e.g., data-mining in extensive data sets), (Fitz-enz, 2010; Marler & Boudreau, 2016; Scholz, 2017; Strohmeier & Piazza, 2013, 2015b), the Internet of Things (Strohmeier et al., 2017), or Artificial Intelligence (Meister, 2017; Strohmeier & Piazza, 2015a) currently diffuse into the HRM function.

Extensive developments and growing complexity of these systems invoke critical questions concerning the role and status of technology in HRM research (Bondarouk & Brewster, 2016; Stone, Deadrick, Lukaszewski, & Johnson, 2015). In these premises, kindred research fields point to the high importance of adequately considering technology in both theoretical contemplation and empirical analyses. For instance, different streams in Information Systems theory stress the importance of understanding technology as deeply entangled and situated in ongoing management and work practices (Cecez-Kecmanovic, Galliers, Henfridsson, Newell, & Vidgen, 2014; Leonardi, 2013; Orlikowski, 2000, 2007). In a similar manner, voices from Science and Technology Studies emphasize that technology should be assigned with sufficient explanatory status to understand stability and change in organizations (Latour, 2005; Law, 1992; Tutnall & Gilding, 1999). In a more straightforward fashion, scholars also realized that being precise about *what* technology (or feature) is actually used and *how* it is used can significantly improve the understanding of the embeddedness of technology in its social environment. For instance, research in group decision support systems shows that modifications of single features have significant impact on decision making and quality (Hassell & Limayem, 2011; Lamprecht & Robra-Bissantz, 2015; Swaab, Galinsky, Medvec, & Diermeier, 2012).

For e-HRM, Strohmeier's review (2007) indicates that research in the domain treats technology as a general and generic entity, barely referring to distinct technologies or single systems. Technology, or: the "e" of e-HRM, seems to be incorporated only in a vague and general manner. These allegedly simplistic views point to specific *assumptions* on the nature and role of technology entrenched in the domain. In general, assumptions have important consequences for the questions scholars ask, the phenomena on which they focus their attention, and the recommendations they give (Fleetwood, 2005; Leonardi, 2013). When technology is merely assumed to be a simple and unproblematic entity hence, the field of vision remains protracted or even limited to the human/social side. The complexities technology evolves in relation to its users and social contexts stay in the dark. Consequently, technology solely considered as a minor matter, as simple utility or self-evident infrastructure, with its relations to the human/social not explicitly problematized, could yield mixed and conflicting results with one-sided contributions made to knowledge (Orlikowski, 2007; Orlikowski & Scott, 2008).

The goal of this chapter is to identify, organize, and scrutinize prevailing assumptions on the nature and role of technology in e-HRM research. In a literature review of 62 empirical e-HRM research papers we systematically disentangle and organize prevailing assumptions in the terminology and qualities related to the "e", in definitions of e-HRM, and in an overview on how technology is linked to other central entities in the literature (embracing organizational structures, factors, and environments, activities and practices, perceptions and attitudes, roles, and relations between actors). The review uncovers three major sets of assumptions (tool, proxy, and ensemble) and two major conceptions of technology (catalyst conception and conformation conception). Based on the results, we identify two shortcomings (black-boxing of the "e" and conceptual oscillation) and discuss their potential consequences for research in e-HRM.

Our review contributes to the e-HRM literature in two ways. First, since prevailing assumptions are critical prerequisites for the knowledge produced (Fleetwood, 2005; Leonardi, 2013), we provide researchers with greater clarity of existing assumptions on technology in e-HRM. By putting the "e" of e-HRM into the center of attention, we aim to show some benefits of paying more attention to the "e" in e-HRM in future research. Second, by suggesting different theoretical approaches to address the "e" beyond existing conceptions, we advance the theoretical spectrum of the e-HRM domain and contribute to closing theoretical gaps a number of scholars have identified in e-HRM throughout the past decade (Marler & Fisher, 2013; Ruël, Bondarouk, & van der Velde, 2007; Stone & Dulebohn, 2013; Strohmeier, 2007). We conclude that the perspectives suggested can bring new explanatory approaches of phenomena and open up the field to new insights at the interfaces between HRM and technology.

LITERATURE REVIEW: UNPACKING THE "E" OF E-HRM

Paper Selection

For the literature review we systematically obtained a sample of 62 research papers from an extensive search in an integrative database system[1] that allows unified access to relevant data-bases in management studies (Business Source Premier, Scopus, Web of Science, ProQuest, etc.). Additionally, we searched the

---

[1] UBSearch is an integrated data-base research interface provided by the University of Salzburg.

TABLE 9.1. Search Terms and Results.

| | | Search Terms | Number of Results | |
			Database System	EBSCO
		E-HRM	137	38
		E-Human Resource Management	5	4
Electronic	AND	HRM	56	56
Electronic	AND	Human Resource Management	111	124
Web-based	AND	HRM	9	15
Web-based	AND	Human Resource Management	12	37
		E-PM	0*	0*
		E-Personnel Management	0	0
Electronic	AND	PM	0*	0*
Electronic	AND	Personnel Management	8	114
Web-based	AND	PM	0*	0*
Web-based	AND	Personnel Management	1	27
		E-Personnel Planning	0	0
Electronic	AND	Personnel Planning	0	0
Web-based	AND	Personnel Planning	1	0
		E-Recruiting	155	37
Electronic	AND	Recruiting	23	285
Web-based	AND	Recruiting	15	16
		E-HRD	0	0
		E-Human Resource Development	0	0
Electronic	AND	HRD	0	13
Electronic	AND	Human Resource Development	14	19
Web-based	AND	HRD	5	9
Web-based	AND	Human Resource Development	7	7
		E-Compensation	1	0*
Electronic	AND	Compensation	0*	0*
Web-based	AND	Compensation	15	0*
		E-Performance Management	5	0
Electronic	AND	Performance Management	0*	160
Web-based	AND	Performance Management	9	0
			589	961
			Total 1,550	

* results of these queries were excluded because they concerned disciplines different from management (e.g., chemistry, physics, material science, geology)

Ebsco database. In both, we used 30 word combinations by complementing the prefixes of "E-", "Electronic", and "Web-based" with the general terms "Human Resource Management" (and "HRM"), "Personnel Management" (and "PM") and with the HRM sub-functions "personnel planning", "recruiting", "Human Resource Development" (and "HRD"), "compensation", and "performance management" (Lepak & Snell, 1998; Thite, Kavanagh, & Johnson, 2009). This search yielded a total of 1,550 results. For a detailed overview see Table 9.1.

In a first step, we excluded all off-topic items, duplicates, conference papers, monographs, edited volumes, and grey literature (e.g., practitioner journals, reports, encyclopedias). Given our intention to trace potential consequences of assumptions in empirical work, we moreover excluded literature reviews and non-empirical accounts in a second step. We moreover limited our analysis to papers published between 2007 and 2016 because several previous literature reviews—with different foci than the one at hand—give a comprehensive overview on the lively discourse on the acronym e-HRM in the periods before (Bondarouk, Parry, et al., 2016; Marler & Fisher, 2013; Strohmeier, 2007). This process resulted in 158 papers. To ensure an appropriate standard for assessment of the research (see Marler & Boudreau, 2016), we limited our sample to papers in journals indexed in the Social Science Citation Index (SSCI). This process yielded 51 papers. In our search, we found several special issues dedicated to the topic "e-HRM" and "e-HR". To enrich our sample, we included all articles of SSCI-indexed special issues that fit our criteria from the first step. This process resulted in a total of 62 papers (see Figure 9.1).

On the basis of our reading, we identified three clusters of information for organizing contents related to the "e": terminology and qualities of the "e", definitions of e-HRM, and technology linked to other entities in research. In the following section we describe the information on technology provided in each cluster.

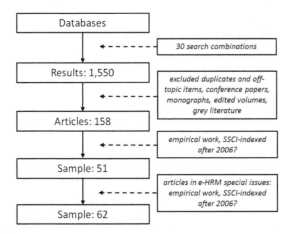

FIGURE 9.1. Paper selection process.

TERMINOLOGY AND QUALITIES OF THE "E"

Terms and Synonyms

In the literature analyzed, the "e" generally assigns the attribute "electronic" to HRM in general or to specific sub-functions (e.g., recruiting, development, learning, etc.). When HRM is "electronic", this means both HRM as management function and the practices executed by HRM and different other actors to be intersected with IT. In the papers, e-HRM also terms the focal technical systems in use. Accordingly, the acronym occurs in combination with a range of terms, e.g., e-HRM systems, implementation, adoption, utilization, use, practices, sophistication, capabilities, design, configuration, diffusion, or attitudes towards e-HRM.

Technically speaking, the "e" embraces both physical (PCs, screens, keyboards, cables, etc.) and non-physical entities (signals, software, data, etc.) and hence appears as a distinct combination of different materiality, including computer hardware, software, and electronic networking resources to process different kinds of data and information for HR purposes. Many papers specifically emphasize the existence of web-based technology (Internet or Intranet) as definitional characteristic for e-HRM. Sometimes, software products serve as indicator for the "e". Examples are modules of ERP systems, employee/manager self-service systems, portals, performance monitoring or appraisal applications, recruiting systems, social networking websites, self-assessment online games, or e-mail. Occasionally, commercial labels or product names like, e.g., "SAP HR" or "PeopleSoft" represent the "e".

Socio-Technical Qualities of the "e"

Since e-HRM terms intersections between IT, HRM, and HRM practices, it appears as a socio-technical phenomenon. The literature suggests several socio-technical qualities e-HRM can shape up to. Most famously, these have been grouped into operational, relational and transformational types of e-HRM (Lepak & Snell, 1998; Ruël, Bondarouk, & Looise, 2004). Operational e-HRM terms the automation of basic HR activities in the administrative area and is mostly concerned with enhancing the effectiveness and efficiency of HRM. Relational e-HRM focuses on the relations between different actors in organizations and refers to technologies supporting basic business processes and services, and the interacting and networking of different actors. Transformational e-HRM concerns activities that support organizational strategy. In the literature reviewed, these type-labels have also been used to differentiate into operational, relational, and transformational e-HRM practices, configurations, goals, impacts, or consequences.

Some contributions emphasize the "e" to create *value* for an organization, whereby different dimensions of value relate to the different socio-technical qualities. Operational e-HRM is associated with leveraging efficiency and effectiveness through standardization, harmonization, automatization, and acceleration of administrative processes. In this direction, a shift in the delivery of transactional

HRM from "labor intensive" to "technology intensive" (Florkowski & Olivas-Luján, 2006) has been observed (Parry, 2011; Parry & Tyson, 2011; Tansley, Huang, & Foster, 2013). In relational e-HRM, the "e" enables new unidirectional or reciprocal relationships between the organization and (future) employees. Accordingly, research emphasizes that new variations of (de)centralized information, communication, and participation patterns can be realized by the implementation of networking structures and interfaces. These can contribute to improve HR services by capitalizing on decoupling of HR activities and its addressees from space- and time-related constraints (Farndale, Paauwe, & Hoeksema, 2009; Holm, 2012; Llorens & Kellough, 2007; Meijerink, Bondarouk, & Maatman, 2013). Transformational e-HRM can create (new) strategic contributions to management. For instance, utilizing IT allows facilitating strategic recruiting, the branding of organizations, or capturing relevant employee data to generate metrics for evidence-based strategic decision-making. Operational e-HRM can support transformational and relational e-HRM by reducing the time spent on the administrative work, e.g., through automatization. These newly attained time resources can be used for process developments, HR policy design, business planning, performance and succession planning, and building human capital (Bondarouk & Ruël, 2013; Parry, 2011).

Composition of the "e" Over Time

In tandem with technological advances, the "e" and its socio-technical qualities have changed their composition over time. Compared to one decade ago, operational, relational, or transformational qualities nowadays include a wider span of technologies and more ways of how these technologies are intersected with HR practices. In a time-sensitive perspective hence, the "e" pronounces sequential generations of IT incorporated in HR practices that provide different scopes of action for organizations and their actors at particular points in time.

Since the 1980s, much of research in e-HRM was concerned with Human Resource Information Systems (HRIS) (Bondarouk, Parry, et al., 2016; Bondarouk & Ruël, 2009; Stone & Dulebohn, 2013), frequently defined as "specialized information system within the traditional functional areas of the organization (…) designed to support the planning, administration, decision-making, and control activities of human resource management" (DeSanctis, 1986). In broader interpretation, HRIS are systems used to acquire, store, retrieve, and distribute pertinent information regarding an organization's human resources and include hardware, software, people, policies, procedures, and data (Thite et al., 2009; Wiblen, Grant, & Dery, 2010) .While earlier e-HRM research considered HRIS as part of e-HRM tools, more recent accounts include HRIS in e-HRM only to the extent they feature web-based IT (Bondarouk & Ruël, 2009). Web-based systems reach all employees at all levels within an organization. They are not limited to HR professionals (Heikkilä, 2013; Marler & Fisher, 2013). Suitably, this "technical unlocking of HRIS for all employees of an organization" (Ruël et al., 2004, p.

365) and the concomitant magnitude and reach of e-HRM systems have been used to demarcate e-HRM from HRIS (Bondarouk & Ruël, 2009). Others, however, partly decouple e-HRM from its web-based foundation and suggest differentiating e-HRM systems in front-end and back-end systems. Front-end systems are usually web-based and their primary purpose is to connect different actors. Back-end systems, e.g., HR data warehouses, embrace systems for storing, processing, and retrieving data. Front-end systems require the support of various back-end systems, underlining the mutual dependence of web-based on non-web-based systems (Panayotopoulou, Galanaki, & Papalexandris, 2010; Strohmeier, 2007).

E-HRM technology occurs in the form of local stand-alone systems or as part of more extensive technical architectures. As indicated in the terms and synonyms section of this chapter, e-HRM systems can be part of large ERP systems, which offer to combine a range of modules for other business areas such as sales, production, and finance (Bondarouk & Ruël, 2013). Recruiting technologies are often embedded in large technological ecosystems as well. Some accounts extensively document how the features and functions of both internal (e.g., applicant tracking systems) and external solutions (e.g., online job boards) have transformed and/ or merged over time (Eckhardt, Laumer, Maier, & Weitzel, 2014; Hwang, 2014; Llorens & Kellough, 2007). Through adding or deleting distinct functions and features or by changing the appearance of user interfaces, graphics, symbols, etc., many e-HRM technologies of different size and reach have changed their compositions over time.

DEFINITIONS OF e-HRM

Definitions of e-HRM represent another source to explore manifestations of the "e" in e-HRM research. In their overview, Bondarouk and Ruël (2009) conclude that no standardized e-HRM definition exists. Several definitions have flourished and fall under one e-HRM label, with different perspectives of IT and HRM and little consistency or agreement. Aiming at unifying varying understandings, they propose to define e-HRM as "an umbrella term covering all possible integration mechanisms and contents between HRM and Information Technologies aiming at creating value within and across organizations for targeted employees and management." (p. 507). In a similar comprehensive manner, Marler and Parry (2016) refer to e-HRM as "configurations of computer hardware, software and electronic networking resources that enable intended or actual HRM activities (e.g. policies, practices and services) through coordinating and controlling individual and group-level data capture and information creation and communication within and across organizational boundaries." (p. 2234). Other very diverse e-HRM definitions found in our literature review could be clustered into three categories: activity-centered, relation-centered, and data-centered. In the following, we explain each category and give some representative examples.

Activity-Centered Definitions

Activity-centered definitions focus on the implementation and support of HR-related activities through technology. In this understanding, e-HRM systems have "facilitated and modified a number of HR processes, including job analysis, recruitment, selection, training, compensation, performance management, and HR planning." (Stone & Dulebohn, 2013, p. 2) A frequently found activity-centered definition was put forward by Ruël et al. (2004). They consider e-HRM as "a way of implementing HR strategies, policies and practices in organizations through a conscious and directed support of and/or with the full use of web-based technology channels." (pp. 365–66) The authors emphasize the broad meaning of "implementing" in this definition, including to make something work, to put something into practice, or to having something realized. In that sense, they regard e-HRM as a way of "doing HRM" (Ruël et al., 2007). In a similar manner, Burbach and Royle (2013) refer to e-HRM as "web-based information technologies to support all HR related activities of a broad range of organizational stakeholders." (p. 433). Olivas-Luján, Ramirez, and Zapata-Cantu (2007) point towards more specific activities and practices and bring a definition of e-HRM as "the application of any technology enabling managers and employees to have direct access to HR and other workplace services for communication, performance, reporting, team management, knowledge management, and learning in addition to administrative applications." (p. 419)

Relation-Centered Definitions

Relation-centered definitions emphasize technology to cohere with relations and communication patterns between HRM and other actors. They underline that e-HRM enables HR practices to be carried out in a decentralized and diffused manner. The unidirectional or reciprocal relationships the "e" establishes between different actors are central. In this understanding, e-HRM is recognized not solely as an "electronization" of HR practices, but as a means to constitute new management systems that open up relationship opportunities between employees and the organization (Bissola & Imperatori, 2014). A widely received relation-centered definition comes from Strohmeier (2007) who regards "e-HRM (...) [as] the (planning, implementation and) application of information technology for both networking and supporting at least two individual or collective actors in their shared performing of HR activities." (p. 20) Marler and Fisher (2013) define e-HRM as "configurations of computer hardware, software, and electronic networking resources that enable intended or actual HRM activities (e.g., policies, practices, and services) through individual and group-level interactions within and across organizational boundaries" (p. 21). Heikkilä and Smale (2011), as another example, regard e-HRM "as the application of Internet and web-based systems to change the nature of interactions between HR professionals, line managers and employees from face-to-face relationships to ones that are increasingly mediated by technology" (p. 306). One important relational HR function is recruiting. Accordingly, Holm (2012) forwards that e-recruitment is "(...) the organization of recruitment process and activities, which, by means of technology and human agents, facilitate time- and space-independent collaboration and interaction in order to identify, attract, and influence competent candidates." (p. 245)

Data-Centered Definitions

Finally, data-centered definitions emphasize the features and functions of e-HRM devices. In particular, the capturing, storing, and sharing of data and its exploitation for HR purposes is in the center of attention. E-HRM enables HR departments to store and analyze data to increase workforce information flows (Tansley, Kirk, Williams, & Barton, 2014). In stressing a strategic element in data processing, for instance, Panos and Bellou (2016) recognize that e-HRM "offers a holistic approach to HRM issues; it can manage with precision a massive amount of multisource data in real time and, most of all, [e-HRM] can be aligned to the organization's strategic choices" (p. 1090).

TECHNOLOGY LINKED TO OTHER
ENTITIES IN e-HRM RESEARCH

The following section illustrates the links between technology and various entities of interest throughout the papers reviewed. These entities comprise organizational structure, factors, and environments; activities and practices; attitudes and perceptions; roles; and relations between actors. For each link, we give a more detailed description.

Organizational Structure, Factors, and Environments

E-HRM technology is linked to different organizational entities that can be divided into three clusters: organizational structure, organizational factors, and organizational environments. Regarding organizational structure, the literature describes effects of technology on HRM in different forms. Most importantly, IT's impact induces the formation of new internal structures or transforms organizational architectures (Bondarouk, Harms, & Lepak, 2017; Farndale et al., 2009; Lin, 2011). In particular, these impacts or effects push HRM in a more virtual direction, whereby virtual HRM terms a distributed structure of different internal and external actors built on network-based partnerships (Lepak & Snell, 1998). Virtual structures consequently enable connecting and organizing members across different geographical spaces, times, and hierarchical levels to accomplish organizational tasks. As one example, e-recruitment technology is stated to transform the traditional recruitment process into a time- and space-independent, collaborative hiring process (Holm, 2012), enabling organizations to leverage specific advantages of centralization and decentralization in recruiting (Llorens & Kellough, 2007).

Another stream supposes organizational factors to influence the form and use of technology. For instance, e-HRM adoption is assumed to be contingent to organizational size and demography, industry, work organization, employment structure, and HRM practices already in place (Strohmeier & Kabst, 2009). Also, organizational factors like size, sector, the existence of a business and HR strategy, HR and employee influence, and employee structure are presumed to shape operational, relational, or transformational e-HRM configurations, as well as different combinations of these three base types (Strohmeier & Kabst, 2014). In a narrower context, e-HRM adoption is assumed to be influenced by how the technology is communicated through certain channels in organizations (Bondarouk, Schilling, & Ruël, 2016). Moreover, characteristics like organizational reputation, quality-based compensation for recruiters, and workforce planning time orientation are expected to shape what kinds of messages are distributed though recruiting technologies (Dineen & Williamson, 2012).

A third stream presumes external forces to influence the form and use of technology. Forces originating from the external environment are enshrined in social and economic developments, partly emerging worldwide, partly in smaller contexts. These forces comprise globalization, fast-moving and partially unpredictable business developments, accelerated pace of change, increased competition, and the global division of labor. Competitive forces also impose pressure on organizations to attract, manage, and retain highly specialized employees to sustain competitive advantages. In concert with labor market shortages, this leads to more contested recruiting markets (Eckhardt et al., 2014; Simón & Esteves, 2016). Altogether, these developments create forces that impact on the diffusion, implementation, application, and use of technology because they require organizations to carry out their HRM activities as effectively and efficiently as possible. Consequently, process re-engineering, automation, and increased self-service are facilitated to create value for the organization and ensure successful performance in a highly competitive environment (Bondarouk, Schilling et al., 2016; Huang & Martin-Taylor, 2013; Mirrazavi & Beringer, 2007; Tate, Furtmueller, & Wilderom, 2013). External forces also comprise national and cultural conditions and environments that affect the diffusion, implementation and use of e-HRM technology. A number of papers conceptualize economic, social, legal, cultural, and technical environments to shape the use of e-HRM. They show how institutional environments and fields (Burbach & Royle, 2013, 2014; Heikkilä, 2013; Holm, 2014; Marler & Parry, 2016; Simón & Esteves, 2016), cultural mindsets (Bondarouk, Schilling et al., 2016; Olivas-Luján et al., 2007), language (Heikkilä & Smale, 2011), or culture variables such as individualism-collectivism, power distance, uncertainty avoidance, and others (Garavan & O'Brien, 2013; Panayotopoulou et al., 2010) affect the way how technology is used, composed, and how its potentials can be evolved.

Activities and Practices

Regarding the activities and practices of HRM and other actors, research suggests that the influence of technology changes work routines, leading to a radical change of the "heart, pace and radius of HR processes." (Tate et al., 2013, p. 414) More specifically, technology establishes new ways of how people work, communicate, share and gather knowledge, or look for resources within and across organizations (Lin, 2011; Parry, 2011; Ruta, 2009). Technology consequently affects existing HR activities and practices and yields new ones, by impacting both delivery logics and professional logics of HR (Farndale et al., 2009). Especially in e-recruiting, technology is stated to gradually transform recruitment practices as a whole (Holm, 2012). Correspondingly, detailed findings exist on how technology induces changes in recruiting activities and processes in sequential steps over time (Eckhardt et al., 2014). Technology also changes communication patterns between management and candidates, leading to employers proactively getting in touch with promising candidates (Arjomandy, 2016; Holm, 2012; Kim & O'Connor, 2009; Selden & Orenstein, 2011a, 2011b).

At the same time, HRM and other organizational members are understood to actively shape the form and use of technology. For instance, HRM can utilize technology in an ambidextrous way by exploiting present opportunities for effective HR (e.g., automation of operational tasks) while facilitating transformational activities to innovate for the future (Tansley et al., 2014). Literature also shows how activities of different actors shape technology configurations and concomitant use patterns during and after implementation processes. Here, managerial support, the implementation of strategic considerations, and micropolitical exchange relationships are anticipated to have significant impact on e-HRM adoption (Bondarouk, Schilling et al., 2016; Burbach & Royle, 2013; Schalk, Timmerman, & van den Heuvel, 2013). Moreover, activities of HR managers are assumed to inscribe operational, relational, or transformational HR types or configurations into technology. From this perspective, technology shapes up to different forms when HRM, for instance, utilizes the "e" to transform HRM processes and build resources (Ruta, 2009; Tansley et al., 2013), or to support the delivery of remote HR services or HR activities in general (Farndale et al., 2009; Meijerink et al., 2013). HR managers are expected to utilize technology in a way that corresponds with the chosen HR strategy and HR configuration (Ruta, 2009) and with overall (organizational) goals like cost reduction, the improvement of HR services, and strategic orientation (Bondarouk & Ruël, 2013; Parry, 2011). Consequently, the extent to which an organization focuses on each type of e-HRM goals (operational, relational or transformational) critically affects which e-HRM system will be adopted and how HRM activities will be arranged (e.g., face-to-face or web-based) (Ruël et al., 2007; Ruta, 2009).

Perceptions and Attitudes

An influential idea throughout the e-HRM literature is that technology impacts on perceptions and attitudes of organizational members. Accordingly, the perception of HRM activities can be different (Bondarouk, Ruël, & van der Heijden, 2009), depending on whether technology is used to "deliver" them or not. For instance, e-HRM systems can influence employee perceptions of HR departments' work (Bissola & Imperatori, 2013). The influence of technology on perceptions is also important in e-recruiting. For example, research argues that the functions of recruiting websites predict individuals' impressions of an organization (Ehrhart, Mayer, & Ziegert, 2012; Selden & Orenstein, 2011a) or that an organizations' use of social media affects job preferences of the "Generation Y" (Guillot-Soulez & Soulez, 2014). Also, information on potential job candidates on social networking sites can shape the perception of recruiters regarding, e.g., the candidates personality traits, intelligence, and global performance (Kluemper & Rosen, 2009). Electronic performance monitoring systems are assumed to stimulate negative perceptions and affect well-being, when conditions like transparency on their utilization are not met by the organization (Wells, Moorman, & Werner, 2007; Zweig & Scott, 2007). Moreover, technology provides the foundation for the meanings actors construct around HR management practices, e.g., understandings of talent and how it is managed (Wiblen et al., 2010). In e-learning, distinct technology characteristics (reliability, synchronicity) are reasoned to influence the perception of trainees regarding the learning environment (Johnson, Gueutal, & Falbe, 2009). In summary hence, technology is assumed to trigger different perceptions and attitudes in different user populations. However, there is also the notion that technology can streamline individual perceptions of HR and its services when it is utilized as communication tool between HR providers and their "customers" (Bondarouk et al., 2017).

Another widespread assumption regards e-HRM technology as strongly influenced by incumbent attitudes and perceptions towards technology. Discourses, processes of negotiation, sense making, or social constructions are assumed to shape the perceptions and attitudes of actors and consequently the implementation processes and use of technology (Francis, Parkes, & Reddington, 2014; Wiblen, 2016). Of paramount interest in the literature analyzed, however, are the perceptions and attitudes directly related to technology already-in-place. As an example, Bissola and Imperatori (2014) stress employees' attitudes towards technology to moderate the relationship between e-HRM practices and trust in the HR department. Based on the diffusion of innovation model (Rogers, 2003), Bondarouk, Schilling et al. (2016) regard the decision to adopt e-HRM as highly influenced by individual perceptions. Others assume perceived justice, fairness, enjoyment, invasiveness, or security related to technology to have consequences for their use (Laumer, Eckhardt, & Weitzel, 2012; Paschal, Stone, & Stone-Romero, 2009; Zweig & Scott, 2007). The most widespread reasoning of how perceptions and attitudes impact on e-HRM is found in literature drawing on the Technology Acceptance Model (TAM) (Davis, 1989; Davis, Bagozzi, & Warshaw, 1989). At its core, this model argues that when actors perceive a technology as useful and easy to use they are more likely to use and accept IT. In the e-HRM literature reviewed, different versions of TAMs are augmented with a range of variables. This research examines how technology acceptance coheres with, e.g., job satisfaction and turnover intention (Maier, Laumer, Eckhardt, & Weitzel, 2013), national culture variables (Garavan & O'Brien, 2013), perceived enjoyment and fairness (Laumer et al., 2012), preferred HR roles in an organization (Voermans & van Veldhoven, 2007), or HRM system strength and perceived HR service quality (Wahyudi & Park, 2014). Others integrate core assumptions of the TAM in qualitative studies (Heikkilä & Smale, 2011) or action research designs (Huang & Martin-Taylor, 2013).

Management can play a proactive role in shaping and reshaping users' perceptions and influence the acceptance of a technology with systematic interventions (Huang & Martin-Taylor, 2013). For instance, a greater social support from colleagues and managers, and better information provision can lead to greater appreciation of e-HRM applications' content and design (Ruël et al., 2007; Ruël & van der Kaap, 2012; Wahyudi & Park, 2014). For instance, spreading information about organizations' and supervisors' monitoring policies can influence perceptions of fairness and satisfaction with monitoring technology (Zweig & Scott, 2007). Tailored messages on websites can predict fit perceptions and organizational pursuit preference of potential job candidates (Kraichy & Chapman, 2014). Moreover, deliberately changing features of applications can, e.g., positively impact on trainees perceptions and maximize learning outcomes (Johnson et al., 2009). Altering attitudes and perceptions of employees is regarded as a central factor in gaining benefits from technology because implementing an e-HRM strategy needs to be accompanied by a change in the employees' mindsets (Bissola & Imperatori, 2013; Olivas-Luján et al., 2007).

Roles

Another argument for implementing e-HRM found in the literature reviewed is that technology propels HRM towards a more strategic (or transformational) orientation. It is stated that technology changes the role and function of HRM (Panayotopoulou et al., 2010), pushes HRM into a new position (Bondarouk et al., 2017), shifts HR's role to a more strategic level (Parry & Tyson, 2011), enables the transformation into new roles (Maier et al., 2013), or strengthens the position of HRM as a business partner (Bondarouk, Schilling et al., 2016) by moving HRM beyond its traditional supporting role to a more proactive one (Arjomandy, 2016). These role changes are not exclusive to HR managers. The transformation of HR processes through e-HRM facilitates a transfer of transactional HRM-activities to employees, managers, and other third parties and hence includes a shift in responsibilities (Farndale et al., 2009; Heikkilä & Smale, 2011; Ruël & van der

Kaap, 2012). Accordingly, from a service management perspective, e-HRM transforms the roles of line managers to service providers that, now performing HR tasks themselves, respond strongly to individual customer demands of third parties (Bondarouk et al., 2017). Role changes through technology also concern IT project teams situated between IT function and the HR function. Their "hybrid" roles during implementation processes are produced through knowledge practices in interaction with technologies (Tansley et al., 2013).

Research in e-HRM also states that different HR roles in place can influence the form and use of e-HRM in organizations. Specifically, research draws from the four roles of Ulrich (1996) (administrative expert, employee champion, change agent, and strategic player) to test the impact of these roles on the use and configuration of technology. For instance, prevailing HR role preferences are presumed to determine the attitude towards e-HRM by both managers and employees (Voermans & van Veldhoven, 2007) or that HR roles moderate the relationships between e-HRM goals and e-HRM outcomes (Panos & Bellou, 2016).

Relations

Regarding the relations between organizational members, the literature suggests that the adoption of IT changes the employee-organization relationship and its management (Bissola & Imperatori, 2013, 2014; Wahyudi & Park, 2014). As mentioned before, particularly the relational socio-technical qualities of the "e" pronounce a remote access to HR information and increased ability to connect with other parts of the organization to managers and employees (Parry, 2011). Technology has effects on, for instance, internal customer relationship between HRM, line managers, and employees (Bondarouk et al., 2017; Kim & O'Connor, 2009) by opening up HRM practices to a range of actors, through which HRM can be transformed into a practice for all users, not just for HR specialists (Huang & Martin-Taylor, 2013). In this context, Francis et al. (2014) stress the effects of the structural arrangements of technology on the relations between HR specialists and line managers. As face-to-face interactions become replaced by technology-mediated self-service relationships, this impacts on their relational positioning to each other and trust relationships in general (also see Bissola & Imperatori, 2014).

DISCUSSION

In the following section we distill the assumptions of technology prevailing in the literature reviewed. Moreover, we identify and describe two conceptions on how technology is linked to other entities in e-HRM research that became apparent during the literature review.

Assumptions about Technology: Tools, Proxies, and Ensembles

One central assumption in the papers is that IT serves as an artifact utilized to support and implement HR-related activities and objectives in organizations.

Hence, it is viewed as a managerial tool, which is also a widespread term used throughout the papers when referring to IT. Orlikowski and Iacono (2006) outline that from a *tool view*, technology emerges as an engineered artifact, expected to do what its designers intend it to do. It assigns separate, definable, and unchanging characteristics to technology over which humans have control. Accordingly, specific features of a technology are assumed to produce certain outcomes. As a consequence, IT presents an unproblematic computing resource that provides specifiable information processing capabilities. In e-HRM, technology is viewed as an *information processing tool*. In this understanding IT enhances the way that HRM processes information. For instance, e-HRM technologies are widely regarded as systems to acquire, store, retrieve, and distribute pertinent information regarding an organization's human resources. This particularly appears in the data-centered definitions that focus on the capturing, storing, and sharing of data and its exploitation through the "e" for HR purposes. Moreover, technology is also seen as a *productivity tool* that extends the reach and performance of HRM. For example, the analysis of the socio-technical qualities suggests that technology can be utilized to create different forms of value for the organization, corresponding to different types of e-HRM (operational, relational, and transformational). The assumption of IT as productivity tool can be found in the definitions as well. Especially the activity-centered definitions underline the implementation or support of "HR doings" through IT towards specific ends. Accordingly, this understanding also appears in research examining how HRM utilizes technology to reshape different HR practices and related structures (see 2.4.2). Another variety of a tool-view grasps IT as a tool to model *social relations*. This assumption is, for instance, implicitly present in the activity-centered definitions, since they stress IT to support the sharing of HR activities and practices between different actors. Clearly more explicit it can be found in relation-centered definitions that focus on the (reciprocal) relationships the "e" establishes, as well as in research addressing the question if or how e-HRM alters the roles of certain actors or their relations.

Other research in e-HRM follows a *proxy view* on technology. From this view, one or more key elements represent the essential aspect, property, or value of IT. The core assumption here is that IT can be captured through surrogate measures (Orlikowski & Iacono, 2006). One proxy for IT is *perception*. While this assumption is not present in the terms and qualities or definitions related to the "e", it is deeply incorporated in work addressing perceptions and attitudes towards e-HRM. Mostly, this concerns literature drawing on the TAM, which assumes that users' perceptions of a technology can predict their intention to use (or accept) it. Another proxy emerging in the literature reviewed is *diffusion*. Diffusion measures the penetration of a particular type of IT within socio-institutional contexts. Research in e-HRM that follows this set of assumptions examines, for instance, organizational factors of diffusion or their barriers that are conceptualized in economic, cultural, or organizational terms.

A final stream of work follows an *ensemble view* of technology. This approach incorporates the assumption that IT works as an ensemble of different elements making up how a technology comes to be used (Orlikowski & Iacono, 2006). Within this stream, technology can be viewed as a *development project*. This understanding is implicitly present in some papers extensively examining implementation projects of IT (e.g., Huang & Martin-Taylor, 2013). Another variation of the ensemble view is that of an *embedded system*. This means, that technology is assumed to be enmeshed in the conditions of its use and concern how technologies come to be used. In the e-HRM literature, this notion, also implicitly, appears mostly in descriptions of multi-level and multi-factorial research frameworks (e.g., Burbach & Royle, 2013; Holm, 2012; Voermans & van Veldhoven, 2007) or in research drawing on a "networked" approach towards technology and its users (Dery, Hall, Wailes, & Wiblen, 2013). It can also be found in extensive definitions, e.g., when HRIS are understood as systems that process pertinent HR information and include hardware, software, people, policies, procedures, and data (Wiblen et al., 2010).

Conceptions of Technology: Catalysts and Conformations

Regarding the question *how* technology is linked to other entities, the review showed two major conceptions in accordance with two basic mechanisms described in previous studies (Marler & Fisher, 2013; Marler & Parry, 2016; Strohmeier, 2009): *Determinism* and *voluntarism*. Determinism conveys the assumption of technological primacy. Following its own teleological trajectory, technology is a source of propelling effects on organizations and human beings that consequently adapt to these changes. Human will and action are to a certain degree determined and sequestrated by preceding events emanating from technology. *Voluntarism*, on the contrary, conveys the assumption of human primacy. This postulates organizations and humans to be capable of utilizing technology to their ends and implicates a free will of humans to act primarily self-directed. These mechanisms emphasize the human/social factors and enunciate either technology's effects on the human/social realm; or conversely, how technology is affected and/or utilized by the human/social.

These assumptions about how technology is linked to the human/social realm are also associated with assumptions about the "e" itself. Determinism charges technology with activity, something that actively affects and determines specific outcomes in the human/social realm. Technology represents a factor that sets in motion shifts in different places in the human/social realm. For this conception, we propose the metaphor of a *catalyst*, since a catalyst defines an entity that induces activity of other entities without being consumed or transformed in the process. Voluntarism conceptualizes the "e" as something that aligns to forces and agencies situated both internal and external to an organization. This associates with the assumption that technology is a means to the service of human ends, a passive universe of objects whose functions and purposes are enacted in the ongoing pursuits of humans in their contexts (Kallinikos, 2011). When (collective) actors (deliberately) exert force on technology, they enable or constrain how technology can be utilized for achieving certain objectives. Closely related

TABLE 9.2. Conceptions of Technology in e-HRM.

	Catalyst	Conformation
Metaphor description	Induces an activity of other entities without being consumed or transformed in the process	Conforms according to pre-given or emerging forces or principles
Core assumption	Technology is a discrete, stable, and active entity, affecting entities in the human/social realm	Technology is a discrete, stable, and passive entity, formed by forces and agencies emerging from the human/social realm
Underlying mechanism	Determinism	Voluntarism

to a tool-view described above, technology hence appears as a passive entity, utilized by the human/social realm to support specific ends. We propose to term this conception *conformation*. This metaphor encapsulates a produced conformity of technology induced by different social and human forces. A description of the conceptions can be found in Table 9.2.

Notably, studies using a catalyst conception often use active voice because technology is "doing" something. Especially at the beginning of papers it is stated that technology intensely and ubiquitously, sometimes inevitably, changes contemporary organizations' life and consequently the way of doing HRM on different levels and in numerous dimensions. In e-HRM research, different kinds of technology are assumed to have significant influence on HRM (Wickramasinghe, 2010), affecting the entire HRM function (de Alwis, 2010), propelling HR systems towards new approaches and practices (Arjomandy, 2016; Bissola & Imperatori, 2013), impacting on the ways of working, relationships, and routines (Reddick, 2009; Ruta, 2009) and, as we have shown, on organizational structure. In particular, IT pushes HRM structures in a more virtual direction (virtual HRM) and alters space and time dimensions in numerous HR practices. Implicitly in these assumptions is that technology represents, to some extent, a material determinant of an organization's structure (Orlikowski & Robey, 1991; Zammuto, Griffith, Majchrzak, Dougherty, & Faraj, 2007). Technology moreover impacts on activities and practices of HRM and other actors, since IT is stated to establish new ways of how people work, communicate, share and gather knowledge, or look for resources within and across organizations. Technology is also assumed to catalyze on the attitudes and perceptions of (future) organizational members, for instance, how employees perceive the work of HR departments when using e-HRM technology for e-recruiting or performance management. Finally, technology as a catalyst impacts on roles of actors and on the relations between them. In particular, research conveys the assumption that e-HRM technology transforms or propels HRM towards a more strategic (or transformational) orientation.

In the conformation conception, technology in e-HRM research conforms to different forces and agencies, emanating, for instance, from organizational environments or organizational factors that define how technology is configured and used.

A central and recurring theme is that organizations and/or HR managers deliberatively can utilize IT to their ends. Accordingly, form and use of technology are reasoned to be shaped by the activities and practices of HRM and other organizational members, e.g., with supportive and systematic interventions. The same holds for perceptions and attitudes, where e-HRM scholars regard incumbent perceptions and attitudes as highly influential regarding technology use. One salient example here is the literature drawing form TAMs. Moreover, technology is assumed to indirectly conform to existing HR roles (Ulrich, 1996). In particular, HR roles influence user attitudes and consequently the outcomes of e-HRM. Finally, regarding the relations between organizational members, it is assumed that the adoption of IT impacts on exchange patters between HR and other actors by providing remote access to HR information and practices. The review and discussion on the assumptions on technology in e-HRM research is summed up in an overview in Figure 9.2.

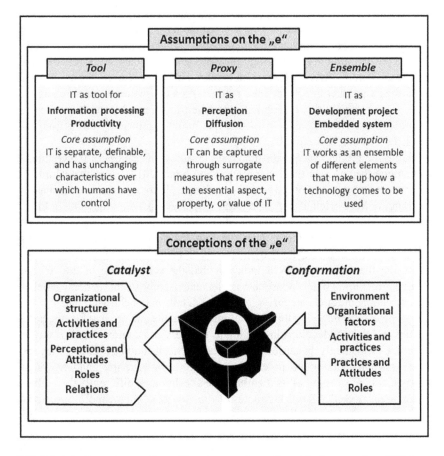

FIGURE 9.2. Overview on Prevailing Assumptions About Technology in e-HRM research.

POTENTIAL CHALLENGES RELATED TO EXISTING
ASSUMPTIONS AND CONCEPTIONS

The review uncovers manifold and nuanced assumptions on technology in e-HRM research. However, a more detailed analysis confirms Strohmeier's (2007) finding that technology itself is addressed only at a very general and generic level. Although distinct technologies or single systems are regularly described, technology tends to be considered only as a simple utility or tool or linked only with basic properties to variables of interest. This becomes apparent, for instance, when scholars exclusively use product names (e.g., e-HRM, ERP, etc.), or some specific features of a product, as placeholder for technology in their research. In this direction, Faraj and Azad (2012) ascertain that there is generally a wide acceptance in Information Systems research to use IT product categories or classes as primary objects of analysis. They warn, however, that this product *conflation* fosters an *acontextualization of technology* because the use of general vocabulary deriving from commercial nomenclatures (or the prima facie) suggests what we already mentioned when outlining the tool view of technology: that technology appears as discrete, finished entity, endowed with universal, inherent properties. This facilitates the presumption that technology provides a well-defined set of features that meet a user's individual or organizational need. Accordingly, users are assumed to only utilize a product in a predefined manner. As a consequence, researchers are unable to analytically distinguish between taken-for-granted features (and product classes) and actual *categories-in-use* that might significantly differ from the intended use (Faraj & Azad, 2012).

Employing product categories moreover erasures differences in the compositions among the "e" over time. Here, Faraj and Azad (2012) give the example of word processing systems. Word processing systems embrace numerous technologies, ranging from original text processing machines (like the Wang Office Information System) to newer versions of Microsoft Word. By drawing exclusively on product labels hence, researchers run into risk to remain blind for specific compositions that may significantly matter when addressing empirical reality. As shown, the literature on e-HRM indicates that the composition of the "e" has changed over time. When researchers refer exclusively to the general label e-HRM or simple product categories, important details may be missed out.

In summary, by implying that technologies are stable and predictable, the complexities technology develops in relation to its users and contexts tend to stay in the dark. Consequently, because the nodes between a technology's properties and its users remain unaddressed, potential explanations for, e.g., how and why different organizations or some of its members use a technology differently than others remain undiscovered. All this facilitates a *"black-boxing"* of technology and protracts the analytical focus almost exclusively to the human/social (Faraj & Azad, 2012; Orlikowski & Iacono, 2006; Orlikowski & Scott, 2008).

Moreover, the review revealed that researchers often do not homogenously draw on either a catalyst or conformation conception but oscillate between them.

TABLE 9.3. Challenges Related to Prevailing Assumptions on Technology in e-HRM and Their Potential Consequences for Research

Challenge	Potential Consequences for Research
Black-boxing of technology	• Acontextualization of technology • Prioritization of features instead of categories-in-use • Actual composition of technology tends to remain unaddressed
Oscillations between catalyst and conformation-conceptions	• Presumed direction of influence of/on technology in research undertaking gets blurred • Ambiguous or weak explanations for inconclusive and complex results

Empirical papers usually start with clear catalyst or conformation conceptions in their models and methods. In case of puzzling results, however, the assumed direction of the relation between technology and the human/social is often changed. This oscillation weakens both the conceptual models derived and the results obtained, giving ambiguous explanations for results that do not fit the chosen conception. Others explain puzzling results with acknowledging that technological, organizational, and human factors are equally important and mutually influence each other, but remain unable explicate concrete mechanisms working on the intersection between technology and the human/social. These findings point to a gap in theory, hindering researchers to render visible sociotechnical relations without referring to unidirectional conceptions of technological or human/social primacy. In the next section hence, we provide some suggestions for theoretical avenues that may support to address the challenges discovered (see Table 9.3).

RECOMMENDATIONS FOR FUTURE RESEARCH

Drawing from research in Information Systems and Science and Technology Studies, the following sections suggest concepts and theoretical perspectives that can help opening up the black box of "e" in e-HRM research to some extent, preventing the use of generic labels in empirical analysis, and provide alternative theoretical avenues beyond unidirectional conceptions that may allow understanding the intersections between IT and HRM in more situated, processual, and dynamic ways.

Avenues for Opening the Black Box "e"

One promising avenue to open the black box "e" to some extent is to provide more detailed descriptions of technology *in situ*. Instead of referring to generic labels, researchers could put the *affordances* of technology in the center of attention. Affordances term the possibilities of action an artifact offers to a subject emerging from their reciprocal and immediate relations (Bucher & Helmond, 2017; Faraj &

Azad, 2012; Hutchby, 2001). An analysis of these relations can uncover complex categories-in-use that emerge when individuals or groups encounter technologies. For a plane example, take a tree, a loin, and a monkey. Apparently, the tree affords different actions to a lion than it does to a monkey. For the lion, the tree is a shady place to rest or an occasion to sharpen his claws on the trunk. For the monkey, the tree affords a safe place and may provide food (see Gibson, 1979). Faraj and Azad (2012) give an example of affordances with information technology. They describe an e-mail protest of faculty members directed to the Vice-President of Communication because of an incident in a university. They argue that, from an affordance perspective, the mail software does not appear as a simple communication tool anymore. Depending on the users and their positions, it rather appears as an artifact to inform, misinform, advertise, campaign, or collaborate. From an affordance perspective hence, technology is not a generic, universal bundle of features; rather, it manifests as an artifact that unfolds its actual, situated utility only when considering its relation to its users and their surroundings. An affordance perspective hence can help to develop a more grounded understanding of, e.g., use patterns of IT in daily work and management practices.

Following a similar idea, researchers can turn to *technical identities* (Faulkner & Runde, 2009, 2013). Technological objects have a dual nature in being constituted by both their physical form and by having a use or function. This function is assigned by the members of social groups whose activities contribute to sustaining the function of the object. Consequently, this results in a technical identity "that flows from the combination of their physical form and the use to which they are put within that group" (Faulkner & Runde, 2009, p. 444). This perspective particularly sensitizes for the link between the physical form of technologies and their use in group settings in which members draw on social rules and routinized practices in the adoption of new technologies.

In our review, we found some passages that implicitly employ the notions described. In acknowledging affordances for instance, Johnson et al. (2009) note that "[r]egardless of the "objective" properties of the technology, individuals have very different perceptions of the technology's capabilities (...)" (p. 549) and may thus leverage technologies to their "own" ends. Ruta (2009), in another example, gives a detailed overview on single features of an HR portal and shows how they support the development of intellectual capital from an HR perspective. In a similar example, Wiblen (2016) insinuates the affordances of a talent management e-HRM system for managers when describing the software's "ability to measure employee performance; facilitating a formalized ranking process; a framework to undertake workforce differentiation; and standardized defining characteristics of talented employees that enable the enactment of systemic and consistent talent identification processes underpinned by objective metrics." (pp. 99–100). In contrast to a simple descriptive view, these framings unpack the affordances of a specific technology for HRM when trying to solve the problem of intellectual capital development or talent management.

In summary, theorizing an artifact's relations to its user(s) can provide a range of useful vehicles for e-HRM research. When it is particularly clear *what* certain technologies afford to different users (in contrast to describe plane features), or what kinds of technical identities emerge from the form and assigned functions of a focal system, more context-sensitive accounts of prevailing use patterns can result. These may, for instance, contribute to explaining stability or conflict in numerous e-HRM-related activities. In long-term studies, they can bring a fresh look on the consequences of changes in technological systems. When the physical form of a technical object is altered (e.g., adding or deleting features or altering interfaces), this may yield new affordances to users or technological identities in groups. Finally, an affordance perspective can enrich research based on TAMs. When considering affordances, research could yield more nuanced results on how and why different features are (not) accepted by users, while at the same time obtaining the TAMs' analytical strengths.

Sociomaterial Perspectives for Relational Conceptions of the IT-HRM-Relationship

Finally, we promote theoretical lenses that scrutinize the relations between technology and the human/social in a more fundamental manner. The vast majority of assumptions in e-HRM research, as well as the affordance or technical identities perspective outlined in the previous section, rely on a substantialist ontology, viewing the world as made of static and separate things that exist first and relations among them subsequently. By contrast, a relational ontology shifts the emphasis on the relations between entities and constitutes reality in dynamic, continuous, and processual terms (Emirbayer, 1997). In Information Systems research, one stream of work drawing from a relational understanding of reality is subsumed under the umbrella term of *sociomateriality* (Cecez-Kecmanovic et al., 2014; Orlikowski, 2007, 2010; Orlikowski & Scott, 2008). By aiming to challenge "the deeply taken-for-granted assumption that technology, work, and organizations should be conceptualized separately" (Orlikowski & Scott, 2008, p. 434), this stream promotes that identities, meaning, and significance of any entity is not given, but derive from in the dynamic process of practice (Feldman & Orlikowski, 2011; Orlikowski & Scott, 2015). Consequently, "people and things are brought into being through everyday activity. They do not pre-exist action, but are enacted." (Schultze, 2017, p. 61) Concerning assumptions on technology, this thinking forwards that boundaries of technologies are not pre-given or fixed, but enacted in ongoing reconfigurations in practice. As Orlikowski (2000) points out:

> [t]echnologies are (…) never fully stabilized or "complete", even though we may choose to treat them as fixed, black boxes for a period of time. By temporarily bracketing the dynamic nature of technology, we assign a "stabilized-for-now" status (…) to our technological artifacts. This is an analytic and practical convenience only,

because technologies continue to evolve, are tinkered with (e.g., by users, designers, regulators, and hackers), modified, improved, damaged, rebuilt, etc. (pp. 411–412)

In an empirical example of a sociomaterial view, Mazmanian, Orlikowski, and Yates (2006) address changes in communication practices related to the introduction of e-mail on mobile devices in a private equity firm. From a sociomaterial perspective, these changes do not appear as a matter of the material features of the technology having certain social impacts, or the new affordances of mobile e-mail devices making communication more efficient or effective; but "[t]he performativity of the [devices] is sociomaterial, shaped by the particular contingent way in which (…) the service [of the devices] is designed, configured, and engaged in practice." (Orlikowski, 2007, p. 1444) With these notions, a sociomaterial perspective specifically allows for researching how HR practices, inextricably entangled with IT and meaning, enact the specific e-HRM phenomena in everyday organizing practices. In e-HRM, a focus on sociomaterial practices can provide a fruitful vehicle to analyze and understand the situated conditions of technology use. In particular, as suggested by Gregeby and Hugosson (2017), research can target e-HRM as intersection between the human/social and materiality constituted by practices that are intentionally co-constituted with historical factors as important conditions and with future ends in sight.

Rooting in Science and Technology Studies, Actor-Network Theory (ANT) (Callon, 1984; Latour, 2005; Law, 1992) offers another fruitful avenue to promote a sociomaterial understanding of technology-HRM interfaces. At its core, ANT assumes the world as consisting of heterogeneous networks of human and non-human actors. In following a relational mindset, reality is not the punctual pattern or sum of discrete human and non-human entities, but the product of their aggregated and interrelated agencies fluently joining together in ongoing processes. Thereby, ANT assumes a "generalized symmetry" of actors, assigning little or no qualitative distinction between humans and non-humans and their activities. Of paramount interest in ANT are mechanisms, through which heterogeneous networks become stabilized, or: translated. In translation processes, actors become enrolled within networks and their agencies become mobilized in order to generate specific outcomes (Callon, 1984). This notion also sensitizes for interruptions in networks, for instance, when certain actors are replaced. In a unique and salient example of e-HRM in our review, Dery et al. (2013) draw from ANT to show how Actor-Networks form and re-form during an implementation of a HRIS. They show how the aim to transform HR into a strategic business partner through a new HRIS system failed because of changing relations between human and non-human actors in the translation process. This example indicates that ANT's core concepts can bring a fresh look on common issues in e-HRM. This also holds for current technical developments we mentioned at the beginning of this chapter. Given the fact that technology is increasingly equipped with agency (e.g., decision-making by algorithms, robots as collaborators, etc.), ANT's notion of objects actively participating in social reality can contribute to better understand e-HRM phenomena in future research.

In e-HRM, sociomaterial notions are acknowledged in a range of accounts (Bondarouk, 2011; Bondarouk et al., 2017; Marler & Fisher, 2013; Marler & Parry, 2016; Ruël & van der Kaap, 2012; Strohmeier, 2009), however, they tend to be background foils rather than a central lens of analyses. Thus, the potential of this perspective is not fully exploited. A particular benefit of sociomaterial thinking is that it shifts away the analytical gaze from static relations between discrete technological and human/social entities to either ongoing practices deeply intertwined and constituted by technology or to ongoing interactions between (analytically) coequal human and non-human actors participating in networks. With these assumptional shifts, sociomaterial analysis can help to gain new insights at the interfaces between HRM and IT.

CONCLUSION

In our contribution, we drew attention to the "e" in e-HRM research by reviewing prevailing assumptions on technology in e-HRM terminologies and qualities, definitions, and conceptions of how the "e" is linked to other relevant entities of interest. Our review sheds light on the diverse assumptions authors—partly unconsciously—hold about technology. It also reveals a black-boxing of technology through the use of general terms as synonyms for technology and that researchers tend to oscillate between catalyst-conceptions and conformation-conceptions. We discussed the potential consequences of these tendencies and provided suggestions on how the black-boxed "e" could be opened up to some extent with the application of different conceptual and theoretical lenses.

Altogether, we invite researches to put more attention on the "e" in e-HRM. As we have shown, notions of some of our suggestions already exist in the e-HRM field in an implicit manner. While we suggested alternative theoretical avenues to unidirectional conceptions, we also wish to underline the indispensable analytical strengths and advantages of existing assumptions and conceptions. With our review, we hope to provide more clarity on the assumptions that come with certain conceptions and on their consequences for the knowledge produced.

REFERENCES

Arjomandy, D. (2016). Social media integration in electronic human resource management: Development of a social eHRM framework. *Canadian Journal of Administrative Sciences, 33*(2), 108–123.

Bissola, R., & Imperatori, B. (2013). Facing e-HRM: The consequences on employee attitude towards the organisation and the HR department in Italian SMEs. *European Journal of International Management, 7*(4), 450.

Bissola, R., & Imperatori, B. (2014). The unexpected side of relational e-HRM: Developing trust in the HR department. *Employee Relations, 36*(4), 376–397.

Bondarouk, T., & Brewster, C. (2016). Conceptualising the future of HRM and technology research. *The International Journal of Human Resource Management, 27*(21), 2652–2671.

Bondarouk, T. V. (2011). Theoretical approaches to e-HRM implementations. In H. J.M. Ruël, J. K. Looise, & T. V. Bondarouk (Eds.), *Advanced series in management. Electronic HRM in theory and practice* (pp. 1–20). Bingley: Emerald.

Bondarouk, T. V., Harms, R., & Lepak, D. (2017). Does e-HRM lead to better HRM service? *The International Journal of Human Resource Management, 28*(9), 1–31.

Bondarouk, T. V., Parry, E., & Furtmueller, E. (2016). Electronic HRM: Four decades of research on adoption and consequences. *The International Journal of Human Resource Management, 28*(1), 98–131.

Bondarouk, T. V., & Ruël, H. J. M. (2009). Electronic human resource management: Challenges in the digital era. *The International Journal of Human Resource Management, 20*(3), 505–514.

Bondarouk, T. V., & Ruël, H. J.M. (2013). The strategic value of e-HRM: Results from an exploratory study in a governmental organization. *The International Journal of Human Resource Management, 24*(2), 391–414.

Bondarouk, T. V., Ruël, H. J.M., & van der Heijden, B. (2009). e-HRM effectiveness in a public sector organization: A multi-stakeholder perspective. *The International Journal of Human Resource Management, 20*(3), 578–590.

Bondarouk, T. V., Schilling, D., & Ruël, H. J.M. (2016). eHRM adoption in emerging economies: The case of subsidiaries of multinational corporations in Indonesia. *Canadian Journal of Administrative Sciences, 33*(2), 124–137.

Bucher, T., & Helmond, A. (2017). The affordances of social media platforms. In J. Burgess, T. Poell, & A. Marwick (Eds.), *The SAGE Handbook of Social Media.* London, New York: SAGE Publications Ltd.

Burbach, R., & Royle, T. (2013). Levels of e-HRM adoption in subsidiaries of a US multinational corporation: The mediating role of power, politics and institutions. *European Journal of International Management, 7*(4), 432–449.

Burbach, R., & Royle, T. (2014). Institutional determinants of e-HRM diffusion success. *Employee Relations, 36*(4), 354–375.

Callon, M. (1984). Some elements of a sociology of translation: Domestication of the scallops and the fishermen of St Brieuc Bay. *The Sociological Review, 32*, 196–233.

Cecez-Kecmanovic, D., Galliers, R. D., Henfridsson, O., Newell, S., & Vidgen, R. (2014). The sociomateriality of information systems: Current status, future directions. *MIS Quarterly, 38*(3), 809–830.

Davis, F. D. (1989). Perceived usefulness, perceived ease of use, and user acceptance of information technology. *MIS Quarterly, 13*(3), 319–340.

Davis, F. D., Bagozzi, R. P., & Warshaw, P. R. (1989). User acceptance of computer technology: A comparison of two theoretical models. *Management Science, 35*(8), 982–1003.

de Alwis, A. C. (2010). The impact of electronic human resource management on the role of human resource managers. *Ekonomie a Management, 10*(4), 47–60.

Dery, K., Hall, R., Wailes, N., & Wiblen, S. (2013). Lost in translation? An actor-network approach to HRIS implementation. *The Journal of Strategic Information Systems, 22*(3), 225–237.

DeSanctis, G. (1986). Human resource information systems: A current assessment. *MIS Quarterly, 10*(1), 15–27.

Dineen, B. R., & Williamson, I. O. (2012). Screening-oriented recruitment messages: Antecedents and relationships with applicant pool quality. *Human Resource Management, 51*(3), 343–360.

Eckhardt, A., Laumer, S., Maier, C., & Weitzel, T. (2014). The transformation of people, processes, and IT in e-recruiting. *Employee Relations, 36*(4), 415–431.

Ehrhart, K. H., Mayer, D. M., & Ziegert, J. C. (2012). Web-based recruitment in the Millennial generation: Work–life balance, website usability, and organizational attraction. *European Journal of Work and Organizational Psychology, 21*(6), 850–874.

Emirbayer, M. (1997). Manifesto for a relational sociology. *American Journal of Sociology, 103*(2), 281–317.

Faraj, S., & Azad, B. (2012). The materiality of technology: An affordance perspective. In P. M. Leonardi, B. A. Nardi, & J. Kallinikos (Eds.), *Materiality and organizing. Social interaction in a technological world* (pp. 237–258). Oxford, UK: Oxford University Press.

Farndale, E., Paauwe, J., & Hoeksema, L. (2009). In-sourcing HR: Shared service centres in the Netherlands. *The International Journal of Human Resource Management, 20*(3), 544–561.

Faulkner, P., & Runde, J. (2009). On the identity of technological objects and user innovations in function. *Academy of Management Review, 34*(3), 442–462.

Faulkner, P., & Runde, J. (2013). Technological objects, social positions, and the transformational model of social activity. *MIS Quarterly, 37*(3), 803–818.

Feldman, M. S., & Orlikowski, W. J. (2011). Theorizing practice and practicing theory. *Organization Science, 22*(5), 1240–1253.

Fitz-enz, J. (2010). *The new HR analytics: Predicting the economic value of your company's human capital investments.* New York, Atlanta, Brussels, Mexico City, San Francisco, Shanghai, Tokyo, Toronto, Washington D.C.: AMACOM.

Fleetwood, S. (2005). Ontology in organization and management studies: A critical realist perspective. *Organization, 12*(2), 197–222.

Florkowski, G. W., & Olivas-Luján, M. R. (2006). The diffusion of human resource information technology innovations in US and non-US firms. *Personnel Review, 35*(6), 684–710.

Francis, H., Parkes, C., & Reddington, M. (2014). E-HR and international HRM: A critical perspective on the discursive framing of e-HR. *The International Journal of Human Resource Management, 25*(10), 1327–1350.

Garavan, T. N., & O'Brien, F. (2013). The use of Manager Self-Service (MSS) HR portals in MNCs: The influence of attitudinal, normative, behavioural and national cultural factors. *European Journal of International Management, 7*(4), 393–412.

Gibson, J. J. (1979). *The ecological approach to visual perception.* Boston, MA: Houghton Mifflin.

Gregeby, J., & Hugosson, M. (2017). What about agency in e-HRM research? In T. V. Bondarouk, H. J.M. Ruël, & E. Parry (Eds.), *Electronic HRM in the Smart Era.* Bingley: Emerald.

Gueutal, H. G., & Stone, D. L. (2005). *The brave new world of eHR: Human resources management in the digital age.* San Francisco: Jossey-Bass.

Guillot-Soulez, C., & Soulez, S. (2014). On the heterogeneity of Generation Y job preferences. *Employee Relations*, *36*(4), 319–332.

Hassell, M. D., & Limayem, M. (2011). A portfolio of media: Effects of media synchronicity on communication performance. *Proceedings of the 32nd International Conference on Information Systems, Shanghai*. Retrieved from http://citeseerx.ist.psu.edu/viewdoc/download?doi=10.1.1.664.9105&rep=rep1&type=pdf"

Heikkilä, J.-P. (2013). An institutional theory perspective on e-HRM's strategic potential in MNC subsidiaries. *The Journal of Strategic Information Systems*, *22*(3), 238–251.

Heikkilä, J.-P., & Smale, A. (2011). The effects of 'language standardization' on the acceptance and use of e-HRM systems in foreign subsidiaries. *Journal of World Business*, *46*(3), 305–313.

Holm, A. B. (2012). E-recruitment: Towards an ubiquitous recruitment process and candidate relationship management. *Zeitschrift für Personalforschung*, *26*(3), 241–259.

Holm, A. B. (2014). Institutional context and e-recruitment practices of Danish organizations. *Employee Relations*, *36*(4), 432–455.

Huang, J., & Martin-Taylor, M. (2013). Turnaround user acceptance in the context of HR self-service technology adoption: An action research approach. *The International Journal of Human Resource Management*, *24*(3), 621–642.

Hutchby, I. (2001). Technology, texts and affordances. *Sociology*, *35*(2), 441–456.

Hwang, Y. (2014). Understanding the electronic recruiting marketplace strategy: The case of JobKorea. *Information Technology for Development*, *20*(4), 353–361.

Johnson, R. D., Gueutal, H., & Falbe, C. M. (2009). Technology, trainees, metacognitive activity and e-learning effectiveness. *Journal of Managerial Psychology*, *24*(6), 545–566.

Kallinikos, J. (2011). *Governing through technology: Information artefacts and social practice*. Basingstoke: Palgrave Macmillan.

Kim, S., & O'Connor, J. G. (2009). Assessing electronic recruitment implementation in state governments: Issues and challenges. *Public Personnel Management*, *38*(1), 47–66.

Kluemper, D. H., & Rosen, P. A. (2009). Future employment selection methods: Evaluating social networking web sites. *Journal of Managerial Psychology*, *24*(6), 567–580.

Kraichy, D., & Chapman, D. S. (2014). Tailoring web-based recruiting messages: Individual differences in the persuasiveness of affective and cognitive messages. *Journal of Business and Psychology*, *29*(2), 253–268.

Lamprecht, J., & Robra-Bissantz, S. (2015). Biased group decision-making and the effect of computer-mediated communication: Separating the effects of anonymity, voting and blind picking. In B. Donnellan, R. Gleasure, M. Helfert, J. Kenneally, M. Rothenberger, M. Chiarini-Trembaly,. . . R. Winter (Eds.), *At the Vanguard of Design Science. First Impressions and Early Findings from Ongoing Research Research-in-Progress* (pp. 41–46). Dublin, Ireland: Lettertec Irl. Ltd.

Latour, B. (2005). *Reassembling the social: An introduction to actor-network-theory*. Oxford: Oxford University Press.

Laumer, S., Eckhardt, A., & Weitzel, T. (2012). Online gaming to find a new job: Examining job seekers' intention to use serious games as a self-assessment tool. *Zeitschrift für Personalforschung*, *26*(3), 218–240.

Law, J. (1992). Notes on the theory of the actor-network: Ordering, strategy, and heterogeneity. *Systems Practice*, *5*(4), 379–393.

Lengnick-Hall, M. L., & Moritz, S. (2003). The impact of e-HR on the human resource management function. *Journal of Labor Research, 24*(3), 365–379.

Leonardi, P. M. (2013). Theoretical foundations for the study of sociomateriality. *Information and Organization, 23*(2), 59–76.

Lepak, D. P., & Snell, S. A. (1998). Virtual HR: Strategic human resource management in the 21st century. *Human Resource Management Review, 8*(3), 215–234.

Lin, L.-H. (2011). Electronic human resource management and organizational innovation: The roles of information technology and virtual organizational structure. *The International Journal of Human Resource Management, 22*(2), 235–257.

Llorens, J. J., & Kellough, E. (2007). A revolution in public personnel administration: The growth of web-based recruitment and selection processes in the federal service. *Public Personnel Management, 36*(3), 207–221.

Maier, C., Laumer, S., Eckhardt, A., & Weitzel, T. (2013). Analyzing the impact of HRIS implementations on HR personnel's job satisfaction and turnover intention. *The Journal of Strategic Information Systems, 22*(3), 193–207.

Marler, J. H., & Boudreau, J. W. (2016). An evidence-based review of HR Analytics. *The International Journal of Human Resource Management, 28*(1), 3–26.

Marler, J. H., & Fisher, S. L. (2013). An evidence-based review of e-HRM and strategic human resource management. *Human Resource Management Review, 23*(1), 18–36.

Marler, J. H., & Parry, E. (2016). Human resource management, strategic involvement and e-HRM technology. *The International Journal of Human Resource Management, 27*(19), 2233–2253.

Mazmanian, M., Orlikowski, W. J., & Yates, J. (2006). Ubiquitous email: Individual experiences and organizational consequences of BlackBerry use. *Best Paper Proceedings of the 65th Annual Meeting of the Academy of Management*, Atlanta.

Meijerink, J., Bondarouk, T. V., & Maatman, M. (2013). Exploring and comparing HR shared services in subsidiaries of multinational corporations and indigenous organisations in The Netherlands: A strategic response analysis. *European Journal of International Management, 7*(4), 469–492.

Meister, J. (2017, March 1). The future of work: The intersection of artificial intelligence and human resources. *Forbes Blog*. Retrieved from https://www.forbes.com/sites/jeannemeister/2017/03/01/the-future-of-work-the-intersection-of-artificial-intelligence-and-human-resources/#3ed555f46ad2

Mirrazavi, S. K., & Beringer, H. (2007). A web-based workforce management system for Sainsburys Supermarkets Ltd. *Annals of Operations Research, 155*(1), 437–457.

Olivas-Luján, M. R., Ramirez, J., & Zapata-Cantu, L. (2007). e-HRM in Mexico: Adapting innovations for global competitiveness. *International Journal of Manpower, 28*(5), 418–434.

Orlikowski, W. J. (2000). Using technology and constituting structures: A practice lens for studying technology in organizations. *Organization Science, 11*(4), 404–428.

Orlikowski, W. J. (2007). Sociomaterial practices: Exploring technology at work. *Organization Studies, 28*(9), 1435–1448.

Orlikowski, W. J. (2010). The sociomateriality of organisational life: Considering technology in management research. *Cambridge Journal of Economics, 34*(1), 125–141.

Orlikowski, W. J., & Iacono, S. (2006). Desperately seeking the 'IT' in IT research: A call to theorizing the IT artifact. In J. L. King & K. Lyytinen (Eds.), *Information systems. The state of the field*. West Sussex: John Wiley & Sons.

Orlikowski, W. J., & Robey, D. (1991). Information technology and the structuring of organizations. *Information Systems Research*, *2*(2), 143–169.

Orlikowski, W. J., & Scott, S. V. (2008). Sociomateriality: Challenging the separation of technology, work and organization. *The Academy of Management Annals*, *2*(1), 433–474.

Orlikowski, W. J., & Scott, S. V. (2015). Exploring material-discursive practices. *Journal of Management Studies*, *52*(5), 697–705.

Panayotopoulou, L., Galanaki, E., & Papalexandris, N. (2010). Adoption of electronic systems in HRM: is national background of the firm relevant? *New Technology, Work and Employment*, *25*(3), 253–269.

Panos, S., & Bellou, V. (2016). Maximizing e-HRM outcomes: A moderated mediation path. *Management Decision*, *54*(5), 1088–1109.

Parry, E. (2011). An examination of e-HRM as a means to increase the value of the HR function. *The International Journal of Human Resource Management*, *22*(5), 1146–1162.

Parry, E., & Tyson, S. (2011). Desired goals and actual outcomes of e-HRM. *Human Resource Management Journal*, *21*(3), 335–354.

Paschal, J. L., Stone, D. L., & Stone-Romero, E. F. (2009). Effects of electronic mail policies on invasiveness and fairness. *Journal of Managerial Psychology*, *24*(6), 502–525.

Reddick, C. (2009). Human resources information systems in Texas city governments: Scope and perception of its effectiveness. *Public Personnel Management*, *38*(4), 19–34.

Rogers, E. M. (2003). *Diffusion of innovations*. New York, London: Free Press; Collier Macmillan.

Ruël, H. J.M., Bondarouk, T. V., & Looise, J. K. (2004). E-HRM: Innovation or irritation? An explorative empirical study in five large companies on webbased HRM. *Management Revue*, *15*(3), 364–380.

Ruël, H. J.M., Bondarouk, T. V., & van der Velde, M. (2007). The contribution of e-HRM to HRM effectiveness. *Employee Relations*, *29*(3), 280–291.

Ruël, H. J.M., & van der Kaap, H. (2012). E-HRM usage and value creation: Does a facilitating context matter? *Zeitschrift für Personalforschung*, *26*(3), 260–281.

Ruta, C. D. (2009). HR portal alignment for the creation and development of intellectual capital. *The International Journal of Human Resource Management*, *20*(3), 562–577.

Schalk, R., Timmerman, V., & van den Heuvel, S. (2013). How strategic considerations influence decision making on e-HRM applications. *Human Resource Management Review*, *23*(1), 84–92.

Scholz, T. M. (2017). *Big Data in organizations and the role of human resource management: A complex systems theory-based conceptualization*. New York: Peter Lang.

Schultze, U. (2017). What kind of world do we want to help make with our theories? *Information and Organization*, *27*(1), 60–66.

Selden, S., & Orenstein, J. (2011a). Government e-recruiting web sites: The influence of erecruitment content and usability on recruiting and hiring outcomes in US state governments. *International Journal of Selection and Assesment*, *19*(1), 31–40.

Selden, S., & Orenstein, J. (2011b). Content, usability, and innovation: An evaluative methodology for government recruiting websites. *Review of Public Personnel Administration, 31*(2), 209–223.

Simón, C., & Esteves, J. (2016). The limits of institutional isomorphism in the design of e-recruitment websites: A comparative analysis of the USA and Spain. *The International Journal of Human Resource Management, 27*(1), 23–44.

Stone, D. L., Deadrick, D. L., Lukaszewski, K. M., & Johnson, R. (2015). The influence of technology on the future of human resource management. *Human Resource Management Review, 25*(2), 216–231.

Stone, D. L., & Dulebohn, J. H. (2013). Emerging issues in theory and research on electronic human resource management (eHRM). *Human Resource Management Review, 23*(1), 1–5.

Strohmeier, S. (2007). Research in e-HRM: Review and implications. *Human Resource Management Review, 17*(1), 19–37.

Strohmeier, S. (2009). Concepts of e-HRM consequences: A categorisation, review and suggestion. *The International Journal of Human Resource Management, 20*(3), 528–543.

Strohmeier, S., & Kabst, R. (2009). Organizational adoption of e-HRM in Europe: An empirical exploration of major adoption factors. *Journal of Managerial Psychology, 24*(6), 482–501.

Strohmeier, S., & Kabst, R. (2014). Configurations of e-HRM—An empirical exploration. *Employee Relations, 36*(4), 333–353.

Strohmeier, S., & Piazza, F. (2013). Domain driven data mining in human resource management: A review of current research. *Expert Systems with Applications, 40*(7), 2410–2420.

Strohmeier, S., & Piazza, F. (2015a). Artificial intelligence techniques in human resource management? A conceptual exploration. In C. Kahraman & S. C. Onar (Eds.), *Intelligent systems reference library. Intelligent techniques in engineering management. Theory and applications* (pp. 149–172). Cham: Springer.

Strohmeier, S., & Piazza, F. (Eds.). (2015b). *Human resource intelligence und analytics: Grundlagen, Anbieter, Erfahrungen und Trends.* Wiesbaden: Springer Gabler.

Strohmeier, S., Piazza, F., Majstorovic, D., Schreiner, J. (2016). *Smart HRM. A Delphi Study on the Future of Digital Human Resource Management (HRM 4.0).* Retrieved from http://www.uni-saarland.de/fileadmin/user_upload/Professoren/fr13_ProfStrohmeier/Aktuelles/Final_report_Smart_HRM_EN.pdf

Swaab, R. I., Galinsky, A. D., Medvec, V., & Diermeier, D. A. (2012). The communication orientation model: Explaining the diverse effects of sight, sound, and synchronicity on negotiation and group decision-making outcomes. *Personality and social psychology review, 16*(1), 25–53.

Tansley, C., Huang, J., & Foster, C. (2013). Identity ambiguity and the promises and practices of hybrid e-HRM project teams. *The Journal of Strategic Information Systems, 22*(3), 208–224.

Tansley, C., Kirk, S., Williams, H., & Barton, H. (2014). Tipping the scales: Ambidexterity practices on e-HRM projects. *Employee Relations, 36*(4), 398–414.

Tate, M., Furtmueller, E., & Wilderom, C. (2013). Localizing versus standardizing electronic human resource management: Complexities and tensions between HRM and IT departments. *European Journal of International Management, 7*(4), 413–431.

Thite, M., Kavanagh, M., & Johnson, R. D. (2009). Evolution of human resource management and human resource information systems: The role of information technology. In M. Kavanagh & M. Thite (Eds.), *Human resource information systems: Basics, applications and future directions* (pp. 2–34). Thousand Oaks: SAGE.

Tutnall, A., & Gilding, A. (1999). Actor-network theory and information systems research. *Proceedings of the 10th Australasian Conference on Information Systems* (pp. 955–966). Retrieved from http://citeseerx.ist.psu.edu/viewdoc/download?doi=10.1.1.10.1265&rep=rep1&type=pdf"

Ulrich, D. (1996). *Human resource champions: The next agenda for adding value and delivering results*. Boston: Harvard Business School Press.

Voermans, M., & van Veldhoven, M. (2007). Attitude towards E-HRM: An empirical study at Philips. *Personnel Review, 36*(6), 887–902.

Wahyudi, E., & Park, S. M. (2014). Unveiling the value creation process of electronic human resource management: An indonesian case. *Public Personnel Management, 43*(1), 83–117.

Wells, D. L., Moorman, R. H., & Werner, J. M. (2007). The impact of the perceived purpose of electronic performance monitoring on an array of attitudinal variables. *Human Resource Development Quarterly, 18*(1), 121–138.

Wiblen, S. (2016). Framing the usefulness of eHRM in talent management: A case study of talent identification in a professional services firm. *Canadian Journal of Administrative Sciences, 33*(2), 95–107.

Wiblen, S., Grant, D., & Dery, K. (2010). Transitioning the new HRIS: The reshaping of human resources and information technology talent. *Journal of Electronic Commerce Research, 11*(4), 251–267.

Wickramasinghe, V. (2010). Employee perceptions towards web-based human resource management systems in Sri Lanka. *The International Journal of Human Resource Management, 21*(10), 1617–1630.

Zammuto, R. F., Griffith, T. L., Majchrzak, A., Dougherty, D. J., & Faraj, S. (2007). Information technology and the changing fabric of organization. *Organization Science, 18*(5), 749–762.

Zweig, D., & Scott, K. (2007). When unfairness matters most: Supervisory violations of electronic monitoring practices. *Human Resource Management Journal, 17*(3), 227–247.

CHAPTER 10

AN EXAMINATION OF WORKPLACE CYBERDEVIANCE

Amber N. Schroeder and Julia H. Whitaker

ABSTRACT

Whereas the use of technology in organizations has many advantages, it also provides employees with new outlets to engage in technology-enabled forms of workplace deviance. This chapter examines various forms of cyber misbehavior through the lens of the four primary dimensions of workplace deviance put forth by Robinson and Bennett (1995). We also expand on Robinson and Bennett's (1995) classic model of workplace deviance by discussing features unique to cyberdeviance engagement. A review of both individual- and organization-directed forms of cyberdeviance is provided, including cyberbullying, online incivility, cyberloafing, and cybercrime. A brief discussion of the known antecedents and outcomes for each construct, as well as recommendations for applied practice and future research are provided.

Whereas the introduction of new technology provides many opportunities for organizational growth and development, it also presents new means for employees to engage in various types of workplace misbehavior. Workplace cyberdeviance,

The Brave New World of eHRM 2.0, pages 279–312.

which is employee misbehavior conducted using electronic means, is important for organizations to address, as it can result in a number of negative outcomes for both organizations and employees. Notably, because of differences in online and offline contexts, cyberdeviance may not simply be the manifestation of offline workplace deviance in an online realm. For instance, online interpersonal communication differs from offline communication in several key ways: (a) messages are text-based, (b) there can be multiple recipients, (c) communication can be easily forwarded to others, (d) there may be a greater risk for misinterpretation due to missing paralinguistic information, and (e) source anonymity may be possible (Kowalski, Limber, & Agatston, 2008; Kruger, Epley, Parker, & Ng, 2005; Privitera & Campbell, 2009). Likewise, non-communicative online behaviors can differ from non-communicative offline behaviors in that online misbehavior can occur at other geographic locations without the perpetrator being present, and some forms of online misbehavior require a high level of technical expertise. Thus, although workplace cyberdeviance shares many commonalities with offline workplace deviance, a special consideration of the unique features of cyberdeviance is warranted. In this chapter, we will first introduce the topic of workplace deviance, followed by a more detailed discussion of workplace cyberdeviance.

WORKPLACE DEVIANCE

Workplace deviance has been defined as norm-breaching volitional behavior that negatively impacts the organization and/or its stakeholders (Robinson & Bennett, 1995). Although a number of conceptual models have been proposed (see e.g., Baron, Neuman, & Geddes, 1999; Björkqvist, Österman, & Hjelt-Bäck, 1994), one of the most well-known taxonomies of workplace deviance was put forth by Robinson and Bennett (1995). In this model, deviant workplace behavior varies along two dimensions—seriousness of the offense and whether the offense is directed toward organizational or interpersonal targets. Thus, deviant workplace behaviors can be sorted into four categories:

1. Personal aggression, which includes severe, interpersonally-targeted actions, such as verbal abuse or sexual harassment,
2. Political deviance, which refers to minor, interpersonally-directed behaviors, such as gossip or inappropriate blame assignment,
3. Production deviance, which includes minor offenses targeted at the organization, such as taking extra work breaks or putting in minimal effort, and
4. Property deviance, which refers to serious, organization-directed behaviors, such as theft or sabotage.

For the purpose of this review, we focus primarily on forms of cyberdeviance that occur internally (i.e., conducted by organizational employees) as opposed to externally (i.e., conducted by organizational outsiders).

A notable issue in the realm of deviance research is the lack of clarity regarding conceptual overlap. For instance, Einarsen, Hoel, Zapf, and Cooper (2011) suggested that the concepts of bullying, harassment, and mobbing share enough conceptual similarity to be used interchangeably. Additionally, Hershcovis (2011) highlighted the degree of item overlap in various measures of incivility, abusive supervision, bullying, and interpersonal conflict, and also provided meta-analytic evidence suggesting that these four constructs did not significantly differ in terms of their relations with 18 of 25 deviance outcomes. As workplace deviance construct definitions frequently include attributes such as intent, severity, frequency, perceived anonymity, and characteristics related to perpetrator–victim relationships, Hershcovis (2011) argued that research would benefit from the consideration of these factors as moderators in an examination of the broader construct of workplace aggression and its corresponding outcomes.

Likewise, researchers have debated the nature of the relation between workplace deviance and organizational citizenship behavior, or discretionary extra-role behaviors that positively impact the organization (Organ, 1997). Some have conceptualized these two constructs as existing on opposite ends of a continuum (see e.g., Ball, Trevino, & Sims, 1994; Bennett & Stamper, 2001), whereas other work has suggested that these two constructs are orthogonal, with only moderate correlations (see e.g., Kelloway, Loughlin, Barling, & Nault, 2002; Miles, Borman, Spector, & Fox, 2002; Sackett, Berry, Wiemann, & Laczo, 2006). For the purpose of this review, cyberdeviance will be conceptualized as being distinct from cyber organizational citizenship behavior.

In an information and communication technologies (ICT) context, conceptual overlap is also an issue (see e.g., Durkin & Patterson, 2011). However, although research would benefit from the refinement of the nomological network for workplace cyberdeviance, such an endeavor is beyond the scope of the current chapter. Rather, we provide an overview of various forms of workplace cyberdeviance, including a discussion of antecedents, outcomes, policy implications, and future research directions. Each behavior will be discussed in relation to Robinson and Bennett's (1995) taxonomy of workplace deviance.

WORKPLACE CYBERDEVIANCE

Whereas many workplace cyberdeviance researchers have utilized Robinson and Bennett's (1995) workplace deviance taxonomy as a guiding framework, there are several distinctions worth noting in an ICT context. First, in regard to cyberdeviance targets (i.e., the first dimension of Robinson and Bennett's [1995] model), as noted by Weatherbee (2010), there is greater boundary permeability and potential for indirect effects in an ICT context. More specifically, an act of cyberdeviance may initially have multiple targets, which allows an act to encompass multiple deviance categories (e.g., discussing workplace issues in online forums could impact an individual and/or the organization's reputation), or the effect of an act of cyberdeviance could shift to a secondary target(s) over time (e.g., in the case of a personal email later being disseminated to external stakeholders). Another defining feature unique to cyberdeviance is the wider accessibility of targets (Campbell, 2005; Dooley, Pyzalski, & Cross, 2009; Tokunaga, 2010), which may present more opportunity for this type of workplace misbehavior to occur (e.g., an employee can hack company records from an offsite location during nonwork hours).

The greater boundary permeability in an ICT context introduces several features that can also impact a behavior's perceived severity (i.e., the second dimension of Robinson and Bennett's [1995] model). We argue that the first feature is the visibility of the act, a characteristic that is greatly impacted by ICT capabilities. For instance, the perceived severity of a private email containing disrespectful remarks may increase if the message was instead posted in a public forum where others are able to witness the target's abuse and thereby increase the victim's embarrassment. The permanence of ICT-based workplace deviance is a second feature impacting perceived severity. Namely, as noted by several scholars (e.g., Campbell, 2005; Dooley et al., 2009; Tokunaga, 2010), behaviors occurring in cyberspace have a high degree of permanence, which presents an opportunity for such behaviors to be re-experienced by cyberdeviance targets over time, thereby contributing to an increase in perceived severity and potential for harm.

To better understand workplace deviance in an ICT context, several researchers have described cyberdeviance behaviors in terms of Robinson and Bennett's (1995) taxonomy (see e.g., Lim, 2002; Weatherbee, 2010). Examples of personal aggression include cyberharassment and cyberaggression, political deviance examples include gossip and blame re-assignment, production deviance behaviors include cyberloafing and Internet shopping, and property deviance examples include hacking and software theft (Weatherbee, 2010). However, in an attempt to circumvent issues related to conceptual overlap and instead provide a more parsimonious discussion of cyberdeviance, we will discuss what we perceive to be the key behaviors within each of Robinson and Bennett's (1995) workplace deviance dimensions (i.e., personal aggression, political deviance, production deviance, and property deviance), noting issues related to conceptual overlap, when relevant (see Figure 10.1). A review of the antecedents, outcomes, and key implications for electronic human resource management (eHRM) practices will be presented for each of the key behaviors (see Table 10.1 for a summary).

Personal Aggression

Robinson and Bennett (1995) identified sexual harassment, verbal abuse, stealing from co-workers, and endangering co-workers as key personal aggression behaviors. In an ICT context, a common way that personal aggression behaviors may manifest is in the form of cyberbullying, which is also known as online bullying or electronic bullying (Notar, Padgett, & Roden, 2013). Cyberbullying has significant conceptual overlap with constructs such as cyberharassment, cyberstalking, (Durkin & Patterson, 2011; Willard, 2007), and cybersmearing (Naples & Maher, 2002). Such behaviors clearly fall under Robinson and Bennett's (1995)

TABLE 10.1. Workplace Cyberdeviance Antecedents, Outcomes, and Implications on eHRM Functions

Deviance Category	Key Attributes	Relevant Cyberbehavior	Antecedents	Outcomes	eHRM Practices		
					Employee Selection	Training & Employee Development	Leadership & Organizational Climate
Personal aggression	Extreme; interpersonal target(s)	Cyberbullying	• E.g., offline and online bullying experience, aggression-related beliefs	• E.g., stress, substance abuse, somatic symptoms	• Evaluate applicant social skills	• Provide social skill development opportunities • Provide training on anti-bullying and online behavior policies	• Develop anti-bullying and online behavior policies • Ensure leaders promote a safe work climate
Political deviance	Minor; interpersonal target(s)	Online incivility	• E.g., neuroticism, workload, role stress	• E.g., mental distress, burnout, offline workplace deviance	• Evaluate applicant social skills • Evaluate applicant personality (e.g., neuroticism)	• Provide social skill development opportunities • Provide training on anti-bullying and online behavior policies	• Develop anti-bullying and online behavior policies • Ensure leaders promote a safe work climate • Monitor work demands
Production deviance	Minor; organizational target(s)	Cyberloafing	• E.g., conscientiousness, extraversion, cyberloafing intentions, attitudes towards cyberloafing	• E.g., productivity loss, perceived stress relief	• Evaluate applicant problematic Internet use • Evaluate applicant conscientiousness and extraversion	• Allocate time for employees to access the Internet for non-work-related purposes	• Develop acceptable Internet use policies • Ensure upper management abides by policies
Property deviance	Extreme; organizational target(s)	Cybercrime	• E.g., conscientiousness, extraversion, organizational innovation, organizational security profile	• E.g., information loss, business disruption, loss of revenue	• Conduct background checks • Evaluate applicant conscientiousness and extraversion	• Provide employee awareness training on information security issues	• Focus on maintaining high employee morale and well-being • Maintain a high security profile

FIGURE 10.1. Typology of deviant offline and online workplace behavior. Note that this figure lists examples within each deviance category and is not an exhaustive list.

personal aggression dimension, as they are serious, interpersonally-targeted actions (see Figure 10.1).

What is cyberbullying? Workplace bullying has been defined as harassing physical or verbal behavior that can include threats, humiliation, ostracism, sarcasm, manipulation, or other actions that are intended to harm the target individual (Li, 2007). Cyberbullying, which has been referred to as an "invisible fist" (Hong, Lin, Hwang, Hu, & Chen, 2014, p. 308), is a special form of workplace bullying that is conducted using electronic forms of communication (e.g., email, text messages, social media websites; Willard, 2007). Although cyberbullying has been defined in a number of ways, in most definitions of cyberbullying, such behaviors must repeatedly occur, and a power imbalance must exist between the victim and perpetrator (Privitera & Campbell, 2009; Smith et al., 2008). However, others (e.g., Staude-Müller, Hansen, & Voss, 2012) have argued that repetition and perpetrator-victim power differentials are not a requirement for a behavior to be classified as cyberbullying. Although cyberbullying and offline bullying are distinct types of behavior, cyberbullying research largely developed on the shoulders of the empirical work on offline bullying. As such, perhaps the power differential definitional component is a remnant of the traditional definition of bullying. As ICTs provide a less observable venue for bullying behaviors, and as even solitary acts of cyberbullying can have detrimental effects, we argue that any harassing behavior conducted via ICTs, regardless of frequency or source, should be classified as cyberbullying behavior.

Whereas there has been a greater focus on cyberbullying among youth than adult populations (Kowalski, Giumetti, Schroeder, & Lattanner, 2014), recent research has highlighted that cyberbullying occurs across the life cycle. For instance, one study found that roughly 10% of employees in a manufacturing union had been cyberbullied (Privitera & Campbell, 2009). Likewise, in a study of individuals ranging in age from 10 to 50 years, Staude-Müller et al. (2012) found that 81.5% of respondents had been verbally harassed online, and 68.3% reported having been sexually harassed online. Thus, these studies highlight that cyberbullying is an issue worthy of discussion in the context of eHRM.

Antecedents of cyberbullying. In examining the antecedents of workplace cyberbullying, it is important to distinguish between predictors of bullying perpetration and factors linked to a greater likelihood of victimization. Zapf and Einarson (2003) suggested that there are three primary individual-level antecedents of offline bullying perpetration:

1. Threatened self-esteem,
2. Social ineptitude, and
3. A focus on self-promotion and organizational advancement.

Other antecedents include previous bullying victimization (Hauge, Skogstad, & Einarsen, 2009) that results in the use of proactive bullying perpetration as a self-protective mechanism (Aquino & Thau, 2009; Lee & Brotheridge, 2006) and perpetrator gender (i.e., a greater prevalence for males; De Cuyper, Baillien, & De Witte, 2009; Hauge et al., 2009; Li, 2007; Rayner, 1997). In terms of work environment antecedents, Hauge et al. (2009) found that bullying perpetration was positively linked to both role conflict and interpersonal conflict. Organizational policies can also promote workplace bullying perpetration, as research has linked the use of forced distribution rating systems (FDRSs) to increased rates of employee sabotage (Berger, Harbring, & Sliwka, 2013). For instance, in the early 2000s, Microsoft implemented an FDRS for its employees, which resulted in employees focusing not only on reaching their own performance goals, but also the unintended consequence of employees actively "work[ing] hard to make sure their colleagues did not" (Eichenwald, 2012, "The Bell Curve," para. 8).

Likewise, Zapf and Einarson (2003) identified three groups of individual-level predictors of offline bullying victimization:

1. Outgroup membership,
2. Poor social skills and a lack of assertiveness, and
3. A high level of achievement and an inability to conform to group norms.

Other individual-level predictors include victim negative and positive affect, gender (i.e., greater prevalence for males), age (i.e., greater prevalence for younger employees), and tenure (i.e., greater prevalence for longer-tenured employees; Bowling & Beehr, 2006). Antecedents related to the work environment have also been linked to bullying victimization, including role conflict, interpersonal conflict, leader behavior (Hauge, Skogstad, & Einarsen, 2007), workload (Einarsen, Raknes, & Matthiesen, 1994; Salin, 2003), social support (Hansen et al., 2006; Zapf, Knorz, & Kulla, 1996), and role ambiguity (Einarsen et al., 1994; Jennifer, Cowie, & Ananiadou, 2003).

With the exception of Li (2007), who found that the joint experience of offline bullying perpetration and victimization, gender (i.e., greater prevalence for males), and nationality predicted cyberbullying perpetration, and that offline bullying victimization and joint experience as an offline bullying victim and perpetrator predicted cyberbullying victimization, much of the research in this area has focused on offline workplace bullying antecedents or on cyberbullying among youth. For instance, Kowalski et al.'s (2014) meta-analysis of youth cyberbullying behaviors found that experience-related factors such as online and offline bullying exposure, risky Internet behavior, and frequency of online activity, as well as environmental factors, such as parental supervision and perceived support, were linked to both cyberbullying perpetration and victimization.

Even though many of the antecedents described above were linked to offline bullying experiences or youth populations, it can be expected that many of these factors would also predict cyberbullying perpetration and victimization in organizational settings, as both offline bullying and cyberbullying behaviors would fall under Robinson and Bennett's (1995) personal aggression dimension. In terms of the relative magnitude of the predictors of cyberbullying behavior, in a meta-analytic study, Kowalski et al. (2014) found that experience-related factors such as cybervictimization and offline bullying perpetration were the strongest predictors of cyberbullying perpetration, with smaller effects for individual-level factors such as aggression-related beliefs and moral disengagement, as well as behavioral factors such as risky Internet behavior and frequency of Internet use. Even smaller effects were found for environmental factors such as perceptions of safety and climate. Likewise, offline bullying victimization and perpetration were the strongest cyberbullying victimization antecedents, albeit with slightly smaller effect sizes than was the case with cyberbullying perpetration. Therefore, in general, for both cyberbullying victimization and perpetration, environmental factors (other than offline or online bullying exposure) tended to have smaller effects than dispositional and behavioral antecedents.

Outcomes of cyberbullying. Workplace bullying has also been linked to a number of psychological, physiological, and behavioral outcomes. Psychological responses include increased negative emotions, such as stress, anger, confusion, powerlessness, and depression (Ayoko, Callan, & Hartel, 2003), decreased job satisfaction and organizational commitment, and higher levels of anxiety and burnout (Bowling & Beehr, 2006). Workplace bullying has also been positively linked to employee illness (Kivimaki, Elovainio, & Vahtera, 2000) and physical injury (Bailey, Dollard, McLinton, & Richards, 2015), as well as behavioral correlates such as individual and group performance (Coyne, Craig, & Smith-Lee Chong, 2004), absenteeism (Kivimaki, Elovainio, & Vahtera, 2000; Ortega, Christensen, Hogh, Rugulies, & Borg, 2011), turnover intentions (Djurkovic, McCormack, & Casimir, 2004), and turnover behavior (Rayner, 1997).

In studies looking specifically at cyberbullying-related outcomes across contexts, victimization has been positively associated with depression, anxiety, loneliness, drug and alcohol use, somatic symptoms, stress, and suicidal ideation, and inversely linked to self-esteem, life satisfaction, and prosocial behavior (Kowalski et al., 2014). In addition, Hong et al. (2014) found that as the amount of workplace cyberbullying victimization increased, the negative outcomes related to experiencing cyberbullying strengthened, but that a positive organizational climate often served as a buffer against negative psychological outcomes. Likewise, albeit in an adolescent sample, Calvete, Orue, Estévez, Villardón, and Padilla (2010) found that perceived social support was inversely linked to cyberbullying perpetration. Thus, having a supportive climate may be beneficial for both cyberbullying prevention and the reduction of negative effects for victims. Also noteworthy is that females and older victims, as well as individuals with higher levels of neuroticism, stress, and previous cyberbullying experience, and lower levels of Internet literacy have been shown to be more likely to experience emotional distress as a result of being a victim of cyberbullying (Staude-Müller et al., 2012). As such, both individual and situational factors may moderate the negative effects of cyberbullying. Notably, researchers have argued that the negative effects of cyberbullying may be more severe than offline bullying effects due to cyberbullying behaviors' greater visibility to bystanders, the increased access to victims that technology affords, and the opportunity for re-experiencing the cyberbullying event due to the permanence of information in cyberspace (Campbell, 2005; Dooley et al., 2009; Tokunaga, 2010).

In comparing the effect sizes of various cyberbullying outcomes, Kowalski et al.'s (2014) meta-analysis of cyberbullying among youth identified mental health-related outcomes such as stress, suicidal ideation, depression, anxiety, and loneliness as having the strongest links to cyberbullying victimization, with additional effects for somatic symptoms and behavioral issues such as drug and alcohol use, among other predictors. Cyberbullying perpetration outcomes generally had smaller effects, with drug and alcohol use, anxiety, and depression having the strongest links. Thus, these findings indicate that a variety of negative mental health outcomes, as well as behavioral coping mechanisms may be the most likely outcomes of cyberbullying behaviors.

Cyberbullying and eHRM. In a review of court cases involving workplace bullying, Martin and LaVan (2010) found that 64% of the organizations involved in litigation did not have an anti-bullying policy, even though evidence has been presented to suggest that such policies can be beneficial for employees (see e.g., Meloni & Austin, 2011). To date, 30 states in the U.S. have enacted workplace anti-bullying legislation (Healthy Workplace Bill, n.d.; see Gilani, Cavico & Mujtaba, 2014, for a review of criminal liability issues). The introduction of organizational anti-bullying policies could also impact the work climate. Notably, a recent study indicated that a positive work climate was not only inversely related to workplace bullying prevalence, but through bullying's positive relation with emotional exhaustion, work climate was also indirectly linked to the prevalence of workers' compensation claims for physical injuries (Bailey et al., 2015). In this case, positive work climate was described as the utilization of participative management practices related to psychosocial safety, which illustrates the impact organizational leadership can have on workplace bullying. Given that mental health issues can result in workers' compensation claims, there may be an indirect link between negative mental health outcomes associated with cyberbullying that could result in compensation claims. For example, Bailey et al. (2015) reported that a number of mental stress conditions (several of which have been linked to cyberbullying) were positively associated with the likelihood of workers' compensation claims being filed, which highlights the severity of the negative health effects that bullying can have on employees, as well as on organizations' financial responsibility. Additionally, depression, alcoholism, and anxiety disorders, which have all been linked to cyberbullying exposure, have been identified as three of the top 10 most expensive mental health issues for U.S. organizations in terms of healthcare, absenteeism, and short-term disability costs (Goetzel, Hawkins, Ozminkowski, & Wang, 2003), with depression and mental illness costing organizations approximately $348 per employee each year (Goetzel et al., 2004).

To help foster a positive work climate, we recommend that organizations develop and provide training on anti-bullying policies, as well as standards for acceptable online behavior. This should include a discussion of punitive actions and available resources. In addition, as social ineptitude and interpersonal conflict have been linked to both workplace bullying victimization and perpetration, organizations may consider giving more weight to social skills in the employee selection process and/or providing more employee development opportunities related to the development of social skills, especially in an online context. See Table 10.1 for a review of workplace cyberbullying antecedents, outcomes, and eHRM recommendations.

Political Deviance

Examples of political deviance from Robinson and Bennett's typology include showing favoritism, gossiping about co-workers, blaming co-workers, and competing nonbeneficially. In an ICT context, workplace online incivility can be considered a form of political deviance due to its characterization as involving minor, interpersonally-targeted deviant behavior. This categorization is consistent with previous work describing online gossiping and the selective communication of information as acts of online political deviance (Weatherbee, 2010). Synonymous or related constructs include cyber incivility (see e.g., Giumetti, McKibben, Hatfield, Schroeder, & Kowalski, 2012) and cyberostracism (see e.g., Williams, Cheung, & Choi, 2000); however, for the purpose of this review, these constructs will be considered forms of online incivility (see Figure 10.1).

What is online incivility? Online incivility refers to impolite or disrespectful behavior performed via technological means (Giumetti et al., 2012; Lim & Teo, 2009). Online incivility involves one or more intentional or unintentional low intensity actions from any source (Hershcovis, 2011). A notable difference between online incivility and other forms of workplace mistreatment is that online incivility is typically characterized by higher prevalence rates, with some indicating daily occurrences (Baron & Neuman, 1996; Lim & Cortina, 2005). With an estimated 98 percent of employees being victimized by workplace incivility (Porath & Pearson, 2013), it has been argued that workplace incivility is a modern-day tool for veiled discrimination (Cortina, 2008).

Antecedents of online incivility. Looking first at the predictors of workplace online incivility perpetration, research has identified several individual-level antecedents. For instance, amount of work experience has been positively linked to engagement in online incivility behaviors (Krishnan, 2016). In addition, gender has been linked to the type of online incivility performed, with females engaging in more passive behaviors (e.g., not responding to emails) and males engaging in more active forms of online incivility (e.g., unkind communication; Lim & Teo, 2009). Online incivility perpetration has also been inversely linked to conscientiousness, as well as negatively associated with both extraversion and emotional stability in circumstances where perpetrator conscientiousness is low (Krishnan, 2016). Likewise, Taylor and Kluemper (2012) found that neuroticism moderated the link between role stress and offline workplace incivility perpetration, such that individuals high in neuroticism were more likely to engage in workplace incivility perpetration in response to their exposure to environmental stressors. Environmental predictors of workplace online incivility perpetration include workload and online incivility victimization (Francis, Holmvall, & O'Brien, 2015). Likewise, environmental antecedents of offline workplace incivility include role stress (Taylor & Kluemper, 2012), organizational injustice, job dissatisfaction, and work exhaustion (Blau & Andersson, 2005).

Although research on the antecedents of workplace online incivility victimization is limited, research has suggested that employee neuroticism and work stress are positively linked to the prevalence of online incivility victimization from one's supervisor (Giumetti et al., 2012). Research on offline workplace incivility victimization has also identified a number of relevant predictors. Namely, offline workplace incivility victimization has been inversely linked to agreeableness and emotional stability through the mediating effect of others' perceptions of provocative target behavior (e.g., a tendency to anger others; Milam, Spitzmueller, & Penney, 2009). In addition, research suggests that offline workplace incivility victimization is higher for racial minorities (Cortina, Kabat-Farr, Leskinen, Huerta, & Magley, 2013), younger individuals (Lim & Lee, 2011), and those with a higher body weight (Sliter, Sliter, Withrow, & Jex, 2012). Findings are mixed regarding the link between gender and offline incivility victimization (see e.g., Cortina et al., 2013; Lim & Lee, 2011). Offline workplace incivility victimization is also more likely for individuals who engage in counterproductive work behavior (Meier & Spector, 2013) and those with certain conflict management styles (Trudel & Reio, 2011). More specifically, Trudel and Reio (2011) found that individuals who have a dominating conflict management style in which one demonstrates little concern for others' goals are more likely to be targeted by offline workplace incivility perpetrators, whereas those who have an integrating conflict management style in which one works to achieve mutually beneficial outcomes are less likely to become victims of offline workplace incivility. Contextual antecedents positively linked to offline workplace incivility victimization include role stress (Taylor & Klemper, 2012) and civility climate (Walsh et al., 2012).

Even though it is difficult to draw conclusions regarding overarching trends related to the antecedents of online incivility, it is noteworthy that several studies have identified neuroticism and factors related to work demands (e.g., workload, work stress) as key predictors of both perpetration and victimization in both offline and online contexts. As such, whereas future work will undoubtedly uncover other important antecedents, these factors provide an important first step in broadening our understanding of the occurrence of online incivility.

Outcomes of online incivility. A variety of negative outcomes have been linked to online incivility victimization. Mental health and attitudinal outcomes include increased psychological distress (Park, Fritz, & Jex, 2015), negative affect (Giumetti et al., 2013), and burnout (Giumetti et al., 2012). Behavioral outcomes linked to online incivility victimization include absenteeism (Giumetti et al., 2012), turnover intentions (Giumetti et al., 2012; Lim & Teo, 2009), engagement in more severe forms of workplace deviance (Lim & Teo, 2009), and likelihood of conforming in future group interactions (e.g., choosing an obvious incorrect decision in order to follow along with other group members; Williams, Cheung, & Choi, 2000). Inverse links have also been demonstrated between online incivility victimization and cognitive performance, engagement, energy (Giumetti et al., 2013), job satisfaction, organizational commitment (Lim & Teo, 2009), mood, and group cohesion (Williams et al., 2000). Interestingly, neuroticism has also been identified as a moderator of the link between online incivility victimization and corresponding outcomes, with those high in neuroticism experiencing stronger negative effects (Giumetti et al., 2012).

Because of the relative paucity of research on online workplace incivility, a discussion of relevant outcomes identified for offline incivility is warranted. Notable offline incivility mental health outcomes include increased psychological distress (Caza & Cortina, 2007; Cortina, Magley, Williams, & Langhout, 2001; Kern & Grandey, 2009; Lim, Cortina, & Magley, 2008) and emotional exhaustion (Kern

& Grandey, 2009; Sliter, Jex, Wolford, & McInnerney, 2010). Other behavioral and relational outcomes include increased job withdrawal (Cortina et al., 2001; Sliter, Sliter, & Jex, 2012), work-to-family conflict (Lim & Lee, 2011), turnover intentions (Lim et al., 2008), incivility perpetration (van Jaarsveld, Walker, & Skarlicki, 2010), and engagement in more extreme acts of workplace deviance (Sakurai & Jex, 2012; Taylor & Kluemper, 2012). Offline incivility victimization has also been inversely related to career focus (Cortina et al., 2001), work effort (Sakurai & Jex, 2012), job satisfaction (Lim et al., 2008; Penney & Spector, 2005), organizational justice perceptions (Lim & Lee, 2011), engagement, and (indirectly) performance (Caza & Cortina, 2007; Sliter et al., 2010; Sliter et al. 2012).

Research has also identified factors that may moderate the link between incivility victimization and negative outcomes. For instance, Kern and Grandey (2009) found that higher racial group identification among minorities exacerbated incivility's positive link to emotional exhaustion. In addition, Taylor and Kluemper (2012) found that high neuroticism and low agreeableness and conscientiousness were linked to an even higher likelihood that incivility would escalate to engagement in more severe forms of workplace deviance. Thus, commonly identified incivility outcomes that occur in both online and offline contexts include mental distress, various types of job and work withdrawal, job dissatisfaction, and engagement in more extreme forms of workplace deviance. Moreover, these outcomes often demonstrate medium to large effects (i.e., standardized coefficients greater than .3 in many cases), which highlights the potential severity of what is considered to be low intensity deviant behavior.

Online incivility and eHRM. As highlighted in the previous section, "although incivility may be subtle, its effects are not" (Cortina & Magley, 2009, p. 272). Thus, introducing organizational mechanisms that discourage workplace online incivility is important. Notably, a recent study found that, on average, less than 3 percent of incivility victims filed formal complaints with their employer, and those who did file a report had often been the target of workplace incivility for an extended period of time before reporting (Cortina & Magley, 2009). This highlights the need for organizations to be proactive in preventing workplace incivility. For instance, Leiter, Laschinger, Day, and Oore (2011) provided evidence to suggest that civility interventions can have a positive impact on reducing incivility, thereby positively impacting outcomes such as job satisfaction, trust in management, and absenteeism. In addition, studies have shown that supervisor social support, increased job control, and post-work psychological detachment may weaken the negative effects of online incivility (Park et al., 2015; Sakurai & Jex, 2012).

Pearson, Andersson, and Porath (2000) provided a number of recommendations for addressing workplace incivility:

a. Develop clear policies regarding organizational norms for interpersonal interactions,
b. Include interpersonal skills as a criterion in the employee selection process,
c. Provide employees with social skills training and communicate the company's interpersonal interaction policies during the new hire orientation process,
d. Utilize mechanisms that discourage uncivil behavior (e.g., feedback from 360-degree surveys), and
e. Punish incivility perpetrators.

Based on our review of workplace incivility antecedents, we also recommend that relevant personality variables (e.g., neuroticism) be included in employee selection practices and that organizations monitor factors related to employee work demands (e.g., workload, work stress) in order to identify at risk individuals. See Table 10.1 for a review of workplace online incivility antecedents, outcomes, and eHRM recommendations.

Production Deviance

Robinson and Bennett (1995) identified leaving early, taking excessive work breaks, intentionally working slowly, and wasting resources as examples of production deviance behaviors. In an ICT context, cyberloafing can be considered a form of production deviance, as this type of employee misbehavior refers to organization-directed behaviors that negatively impact organizational productivity. Cyberloafing refers to a situation in which employees use technology for activities that do not contribute to work productivity (Lim, 2002). Other related constructs include cyberslacking (see e.g., O'Neill, Hambley, & Chatellier, 2014) and Internet misuse (see e.g., Young & Case, 2009); for the purpose of this review, these constructs will be broadly examined as cyberloafing (see Figure 10.1).

What is cyberloafing? Cyberloafing is defined as any voluntary act in which employees use their company's Internet to engage in non-job-related activities during work hours (Lim, 2002). Page (2015) found that 73.8% of employees engaged in cyberloafing behaviors. Examples of cyberloafing include checking non-work-related email, viewing sports-related websites, visiting personal banking sites, participating in online gambling, booking vacations, looking for other employment, viewing social networking sites, downloading music, and viewing explicit adult websites (Blanchard & Henle, 2008; Lim & Chen, 2012; Sheikh, Atashagah, & Abidzadegan, 2015). Not surprisingly, such behaviors can be concerning for organizations due to a loss of productivity and resources, as organizations lose an estimated one billion dollars annually due to such activities (Ananadarajan, Simmers, & Igbaria, 2000). Cyberloafing has also been further classified in two main categories of minor and serious acts (Blanchard & Henle, 2008). Minor cyberloafing behaviors tend to occur more frequently, such as using personal email or viewing news sites, whereas serious cyberloafing behaviors are less prevalent and can include behaviors such as viewing pornographic sites or downloading illegal music.

Antecedents of cyberloafing. In examining offline loafing behaviors, research has identified several individual- and organization-level antecedents. For example, production deviance has been inversely linked to extraversion, conscientiousness, and agreeableness, as well as positively related to openness and job dissatisfaction (Bolton, Becker, & Barber, 2010). Organization-level antecedents include social norms regarding others' perceived approval of loafing behavior and the ease in which loafing can be executed without detection (Henle, Reeve, & Pitts, 2010). Additionally, in examining sanction type as a predictor of production deviance engagement, informal sanctions (e.g., co-worker threat, such as informing an authority figure about misconduct) have been shown to be stronger deterrents than formal sanctions (e.g., management threat, such as employee termination; Hollinger & Clark, 1982). Similarly, social loafing can be considered a form of productivity loss that stems from the deindividuation that occurs when working with a group (Liden, Wayne, Jaworski, & Bennett, 2004). Select predictors of social loafing include low conscientiousness, felt responsibility (Hoon & Tan, 2008), and a lack of identifiability for individual contributions (Williams, Harkins, & Latané, 1981).

Specifically related to online loafing behaviors, research has identified various demographic characteristics and individual differences related to cyberloafing behaviors. Namely, cyberloafing prevalence has been found to be higher for men and racial minorities (Baturay & Toker, 2015; Blanchard & Henle, 2008; Vitak, Crouse, & LaRose, 2011), younger individuals (Andreassen, Torsheim, & Pallesen, 2014; Liberman, Seidmen, McKenna, & Buffardi, 2011), those who are not in a romantic relationship (Andreassen et al., 2014), higher status employees, managers, and those with higher salaries and education (Garrett & Danziger, 2008). In addition, those who use the Internet on a daily basis (Baturay & Toker, 2015), those who participate in non-Internet loafing behaviors (Liberman et al., 2011), individuals who work in jobs that are repetitive (Vitak, Crouse, & LaRose, 2011), and those who experience sleep deficits (Wagner, Barnes, Lim, & Ferris, 2012) are also more likely to engage in cyberloafing. In regard to motivation and personality, cyberloafing engagement is more likely to occur for those with low intrinsic motivation (Liberman et al., 2011), an external locus of control (Blanchard & Henle, 2008), low levels of conscientiousness and emotional stability, and high extraversion (Andreassen et al., 2014; Jia, Jia, & Karau, 2013). Honesty and procrastination have also been demonstrated to provide incremental prediction above personality traits in predicting cyberloafing, with honesty being negatively and procrastination being positively related to cyberloafing (O'Neill, Hambley, & Chatellier, 2014). In terms of attitudinal antecedents, positive attitudes towards cyberloafing (Blanchard & Henle, 2008; Liberman et al., 2011; Sheikh, Atashgah, & Adibzadegan, 2015), and positive attitudes about using the

Internet at work for personal reasons (Askew et al., 2014; Sheikh et al., 2015) have been linked to increased cyberloafing engagement.

In addition to the individual-level antecedents of cyberloafing, there is also evidence of organization-level factors contributing to cyberloafing behaviors. For example, when perceptions of organizational justice are high, people tend to engage in lower levels of cyberloafing (Blau, Yang, & Ward-Cook, 2006), and cyberloafing is reduced even further in high justice conditions when individuals are high in conscientiousness (Kim, Triana, Chung, & Oh, 2016). Several studies have found that employees are more likely to engage in cyberloafing behaviors when they believe that their coworkers and supervisors approve of cyberloafing (Askew et al., 2014; Blanchard & Henle, 2008; Liberman et al., 2011; Sheikh et al., 2015), as well as when employees believe they are able to hide their cyberloafing activities (Askew et al., 2014; Sheikh et al., 2015). In addition, Henle and Blanchard (2008) found that role ambiguity and role conflict were positively linked to cyberloafing, whereas role overload had an inverse relation with cyberloafing.

Examining common antecedents across both offline and online contexts, research has identified behavioral intentions and normative attitudes (e.g., perceiving loafing behaviors to be acceptable) as key predictors of loafing behavior, as several studies have demonstrated moderately large effects. Albeit with smaller effect sizes, conscientiousness and extraversion have also emerged across both contexts as personality antecedents of loafing behavior. Nevertheless, more research is needed to uncover additional antecedents of loafing behavior.

Outcomes of cyberloafing. As research regarding outcomes specifically pertaining to cyberloafing is limited, a brief review of outcomes associated with offline loafing behaviors is needed. For instance, outcomes associated with absenteeism (i.e., a type of loafing behavior) can include decreased performance (Tharenou, 1993), reduced group productivity (Goodman & Leyden, 1991), and an increase in workplace accidents due to reduced familiarity with equipment (Goodman & Garber, 1988). In fact, it has been estimated that approximately 36.6% of payroll expenditures go toward unplanned employee absences (Society for Human Resource Management [SHRM], 2014). Similarly, social loafing can lead to decreased productivity, decreased individual effort, and poor group coordination (Latané, Williams, & Harkins, 1979).

Organizations lose an estimated one billion dollars annually due to cyberloafing activities (Ananadarajan et al., 2000). Cyberloafing behaviors can also result in decreased bandwidth, security violations, or even trade secret violations (Sipior & Ward, 2002). Similarly, it has been estimated that if an employee cyberloafs daily for one hour, it costs the organization roughly $9,600 annually (Sipior & Ward, 2002). Aside from the costly outcomes of productivity loss, there are other negative consequences that result from cyberloafing. For instance, Griffiths (2003) described how employee cyberloafing can detract from performance on work tasks. Young (2010) suggested that this type of behavior can translate into poor customer service or less than optimal work quality, which can reflect poorly on organizational credibility and decrease customer satisfaction. In addition, Young and Case (2009) suggested that more extreme cyberloafing behaviors, such as downloading illegal music or viewing pornographic websites, can place organizations at risk for legal liability.

Although cyberloafing is typically viewed as a deviant workplace behavior that results in a loss of productivity, some researchers argue that it can also have positive outcomes, including increased productivity (Page, 2015) and reduced stress (Lavoie & Pychyl, 2001). Likewise, Coker (2013) proposed that cyberloafing can be beneficial to employees, as it can replenish their attentional resources. In a controlled experiment, Coker (2013) found that employees who were able to cyberloaf during a break had greater sustained vigilance compared to a control group. Research has also suggested that employees may cyberloaf in an effort to cope with workplace stressors (Henle & Blanchard, 2008).

Thus, in examining the effects of both offline and online loafing behaviors, it is clear that the costs associated with production loss is substantial in both contexts. Interestingly, however, links to positive outcomes such as increased productivity and stress relief have also been identified, often with moderately large to large effects. As such, further research is needed to provide a more comprehensive understanding of both the positive and negative effects of loafing behaviors.

Cyberloafing and eHRM. Due to the prevalence of cyberloafing, some organizations have begun to develop and implement policies that attempt to manage these behaviors at work (Henle, Kohut, & Booth, 2009). Internet policies can vary in their purpose, such as utilizing software that restricts access to certain websites, monitoring employee Internet use, establishing sanction systems that threaten punishment for certain types of Internet use, or even policies that fully restrict the use of the Internet for personal use at work (D'Arcy, Hovav, & Galletta, 2009; Henle et al., 2009; Henle & Kedharnath, 2012). However, whereas some research has suggested that the presence of Internet use policies has been associated with a decrease in cyberloafing (Andreasseen et al., 2014; Jia et al., 2013), others studies (e.g., Young & Case, 2004) have indicated that such policies were not effective in reducing cyberloafing. Notably, Manrique de Lara (2006) found that the fear of threatened organizational punishment often associated with Internet use policies can actually increase cyberloafing.

In an effort to understand how Internet use policies impact cyberloafing behaviors, Ugrin and Pearson (2008) investigated the interactive effects of sanctioning systems related to personal Internet use at work, the detection of cyberloafing behaviors, and the enforcement of Internet use policies. They found that enforcement of acceptable use policies (AUPs) produced the greatest reduction in cyberloafing when employees were presented with a scenario that indicated previous employees had been terminated for engaging in non-accepted Internet use at work. The second most impactful factor was the severity of sanctions, followed by the use of detection systems, such as programs that monitor employee computer use.

In sum, the authors argued that organizations should not only utilize AUPs in an attempt to manage cyberloafing, but they need to include potential sanctions that the organization will enforce when employees violate the policy (Ugrin & Pearson, 2008). Similarly, Patrick (n.d.) recommended the use of employee Internet management (EIM) software that can be set up in coordination with AUPs. For example, some EIM products allow organizations to set up time-based quotas that allow employees to access non-work related sites for an allotted amount of time, or to utilize filtering systems that prevent non-work related web browsing during work hours.

It is our recommendation that organizations develop and enforce an Internet use policy that specifically outlines restrictions and limitations regarding non-work-related Internet use. Organizations should carefully consider the strictness of these policies, as well as establish a punitive system that is used when employees violate the terms of the policy. Likewise, it may also be worthwhile to consider some of the potential positive outcomes that results from non-work-related Internet use, as emerging evidence suggests that the impact of cyberloafing is not solely negative. For example, if organizations implement filtering software that prohibits non-work-related web browsing, organizations could consider removing the filters during employee breaks so they are given the opportunity to check personal email or access social media. It should also be noted that although organizations have the capability to strictly monitor employee Internet use on company equipment, personal devices such as cellphones create other avenues for cyberloafing to occur. Thus, organizations may consider including cellphone use restrictions within Internet use policies. In addition, as previously mentioned, managers are more likely to engage in cyberloafing behavior than lower level employees. Thus, it may be particularly important that managers abide by the enforced policies to set an example for other employees. Finally, if cyberloafing is a major concern, Davis, Flett, and Besser (2002) validated a measure of problematic Internet use that could be used in the selection process to detect potential offenders as a preventative effort to screen out cyberloafers. Similarly, as conscientiousness and extraversion are related to cyberloafing behaviors, employers may consider evaluating applicant personality traits as part of the formal selection process. See Table 10.1 for a review of workplace cyberloafing antecedents, outcomes, and eHRM recommendations.

Property Deviance

Property deviance involves employee behaviors that damage company property or result in the attainment of assets without the permission of the organization (Hollinger & Clark, 1982). According to Robinson and Bennett's (1995) typology of workplace deviance, property deviance can include organization-targeted behaviors such as sabotaging equipment, accepting kickbacks, lying about hours worked, or stealing from the company. In a cyber context, we argue that property deviance often manifests as cybercrime, which is consistent with Weatherbee's

(2010) model of cyberdeviance. However, in contrast to Robinson and Bennett's (1995) original conceptualization of property deviance, cybercrime can also occur external to the organization (i.e., by non-organizational members). For example, in 2014, Home Depot suffered from a data breach in which cybercriminals used malware to steal an estimated 56 million debit and credit cards from customers (Krebs, 2014), which resulted in a $19.5 million settlement (Reuters, 2016). Similarly, Target suffered from a data breach that compromised 40 million customer credit card accounts and ended with a $10 million settlement (Reuters, 2016). Cybercrime has been argued to include a variety of activities, including hacking, phishing (Khey & Sainato, 2013), software piracy (Donner, Marcum, Jennings, Higgins, & Banfield, 2014), and data breaching (Martin & Rice, 2011); however, for the purpose of this review, we broadly examine these constructs as cybercrime (see Figure 10.1).

What is cybercrime? Cybercrime, sometimes referred to as cyberattacks, can be defined as online criminal activity that can include malware attacks, stealing data from organizations, confiscating online bank accounts, releasing organizations' confidential information, phishing, using botnets, stealing company equipment, and using malicious code (Ponemon Institute, 2016). Similarly, data breaches involves acquiring data that can compromise the confidentiality, security, or integrity of personal information (Romanosky, Telang, & Acquisti, 2011). Data breaches can include hacking or malware, for example, and can be executed from a variety of sources, including insiders, outsiders, or third parties (Baker et al., 2010).

Antecedents of cybercrime. Research has identified dispositional antecedents of offline property deviance to include low self-control (Gottfredson & Hirschi, 1990), low conscientiousness (Bolton, Becker, & Barber, 2010), high Machiavellianism, and an external locus of control (Jones & Kavanagh, 1996). Environmental antecedents include perceptions of organizational injustice (Greenberg, 1990) and employee dissatisfaction (Hanisch & Hulin, 1991; Jones & Kavanagh, 1996). White-collar crimes, which can be defined as the violation of laws in the course of occupational activities (Griffin, 2002) can also be considered a form of property deviance. White-collar crimes can include activities such as insider trading, theft, or bank fraud (Bashir, Shahzaz, Abbass, Abbass, & Saeed, 2011). Antecedents of white-collar crime have been suggested to include an unhealthy organizational culture, a lack of employee accountability (e.g., employees not being held liable for their actions), and a lack of criminal activity reporting by organizations (Bashir et al., 2011). In addition, Bashir et al. (2011) suggested that when there is high degree of peer support, white-collar crimes are more likely to occur, as individuals are not likely to report crimes committed by close peers.

Regarding cybercrime, Fowler (2016) classified those who are likely to commit cybercrimes into four groups:

1. Petty criminals (i.e., a single person or small group that targets individuals or organizations and usually has limited resources),
2. Organized criminals (i.e., those who engage in cybercrimes but are generally part of a larger group that has plentiful financial resources),
3. Hacktivists (i.e., those who carry out cybercrimes in support of political causes), and
4. Nation-state sponsored criminals (i.e., highly skilled individuals who are hired to target attacks to fit country agendas).

Researchers have also examined the impact of organizational membership as a predictor of cybercrime. For instance, Widup (2010) found that outsiders of organizations were responsible for 48% of reported data breaches, whereas organizational insiders were responsible for 29% of reported data breaches. However, it should be noted that of the data breaches by insiders, approximately 77% were accidental, rather than malicious (Widup, 2010). Baker and colleagues (2010) found that 48% of breaches occur due to the abuse of privilege from insiders, and 40% resulted from hacking. In addition, they found that roughly 70% of cybercrimes were executed from outsiders, or more specifically, from unknown entities or organized criminal groups.

Several environmental factors have also been identified as antecedents of cybercrime perpetration. Namely, Widup (2010) found that data breach incidents could be classified into four sectors: business, education, government, and healthcare. Of those four categories, the business sector was found to be the most susceptible to data breaches, followed by education. In contrast, Khey and Sainato (2013) found that the two most victimized industries were healthcare and education. In addition, they found that within the US, data breaches were the most likely to occur on the West Coast, the Northeast, and South Florida. Collins, Sainato, and Khey (2011) found that specific types of breaches, such as hacking, unintended disclosure of information, and theft were the most probable in educational settings; insider abuse, loss of records, and compromised devices, however, were the most likely to occur in healthcare contexts. The Ponemon Institute (2016) found that organization size, level of innovation (e.g., taking on new partners or launching a new product), and a lack of organizational security were positively associated with cybercrime. In addition, they found that with the passing of legislation to require reports of data breaches within specific industries, the amount of reported data breaches increased. Finally, Willison (2000) suggested that both external factors, such as an unfavorable economic climate, and internal factors, such as feeling pressure from work, may be underlying factors that motivate potential offenders to engage in cybercrimes.

Given the various forms of offline and online property deviance (e.g., theft, sabotage), it is difficult to identify common predictors that fully encompass these behaviors. However, in offline contexts, personality characteristics such as conscientiousness and extraversion have been inversely linked to property deviance engagement, with small to moderate effect sizes. Another offline property deviance predictor, albeit with typically only a small effect size, is employee dissatisfaction. Interestingly, in order to understand the conditions that are more likely to result in cybercrime, the Ponemon Institute (2016) found that highly innovative organizations and companies with a low security profile experienced the most costs associated with cybercrime. Future research should identify predictors that can be generalized across contexts to help organizations combat cybercrime from a broad perspective.

Outcomes of cybercrime. Theft, one form of offline property deviance, can result in substantial losses of organizational profits (Greenberg & Barling, 1996), including indirect costs due to productivity loss (e.g., inability to work due to stolen equipment; Dunlop & Lee, 2004). This form of property deviance can negatively affect customers through increased prices that attempt to cover losses associated with employee theft (Brown & Pardue, 1985). Similarly, acts of employee sabotage can result in lost or altered confidential information, damaged equipment, or even disruptions in production and distribution methods (Crino, 1994). In addition, acts of service sabotage (e.g., rude behavior toward customers) are negatively associated with perceived company performance and employee-customer rapport (Harris & Ogbonna, 2006). As with various forms of cyberdeviance, sabotage can also be executed by non-organizational members, which can negatively affect organizational functioning, thereby causing production delays or missed deadlines (Klein, Leong, & Silva, 1996).

As technology has become more mainstream, organization-directed crimes have manifested in ICT contexts, with cybercrimes costing an estimated $445 billion globally each year (Sandle, 2014). The Ponemon Institute (2016) investigated the consequences of cyberattacks on organizations and how they financially impact the organization. Specifically, they identified four primary consequences of cyberattacks on organizations:

1. Business disruptions (e.g., the economic impact of unplanned outages),
2. Loss of information (e.g., losing confidential employee or customer information),
3. Loss of revenue (e.g., losing customers due to cyberattacks), and
4. Damage to equipment (e.g., cost to restore equipment or software after a cyberattack).

In addition to direct costs associated with cybercrimes, there are also indirect costs. Fowler (2016) discussed how organizations often lose business, witness a decrease in employee productivity, and experience damage to both their company reputation and brand value as a result of cybercrimes. For example, Gemalto (2014) found that 65% of respondents would never or would be very unlikely to continue doing business with a company that had suffered from a data breach. In addition, Fowler (2016) discussed how employees are often reassigned to assist data breach repair efforts, which takes them away from their normal job duties and can reduce overall employee productivity.

Across both offline and online property deviance contexts, the most significant outcome associated with these behaviors is their financial impact. For instance, the Ponemon Institute (2016) found that of the total costs associated with cybercrime in organizations, 39% are attributed to information loss, 36% to business disruptions, and 20% to loss of revenue. Future research should attempt to investigate non-financial outcomes (e.g., decreased productivity, damage to reputation) empirically in order to further our understanding and impact of cybercrime in the workplace.

Cybercrime and eHRM. According to crime theory, the opportunity for crime to occur is said to require three elements: (1) a likely offender, (2) a suitable target, and (3) the absence of a guardian (Felson & Clarke, 1998). As such, situational crime prevention (SCP) programs have emerged in an effort to reduce the likelihood and frequency of opportunities to commit crimes (Collins et al., 2011), and researchers have begun to structure recommendations to reduce and prevent cybercrime by employing SCP tactics. For instance, Felson (1998) developed a model that describes the relationship between offenders, targets, and guardians. Based on this model, one can attempt to understand situations that facilitate crime.

Hinduja and Kooi (2013) provided a holistic framework for the utilization of SCP and described specific policy-related strategies that can be used to prevent online and information security vulnerabilities. Specifically, they described 16 workplace SCP techniques that can be grouped into four categories:

1. Increasing perceived effort (e.g., conducting background checks on job applicants to screen for past cybercrime-related behaviors),
2. Increasing perceived risks associated with carrying out cybercrime (e.g., providing a hotline for employees to use to report any suspicious information or to include intrusion detection systems),
3. Reducing anticipated rewards (e.g., safeguarding the location of secure systems or using invisible watermarks on documents), and
4. Removing excuses (e.g., implementing acceptable use policies or encouraging a healthy work environment by increasing employee morale and individual well-being).

Collins et al. (2011) also recommended the use of SCP programs, as well as the implementation of virtual private networks. In addition, Widup (2010) suggested that organizations develop data breaching contingency plans to help prevent cyber vulnerabilities.

Addressing cybercrime, our recommendations coincide with strategies previously mentioned. More specifically, we encourage organizations to employ SCP tactics that attempt to prevent and detect cybercrimes. This could be accomplished through a variety of means such as conducting background checks on job applicants to screen for previous offenders, safeguarding confidential information, or utilizing detection systems. In addition, we recommend developing acceptable use policies and conducting employee awareness training programs that make cybercrime issues salient. It is especially important for eHRM professionals to be mindful of a key attribute of property deviance: the ability for cybercrimes to occur both internal and external to organizations. As such, attention should be devoted to the prevention of cybercrime by both employees and non-organizational members. Given the link between personality characteristics and the engagement in property deviance, employers may consider evaluating applicant personality in the selection process. Additionally, organizations should maintain a high security profile, as this is related to lower costs associated with cybercrime. Lastly, as Hinduja and Kooi (2013) recommend, fostering a healthy work environment by increasing employee morale is likely to aid in the prevention of cybercrimes. See Table 10.1 for a review of workplace cybercrime antecedents, outcomes, and eHRM recommendations.

CONCLUSIONS & FUTURE RESEARCH DIRECTIONS

Workplace cyberdeviance is an important topic, as this type of misbehavior can lead to a number of negative work outcomes. In this chapter, we examined four key cyberdeviance behaviors in relation to Robinson and Bennett's (1995) taxonomy of workplace deviance: (1) cyberbullying, (2) online incivility, (3) cyberloafing, and (4) cybercrime. In addition to discussing how Robinson and Bennett's (1995) model can be extended to an ICT context, we also briefly addressed some of the conceptual overlap among similar cyberdeviance constructs. A summary of our review of cyberdeviance antecedents and outcomes, as well as our recommendations regarding the management of workplace cyberdeviance in eHRM practices can be found in Table 10.1.

As workplace cyberdeviance is a relatively new topic due to emerging technologies over the past several decades, there are many avenues for future research. For instance, it is worth acknowledging that the use of typologies is sometimes subject to criticism (see e.g., McKelvey, 1982). For example, it has been argued that typologies are limited to providing descriptions rather than explaining underlying phenomena (Bacharach, 1989) or causal processes (Scott, 1981), and they do not account for variability among categories within the typology (McKelvey, 1982). However, typologies can be more than a means of storing and classifying information; rather, they can serve as a theoretical foundation that can and should undergo strict empirical testing (Doty & Glick, 1994). Nevertheless, we encourage researchers in this area to also examine cyberdeviance through the lens of a relational model that explores the underlying causal processes associated with workplace cyberdeviance (e.g., what impacts perceptions of cyberdeviance consequences, and how do those attitudes then affect cyberdeviance engagement?).

Specific to interpersonal workplace cyberdeviance, future research should address questions such as: What is the relation between perpetration and/or victimization across offline and ICT contexts for both workplace cyberbullying and online incivility? Are their additional antecedents of workplace cyberbullying and online incivility that are unique to ICT contexts (e.g., perceptions of organizational cybermonitoring)? How effective are various preventative mechanisms (e.g., anti-bullying workplace policies), and what contributes to increased success in such programs? In addition, as cross-sectional research designs have largely dominated this area of research, longitudinal and multi-source designs are especially encouraged to help us gain a richer understanding of the impact of interpersonal cyberdeviance at work.

In regard to organization-directed workplace cyberdeviance, there are also many opportunities for research advancement. For instance, evidence has emerged highlighting both positive (e.g., reduced stress) and negative (e.g., decreased productivity) outcomes of cyberloafing. However, little is known as to whether there is a threshold that indicates when personal Internet browsing at work becomes detrimental to employee productivity. In addition, as research has indicated that the effectiveness of acceptable use policies varies, future research should work to identify the factors that contribute to the success (or lack thereof) of such policies. Additionally, as a moderate amount of the cybercrimes that occur in organizations are accidental, are there certain situations in which employees are more susceptible to unintentionally carrying out behaviors that may result in cybercrime? Are organizational policies related to preventing situations that may result in cybercrime effective? In sum, there are many research avenues that would further our understanding of both individual- and organization-directed acts of cyberdeviance, and greater knowledge and awareness of these constructs will undoubtedly contribute to bettering organizational eHRM practices.

REFERENCES

Ananadarajan, M., Simmers, C. A., & Igbaria, M. (2000). An exploratory investigation of the antecedents and impact of Internet usage: An individual perspective. *Behavior & Information Technology, 19,* 69–85. doi:10.1109/hicss.1998.655247

Andreassen, C. S., Torsheim, T., & Pallesen, S. (2014). Predictors of use of social network sites at work—A specific type of cyberloafing. *Journal of Computer-Mediated Communication, 19,* 906–921. doi:10.1111/jcc4.12085

Aquino, K., & Thau, S. (2009). Workplace victimization: Aggression from the target's perspective. *Annual Review of Psychology, 60,* 717–741. doi:10.1146/annurev. psych.60.110707.163703

Askew, K., Buckner, J. E., Taing, M. U., Ilie, A., Bauer, J. A., & Coovert, M. D. (2014). Explaining cyberloafing: The role of the theory of planned behavior. *Computers in Human Behavior, 36,* 510–519. doi:10.1016/j.chb.2014.04.006

Ayoko, O. B., Callan, V. J., & Hartel, C. E. J. (2003). Workplace conflict, bullying, and counterproductive behaviors. *International Journal of Organizational Analysis, 11,* 283–301. doi:10.1108/eb028976

Bacharach, S. B. (1989). Organizational theories: Some criteria for evaluation. *The Academy of Management Review, 14*(4), 496–515. doi:10.2307/258555

Bailey, T. S., Dollard, M. F., McLinton, S. S., & Richards, P. A. M. (2015). Psychosocial safety climate, psychosocial and physical factors in the aetiology of musculoskeletal disorder symptoms and workplace injury compensation claims. *Work & Stress, 29,* 190–211. doi:10.1080/02678373.2015.1031855

Baker, W., Goudie, M., Hutton, A., Hylender, C. D., Niemantsverdriet, J. Novak, C.... Men and women of the United States Secret Service. (2010). *Data Breach Investigations Report. Verizon Business RISK Team.* Retrieved from www.verizonenterprise.com/resources/reports/rp_2010-data-breach_en_xg.pdf

Ball, G. A., Trevino, L. K., & Sims, Jr., H. P. (1994). Just and unjust punishment: Influences on subordinate performance and citizenship. *Academy of Management Journal, 37,* 299–322. doi:10.2307/256831

Baron, R. A., & Neuman, J. A. (1996). Workplace violence and workplace aggression: Evidence on their relative frequency and potential causes. *Aggressive Behavior, 22,* 161–173. doi:10.1002/(sici)1098–2337(1996)22:3<161::aid-ab1>3.3.co;2–2

Baron, R. A., Neuman, J. H., & Geddes, D. (1999). Social and personal determinants of workplace aggression: Evidence for the impact of perceived injustice and the Type A behavior pattern. *Aggressive Behavior, 25,* 281–296.

Bashir, S., Shahzaz, K., Abbass, M., Abbass, N., & Saeed, S. (2011). Antecedents of white collar crime in organizations: A literature review. *African Journal of Business Management, 5,* 13359–13363.

Baturay, M. H., & Toker, S. (2015). An investigation of the impact of demographics on cyberloafing from an educational setting angle. *Computer in Human Behavior, 50,* 358–366. doi:0.1016/j.chb.2015.03.081

Bennett, R., & Stamper, C. L. (2001). Corporate citizenship and deviancy: A study of discretionary work behavior. In S. Craig, Galbraith, & Mike Ryan (Eds.), *Strategies and organizations in transition* (Vol. 3, pp. 269–290). Amsterdam: Elsevier Science.

Berger, J., Harbring, C., & Sliwka, D. (2013). Performance appraisals and the impact of forced distribution–An experimental investigation. *Management Science, 59,* 54–68. doi:10.1287/mnsc.1120.1624

Björkqvist, K., Österman, K., & Hjelt-Bäck,M. (1994). Aggression among university employees. *Aggressive Behavior, 20,* 173–184. doi:10.1002/(sici)1098–2337(1999)25:4<281::aid-ab4>3.3.co;2-a

Blanchard, A. L., & Henle, C. A. (2008). Correlates of different forms of cyberloafing: The role of norms and external locus of control. *Computers in Human Behavior, 24,* 1067–1084. doi:10.1016/j.chb.2007.03.008

Blau, G., & Andersson, L. (2005). Testing a measure of instigated workplace incivility. *Journal of Occupational and Organizational Psychology, 78,* 595–614. doi:10.1348/096317905X26822

Blau, G., Yang, Y., & Ward-Cook, K. (2006). Testing a measure of cyberloafing. *Journal of Allied Health, 35,* 9–17.

Bolton, L. R., Becker, L. K., & Barber, L. K. (2010). Big Five trait predictors of differential counterproductive work behavior dimensions. *Personality and Individual Differences, 49,* 537–541. doi:10.1016/j.paid.2010.03.047

Bowling, N. A., & Beehr, T. A. (2006). Workplace harassment from the victim's perspective: A theoretical model and meta-analysis. *Journal of Applied Psychology, 91,* 998–1012. doi:10.1037/0021–9010.91.5.998

Brown, T. S., & Pardue, J. (1985). Effectiveness of personnel selection inventory in reducing drug store theft. *Psychological Reports, 56,* 875–881. doi:10.2466/pr0.1985.56.3.875

Calvete, E., Orue, I., Estévez, A., Villardón, L., and Padilla, P. (2010). Cyberbullying in adolescents: Modalities and aggressors' profile. *Computers in Human Behavior, 26,* 1128–1135. doi:10.1016/j.chb.2010.03.017

Campbell, M. A. (2005). Cyber bullying: An old problem in a new guise? *Australian Journal of Guidance and Counselling, 15,* 68–76. doi:10.1375/ajgc.15.1.68

Caza, B. B., & Cortina, L. M. (2007). From insult to injury: Explaining the impact of incivility. *Basic and Applied Social Psychology, 29,* 335–350. doi:10.1080/01973530701665108

Coker, B. L. S. (2013). Workplace Internet leisure browsing. *Human Performance, 26,* 114–125. doi:10.1080/08959285.2013.765878

Collins, J. D., Sainato, V. A., & Khey, D. N. (2011). Organizational data breaches 2005–1010: Applying SCP to the healthcare and education sectors. *International Journal of Cyber Criminology, 5,* 794–810.

Cortina, L. M. (2008). Unseen injustice: Incivility as modern discrimination in organizations. *Academy of Management Review, 33,* 55–75. doi:10.5465/amr.2008.27745097

Cortina, L. M., Kabat-Farr, D., Leskinen, E. A., Huerta, M., & Magley, V. J. (2013). Selective incivility as modern discrimination in organizations evidence and impact. *Journal of Management, 39,* 1579–1605. doi:10.1177/0149206311418835

Cortina, L. M., & Magley, V. J. (2009). Patterns and profiles of response to incivility in the workplace. *Journal of Occupational Health Psychology, 14,* 272–288. doi:10.1037/a0014934

Cortina, L. M., Magley, V. J., Williams, J. H, & Langhout, R. D. (2001). Incivility in the workplace: Incidence and impact. *Journal of Occupational Health Psychology, 6,* 64–80. doi:10.1037/1076–8998.6.1.64

Coyne, I., Craig, J., & Smith-Lee Chong, P. (2004). Workplace bullying in a group context. *British Journal of Guidance and Counselling, 32,* 301–317. doi:10.1080/03069880410001723530

Crino, M. D. (1994). Employee sabotage: A random or preventable phenomenon? *Journal of Managerial Issues, 3,* 311–330.

D'Arcy, J., Hovav, A., & Galletta, D. (2009). User awareness of security countermeasures and its impact on information systems misuse: A deterrence approach. *Information Systems Research, 20,* 79–98. doi:10.1287/isre.l070.0160

Davis, R. A., Flett, G. L., & Besser, A. (2002). Validation of a new scale or measuring problematic Internet use: Implications for pre-employment screening. *CyberPsychology & Behavior, 5,* 331–345.

De Cuyper, N., Baillien, E., & De Witte, H. (2009). Job insecurity, perceived employability and targets' and perpetrators' experiences of workplace bullying. *Work & Stress, 23,* 206–224. doi:10.1080/02678370903257578

Djurkovic, N., McCormack, D., & Casimir, G. (2004). The physical and psychological effects of workplace bullying and their relationship to intention to leave: A test of the psychosomatic and disability hypotheses. *International Journal of Organizational Theory and Behavior, 7,* 469–497.

Donner, C. M., Marcum, C. D., Jennings, W. G., Higgins, G. E., & Banfield, J. (2014). Low self-control and cybercrime: Exploring the utility of the general theory of crime beyond digital piracy. *Computers in Human Behavior, 34,* 165–172. doi:10.1016/j. chb.2014.01.040

Dooley, J. J., Pyzalski J., & Cross, D. (2009). Cyberbullying versus face-to-face bullying: A theoretical and conceptual review. *Journal of Psychology, 217,* 182–188. doi:10.1027/0044–3409.217.4.182

Doty, D. H., & Glick, W. H. (1994). Typologies as a unique form of theory building: Toward improved understanding and modeling. *The Academy of Management Review, 19,* 230–251. doi:10.2307/258704

Dunlop, P. D., & Lee, K. (2004). Workplace deviance, organizational citizenship behavior, and business unit performance: The bad apples do spoil the whole barrel. *Journal of Organizational Behavior, 25,* 67–80. doi:10.1002/job.243

Durkin, K., & Patterson, D. (2011). Cyberbullying, cyberharassing, and cyberstalking. In C. D. Bryant (Ed.), *The Routledge handbook of deviant behavior* (pp. 450–455). London: Routledge.

Eichenwald, K. (2012, July). Microsoft's lost decade. *Vanity Fair.* Retrieved from http://www.vanityfair.com/news/business/2012/08/microsoft-lost-mojo-steve-ballmer

Einarsen, S., Hoel, H., Zapf, D., & Cooper, C. L. (2011). The concept of bullying and harassment at work: The European tradition. In S. Einarsen, H. Hoel, D. Zapf & C. L. Cooper (Eds.), *Bullying and harassment in the workplace* (pp. 3–40). Boca Raton, FL: Taylor & Francis.

Einarsen, S., Raknes, B. I., & Matthiesen, S. B. (1994). Bullying and harassment at work and their relationship to work environment quality: An exploratory study. *European Work and Organizational Psychologist, 4,* 381–401. doi:10.1080/13594329408410497

Felson, M. (1998). *Crime and everyday life* (2nd ed.). Thousand Oaks, CA: Pine Forge Press.

Felson, M., & Clarke, R. (1998). *Opportunity makes the thief: Practical theory for crime prevention.* Great Britain: Home Office, Policing and Reducing Crime Unit.

Fowler, K. (2016). An overview of data breaches. In *Data breach preparation and response* (pp. 1–26). Cambridge, MA: Syngress is an imprint of Elsevier.

Francis, L., Holmvall, C. M., & O'Brien, L. E. (2015). The influence of workload and civility of treatment on the perpetration of email incivility. *Computers in Human Behavior, 46,* 191–201. doi:10.1016/j.chb.2014.12.044

Garrett, R. K., & Danziger, J. N. (2008). On cyberslacking: Workplace status and personal Internet use at work. *CyberPsychology & Behavior, 11,* 287–292. doi:10.1089/cpb.2007.0146

Gemalto. (2014). Global survey results reveals impact of data breaches on customer loyalty. *Gemalto.* Retrieved from https://safenet.gemlato.com/news/2014/data-breaches-impact-on-customer-loyalty-survey/

Gilani, S. R. S., Cavico, F. J., & Mujtaba, B. G. (2014). Harassment at the workplace: A practical review of the laws in the United Kingdom and the United States of America. *Public Organization Review, 14,* 1–18. doi:10.1007/s11115-012-0202-y

Giumetti, G. W., Hatfield, A. L., Scisco, J. L., Schroeder, A. N., Muth, E. R., & Kowalski, R. M. (2013). What a rude e-mail! Examining the differential effects of incivility versus support on mood, energy, engagement, and performance in an online context. *Journal of Occupational Health Psychology, 18,* 297–309. doi:10.1037/a0032851

Giumetti, G. W., McKibben, E. S., Hatfield, A. L., Schroeder, A. N., & Kowalski, R. M. (2012). Cyber incivility @ work: The new age of interpersonal deviance. *Cy-*

berpsychology, Behavior, and Social Networking, 15, 148–154. doi:10.1089/cyber.2011.0336

Goetzel, R., Z., Hawkins, K., Ozminkowski, R. J., & Wang, S. (2003). The health and productivity cost burden of the "Top 10" physical and mental health conditions affecting six large U.S. employers in 1999. *Journal of Occupational and Environmental Medicine, 45,* 5–15. doi:10.1097/01.jom.0000048178.88600.6e

Goetzel, R. Z., Long, S. R., Ozminkowski, R. J., Hawkins, K, Wang, S., & Lynch, W. (2004). Health, absence, disability, and presenteeism cost estimates of certain physical and mental health conditions affecting U.S. employers. *Journal of Occupational and Environmental Medicine, 46,* 398–412. doi: 10.1097/01.jom.0000121151.40413.bd

Goodman, P. S., & Garber, S. (1988). Absenteeism and accidents in a dangerous environment: Empirical analysis of underground coal mines. *Journal of Applied Psychology, 73*(1), 81–86. doi:10.1037/0021–9010.73.1.81

Goodman, P. S., & Leyden, D. P. (1991). Familiarity and group productivity. *Journal of Applied Psychology, 76*(4), 578–586. doi:10.1037/0021–9010.76.4.578

Gottfredson, M. R., & Hirschi, T. (1990). *A General Theory of Crime.* Standford, CA: Standford University Press.

Greenberg, J. (1990). Employee theft as a reaction to underpayment inequity: The hidden cost of pay cuts. *Journal of Applied Psychology, 75,* 561–568.

Greenberg, J., & Barling, J. (1996). Employee theft. In C. L. Cooper & D. M. Rousseau (Eds.), *Trends in Organizational Behavior* (Vol. 3, pp. 49–65). Chichester, NY: Wiley.

Griffin, S. P. (2002). Actors or activities? On the social construction of "white-collar crime" in the United States. *Crime, Law and Social Change, 37,* 245–276. doi:10.1023/A:1015029710490

Griffiths, M. (2003). Internet abuse in the workplace: Issues and concerns for employers and employment counselors. *Journal of Employment Counseling, 40,* 87–96. doi:10.4018/9781591401483.ch012

Hanisch, K. A., & Hulin, C. L. (1991). General attitudes and organizational withdrawal: An evaluation of a causal model. *Journal of Vocational Behavior, 39(1),* 110–128. doi:10.1016/0001–8791(91)90006–8

Hansen, Å. M., Hogh, A., Persson, R., Karlson, B., Garde, A. H., & Ørbæk, P. (2006). Bullying at work, health outcomes, and physiological stress response. *Journal of Psychosomatic Research, 60,* 63–72. doi:10.1016/j.jpsychores.2005.06.078

Harris, L. C., & Ogbonna, E. (2006). Service sabotage: A study of antecedents and consequences. *Journal of the Academy of Marketing Science, 34,* 543–558. doi:10.1177/0092070306287324

Hauge, L. J., Skogstad, A., & Einarsen, S. (2007). Relationships between stressful work environments and bullying: Results of a large representative study. *Work & Stress, 21,* 220–242. doi:10.1080/02678370701705810

Hauge, L. J., Skogstad, A., & Einarsen, S. (2009). Individual and situational predictors of workplace bullying: Why do perpetrators engage in the bullying of others? *Work & Stress, 23,* 349–358. doi:10.1080/02678370903395568

Healthy Workplace Bill. (n.d.). Retrieved from http://healthyworkplacebill.org.

Henle, C. A., & Blanchard, A. L. (2008). The interaction of work stressors and organizational sanctions on cyberloafing. *Journal of Managerial Issues, 20,* 383–400.

Henle, C. A., & Kedharnath, U. (2012). Cyberloafing in the workplace. *Encyclopedia of Cyber Behavior*, 560–573. doi:10.4018/978-1-4666-0315-8

Henle, C. A., Kohut, G., & Booth, R. (2009). Designing electronic use policies to enhance employee perceptions of fairness and to reduce cyberloafing: An empirical test of justice theory. *Computers in Human Behavior, 25*, 902–910. doi:10.1016/j.chb.2009.03.005

Henle, C. A., Reeve, C. L., & Pitts, V. E. (2010). Stealing time at work: Attitudes, social pressure, and perceived control as predictors of time theft. *Journal of Business Ethics, 94*(1), 53–67. doi:10.1007/s10551-009-0249-z

Hershcovis, M. S. (2011). "Incivility, social undermining, bullying. . .oh my!": A call to reconcile constructs within workplace aggression research. *Journal of Organizational Behavior, 32*, 499–519. doi:10.1002/job.689

Hinduja, S., & Kooi, B. (2013). Curtailing cyber and information security vulnerabilities through situational crime prevention. *Security Journal, 26*, 383–402. doi:10.1057/sj.2013.25

Hollinger, R. C., & Clark, J. P. (1982). Formal and informal social controls of employee deviance. *Sociological Quarterly, 23*, 333–343.

Hoon, H., & Tan, T. M. L. (2008). Organizational citizenship behavior and social loafing: The role of personality, motives, and contextual factors. *The Journal of Psychology, 142*, 89–108. doi:10.3200/jrlp.142.1.89-112

Hong, J.-C., Lin, C.-H., Hwang, M.-Y., Hu, R.-P., & Chen, Y.-L. (2014). Positive affect predicting worker psychological response to cyber-bullying in the high-tech industry in Northern Taiwan. *Computers in Human Behavior, 30*, 307–314. doi:10.1016/j.chb.2013.09.011

Jennifer, D., Cowie, H., & Ananiadou, K. (2003). Perceptions and experience of workplace bullying in five different working populations. *Aggressive Behavior, 29*, 489–496. doi:10.1002/ab.10055

Jia, H., Jia, R., & Karau, S. (2013). Cyberloafing and personality: The impact of the Big Five traits and workplace situational factors. *Journal of Leadership & Organizational Studies, 20*, 358–365. doi:10.1177/1548051813488208

Jones, G. E., & Kavanagh, M. J. (1996). An experimental examination of the effects of individual and situational factors on unethical behavioral intentions in the workplace. *Journal of Business Ethics, 15*, 657–674. doi:10.1007/978-94-007-4126-3_33

Kelloway, E. K., Loughlin, C., Barling, J., & Nault, A. (2002). Self-reported counterproductive behaviors and organizational citizenship behaviors: Separate but related constructs. *International Journal of Selection and Assessment, 10*, 143–151. doi:10.1111/1468-2389.00201

Kern, J. H., & Grandey, A. A. (2009). Customer incivility as a social stressor: The role of race and racial identity for service employees. *Journal of Occupational Health Psychology, 14*, 46–57. doi:10.1037/a0012684

Khey, D. N., & Sainato, V. A. (2013). Examining the correlates and spatial distribution of organizational data breaches in the United States. *Security Journal, 26*, 367–382. doi:10.1057/sj.2013.24

Kim, K., del Carmen Triana, M., Chung, K., & Oh, N. (2016). When do employees cyberloaf? An interactionst perspective examining personality, justice, and empowerment. *Human Resource Management, 55*, 1041–1058. doi:10.1002/hrm/21699

Kivimaki, M., Elovainio, M., & Vahtera, J. (2000). Workplace bullying and sickness absence in hospital staff. *Occupational and Environmental Medicine, 57,* 656–660. doi:10.1136/oem.57.10.656

Klein, R. L., Leong, G. B., & Silva, J. A. (1996). Employee sabotage in the workplace: A biopsychosocial model. *Journal of Forensic Sciences, 41,* 52–55. doi:10.1520/jfs13896j

Kowalski, R. M., Giumetti, G. W., Schroeder, A. N., & Lattanner, M. R. (2014). Bullying in the digital age: A critical review and meta-analysis of cyberbullying research among youth. *Psychological Bulletin, 140,* 1073–1137. doi:10.1037/a0035618

Kowalski, R. M., Limber, S. P., & Agatston, P. W. (2008). *Cyber bullying: Bullying in the digital age.* Malden, MA: Blackwell.

Krebs. (2014). Home Depot: 56M cards impacted, malware contained. *Krebs on Security.* Retrieved from http://krebsonsecurity.com/2014/09/home-depot-56m-cards-impacted-malware-contained/

Krishnan, S. (2016). Electronic warfare: A personality model of cyber incivility. *Computers in Human Behavior, 64,* 537–546. doi:10.1016/j.chb.2016.07.031

Kruger, J., Epley, N., Parker, J., & Ng, Z.-W. (2005). Egocentrism over e-mail: Can we communicate as well as we think? *Journal of Personality and Social Psychology, 89,* 925–936. doi:10.1037/0022–3514.89.6.925

Latané, B., Williams, K., & Harkins, S. (1979). Many hands make light the work: The causes and consequences of social loafing. *Journal of Personality and Social Psychology, 37*(6), 822–832. doi:10.1037/0022–3514.37.6.822

Lavoie, J. A. A., & Pychyl, T. A. (2001). Cyberslacking and the procrastination superhighway: A web-based survey of online procrastination, attitudes, and emotion. *Social Science Computer Review, 19,* 431–444. doi:10.1177/089443930101900403

Lee, R.T., & Brotheridge, C.M. (2006). When prey turns predatory: Workplace bullying as a predictor of counteraggression/bullying, coping, and well-being. *European Journal of Work and Organizational Psychology, 15,* 352–377. doi:10.1080/13594320600636531

Leiter, M. P., Laschinger, H. K. S., Day, A., & Oore, D. G. (2011). The impact of civility interventions on employee social behavior, distress, and attitudes. *Journal of Applied Psychology, 96,* 1258–1274. doi:10.1037/a0024442

Li, Q. (2007). Bullying in the new playground: Research into cyberbullying and cyber victimization. *Australasian Journal of Educational Technology, 23,* 435–454. doi:10.14742/ajet.1245

Liberman, B., Seidman, G., McKenna, K. Y. A., & Buffardi, L. E. (2011). Employee job attitudes and organizational characteristics as predictors of cyberloafing. *Computers in Human Behavior, 27,* 2192–2199. doi:10.1016/j.chb.2011.06.015

Liden, R. C., Wayne, S. J., Jaworski, R. A., & Bennett, N. (2004). Social Loafing: A field investigation. *Journal of Management, 30*(2), 285–304. doi:10.1016/j.jm.2003.02.002

Lim, S., & Cortina, L. M. (2005). Interpersonal mistreatment in the workplace: The interface and impact of general incivility and sexual harassment. *Journal of Applied Psychology, 90,* 483–496. doi:10.1037/0021–9010.90.3.483

Lim, S., Cortina, L. M., & Magley, V. J. (2008). Personal and workgroup incivility: Impact on work and health outcomes. *Journal of Applied Psychology, 93,* 95–107. doi:10.1037/0021–9010.93.1.95

Lim, S., & Lee, A. (2011). Work and nonwork outcomes of workplace incivility: Does family support help? *Journal of Occupational Health Psychology, 16,* 95–111. doi:10.1037/a0021726

Lim, V. K. G. (2002). The IT way of loafing on the job: Cyberloafing, neutralizing and organizational justice. *Journal of Organizational Behavior, 23,* 675–694. doi:10.1002/job.161

Lim, V. K. G., & Chen, D. J. Q. (2012). Cyberloafing at the workplace: Gain or drain on work? *Behaviour & Information Technology, 31,* 343–353. doi:10.1080/01449290903353054

Lim, V. K. G., & Teo, T. S. H. (2009). Mind your E-manners: Impact of cyber incivility on employees' work attitude and behavior. *Information & Management, 46,* 419–425. doi:10.1016/j.im.2009.06.006

Manrique de Lara, P. Z. (2006). Fear in organizations: Does intimidation by formal punishment mediate the relationship between interactional justice and workplace Internet deviance? *Journal of Managerial Psychology, 21,* 580–592. doi:10.1108/02683940610684418

Martin, W., & LaVan, H. (2010). Workplace bullying: A review of litigated cases. *Employee Responsibilities & Rights Journal, 22,* 175–194. doi:10.1007/s10672-009-9140-4

Martin, N., & Rice, J. (2011). Cybercrime: Understanding and addressing the concerns of stakeholders. *Computers & Security, 30,* 803–814. doi:10.1016/j.cose.2011.07.003

McKelvey, B. (1982). *Organizational systematics–Taxonomy, evolution, classification.* Berkeley, CA: University of California Press.

Meier, L. L., & Spector, P. (2013). Reciprocal effects of work stressors and counterproductive work behavior: A five-wave longitudinal study. *Journal of Applied Psychology, 98,* 529–539. doi:10.1037/a0031732

Meloni, M., & Austin, M. (2011). Implementation and outcomes of a zero tolerance of bullying and harassment program. *Australian Health Review, 35,* 92–94. doi:10.1071/ah10896

Milam, A. C., Spitzmueller, C., & Penney, L. M. (2009). Investigating individual differences among targets of workplace incivility. *Journal of Occupational Health Psychology, 14*(1), 58–69. doi:10.1037/a0012683

Miles, D. E., Borman, W. E., Spector, P. E., & Fox, S. (2002). Building an integrative model of extra role work behaviors: A comparison of counterproductive work behavior with organizational citizenship behavior. *International Journal of Selection and Assessment, 10,* 5–57. doi:10.1111/1468-2389.00193

Naples, G. J., & Maher, M. (2002). Cybersmearing: A legal conflict between individuals and corporations. *Journal of Information, Law & Technology, 2,* 1–11.

Notar, C. E., Padgett, S., & Roden, J. (2013). Cyberbullying: A review of the literature. *Universal Journal of Educational Research, 1,* 1–9. doi:10.13189/ujer.2013.010101

O'Neill, T. A., Hambley, L. A., & Chatellier, G. S. (2014). Cyberslacking, engagement, and personality in distributed work environments. *Computers in Human Behavior, 40,* 152–160. doi:10.1016/j.chb.2014.08.005

Organ, D. (1997). Organizational citizenship behavior: It's construct clean-up time. *Human Performance, 10,* 85–97. doi:10.1207/s15327043hup1002_2

Ortega, A., Christensen, K. B., Hogh, A., Rugulies, R., & Borg, V. (2011). One-year prospective study on the effect of workplace bullying on long-term sickness absence. *Journal of Nursing Management, 19,* 752–759. doi:10.1111/j.1365-2834.2010.01179.x

Page, D. (2015). Teachers' personal web use at work. *Behaviour & Information Technology, 34*, 443–453. doi:10.1080/0144929X.2014.928744

Park, Y., Fritz, C., & Jex, S. M. (2015). Daily cyber incivility and distress: The moderating roles of resources at work and home. *Journal of Management.* Advance online publication. doi:10.1177/0149206315576796

Patrick, E. (n. d.). Employee Internet management: Now an HR issue. *Society for Human Resource Management.* Retrieved from https://www.shrm.org/hr-today/news/hr-magazine/pages/cms_006514.aspx

Pearson, C. M., Andersson, L. M., & Porath, C. L. (2000). Assessing and attacking workplace incivility. *Organizational Dynamics, 29,* 123–137. doi:10.1016/s0090-2616(00)00019-x

Penney, L. M., & Spector, P. E. (2005). Job stress, incivility, and counterproductive work behavior (CWB): The moderating role of negative affectivity. *Journal of Organizational Behavior, 26,* 777–796. doi:10.1002/job.336

Ponemon Institute. (2016). 2016 cost of cybercrime study & the risk of business innovation. *Ponemon Institute.* Retrieved from www.ponemon.org/library/2016-cost-of-cyber-crime-study-the-risk-of-business-innovation.

Porath, C. L., & Pearson C. (2013). The price of incivility. *Harvard Business Review, 91,* 115–121.

Privitera, C., & Campbell, M. A. (2009). Cyberbullying: The new face of workplace bullying? *CyberPsychology & Behavior, 12,* 395–400. doi:10.1089/cpb.2009.0025

Rayner, C. (1997). The incidence of workplace bullying. *Journal of Community & Applied Social Psychology, 7,* 199–208. doi:10.1002/(sici)1099–1298(199706)7:3<199::aid-casp418>3.3.co;2–8

Reuters. (2016). Home Depot to pay millions for data breach. *Fortune.* Retrieved from http://fortune.com/2016/03/08/home-depot-data-breach-2/

Robinson, S. L., & Bennett, R. J. (1995). A typology of deviant workplace behaviors: A multidimensional scaling study. *Academy of Management Journal, 38,* 555–572. doi:10.2307/256693

Romanosky, S., Telang, R., & Acquisti, A. (2011). Do data breach disclosure laws reduce identity theft? *Journal of Policy Analysis and Management 30,* 256–286. doi:10.1002/pam.20567

Sackett, P. R., Berry, C. M., Wiemann, S. A., & Laczo, R. M. (2006). Citizenship and counterproductive behavior: Clarifying relations between the two domains. *Human Performance, 19,* 441–464. doi:10.1207/s15327043hup1904_7

Sakurai, K., & Jex, S. M. (2012). Coworker incivility and incivility targets' work effort and counterproductive work behaviors: The moderating role of supervisor social support. *Journal of Occupational Health Psychology, 17,* 150–161. doi:10.1037/a0027350

Salin, D. (2003). Bullying and organisational politics in competitive and rapidly changing work environments. *International Journal of Management and Decision Making, 4,* 35–46. doi:10.1504/ijmdm.2003.002487

Sandle, P. (2014). Cyber crime costs global economy $445 billion a year: Report. *Reuters.* Retrieved from www.reuters.com/articles/us-cybersecurity-mcafee-csis-idUSK-BN0EK0SV20140609

Scott, W. R. (1981). *Organizations: Rational, natural, and open systems.* Englewood Cliffs, NJ: Prentice Hall.

Sheikh, A., Atashgah, M. S., & Adibzadegan, M. (2015). The antecedents of cyberloafing: A case study in an Iranian copper. *Computers in Human Behavior, 51,* 172–179. doi:10.1016/j.chb.2015.04.042

Sipior, J. C. & Ward, B. T. (2002). A strategic response to the broad spectrum of Internet abuse. *Information Systems Management, 19,* 71–79. doi: 10.1201/1078/43202.19. 4.20020901/38837.9

Sliter, K. A., Sliter, M. T., Withrow, S. A., & Jex, S. M. (2012). Employee adiposity and incivility: Establishing a link and identifying demographic moderators and negative consequences. *Journal of Occupational Health Psychology, 17,* 409–424. doi:10.1037/a0029862

Sliter, M., Jex, S., Wolford, K., & McInnerney, J. (2010). How rude! Emotional labor as a mediator between customer incivility and employee outcomes. *Journal of Occupational Health Psychology, 15,* 468–481. doi:10.1037/a0020723

Sliter, M., Sliter, K., & Jex, S. (2012). The employee as a punching bag: The effect of multiple sources of incivility on employee withdrawal behavior and sales performance. *Journal of Organizational Behavior, 33,* 121–139. doi:10.1002/job.767

Smith, P., Mahdavi, J., Carvalho, M., Fisher, S., Russell, S., & Tippett, N. (2008). Cyberbullying: Its nature and impact in secondary school pupils. *Journal of Child Psychology and Psychiatry, 49,* 376–385. doi:10.1111/j.1469-7610.2007.01846.x

Society for Human Resource Management (SHRM), (2014). *Employee absences have consequences for productivity and revenue, SHRM research shows.* Society for Human Resource Management. Retrieved from https://www.shrm.org/about-shrm/pressroom/press-releases/pages/employeeabsencessurvey.aspx

Staude-Müller, F., Hansen, B., & Voss, M. (2012). How stressful is online victimization? Effects of victim's personality and properties of the incident. *European Journal of Developmental Psychology, 9,* 260–274. doi:10.1080/17405629.2011.643170

Taylor, S. G., & Kluemper, D. H. (2012). Linking perceptions of role stress and incivility to workplace aggression: The moderating role of personality. *Journal of Occupational Health Psychology, 17,* 316–329. doi:10.1037/a0028211

Tharenou, P. (1993). A test of reciprocal causality for absenteeism. *Journal of Organizational Behavior, 14,* 269–287. doi:10.1002/job.4030140306

Tokunaga, R. S. (2010). Following you home from school: A critical review and synthesis of research on cyberbullying victimization. *Computers in Human Behavior, 26,* 277–287. doi:10.1016/j.chb.2009.11.014

Trudel, J., & Reio, T. G. (2011). Managing workplace incivility: The role of conflict management styles—Antecedent or antidote? *Human Resource Development Quarterly, 22,* 395–423. doi:10.1002/hrdq.20081

Ugrin, J. C., & Pearson, J. M. (2008). Exploring Internet abuse in the workplace: How can we maximize deterrence efforts? *Review of Business, 28,* 29–40.

van Jaarsveld, D. D., Walker, D. D., & Skarlicki, D. P. (2010). The role of job demands and emotional exhaustion in the relationship between customer and employee incivility. *Journal of Management, 36,* 1486–1504. doi:10.1177/0149206310368998

Vitak, J., Crouse, J., & LaRose, R. (2011). Personal Internet use at work: Understanding cyberslacking. *Computers in Human Behavior, 27,* 1751–1759. doi:10.1016/j.chb.2011.03.002

Wagner, D. T., Barnes, C. M., Lim, V. K. G., & Ferris, D. L. (2012). Lost sleep and cyber-loafing: Evidence from the laboratory and a daylight saving time quasiexperiment. *Journal of Applied Psychology, 97*, 1068–1076. doi:10.1037/a/0027557

Walsh, B. M., Magley, V. J., Reeves, D. W., Davies-Schrils, K. A., Marmet, M. D., & Gallus, J. A. (2012). Assessing workgroup norms for civility: The development of the Civility Norms Questionnaire-Brief. *Journal of Business and Psychology, 27*, 407–420. doi:10.1007/s10869-011-9251-4

Weatherbee, T. G. (2010). Counterproductive use of technology at work: Information & communications technologies and cyberdeviancy. *Human Resource Management Review, 20(*1), 35–44. doi:10.1016/j.hrmr.2009.03.012

Widup, S. (2010). *The leaking vault: Five years of data breaches. Disgital Forensics Association.* Retrieved from http://www.digitalforensicsassociation.org.

Willard, N. (2007). *Cyberbullying and cyber-threats: Responding to the challenge of online social aggression, threats, and distress.* Champaign, IL: Research Press.

Williams, K., Harkins, S. G., & Latané, B. (1981). Identifiability as a deterrent to social loafing: Two cheering experiments. *Journal of Personality and Social Psychology, 40*, 303–311. doi:10.1037/0022-3514.40.2.303

Williams, K. D., Cheung, C. K. T., & Choi, W. (2000). Cyberostracism: Effects of being ignored over the Internet. *Journal of Personality and Social Psychology, 79*, 748–762. doi:10.1037//0022-3514.79.5.748

Willison, R. (2000). Understanding and addressing criminal opportunity: The application of situational crime prevention to IS security. *Journal of Financial Crime, 7*, 201–210. doi:10.1108/eb025940.

Young, K. (2010). Policies and procedures to manage employee Internet abuse. *Computers in Human Behavior, 26*, 1467–1471. doi:10.1016/j.chb.2010.04.025

Young, K. S., & Case, C. J. (2004). Internet abuse in the workplace: New trends in risk management. *CyberPsychology & Behavior, 7*, 105–111. doi:10.1089/109493104322820174

Young, K. S., & Case, C. J. (2009). Computer ethics: Gender effects and employee Internet misuse. *Issues in Information Systems, 10*, 598–603.

Zapf, D., & Einarsen, S. (2003). Individual antecedents of bullying: Victims and perpetrators. In S. Einarsen, H. Hoel, D. Zapf & C. L. Cooper (Eds.), *Bullying and emotional abuse in the workplace. International perspectives in research and practice* (pp. 165–184). London: Taylor & Francis.

Zapf, D., Knorz, C., & Kulla, M. (1996). On the relationship between mobbing factors, and job content, the social work environment and health outcomes. *European Journal of Work and Organizational Psychology, 5*, 215–237. doi:10.1080/13594329608414856

CPSIA information can be obtained
at www.ICGtesting.com
Printed in the USA
BVHW070027180120
569783BV00005B/15

9 781641 131551